Peloubet's

Sunday School Notes 1999–2000

Based on the International Bible Lessons
for Christian Teaching Uniform Series

James Reapsome

126th Annual Volume
Founded by Francis N. Peloubet

David C. Cook Church Ministries
Colorado Springs, Colorado/Paris, Ontario

Peloubet's Sunday School Notes

© 1999 David C. Cook Publishing
Co., 4050 Lee Vance View,
Colorado Springs, CO 80918,
U.S.A. All rights reserved. Printed
in U.S.A. May not be reproduced
without permission. Lessons based
on International Sunday School
Lessons: the International Bible
Lessons for Christian Teaching,
© 1996 by the Committee on the
Uniform Series.

Edited and desktop-published by
Dave and Neta Jackson.

Cover photography ©1998 by
Dan Stultz

Cover design by Jeffrey P. Barnes

Scripture quotations, unless other-
wise noted, are from THE HOLY
BIBLE, NEW INTERNATIONAL
VERSION, © 1973, 1978, 1984 by
International Bible Society. Used
by permission of Zondervan
Publishing House. All rights
reserved.

ISBN: 0-7814-5482-4

From Slavery to Promised Land

Unit I: Liberation and Covenant

Unit II: Wilderness Wanderings

Unit III: Entering the Promised Land

Studies in Matthew

Unit I: Beginnings: Birth and Ministry

Unit II: Jesus' Teachings and Ministry

Unit III: Fulfillment of Jesus' Mission

Continuing Jesus' Work

New Life in Christ

Use Peloubet's with Materials from These Publishers

Sunday school materials from the following denominations and publishers follow International Sunday School Lesson outlines (sometimes known as Uniform Series). Because *Peloubet's Sunday School Notes* follow the same outlines, you can use *Peloubet's Sunday School Notes* as an excellent teacher resource to supplement the materials from these publishing houses.

DENOMINATIONAL:

Advent Christian General Conference: *Adult*

American Baptist *(Judson Press): Adult*

United Holy Church of America: *Adult*

Church of God in Christ *(Church of God in Christ Publishing House): Adult*

Church of Christ Holiness: *Adult*

Church of God *(Warner Press): Adult*

Church of God by Faith: *Adult*

National Baptist Convention of America *(Boyd): All ages*

National Primitive Baptist Convention: *Adult*

Progressive National Baptist Convention: *Adult*

Presbyterian Church *(U.S.A.) (Bible Discovery Series—Presbyterian Publishing House or P.R.E.M.): Adult*

Southern Baptist *(Baptist Sunday School Board): All ages*

Union Gospel Press: *All ages*

United Holy Church of America: *Adult*

United Methodist *(Cokesbury): All ages*

NONDENOMINATIONAL:

David C. Cook Publishing Co.: *Adult*

Echoes Literature: *Adult*

Standard Publishing: *Adult*

Urban Ministries: *All ages*

From Slavery to Promised Land

God Calls Moses

DEVOTIONAL READING
Exodus 6:2-8

DAILY BIBLE READINGS
Monday August 30
Exodus 2:1-10 Birth and Youth of Moses

Tuesday August 31
Exodus 2:11-15 Moses Flees to Midian

Wednesday September 1
Exodus 2:16-25 Moses Settles in Midian

Thursday September 2
Exodus 3:1-12 Moses at the Burning Bush

Friday September 3
Exodus 3:13-22 Moses Called to Deliver Israel

Saturday September 4
Exodus 4:1-9 Moses Empowered by God

Sunday September 5
Exodus 4:10-20 Moses Responds to God's Call

Scripture
Background Scripture: *Exodus 3*
Scripture Lesson: *Exodus 3:1-12*
Key Verse: *God said to Moses, "I AM WHO I AM. This is what you are to say to the Israelites: 'I AM has sent me to you.'"* Exodus 3:14.
Key Verse for Children: *"So now, go. I am sending you to Pharaoh to bring my people the Israelites out of Egypt."* Exodus 3:10.

Lesson Aim
To examine our motives and our walk with Christ, so we can answer yes when God calls.

Lesson Setting
Time: *1450 B.C.*
Place: *Egypt*

Lesson Outline
God Calls Moses
   I.   God Appeared to Moses: Exodus 3:1-6
      A. He Was a Shepherd: vs. 1
      B. He Saw a Burning Bush: vss. 2-3
      C. God Spoke to Him: vss. 4-6
  II. God Called Moses: Exodus 3:7-10
      A. He Saw His Suffering People: vss. 7-9
      B. He Wanted Moses to Lead Them: vs. 10
 III. Moses Was Reluctant: Exodus 3:11-12
      A. He Was a Nobody: vs. 11
      B. God Reassured Him: vs. 12

Introduction for Adults

Topic: *Called to Obedience*

Israel's liberator, Moses, did not have a business card when he introduced himself to Pharaoh after a 40-year flight. But he did have a striking introduction: "I AM has sent me to you" (Exod. 3:14).

The story behind his "calling card" began with a flaming desert shrub that was not burned up. Then God spoke to him. After considerable give-and-take about Moses' unsuitability for the task, he enlisted in God's cause to free His people.

Believers of all generations have also learned that God intervenes to establish His authority in their lives. They have been sufficiently impressed, as Moses was, to find and do what the caller (God Himself) has in mind.

Introduction for Youths

Topic: *Who, Me?*

Divine calls baffle us. What are they like? A voice from a flaming bush? A voice out of a dazzling, blinding light? A voice from God's holy throne? A voice calling your name at night? That's what it was like for Moses, Paul, Isaiah, and Samuel. But not necessarily for us.

On some occasions God may get our attention in some spectacular way, but that's not the norm. The important thing is not the setting, but the deep-seated assurance that you really can hear from God. How? As you read the Bible and meditate on God's words. As you worship. As you do what you know you are supposed to do now. As you obey God's moral and spiritual precepts. As you pray. As you talk with other believers.

We keep asking, "What shall I do, Lord?" with the complete assurance that God will show the way. The one essential ingredient to hearing from God is commitment to do His will.

Concepts for Children

Topic: *Being a Helper*

1. God heard the cries of His children in Egypt and called Moses to deliver them.
2. We can be sure that God hears our prayers when we are in difficulties.
3. Our friends need to know that we worship an all-seeing, all-powerful, all-loving God who cares about people.
4. God is interested in the smallest details of our lives, and wants us to trust Him with everything.
5. God gives us many opportunities to be His helper, as Moses was.
6. God wants us to listen to His Word, so we can recognize God's voice when He speaks to us.

The Lesson Commentary

I. GOD APPEARED TO MOSES: EXODUS 3:1-6

A. He Was a Shepherd: vs. 1

Now Moses was tending the flock of Jethro his father-in-law, the priest of Midian, and he led the flock to the far side of the desert and came to Horeb, the mountain of God.

This quarter covers the history of God's people from the Exodus through entry into the promised land. The study focuses on God's deliverance of Israel from slavery, including the making of the covenant and the fulfillment of the promise of a land for His people. Passages are taken from Exodus, Leviticus, Numbers, Deuteronomy, and Joshua.

The Israelites had been in slavery in Egypt for 400 years (1850 B.C. to 1450 B.C.). Now God was about to act on their behalf. Out of what appeared to be utter hopelessness and despair, He initiated deliverance for His suffering people.

He began by revealing Himself to one man in a special way. Verses 1-6 tell how He gained the attention of Moses by a miracle—a burning bush that was not consumed by the flames.

To retrace the story of Moses, we go back 40 years to the time when he prematurely tried to assume the leadership of the Israelites. In that fiasco, he had rushed to defend one of his countrymen and murdered his oppressor. However, the Israelites turned on Moses, Pharaoh found out about the murder, and Moses fled into the desert to save his life.

According to Stephen's testimony (Acts 7:23-30), Moses lived as a shepherd in exile in Midian for another 40 years. Moses, the writer of Exodus, did not record anything about those years. He married Jethro's daughter Zipporah and worked as a shepherd for his father-in-law. Probably he kept hoping to return to his people, but as the years rolled by no opportunities came. He had settled into his shepherd's routine. However, according to Hebrews 11:27, Moses did not abandon his faith in God. Rather, "he persevered because he saw him who is invisible."

God was with Moses the shepherd, the exile, the refugee. Even though it seemed that God had parked him on a siding, with no apparent service for the Lord, God was preparing His man for history-making leadership. God's people persevere in faith, even when life looks like a dead-end street.

One day Moses took his flock to pasture on the "far side of the desert," that is, the central part of the Sinai Peninsula. He had made a three- or four-day journey to find pasture and water. Midian was across the Gulf of Aqaba on the western edge of Arabia.

Moses arrived at a conspicuous mountain peak, Horeb, another name for the area of Mount Sinai. In retrospect, Moses called it "the mountain of God," because that was where God revealed His glory to him and where God handed down His laws for His people.

B. He Saw a Burning Bush: vss. 2-3

There the angel of the LORD appeared to him in flames of fire from within a bush. Moses saw that though the bush was on fire it did not burn up. So Moses thought, "I will go over and see this strange sight—why the bush does not burn up."

Moses, of course, knew desert terrain and plant life. But he had never seen a bush catch fire and not burn to ashes. So he went to investigate this strange sight.

He did not know that the angel of the Lord was in the flames. This "angel" was not a winged creature, but God Himself (vs. 4). In the Old Testament stories, "the angel of the Lord" was at times identified with the Lord Himself. In some cases, the angel was distinct from the Lord. These appearances, called theophanies [thee-AH-fuh-neez], foreshadowed the coming of the Lord Jesus Christ.

It is also important to consider the symbolism in this story. The bush was not consumed, showing that God is the living God. Fire symbolizes His holiness. These facts became the cornerstone of Moses' leadership later on. The burning bush not only served to get his attention, it also taught him the essentials of his knowledge of the true and living God.

C. God Spoke to Him: vss. 4-6

When the LORD saw that he had gone over to look, God called to him from within the bush, "Moses! Moses!" And Moses said, "Here I am." "Do not come any closer," God said. "Take off your sandals, for the place where you are standing is holy ground." Then he said, "I am the God of your father, the God of Abraham, the God of Isaac and the God of Jacob." At this, Moses hid his face, because he was afraid to look at God.

Having gotten Moses' attention, God called to him by name, and Moses answered Him. God warned him not to come any closer to the bush, because he was standing on holy ground. To acknowledge God's holiness, Moses removed his sandals. The spot itself was not holy, but God's presence made it so.

Standing in awe of God's majesty and holiness, Moses needed reassurance that he would not die in the presence of the divine. He gained that reassurance when God revealed to him that He is not only holy, but also personal and knowable. This was a monumental revelation to Moses which laid the foundation for his call to deliver the Israelites from Egypt.

Somewhat assured, Moses turned his gaze away from the burning bush. "He was afraid to look at God" because, sinner that he was, he knew he might be consumed by God's holiness.

Moses greatly needed this word from the Lord. He had to be sure this experience was not a dream, a fantasy, or an hallucination from heat prostration. Moses needed a keen sense of God's holiness and power to be prepared for leadership. Moses knew what the writer of Hebrews told New Testament believers many centuries later: "God is a consuming fire" (Heb. 12:29).

II. GOD CALLED MOSES: EXODUS 3:7-10

A. He Saw His Suffering People: vss. 7-9

The LORD said, "I have indeed seen the misery of my people in Egypt. I have heard them crying out because of their slave drivers, and I am concerned about their suffering. So I have come down to rescue them from the hand of the Egyptians and to bring them up out of that land into a good and spacious land, a land flowing with milk and honey—the home of the Canaanites, Hittites, Amorites, Perizzites, Hivites and Jebusites. And now the cry of the Israelites has reached me, and I have seen the way the Egyptians are oppressing them."

God's conversation with Moses continued around the bush. God had called Moses' name, told him to take off his sandals, and revealed who He was. These were all necessary precursors to His big announcement: He was going to rescue His people, and Moses would bring them out of Egypt.

What stunning news this was for Moses. God had seen the misery of His people in Egypt; He had heard them crying out for relief; He was concerned about their suffering (vs. 7). He was about to rescue them and give them a wonderful home (vs. 8). He had heard the cries of the Israelites; He had seen how the Egyptians were oppressing them (vs. 9). There was a personal, knowing, loving God in heaven who cared about the tragic plight of His children.

God does not work according to human demands and timetables. Four hundred years of slavery seems an unusually long time to wait for His intervention. But people of faith know that God keeps His own counsel.

Faith, according to the writer of Hebrews, is being certain of what we do not see (Heb. 11:1). That's one of the reasons Moses was commended for his faith. "By faith he left Egypt, not fearing the king's anger; he persevered because he saw him who is invisible" (vs. 27).

God was moved because of the harsh treatment the Israelites received from their Egyptian taskmasters. Probably most of the Hebrews had long ago given up on God's intervention. If He did exist, He did not care about them.

Of course, not all Israelites gave up on God. We don't know how many there were, but God told Moses He had heard their cries. Their cries reflect persistent, prevailing prayer over many generations. Prayer is our main recourse, whatever the cause of our suffering.

Out of this grim picture God wanted Moses to know that He understood and cared about the Israelites. "I am concerned about their suffering" (Exod. 3:7) indicates personal feelings, tenderness, and compassion.

Moses, the leader-to-be, had to know not only God's holiness and majesty, but also His lovingkindness and mercy. God not only cared, but He was about to act. "I have come down to rescue them" (vs. 8). Also implied in this announcement was coming judgment on Egypt. God will deliver and He will judge. No oppression escapes God's notice.

God's plan encompassed not only freedom from slavery in Egypt, but also a new homeland, "a good and spacious land, a land flowing with milk and honey" (vs. 8). That land was occupied by various other tribes, but God implied that He would drive them out and give it to the Hebrews.

B. He Wanted Moses to Lead Them: vs. 10

"So now, go. I am sending you to Pharaoh to bring my people the Israelites out of Egypt."

This was God's call to leadership. Moses was to leave shepherding for Jethro in Midian and go back to Pharaoh in Egypt. Then he would bring God's people out of their distressing bondage.

Moses' momentary rejoicing was cut short by this bombshell of an announcement. Perhaps he had even formulated the first logical question to God's news: "How?" Then he found out that he himself was the "how."

God's plan required a human leader. God could have saved Israel without a leader, but He chose not to work that way. Ever since, God has called men and women to leadership roles in His kingdom.

Why did God declare, "I am sending you?" What qualified Moses for the job? For one thing, he had been brought up in Pharaoh's family and received a good education and training. Although he had presumptuously tried to lead Israel, God did not give up on Moses. Instead, He sent him to "school" for 40 years. Somehow, Moses gained the necessary spiritual qualifications through the disciplines of those years.

Christians must be prepared to pay the price of spiritual preparation and training. No Christian knows when God will say, "I am sending you."

III. Moses Was Reluctant: Exodus 3:11-12

A. He Was a Nobody: vs. 11

But Moses said to God, "Who am I, that I should go to Pharaoh and bring the Israelites out of Egypt?"

In Exodus 3:11—4:17 we have an extended dialogue between God and Moses. The subject was simple: Moses did not want to go and he told God four reasons why he wasn't fit for the task: (1) his lack of stature (3:11); (2) his lack of divine authority (3:13); his fear of failure (4:1); (4) his lack of eloquence (4:10).

When Moses asked, "Who am I to lead the people out of Egypt?" he sounded a different note than he had 40 years earlier. Then he was self-confident and assumed he could save his people by his own efforts. Now he realized there was no way he could do that. After all, he was just a simple, humble shepherd.

His lowly view of himself showed that he had been humbled. He was no longer the take-charge guy, the go-to person. His "Who am I?" shows he had learned humility, a quality much desired in leaders. God's work in his life had achieved this outstanding quality. So much so that later on Moses was called "a very humble man, more humble that anyone else on the face of the earth"

(Num. 12:3). Obviously, Moses had other leadership qualities as well, but we need to remember how high humility stands on God's list.

B. God Reassured Him: vs. 12

And God said, "I will be with you. And this will be the sign to you that it is I who have sent you: When you have brought the people out of Egypt, you will worship God on this mountain."

God did not butter up Moses with affirmations of his leadership skills. Rather, He simply told him that He would be with him. His personal presence would guarantee the success of this mission, which was, after all, God's mission, not Moses'.

Then God made a curious promise. He said that Israel would worship Him on the very spot where they were then standing. Of course, this was intended to show Moses that God was with him and that He would guarantee success.

Could Moses believe this? Would the people really leave Egypt and worship God on Mount Sinai? It was greatly reassuring to know that God would remove all obstacles to deliver His people. Moses was cast completely on God. That is the indispensable quality of all leaders.

Discussion Questions

1. How do you think Moses felt during 40 years of shepherding? Why?
2. As a Christians, what should you do when you feel God has forgotten you?
3. How does God speak to His people today? What is required for His message to get through?
4. How can Christians develop a healthier respect for God's holiness?
5. Is God's call limited to religious vocations? How does one receive a call to be a plumber or a scientist?
6. What must we believe about God before we say yes to His call?

Contemporary Application

Moses had much to learn before he could answer God's call to leadership. Today, however, it's tempting to look for shortcuts. We think we can produce "instant leaders" like we prepare pudding out of a box.

Consequently, people often jump around looking for the most promising positions, rather than growing through the disciplines of faithful learning. In the churches, we sometimes thrust immature people into leadership, disregarding the apostle Paul's counsel in this matter (1 Tim. 3:6).

God's call does not come through popularity contests, nor necessarily to those most highly placed in society and business. God's call to leadership in Israel came to an inconspicuous nobody in the desert.

We all suffer when unqualified people are given authority, but we also suffer when qualified people turn down God's call. How we answer God's call depends to a large degree on our loving obedience to Christ (John 14:21, 23).

Crossing the Red Sea

DEVOTIONAL READING
Psalm 106:1-12

DAILY BIBLE READINGS

Monday September 6
*Exodus 13:3-10 The
Festival of Unleavened
Bread*

Tuesday September 7
*Exodus 13:17-22 Led by
Pillars of Cloud and Fire*

Wednesday September 8
*Exodus 14:1-9 Caught
between Pharaoh and the
Sea*

Thursday September 9
*Exodus 14:10-18 Going
Forward at God's Command*

Friday September 10
*Exodus 14:19-25 Israel
Crosses the Red Sea*

Saturday September 11
*Exodus 14:26-31 God
Saves Israel from the
Egyptians*

Sunday September 12
*Exodus 15:1-13 Moses
Sings of God's Victory*

Scripture

Background Scripture: *Exodus 13:17—14:31*
Scripture Lesson: *Exodus 13:17-22; 14:26-31*
Key Verse: *Moses answered the people, "Do not be
afraid. Stand firm and you will see the deliverance the
LORD will bring you today. The Egyptians you see today
you will never see again."* Exodus 14:13.

Lesson Aim

To find new reasons to trust God for wisdom and
courage in the face of opposition and discouragement.

Lesson Setting

Time: *about 1450 B.C.*
Place: *Egypt*

Lesson Outline

Crossing the Red Sea

  I. The Exit from Egypt: Exodus 13:17-22
     A. The Prescribed Route: vss. 17-19
     B. God's Guidance: vss. 20-22
  II. The Red Sea Crossing: Exodus 14:26-31
     A. The Egyptians Were Destroyed: vss. 26-28
     B. The Israelites Were Saved: vss. 29-30
     C. The People Trusted God: vs. 31

Introduction for Adults

Topic: *Called to Deliverance*

Detours often lead to disasters. An American traveler driving through Germany missed a detour sign because he couldn't read German. Soon he was hopelessly bogged down in a small town where the streets had been torn up.

That's what it must have seemed like to the Israelites. Their detour out of Egypt seemed like a disaster, because the Egyptians quickly overtook them.

However, in their case the supposed detour was really God's leading. Many times when we face unexpected turns in our lives we wonder if God is in control. We have the maps to our lives pretty well figured out, and then God says, "Take a different road. Go south."

The Red Sea crossing proves that it is best to follow God's word. He makes no mistakes. Even when it looks like we are trapped, He is with us and He tells us not to be afraid. He tells us to trust Him and to go forward.

Introduction for Youths

Topic: *Hope out of Despair*

What's it like to be a slave? We cannot imagine the experience, because we enjoy unparalleled freedom. However, depression, fear, and despair come at us from different directions today through broken homes, broken promises, sickness, emotional and physical abuse, violence in our neighborhoods and schools, substance abuse, and suicide.

But the story of Israel's Red Sea crossing gives us many reasons for hope in the midst of despair. Teenagers readily confess their need for courage and hope. They need courage to be faithful to Christ. They need hope to meet some of the severe crises they confront.

But our story strongly reminds us that God is with us today in the person of Jesus. Jesus said He would never leave or forsake His people.

When we are trapped between the Egyptians and the Red Sea, we need to pray and cry out to God for courage, hope, and wisdom.

Concepts for Children

Topic: *Being a Leader*

1. As God's leader, Moses wisely counseled his people to prepare to leave Egypt and to keep the Passover.
2. When panic and fear gripped the Israelites, Moses calmed them down and told them to trust the Lord.
3. After the Red Sea crossing, Moses led the people in worship.
4. God wants us to be His leaders at home, school, and in our neighborhoods.
5. Leaders require courage and faith, so we can ask Jesus to make us bold and faithful.
6. Some of our friends do not confess Jesus as Lord. Being a leader means helping them to put their faith in Him.

The Lesson Commentary

I. THE EXIT FROM EGYPT: EXODUS 13:17-22

A. The Prescribed Route: vss. 17-19

When Pharaoh let the people go, God did not lead them on the road through the Philistine country, though that was shorter. For God said, "If they face war, they might change their minds and return to Egypt." So God led the people around by the desert road toward the Red Sea. The Israelites went up out of Egypt armed for battle. Moses took the bones of Joseph with him because Joseph had made the sons of Israel swear an oath. He had said, "God will surely come to your aid, and then you must carry my bones up with you from this place."

After four centuries of slavery in Egypt, the Lord set the Israelites free. There has never been another event like the exodus from Egypt. It is unique because a helpless nation of slaves gained freedom from a far superior power.

It happened because God intervened and changed the Egyptians by a series of 10 plagues on Egypt. After the tenth plague broke out (the death of the Egyptians' firstborn sons), Pharaoh ordered his slaves to leave (Exod. 12:31-32).

Before this, Moses had demanded that Pharaoh free God's people, but Pharaoh had stubbornly refused. Moses' demand for freedom became a battle of wills, as Pharaoh steadfastly resisted God's will. Pharaoh had defiantly replied, "Who is the LORD, that I should obey him and let Israel go? I do not know the LORD and I will not let Israel go" (Exod. 5:2).

In delivering His people, God had forced them to recognize His sovereignty. God had told Moses, "And the Egyptians will know that I am the LORD when I stretch out my hand against Egypt and bring the Israelites out of it" (Exod. 7:5).

There are two basic issues in this story: (1) God loved His people and responded to their oppression by giving them freedom, and (2) God proved to Israelites and Egyptians alike that He is the all-powerful ruler of the universe who controls the destinies of nations.

Moses instructed the people in God's plan to spare them from the plague of death on Egypt's firstborn children and cattle. The blood of a lamb, spread on the doorposts of their houses, was a sign to the Lord, who said, "When I see the blood, I will pass over you" (Exod. 12:13). This was the institution of the rite of the Passover in Israel.

God's people obeyed these instructions perfectly. Everything happened as Moses said it would. The firstborn in Israel were spared. The Israelites put on their sandals, tucked up their robes, grabbed their staffs, and ate the Lord's Passover in a rush (12:11). They also plundered the Egyptians of their gold and silver (12:35-36). However, they brought nothing else except unleavened dough and their cattle (12:33-39).

"There were about six hundred thousand men on foot, besides women and children" (12:37). This means the total camp came to nearly two million people. It is difficult to apprehend how this mass migration was carried out. However, three times during the plagues Pharaoh had said he would let the people go . . . under certain conditions. This is probably when Moses told the Israelites how to get ready for the march.

They first stopped at Succoth (12:37). This was probably the headquarters for the Israelites in Egypt, and the place where Joseph's bones were kept. However, God did not lead them out of Egypt by the most direct route through the land of the Philistines. He feared that if they had to fight the Philistines, they might quit and go back to Egypt. This is exactly what happened when the Egyptians pursued them (14:11-12).

Instead of taking the shorter, coastal route, the Israelites took the desert route by way of the Red Sea. At God's direction, they moved southward toward the rugged Sinai Peninsula. (Consult a Bible atlas.) However, this meant they had to cross the Red Sea, or Sea of Reeds (as the Hebrew text says), an ancient lake along what is now the Suez Canal. This is not the same body of water now known as the Red Sea (though there is no question about the miracle involved here).

The Israelites departed "armed for battle" (13:18b). In Egypt, they had occupied a frontier district that was exposed to frequent raids, and Pharaoh was afraid that some day they might join forces with these raiders (Exod. 1:10). However, the word "armed" has also been translated "marshaled in an orderly array." This probably fits the context better, because there is no evidence that the Israelites were a strong military force.

Moses made sure to honor the dying request of Joseph (Gen. 50:24-25) who had asked that his bones be carried out of Egypt, He was sure that one day God would bring his descendants into their own land.

B. God's Guidance: vss. 20-22

After leaving Succoth they camped at Etham on the edge of the desert. By day the LORD went ahead of them in a pillar of cloud to guide them on their way and by night in a pillar of fire to give them light, so that they could travel by day or night. Neither the pillar of cloud by day nor the pillar of fire by night left its place in front of the people.

God had told them which route to take, and they moved ahead toward the desert. In addition to their organization and the leadership skills of Moses, God also gave them a special manifestation of His presence.

The cloud and the fire were like powerful searchlights pointing the way through unknown territory. We cannot describe these phenomena precisely, but it is clear that God intended to show Himself as their supreme guide. They could know they were on the right track as long as they followed these signs.

The pillar of cloud separated the Israelites from the pursuing Egyptians (14:19-20). Later on, the pillar of cloud stood at the entrance of the tent where Moses met the Lord (33:9-10). The Lord actually spoke from the cloud (Num. 12:5; 14:14; Ps. 99:7). The cloud and fire stayed with them 40 years, despite their sin and unbelief (Neh. 9:19-21).

II. THE RED SEA CROSSING: EXODUS 14:26-31

A. The Egyptians Were Destroyed: vss. 26-28

Then the LORD said to Moses, "Stretch out your hand over the sea so that the waters may flow back over the Egyptians and their chariots and horsemen." Moses stretched out his hand over the sea, and at daybreak the sea went back to its place. The Egyptians were fleeing toward it, and the LORD swept them into the sea. The water flowed back and covered the chariots and horsemen—the entire army of Pharaoh that had followed the Israelites into the sea. Not one of them survived.

Israel's deliverance from Egypt was not without its terrifying tests. When "the LORD struck down all the firstborn in Egypt" (12:29), the Egyptians predictably wanted to get rid of the Hebrews as fast as possible.

Pharaoh had boasted before Moses and Aaron that the God of Israel was nothing to him. But God had vowed to Moses that one day Pharaoh would acknowledge Him. In bringing the Israelites to freedom, God also taught Egypt and the nations that He really was the supreme ruler of the world. God said He would "gain glory for myself through Pharaoh and all his army, and the Egyptians will know that I am the LORD" (14:4).

God's object lesson was also intended for the Israelites. They panicked when the Egyptians pursued them (vss. 10-12). They turned on Moses and said it would have been better for them to die in Egypt. But Moses encouraged the people to trust God. "The LORD will fight for you; you need only to be still" (vs. 14). Then God gave Moses the frightening command to march straight through the Red Sea on dry ground, because he would "divide the water" (vs. 16). God revealed to Moses His plan for destroying the Egyptians and for bringing glory to Himself (vss. 17-18).

The scene was the northeast corner of Egypt between the Gulf of Suez and the Mediterranean Sea. Moses identified the towns it was near (vss. 1-2), which is now known as the Bitter Lakes region of Egypt, between Qantara (30 miles south of Port Said) and just north of Suez.

When Moses got to the Red Sea, he did as God had commanded. While he put his hand over the water, God drove a path through the sea with a strong east wind that blew all night long. "The waters were divided, and the Israelites went through the sea on dry ground, with a wall of water on their right and on their left" (vss. 21-22).

Moses' staff symbolized God's leading and the authority He had given to Moses. Nevertheless, for them to step between the walls of water was a tremendous test of their faith and obedience.

First, they had been paralyzed by fear and complaining. Next, they responded to Moses and followed him and Aaron into the unknown. Doubtless they did so with great trepidation. God did not fail them. His power sustained not only the wall of water but the courage of the Israelites.

Meanwhile, the Egyptians thought this would be an easy victory. But what looked like a stroll along the Nile turned into disaster. From the pillar of fire and cloud God threw the Egyptian army into total disarray. Their horses bolted and their vaunted chariots broke down.

Sensing they were losing, the Egyptians decided to flee. "The LORD is fighting for them against Egypt," they cried (vs. 25). They had previously experienced God's mighty hand, so they recognized that He was fighting against them now. They had only one recourse, "Run for your life!"

It was too late. God told Moses to stretch out his hand again, so the waters would engulf the Egyptians. Pharaoh's army was wiped out. This was such a devastating disaster that Egypt was not able to mount another expedition into this area for years.

The Red Sea crossing was both God's judgment on Egypt and His deliverance of Israel. This was the initiation of Israel's national self-consciousness. The exodus from Egypt remains the cornerstone of Jewish identity.

To Old Testament believers, the miraculous crossing of the Red Sea stood for God's power and love. It also was the basis of His claim to the worship and obedience of His people. Throughout the Psalms it is celebrated and used as a call to faithfulness (Psalm 66:6; 74:13; 106:9; 136:13). In the New Testament, it is cited as an example of faith (Heb. 11:29).

B. The Israelites Were Saved: vss. 29-30

But the Israelites went through the sea on dry ground, with a wall of water on their right and on their left. That day the LORD saved Israel from the hands of the Egyptians, and Israel saw the Egyptians lying dead on the shore.

Having obeyed the Lord and followed Moses and Aaron, the people safely crossed the Red Sea. It would be exciting to read a journal of their feelings while they walked. Would the walls of water crush them? Would the pursuing Egyptians catch them?

Once they arrived safely on the other side, imagine how they felt when they looked back and saw the Egyptians drowning. Then they knew for certain that God had saved Israel. They had not defeated the Egyptians; God had.

C. The People Trusted God: vs. 31

And when the Israelites saw the great power the LORD displayed against the Egyptians, the people feared the LORD and put their trust in him and in Moses his servant.

Safely on the east side of the Red Sea, the Israelites expressed their commitment to God. They had witnessed God's "great power" in the 10 plagues and in the crossing of the Red Sea. They were set free from the idols of Egypt to worship the one true and living God. That was the fundamental issue they had to settle: Who is the Lord?

They feared the Lord and trusted in Him. Fear speaks of reverential awe.

How could they feel otherwise, in light of what they had just witnessed? Fear speaks of holy respect, of knowing God's power, justice, and holiness.

To trust God meant that they had to follow Him for the rest of the journey. To trust God meant that they had to abandon self-reliance and pride. It meant believing God when it appeared there was no other way out.

The Israelites had to trust God because of the great tests that awaited them. For the sake of organization and unity, they also needed to trust their leader, lest there be rebellion and confusion in the ranks.

We know that later on, when the time came to enter Canaan, they rebelled against God and Moses. Consequently, God consigned them to 40 years of wandering in the desert. But at this point they made a glorious commitment to God and to Moses. A celebration of praise and worship broke out (15:1-21).

In Revelation 15:3 this song of Moses is linked to the final triumph of Christians. Therefore, the Red Sea crossing also sends a strong prophetic signal of the Church's ultimate triumph and deliverance.

Discussion Questions

1. Why do you think God didn't lead the Israelites by a shorter route to Canaan?
2. What kinds of preparations did the Israelites have to make for the Exodus?
3. Why did they need the pillar of cloud and fire to lead them?
4. How would you have felt when trapped between the Egyptians and the Red Sea? Why?
5. How do people today find out who God really is?
6. How does God get glory for Himself in the Church?

Contemporary Application

Old Testament prophets exhorted the people to repent and turn to God because He had redeemed them from Egypt. The Exodus was the cornerstone of their relation to God. They were His people because He had set them free.

Christians belong to God because Jesus Christ purchased their freedom with His death on the cross. We do not belong to ourselves, but to Him who died for us.

We proclaim God's mighty power in the Exodus and the Red Sea crossing. We proclaim God's mighty power in the death and resurrection and ascension of the Lord Jesus Christ.

The spirit of the age denies that God has worked His power at the Red Sea and at Calvary. The spirit of the age says that we can solve our own problems with technology or through social and political engineering.

However, Christians carry a strong voice. Their mission is the same as God's mission was at the Red Sea crossing. The world must know that He is God, and He alone. He has spoken finally in Jesus Christ. One day He shall judge the world, and the question will be: Who is the Lord? And, did you follow Him?

The Covenant

Scripture

Background Scripture: *Exodus 19:1—20:21*
Scripture Lesson: *Exodus 19:3-6; 20:2-4, 7-8, 12-17*
Key Verse: *"Now if you obey me fully and keep my
covenant, then out of all nations you will be my treasured
possession."* Exodus 19:5.

Lesson Aim

To appreciate the personal and social values of the
Ten Commandments, and to seek the higher
standards taught by Jesus (Matt. 5:21-22, 27-28,
43-44).

Lesson Setting

Time: *about 1446 B.C.*
Place: *Mount Sinai*

Lesson Outline

The Covenant
   I. God's Proposal: Exodus 19:3-6
      A. A Look Back: vss. 3-4
      B. A Look Ahead: vss. 5-6
  II. God's Commands: Exodus 20:2-4, 7-8, 12-17
      A. No Other Gods: vss. 2-3
      B. No Idols: vs. 4
      C. No Profanity: vs. 7
      D. Keep the Sabbath: vs. 8
      E. Honor Your Parents: vs. 12
      F. No Murder: vs. 13
      G. No Adultery: vs. 14
      H. No Stealing: vs. 15
      I. No False Testimony: vs. 16
      J. No Coveting: vs. 17

Introduction for Adults

Topic: *Called to Covenant*

In the exhilaration of their newly granted freedom from Egypt, the Israelites were not prepared for the moral and social dangers that would soon confront them. Therefore, God called them to make a monumental covenant, or agreement, with Him. By virtue of the exodus from Egypt, they now belonged to Him and would be expected to live accordingly.

Rarely do we think the stakes are so high. Rarely do we put our commitment to Christ in the terms of a solemn agreement. Rarely do we even recall the covenant we made when we trusted in Christ and joined His church. Rarely do we even hear those vows, except when new members are taken in.

We must see the Ten Commandments as a set of vows the Israelites promised to keep, for their own good and for the good of their society and country.

Introduction for Youths

Topic: *What Are the Limits?*

The only restrictions on youth used to be the age of driving, drinking, and voting. No more. The rules now extend to what you can't wear to school, the weapons and drugs you can't carry into school, the hours you can't keep, the music you can't listen to, and the substances you can't abuse.

It's no use arguing that the reason for some of these rules is their self-protection for young people. If some youths had not started to carry the habits of adult law-breakers into school, the rules would not be necessary.

In somewhat the same way, God saw the moral dangers His people would face. He knew the world was filled with idolaters, murderers, thieves, and adulterers. Therefore, they needed a set of rules. He set the limits so they would know what holiness means.

For Christian youth, their allegiance is to Jesus, because He died for them and rescued them from ungodly lifestyles. To get off to a good start, they need to know and obey the Ten Commandments.

Concepts for Children

Topic: *Following Rules*

1. God loved His people Israel so much that He gave them freedom and also the responsibility to love and obey Him.
2. Jesus loves us and expects us to do His will.
3. Many times we find it hard to obey God's rules, so we must pray and ask for God's help.
4. We can also find help from our parents and older Christians.
5. Other children may not have the same high regard for God's laws as Christian children do, so we must be lovingly patient with them.
6. Inviting other children into our homes is a wonderful way to help them come to know Jesus and His ways.

The Lesson Commentary

I. God's Proposal: Exodus 19:3-6

A. A Look Back: vss. 3-4

Then Moses went up to God, and the LORD called to him from the mountain and said, "This is what you are to say to the house of Jacob and what you are to tell the people of Israel: 'You yourselves have seen what I did to Egypt, and how I carried you on eagles' wings and brought you to myself.'"

Having led the people in a triumphal celebration through the Red Sea to deliver them from Egypt, Moses began the trek into the wilderness of Sinai. At Marah God miraculously gave them drinkable water, and at Elim they found a desert oasis. Half way through their second month, however, they grumbled against Moses and Aaron because they thought they were starving to death. God gave them manna and quail to eat.

Following the cloud by day and the fire by night, they moved on to Rephidim, where once again they complained because there was no water there. However, Moses struck a rock and by God's grace, water flowed freely. While camped there, the Israelites were attacked by the Amalekites, but Joshua defeated the enemy.

Meanwhile, in the third month the camp advanced to Sinai, where God spoke to Moses and revealed His rules for His people to live by. But first He described to Moses the broad outline of His proposal. He began by telling Moses to tell His people to look back on how God had delivered them.

God used a magnificent metaphor to describe what He had done. "I carried you on eagles' wings." Israel could not boast of anything. God had done it all. Israel now belonged to the one true and living God.

B. A Look Ahead: vss. 5-6

" 'Now if you obey me fully and keep my covenant, then out of all nations you will be my treasured possession. Although the whole earth is mine, you will be for me a kingdom of priests and a holy nation.' These are the words you are to speak to the Israelites."

Having reflected on what God had done in the recent past, God through Moses directed Israel to look ahead. This helpless band of refugees would become God's "treasured possession" and "a kingdom of priests and a holy nation."

The apostle Peter used similar language for Christians: "You are a chosen people, a royal priesthood, a holy nation, a people belonging to God" (1 Pet. 2:9).

The Israelites would be priests in the generic sense, not in the sense of a special caste of religious intermediaries. They were to be marked by their holiness.

God made very clear that the fulfillment of His promises rested on the obedience of the Israelites: "Now if you obey me fully . . ." (Exod. 19:5). His covenant was a two-way street. They must keep His commands while He keeps them safe. This covenant would be the focal point of Israel's history from the Exodus to the downfall of Jerusalem about 1,500 years later.

II. GOD'S COMMANDS: EXODUS 20:2-4, 7-8, 12-17

A. No Other Gods: vss. 2-3

"I am the LORD *your God, who brought you out of Egypt, out of the land of slavery. You shall have no other gods before me."*

The elders responded to Moses by promising to do everything the Lord had said (19:8). Moses told the people to wash themselves and to stay away from the mountain where God would speak to him (vss. 10-13). God appeared in what looked like a volcanic eruption and spoke to him, revealing what we call the Ten Commandments. Actually, he revealed a whole lot more (Exodus 20—34). Moses stayed on the mountain with God for 40 days and nights, going without bread or water. At God's command, He wrote on stone tablets the words of the covenant—the Ten Commandments (34:28).

The first command lays the groundwork. It declares that the God who had delivered them from slavery in Egypt was their God. They were not saved by any local pagan god. Only the one true and living God in heaven was their savior and protector. Therefore, they were not to worship any other gods.

This was to become Israel's chief temptation and the cause of her downfall as a nation. They could not keep themselves from dabbling in pagan worship.

B. No Idols: vs. 4

"You shall not make for yourself an idol in the form of anything in heaven above or on the earth beneath or in the waters below."

Egypt was saturated with every imaginable kind of idol. Soon the Israelites would encounter Canaanite idols. People believed strongly that the gods represented by these idols brought good fortune, safety, fertility, good crops, and protection from enemies.

God strictly prohibited the making of and worshiping of idols. The Israelites could not make any representation of earthly, heavenly, or underwater deities.

Not only was God to be their exclusive God, He was not to be portrayed by any physical form. His power and glory could not in any way be compared to a man-made idol, no matter how elaborate the idol. God is spirit, not matter.

C. No Profanity: vs. 7

"You shall not misuse the name of the LORD *your God, for the* LORD *will not hold anyone guiltless who misuses his name."*

Because their redeemer God was sovereign and holy, His name was to be revered and respected. His name stood for who He was. His name represented His nature and character. Therefore, He prohibited the flippant, senseless, light use of His name, and He would judge those who broke this command.

This command also related to how they worshiped the Lord. It prohibits outward, phony, hypocritical worship. Better not to use God's name at all than to make it an external ritual and not a matter of the heart. Consequently, the Israelites developed a tradition of not using God's name at all rather than risk using it in the wrong way.

D. Keep the Sabbath: vs. 8

"Remember the Sabbath day by keeping it holy."

God instituted the Sabbath ("seventh") day in Israel. This was a radical departure from the prevailing customs of the day, but God told Moses to keep the day holy, which means set apart to God. Obedience to this command would send another powerful signal to surrounding peoples that the Israelites really were a different people. They would be a strong witness to the one true God in heaven.

The Sabbath command was based on God's rest from His creation work on the seventh day (vs. 11). God, as it were, built this principle into His creation of human beings. They would be stronger and more faithful to God if they observed the sabbath (rest) principle.

Sadly, this principle was allowed to lapse in Israel, and God judged His people for it. After their captivity in Babylon, the Jews restored this law with a vengeance, so much so that Jesus rebuked their over-zealous legalism.

E. Honor Your Parents: vs. 12

"Honor your father and your mother, so that you may live long in the land the LORD *your God is giving you."*

The first four commands related to Israel's walk and obedience to God. The next six related to their responsibilities to one another in a social context. The first four kept their faith in line, the last six kept their lives in order and guaranteed peace, safety, and overall well-being.

The fifth command revealed God's concern for healthy family life. His people were to honor their parents. By doing so they would enjoy peace and prosperity in the land God intended to give them. This command was the cement of family solidarity, love, trust, and acceptance. It also guaranteed security in old age.

In God's plan, honoring one's parents is a lifelong duty. It does not cease when we reach adulthood. It continues as long as our parents live.

How the people were to honor their parents was not spelled out in detail, but it certainly included love, respect, trust, and security for their physical and emotional needs. It included learning from their wisdom and experience.

F. No Murder: vs. 13

"You shall not murder."

Every human being is created in God's image. Therefore, every person's life is sacred to God. Consequently, God clearly prohibited murder.

This command stands as a cornerstone of society. It told the Israelites they were responsible for the well-being of everyone else. They learned of the supreme value of human life.

G. No Adultery: vs. 14

"You shall not commit adultery."

Well-ordered society depends on marital fidelity. This command made it clear that adultery would not be tolerated in Israel. If faithfulness goes out the window, so does satisfying family life, and society as a whole suffers greatly.

The family is the basic unit of society. God's law in this case was intended to insure that the family stayed together, and that husbands, wives, and children would not suffer the consequences of infidelity.

Of course, the command was also addressed to the deep-seated temptation to sexual sins. The Israelites had lived in a society of sexual permissiveness. The corruption they would see in Canaan was deplorable.

H. No Stealing: vs. 15

"You shall not steal."

God's concern for personal safety extended beyond bodily and marital harm. He included the law against stealing, because one's property becomes a part of one's self-identity. When someone burglarizes your house, you feel personally violated. This command protects individuals against the violation of personhood, as well as the loss of property.

This law also recognizes the human propensity to steal, not just big things like robbing banks, but cheating on taxes, taking employers' property, stealing company time, failing to return a borrowed piece of equipment, and so on. When we obey this command in its broadest sense, we not only protect society but we protect our reputations and give good witness to our faith in God. He takes care of us, so we do not need to steal.

I. No False Testimony: vs. 16

"You shall not give false testimony against your neighbor."

False testimony occurs not only in a court of law, but also on our streets and offices when we spread gossip and outright lies. Because we are made in God's image, our reputations as well as our bodies are sacred to Him.

This command relates to the testimony the Israelites would have to give when someone was charged with breaking any of God's laws. (Skim the rest of Exodus to see how detailed they were.) Witnesses would be called to verify what had happened. A person's life often hung on a neighbor's testimony.

Therefore, God prohibited false witness. This command gave a solid foundation to Israel's justice system.

J. No Coveting: vs. 17

"You shall not covet your neighbor's house. You shall not covet your neighbor's wife, or his manservant or maidservant, his ox or donkey, or anything that belongs to your neighbor."

As the Israelites contemplated moving into a new land, they had to be concerned about living in freedom without the controls the Egyptians had placed on their lives. This new freedom could easily degenerate into wholesale exploitation, greed, and oppression. They had left Egypt with considerable wealth in jewelry and gold. Rare is the person who does not want more.

God commanded them not even to think desiringly or greedily about what their neighbors had. Don't itch for another's house, his wife, his servants, his animals, "or anything that belongs to your neighbor."

Coveting is such a terrible sin because it tears up our minds. It robs us of contentment in God. Coveting tells us lies that we will be happier with another person's spouse or property. Coveting appeals to the desires of the flesh. It completely ignores the fact that Jesus revealed: Our satisfaction in life does not come from abundant possessions.

Discussion Questions

1. Why was the prelude (Exod. 19:3-6) necessary to the giving of the Ten Commandments? What does it tell you about your relation to God?
2. What application of this principle can you make from John 14:21, 23?
3. What "other gods" are we in danger of worshiping today?
4. How can Christians relate positively to the flood of new immigrants who do worship other gods?
5. In what practical ways can Christians help each other to keep God's commandments? What kinds of accountability do we have to each other at home and in the church?
6. How can we help our children to learn and obey the Ten Commandments?

Contemporary Application

God's covenant with Israel was very specific. It is quite different from our modern way of deciding between many options. Ours is a pick and choose society—choose which of God's laws you want to keep, and you forget the rest.

In this kind of cultural climate, it's often hard for Christians to be unequivocal about God's laws. They don't want to be considered narrow-minded, bigoted, and intolerant. On the other hand, they know God's laws are best for society as well as for their individual lives.

Therefore, we cannot afford to explain them away, tone them down, or make exceptions to gain popular approval. So much of society is at risk, and so many people's lives are messed up, that we must insist the only way to improvement lies in following the principles laid down in the Ten Commandments.

The Tabernacle and Obedience

DEVOTIONAL READING

Psalm 84

DAILY BIBLE READINGS

Monday September 20
*Exodus 40:1-15 God's
Command Regarding
Tabernacle and Priests*

Tuesday September 21
*Exodus 40:16-23 Building
the Tabernacle*

Wednesday September 22
*Exodus 40:24-33 Equip-
ping the Tabernacle*

Thursday September 23
*Leviticus 26:1-13 Rewards
for Obedience*

Friday September 24
*Leviticus 26:14-22
Consequences of Disobedi-
ence*

Saturday September 25
*Leviticus 26:27-39 God
Either/Or*

Sunday September 26
*Leviticus 26:40-46
Confession Will Bring
Renewal*

Scripture

Background Scripture: *Exodus 40:1-33; Leviticus 26*
Scripture Lesson: *Exodus 40:1-9; Leviticus 26:2-6,
11-13*
Key Verse: " *'Observe my Sabbaths and have reverence
for my sanctuary. I am the LORD.'* " Leviticus 26:2.

Lesson Aim

To see God's holiness and enjoy His presence as we
worship and obey Him.

Lesson Setting

Time: *about 1446 B.C.*
Place: *Mount Sinai*

Lesson Outline

The Tabernacle and Obedience

  I. Setting Up the Tabernacle: Exodus 40:1-9
     A. *The Ark, Lampstand, and Altar of Incense:
        vss. 1-5*
     B. *The Altar of Burnt Offering: vss. 6-8*
     C. *The Anointing: vs. 9*
 II. God's Promises: Leviticus 26:2-6, 11-13
     A. *Reverence His Sanctuary: vs. 2*
     B. *Keep His Commands: vs. 3*
     C. *His Rich Harvests: vss. 4-5*
     D. *His Peace: vs. 6*
     E. *His Presence: vss. 11-13*

Introduction for Adults

Topic: *Called to Obedience*

Being called to obedience is like being called by your draft board to serve in the Army—not a pleasant prospect. But that's what God requires of His people. He has the right to do this because He purchased us for His own possession by the blood of Christ.

Because we are also called to receive His manifold blessings, which are described as unsearchable riches of Christ (Eph. 3:8), our obedience is not blind drudgery, but joyful anticipation.

Called to obedience is also a call to blessing. In Christ, we have been blessed with all things pertaining to life and godliness (2 Pet. 1:3). In Christ, we have "all the treasures of wisdom and knowledge" (Col. 2:3). We "have been given fullness in Christ" (Col. 2:10). Therefore, why should we not obey Him?

Introduction for Youths

Topic: *A Point of Contact*

Where do we meet God today? Some people say they can meet God in nature, or in drugs. Finding God is somehow thought to be a mystical experience reserved for a few people who are into religion. That leaves out most people.

But the Bible tells us that God is looking for us. He sent Jesus, the Good Shepherd, to find us. He loved us and died for us, so that we might experience God and know Him personally. This is not a religious secret; it is revealed in the Gospel.

Therefore, our task is to help other people experience God in us. How do we do that? By loving and obeying Jesus. He promised that when we do that, it reveals that He and His Father live in us (John 14:21, 23). Then the world will have a point of contact with God.

Concepts for Children

Topic: *Remembering and Worshiping God*

1. God helps us to remember Him by giving us special times and places for worship.
2. God seeks our worship. He is the focal point of worship, not the church building.
3. When we gather with friends to sing, hear God's Word, and pray, we can know that God is among us.
4. The Israelites learned that God is holy and requires sacrifice for sin. The Lord Jesus Christ is the sacrifice for our sins.
5. God loves to bless us, and when we obey Him He takes care of all of our real needs.
6. We can be happiest when we are enjoying God's presence.

The Lesson Commentary

I. SETTING UP THE TABERNACLE: EXODUS 40:1-9

A. The Ark, Lampstand, and Altar of Incense: vss. 1-5

Then the LORD said to Moses: "Set up the tabernacle, the Tent of Meeting, on the first day of the first month. Place the ark of the Testimony in it and shield the ark with the curtain. Bring in the table and set out what belongs on it. Then bring in the lampstand and set up its lamps. Place the gold altar of incense in front of the ark of the Testimony and put the curtain at the entrance to the tabernacle."

God's laws for Israel (Exod. 20—40) began with His giving the Ten Commandments and concluded with the setting up of the tabernacle. "The Book of the Covenant" (20:22—23:33) is the oldest record of Jewish law. It includes judgments (various applications of the law) and statutes (which are direct commands).

All of the laws rested on God's authority. They were not the work of a king or parliament. There was no difference between civil and religious law, because God is concerned for the totality of life. God also revealed the sanctity of human life by establishing fixed, limited punishment.

Of course, it's helpful to understand that the laws were rooted in the settled life Israel was to enjoy in Canaan. Theirs was to be an agricultural community. Therefore, although some of the laws appear to be irrelevant to other cultures, the fixed principles of God's holiness and justice do not change with time.

The people ratified the covenant (Exod. 24), then God gave instructions for making and furnishing the tabernacle (Exod. 25—27). (Look for a picture of the tabernacle and its furnishings in a standard Bible handbook or dictionary.) The next section of the law (Exod. 28—30) covered the priests and their duties.

However, sin erupted in the camp (Exod. 32). Six weeks after pledging to keep the covenant, the people fell to worshiping a golden calf. God's judgment broke out and the idolaters died. Moses smashed the tablets, symbolizing the broken covenant. Moses pleaded with God to spare the people and he saw God's glory (Exod. 33). The tablets were regiven and the covenant was renewed (Exod. 34).

The instructions given for setting up the tabernacle in chapters 25—32 were carried out. Exodus 35—40 tells how the craftsmen went to work. The people gave generously, and everything was completed exactly according to God's specifications. God's visible presence in the cloud rested on the tabernacle, which was filled with His glory. Until it was replaced by Solomon's temple 500 years later, the tabernacle stood as the focal point of Israel's worship.

God told Moses when to set up the tabernacle and where to place the various furnishings. "The first day of the first month" shows that this occasion marked the beginning of Israel's second year in the wilderness (vs. 17; see also Exod. 12:2).

The ark, a wooden box made of acacia wood, was unique in that it housed "the Testimony," that is, God's laws for Israel inscribed on the stone tablets. The box was about four feet long, two feet wide, and two feet high. It was overlaid with gold inside and out, and had a gold molding around it. The ark was covered with a gold atonement plate and decorated with facing cherubim (angels) made of gold. It was shielded by a curtain.

The ark was not an idol or an image. It was the center of Israel's divinely revealed faith. "There, above the cover between the two cherubim that are over the ark of the Testimony, I will meet with you and give you all my commands for the Israelites," God told Moses (25:22).

The lampstand was the only source of light in the tabernacle. All natural light was blocked out. The details of the lampstand in Hebrew are difficult to ascertain with precision, so our best idea is that it looked like a stylized tree (25:31).

In the holy place in front of the curtain stood the altar of incense (30:1-10). It was also made of acacia wood and overlaid with gold, so it was called "the golden altar." It stood a foot and a half wide, a foot and a half long, and three feet high, with ornamental horns and molding. It stood directly opposite the ark.

B. The Altar of Burnt Offering: vss. 6-8

"Place the altar of burnt offering in front of the entrance to the tabernacle, the Tent of Meeting; place the basin between the Tent of Meeting and the altar and put water in it. Set up the courtyard around it and put the curtain at the entrance to the courtyard."

The altar of burnt offering was made of acacia wood and stood four and a half feet high, and about seven and a half feet long and wide (27:1-8). It was overlaid with bronze. All of its fittings were also of bronze.

It resembled a huge barbecue grill and stood to the east of the door of the tabernacle. Its "horns" served to bind sacrificial animals.

The tabernacle itself stood on the western half of a courtyard 150 by 70 feet. The long side ran north and south. The door faced east. The courtyard was set off by a linen screen seven and a half feet high.

C. The Anointing: vs. 9

"Take the anointing oil and anoint the tabernacle and everything in it; consecrate it and all its furnishings, and it will be holy."

Everything in the tabernacle had to be anointed to show its total consecration to God. All of Israel's worship was permeated with a sense of God's holiness and awesome presence. Aaron and his sons were also anointed and consecrated (vss. 12-15).

The tabernacle also speaks profound spiritual truths to believers today. Of course, it proclaims that God is holy, but it also tells us that He is accessible. God indwells His people and He desires our worship according to His will. He loves to meet with us and has made full provision through the death and resurrection of Jesus Christ. The tabernacle prefigured the profound New Testament truth that it is only by sacrifice and shed blood that any one of us can have fellowship with a holy, righteous God (Eph. 2:11-18; Heb. 10:19-25).

II. GOD'S PROMISES: LEVITICUS 26:2-6, 11-13

A. Reverence His Sanctuary: vs. 2

" 'Observe my Sabbaths and have reverence for my sanctuary. I am the LORD.' "

Leviticus is the book of laws given by God to Israel through Moses at Mount Sinai. These laws covered all aspects of life. The book is named after the order of Levitical priests (Aaron, his sons, and their descendants).

These laws signified not only the holiness God expected of His people, but also the way to atone for breaking them. In the long range, they pointed to Christ's substitutionary atonement for our sins.

The laws also showed God's concern for the physical and material well-being of Israel, because they related to life in the natural environment. In many cases, they were good preventive medicine.

Another purpose of the laws was to set God's people apart from the pagan environment and culture of the Egyptians and Canaanites. God's people were a holy nation, standing as a witness to the one holy and true God in heaven.

Because of the pernicious influence of idolatry, God repeated His warning against making and worshiping images (26:1). "I am the LORD" (vs. 2) also demanded that Israel keep His Sabbaths and respect His sanctuary, the tabernacle.

The entire practice of Israel's faith depended on all that took place in and around God's sanctuary, His most holy place.

B. Keep His Commands: vs. 3

" 'If you follow my decrees and are careful to obey my commands, . . .' "

God's promised blessings for Israel rested on Israel's keeping His commands. They were meticulously detailed to cover all aspects of worship and daily life.

The Ten Commandments portrayed God's concern in the broad picture, relating as they did to His supremacy and His wisdom for their social conduct. To these were added the other commands in Exodus and Leviticus. As we skim them, we are overwhelmed with how carefully they were framed for Israel's welfare. At first they seem onerous and restrictive, but on fuller examination we find that they were given to make Israel holy and happy.

C. His Rich Harvests: vss. 4-5

" 'I will send you rain in its season, and the ground will yield its crops and the trees of the field their fruit. Your threshing will continue until grape harvest and the grape harvest will continue until planting, and you will eat all the food you want and live in safety in your land.' "

God promised rich, abundant, year-long harvests and protection for His people in Canaan. What tremendous assurance and hope God gave His people. What anticipation they must have had of this good land that awaited them.

Good harvests depended on timely rain, which God promised to give. Later on, withholding rain was a sign of God's judgment on their sin.

With the proper rain would come fertile crops and fruitful trees. The usual summer drought ended with fall rains. Seeds were planted in late November or December. Heavy winter rains provided needed moisture, and later spring rains brought the crops to maturity.

The main crops were wheat and barley. Wheat was more valuable, but barley grew on poorer soil and had a shorter growing season. Lentils, peas, and beans were secondary crops. They also grew vegetables, especially onions and garlic, plus a wide variety of herbs, seeds, and condiments.

In the Gospel, God's "rich harvest" is not wheat and fruit, but the fruit of the Holy Spirit (Gal. 5:22-23). For our faith and trust in Christ He gives us life "to the full" (John 10:10). For our obedience, God gives us His "kingdom . . . of righteousness, peace and joy in the Holy Spirit" (Rom. 14:17).

D. His Peace: vs. 6

" 'I will grant peace in the land, and you will lie down and no one will make you afraid. I will remove savage beasts from the land, and the sword will not pass through your country.' "

In addition to the temptations to worship idols and follow the corrupt practices of the Canaanites, the Israelites would face dangers from wild animals and enemy fighters. This great promise offered Israel perpetual serenity in the midst of danger. More than physical protection, this promise gave peace of mind. The dangers from attacks would not be removed, but God promised to be Israel's protector.

The New Testament promises do not focus on animals and robbers, but in Christ, God does offer abiding peace of mind, heart, and soul. Peter counsels believers to "cast all your anxiety on him [God] because he cares for you" (1 Pet. 5:7). Lions are not the enemy of Christians, but the "roaring lion," the devil, is (1 Pet. 5:8). But even in the face of the devil's attacks, God promises to make His children "strong, firm and steadfast" (1 Pet. 5:10).

Jesus told us that we do not need to live with troubled hearts, because He gives us His peace (John 14:1, 27). The apostle Paul encouraged believers to "let the peace of Christ rule in your hearts" (Col. 3:15). These are great promises for Christians to claim.

E. His Presence: vss. 11-13

" 'I will put my dwelling place among you, and I will not abhor you. I will walk among you and be your God, and you will be my people. I am the LORD your God, who brought you out of Egypt so that you would no longer be slaves to the Egyptians; I broke the bars of your yoke and enabled you to walk with heads held high.' "

Strong protection, peace of mind, and fruitful harvests: What more could Israel need and desire? God's presence. His greatest promise of all was that He would be with them. He would be their God and they would be His people.

If Israel had all of the other promises fulfilled, but lacked the certainty of

God's presence, all would be in vain. Their hearts, souls, minds, and spirits would be diminished, even while they enjoyed good harvests.

Prosperity and protection cannot make up for God's presence. He alone satisfies the hungry heart and soul. Jesus said we must hunger and thirst after righteousness, not money and the things of this world.

New Testament Christians claim the presence of Christ: "Surely I am with you always" (Matt. 28:20). The writer of Hebrews quoted the Old Testament promise to ancient Israel and applied it to the church: "Never will I leave you; never will I forsake you" (Heb. 13:5). The consequence of this fact is that Christians enjoy the peace God promised to Israel: "The Lord is my helper; I will not be afraid" (Heb. 13:6).

Discussion Questions

1. How might you have responded when the tabernacle was set up? Why?
2. What comfort or peace would you draw from worshiping there? Why?
3. What impressions of God would you receive? Why? How would this influence your behavior?
4. As you reflect on what you would like to receive from God, how do you rate your qualifications for these blessings? On what do His promises depend?
5. How can Christians encourage one another to move ahead by faith into the fullness of God's blessings?
6. At special places and times how have you felt God's presence especially keenly? How do your worship services help you to enjoy God's presence?

Contemporary Application

Many people have never heard of Israel's tabernacle, and they aren't particularly interested in finding out about it. Therefore, as Christians who believe it "was only a copy of the true one . . . heaven itself" (Heb. 9:24), we have to draw out the principles God was trying to teach about Himself. For example, the altar was a place of sacrifice, which was central to Israel's worship. Today, the church points people to the fact that Jesus Christ has fulfilled the purpose of these sacrifices (Heb. 9:11-15). From there, we can affirm the splendid joys of worship in which we express our appreciation for what Jesus has done for us.

We can focus on what God's plan for the tabernacle represented in terms of beauty and human craftsmanship. We can celebrate these gifts in our worship as well. Our sanctuaries help us to praise God for His character, majesty, and saving deeds.

But once we have been to the tabernacle, we realize that it is all worthless without our obedience and faith. The tabernacle (and later the temple) did not save Israel from destruction. If we do not obey Christ and the Gospel, we are likewise doomed.

The Cloud and the Fire

DEVOTIONAL READING

Psalm 107:1-9

DAILY BIBLE READINGS

Monday September 27
*Exodus 40:34-38 God's
Glory Fills the Tabernacle*

Tuesday September 28
*Numbers 9:15-23 Led by
God's Cloud and Fire*

Wednesday September 29
*Numbers 10:29-36
Journeying Away from
Mount Sinai*

Thursday September 30
*Psalm 105:1-15 God Keeps
His Covenant Forever*

Friday October 1
*Psalm 105:16-25 God
Provided for Israel in Egypt*

Saturday October 2
*Psalm 105:26-36 God Sent
Plagues upon Egypt*

Sunday October 3
*Psalm 105:37-45 God
Delivered Israel from Egypt*

Scripture

Background Scripture: *Exodus 40:34-38; Numbers 9:15-23*

Scripture Lesson: *Exodus 40:34-38; Numbers 9:15-19, 22-23*

Key Verse: *So the cloud of the LORD was over the tabernacle by day, and fire was in the cloud by night, in the sight of all the house of Israel during all their travels.* Exodus 40:38.

Key Verse for Children: *In all the travels of the Israelites, whenever the cloud lifted from above the tabernacle, they would set out.* Exodus 40:36.

Lesson Aim

To find wisdom and security in knowing God's good and perfect will.

Lesson Setting

Time: *around 1400 B.C.*
Place: *Wilderness of Sinai*

Lesson Outline

The Cloud and the Fire

   I. The Glory of the Lord: Exodus 40:34-35
      A. *Filled the Tabernacle: vs. 34*
      B. *Kept Moses Out: vs. 35*
  II. The Cloud and the Fire: Exodus 40:36-38
      A. *God's Direction: vss. 36-37*
      B. *God's Presence: vs. 38*
 III. The People Obeyed God: Numbers 9:15-19, 22-23

Introduction for Adults

Topic: *Follow Day by Day*

Anyone who grows up on a dairy farm soon learns the ways of cows. When it's time to come to the barn for milking, they follow the same order every day. No one knows why or how they do this, but they do.

Pretty boring, isn't it? Imagine how boring it seemed to the Israelites when their routine never varied from day to day. Get up in the morning. Look for the cloud over the tabernacle. Not moving? Get ready for the day. Moving? Pack up your stuff.

Faithfulness to God may seem to be boring at times, but when we choose to obey God's will we experience His wisdom, security, and protection. That's what most people say they want more than anything else in life.

The rewards of commitment and obedience far outrank what seems to be boring religious routine. For a fresh touch from God, we must put our lives into His hands and do what He tells us to do.

Introduction for Youths

Topic: *Following Faithfully*

Why go to school when it's such a great day? Warm weather will soon be over; the lake's still warm. One day won't make any difference. This was probably what two boys were thinking when they bagged high school soon after school opened and went for a swim in Lake Michigan, where they drowned in a wicked undertow.

Sadly, this tragedy illustrates a larger principle. When we bag school, so to speak, and seek fun and adventure at the expense of following Jesus, we court disaster. Faithfulness may not seem glamorous and exciting, but faithfulness guarantees God's blessing on our lives.

God gives the deepest happiness and satisfaction when we follow His revealed will and play the game of life by His rules. In the highest sense, joy and excitement are ours when we allow Jesus to lead us.

Concepts for Children

Topic: *Following Directions*

1. God blessed Israel by giving guidance and protection every day.
2. God enriched our lives by sending Jesus to save us from our sins and to guide us in our daily activities.
3. Unbelieving friends may ridicule us for claiming to follow Jesus.
4. It's important to study the Bible and pray so we can know what God wants us to do.
5. We don't follow the cloud and the fire; we follow Jesus, the light of the world.
6. We can find help from older Christians when we are confused about what to believe and what things to do.

The Lesson Commentary

I. THE GLORY OF THE LORD: EXODUS 40:34-35

A. Filled the Tabernacle: vs. 34

Then the cloud covered the Tent of Meeting, and the glory of the LORD filled the tabernacle.

Our next five lessons take us through Israel's wilderness wanderings, which took 40 years—on the journey from Egypt to the promised land in Canaan. The first major stop, of course, was at Mount Sinai for the giving of the law, which included instructions for building the tabernacle, Israel's portable tent of meeting with the Lord.

The people gave generously to build this complex place of worship and sacrifice. Israel's craftsmen worked with gold, precious stones, animal skins, and fine linen. When it was finished, God's glory filled the tabernacle. He had come to dwell with His people.

The story in Exodus closes with this dramatic moment. The cloud that had led Israel's camp since the flight from Egypt hovered over the tabernacle. But what happened in the tabernacle was unique and awe-inspiring. God Almighty manifested His presence there. It is described as God's glory. The original Hebrew word translated "glory" signifies heaviness, or weight, or worth. Ancient people used it to describe their wealth, splendor, or reputation. Sometimes the same word is translated "honor."

For Israel, God's glory accompanied the people out of Egypt in the cloud. The cloud rested on Mount Sinai, where Moses saw God's glory (Exod. 24:15-18). No human being could ever see God's "face" and expect to live, but He did give Moses some vision of His glory (Exod. 34:5-8).

The glory of the Lord filled the tabernacle and appeared especially at the hour of sacrifice (Lev. 9:6, 23). Later on, the temple of Jerusalem became the location of God's glory (1 Kings 8:11; 2 Chron. 7:1-3).

The prophets envisioned God's glory with both mystical and physical manifestations (see for example, Ezek. 1:28). Isaiah's vision of God on his throne apparently combined both ideas (Isa. 6:1-4).

The glory of God was seen by the shepherds at Christ's birth, and by His disciples, especially in His miracles and at His transfiguration.

Since Christ's coming, we do not need a tabernacle to contain God's glory. God, as it were, has pitched His tent in the human flesh of Jesus (John 1:14). Christ's resurrection and ascension also were manifestations of God's glory. Above all, however, we will see His glory fully manifested when He returns to earth (Mark 8:38; 13:26). That is the promise of the New Testament.

B. Kept Moses Out: vs. 35

Moses could not enter the Tent of Meeting because the cloud had settled upon it, and the glory of the LORD filled the tabernacle.

41

With the cloud settled on the tabernacle, and God's glory filling it, Moses found that his way was barred. The barring of Moses signified God's unapproachable holiness and the fact that an insurmountable barrier still existed between God and humans. Access would be severely limited to special people on special days.

This did not mean that Moses was prohibited from any further interaction with God. Quite the contrary. In fact, Moses met with the Lord at the Tent of Meeting for special instructions (Num. 1:1; 9:1; 16:42-45; 20:6).

II. THE CLOUD AND THE FIRE: EXODUS 40:36-38

A. God's Direction: vss. 36-37

In all the travels of the Israelites, whenever the cloud lifted from above the tabernacle, they would set out; but if the cloud did not lift, they did not set out—until the day it lifted.

This description summarizes the pattern followed by Israel in the wilderness. The people were attached to God by the permanent presence of a special cloud, which was illuminated by fire at night. When the cloud moved from over the tabernacle, Israel moved; when it stayed, Israel stayed.

This physical sign was God's provision for all of Israel's movements. This was how God directed His people. He had given them His laws for their moral and spiritual guidance. He had given them the tabernacle for worship. He gave them the cloud and the fire so they could be sure they were following Him.

B. God's Presence: vs. 38

So the cloud of the LORD was over the tabernacle by day, and fire was in the cloud by night, in the sight of all the house of Israel during all their travels.

As important and valuable as God's directions for the journey were, probably the cloud's supreme value was its proof that God was with His people. The trip from Egypt to Canaan would have been disastrous without the presence of the Lord. The cloud was a 24-hour-a-day sign that God was there. No matter where the people camped, they could look up and see the Lord's presence. The evidence was unmistakable and reassuring.

Why was such a sign necessary? We have to remember that this nation was in its infancy. For 400 years they had had no revelation from the Lord, that is, from the time of Joseph to Moses. In Jacob's time, the nation had consisted of one family. Now it consisted of some two million people.

God's presence was totally new to them. They had witnessed His mighty power displayed against the Egyptians in the plagues and in the Red Sea crossing. But those mighty miracles were not the same as being able to see God's presence all day, all night, every day.

Their laws were handed down from Mount Sinai, so they knew the rules of the game, so to speak. But those laws apart from God's presence would not have conquered their fears of the unknown. They could very well have expected never to see God anymore after the exhibitions on Mount Sinai. After all, none of the gods of other nations traveled with the people.

Of course, the cloud's purpose was also to keep the people in line. Otherwise, strong-minded people would have headed in any direction they liked. Chaos would have resulted if every family chief could have taken off with his clan. Unity and solidarity were absolutely essential.

Tabernacle and cloud moved together. In God's wisdom, His presence was not separated from the place of worship. He was anchored to the tabernacle, so to speak, although we know God is present everywhere. But in Israel's case, He chose to dwell in the tabernacle. Without His presence, the tabernacle was useless. "God is with us," the people could say when they saw the cloud joined to the tabernacle.

III. THE PEOPLE OBEYED GOD: NUMBERS 9:15-19, 22-23

On the day the tabernacle, the Tent of the Testimony, was set up, the cloud covered it. From evening till morning the cloud above the tabernacle looked like fire. That is how it continued to be; the cloud covered it, and at night it looked like fire. Whenever the cloud lifted from above the Tent, the Israelites set out; wherever the cloud settled, the Israelites encamped. At the Lord's command the Israelites set out, and at his command they encamped. As long as the cloud stayed over the tabernacle, they remained in camp. When the cloud remained over the tabernacle a long time, the Israelites obeyed the Lord's order and did not set out. . . . Whether the cloud stayed over the tabernacle for two days or a month or a year, the Israelites would remain in camp and not set out; but when it lifted, they would set out. At the Lord's command they encamped, and at the Lord's command they set out. They obeyed the Lord's order, in accordance with his command through Moses.

The book of Numbers takes its name from the fact that Moses took a census in Israel and counted the people (chaps. 1-4). The first part of the book covers the year when Israel was camped at Mount Sinai; the second part describes the journey from Mount Sinai to the east side of the Dead Sea opposite the Jordan River; the third part describes the plans for moving into Canaan and conquering the people there.

Our text comes at the end of the first section (1:1—10:10). Moses commanded the people to celebrate the anniversary of the Passover from Egypt (9:1-5). Finally, on the twentieth day of the second month of the second year the cloud lifted and Israel began its long march from Sinai to Canaan. The order of the march is described in 10:11-36.

Interestingly, Moses enlisted the help of a local scout to find a place to camp (29-33). He also prayed whenever they broke camp, "Rise up, O LORD! May your enemies be scattered; may your foes flee before you" (10:35). He also prayed when they found a place to camp, "Return, O LORD, to the countless thousands of Israel" (10:36).

Moses thus acknowledged Israel's total dependence on God for guidance, protection, and blessing. He also knew that guidance and protection depended on Israel's absolute obedience to the Lord. The story tells not only what happened but why. God's plan succeeded because the people moved and stayed "at the Lord's command" (vs. 23). Obedience was the key to blessing.

The same principle follows in the New Testament. Christians love and obey the Lord, and thus enjoy His presence. Jesus told His disciples to trust Him implicitly (John 14:1, 10-12). Such obedience was the indicator of the indwelling presence of God the Father and God the Son (John 14:21, 23). This special relationship far surpasses anything the Israelites knew. Christians enjoy a sense of intimacy with God that the Israelites never knew by following the cloud. Christians follow Jesus, not a cloud.

Of course, on a universal scale Jesus is like the cloud that directed Israel. Jesus is the light, not just of Israel, but of the world (John 1:9; 3:19; 8:12; 9:5; 11:9; 12:35; 12:46). John declared of Jesus, "In him was life, and that life was the light of men. The light shines in the darkness, but the darkness has not understood it" (John 1:4-5).

When Jesus first publicly pronounced, "I am the light of the world" (John 8:12), it was right after the Feast of Tabernacles (John 7:2). This glorious celebration was fresh in the minds of the people and their leaders. The Feast of Tabernacles recalled God's guidance of Israel by the pillar of cloud and fire. The highlight of the feast was a ceremony of lights, which lit up the entire Temple area in Jerusalem. Therefore, on this occasion Jesus connected Himself directly with the experience of ancient Israel in the wilderness.

God moved Israel from camp to camp through a desert. In His Son, He moves us first to repentance and then to saving faith. Our journey is not to Canaan, but to heaven and the presence of Jesus. Our salvation depends on responding to what God says. "The work of God is this: to believe in the one he has sent" . . . "For my Father's will is that everyone who looks to the Son and believes in him shall have eternal life" (John 6:29, 40).

Jesus called the Holy Spirit a Counselor who will be with us forever (John 14:16). He said the Holy Spirit will be our teacher (John 14:26). He will guide us "into all truth" (John 16:13). He is the source of the only safe, reliable guidance. That's why the apostle Paul told us to "be filled with the Spirit" (Eph. 5:18) and to "live by the Spirit" and be "led by the Spirit" (Gal. 5:16, 18).

You can well imagine more than a few Israelites complaining, "What! Another day camped in this miserable place? Why don't we pack up and move? We'll never get to Canaan at this rate. The cloud is stuck. Let's forget it and move out" (Num. 9:22).

Great faith and patience were required to stick with God's timetable and not rush ahead, especially when to the human eye there appeared to be no logical reason not to move. The cloud tested Israel's faith and obedience.

Likewise, the faith and patience of Christians are tested when it appears that God is silent. Tragically, unbelief and sin often erupt when we run out of patience with God. We take matters into our own hands and plunge ahead.

The key to sticking with the Lord's guidance is Scripture. God does not lead us contrary to His Word. Every other scheme, doctrine, and philosophy must pass the test of Scripture. If it is not clearly taught in the Bible, suspect it.

At the same time, God guides us through the internal direction of the Holy Spirit, through prayer, worship, and fellowship with other believers. Many times our fellow Christians can steady us and keep us from making rash decisions. Our main objective is to stay close to Jesus, just like the ancient Israelites stayed close to the cloud and the fire.

Discussion Questions

1. What does God's glory mean to you? How do you experience it?
2. What does Christian worship contribute to your appreciation of God's glory?
3. In what special ways have you felt God's presence? His direction?
4. What tips would you have for a new believer to find God's will?
5. What "siren songs" try to derail Christians from following Jesus?
6. What is your best protection against being led astray by false teachers and their teachings?

Contemporary Application

Many Christians find it hard to discover God's guidance in their lives. One man tried to ascertain God's will by the kind of stamps that arrived with his letters. His Christian friends thought that bordered on magic, but he called it "putting out the fleece" like Gideon did.

On one hand, some flip open their Bibles at random and put their finger on a verse, while on the otherhand, some consult horoscopes in the daily newspapers. Either way, there's no connection between guidance and their knowledge of Christ and His Word.

Therefore, it is imperative for Christians to be well taught. We all need a consistent, dependable source of information that will help us to determine our next steps. We cannot risk making decisions without seeking God's direction in Scripture and in prayer.

Part of our responsibility also is to declare boldly and publicly what is not God's will. Truth and error cannot coexist. The eternal God has revealed absolutes. Many times our confusion comes because we either don't know what His moral imperatives are, or we refuse to listen and choose our own way instead.

Israel had to choose to follow the cloud and the fire. Christians must choose to follow Jesus, no matter what.

The People Rebel

DEVOTIONAL READING

Numbers 14:5-19

DAILY BIBLE READINGS

Monday October 4
Numbers 12:1-9 Aaron and Miriam Jealous of Moses

Tuesday October 5
Numbers 12:10-15 Miriam Punished with Leprosy

Wednesday October 6
Numbers 13:1-16 Twelve Sent to Spy out Canaan

Thursday October 7
Numbers 13:17-24 The Spies Carry Out Moses' Orders

Friday October 8
Numbers 13:25-33 Fearful Spies and a Negative Report

Saturday October 9
Numbers 14:1-12 Israel Rebels against Moses and Aaron

Sunday October 10
Numbers 14:13-15 Moses Intercedes for Israel

Scripture

Background Scripture: *Numbers 12:1—14:25*
Scripture Lesson: *Numbers 13:1-3, 32—14:4, 20-24*
Key Verse: *"If the LORD is pleased with us, he will lead us into that land, a land flowing with milk and honey, and will give it to us. Only do not rebel against the LORD. And do not be afraid of the people of the land, because we will swallow them up. Their protection is gone, but the LORD is with us. Do not be afraid of them."* Numbers 14:8-9.
Key Verse for Children: *Even a child is known by his actions.* Proverbs 20:11.

Lesson Aim

To trust and obey the Lord, even when the assignment appears impossible.

Lesson Setting

Time: *1400 B.C.*
Place: *Wilderness of Sinai*

Lesson Outline

The People Rebel

  I. The Commission: Numbers 13:1-3
 II. The Fearful Report: Numbers 13:32-33
III. The People's Despair: Numbers 14:1-4
    A. They Wept: *vs. 1*
    B. They Grumbled: *vs. 2*
    C. They Blamed God: *vs. 3*
    D. They Wanted to Return to Egypt: *vs. 4*
IV. God's Judgment: Numbers 14:20-24
    A. No One Will See the Land: *vss. 20-23*
    B. Except Caleb and Joshua: *vs. 24*

Introduction for Adults

Topic: *A Missed Opportunity*

Many times when friends get together people often talk about something they wished they had done in previous years, but did not. "I wish I had invested in IBM stock in 1950" or "I wish I had kept up with piano lessons." Life seems cluttered with missed opportunities.

But we cannot go on living with missed opportunities. We cannot keep looking back and saying, "If only I had . . ." What is really tragic is living with the regrets of not having done something we knew God wanted us to do, but we were afraid to do it.

Have you ever heard Christians in their thirties and forties who wish they had answered God's call to some Christian vocation when they were in their twenties? God doesn't call everyone to full-time professional ministry, but He wants to make His will clear to us, just as He did to Israel when He told them to march into Canaan.

Introduction for Youths

Topic: *Hitting the Panic Button*

The people of Israel hit the panic button just when they were on the verge of success. How like so many of us today! We know God has something very special in store for us. We claim the promises of Jesus for our salvation and eternal life with Him. But suddenly a huge giant stands in our way, and we retreat in fear.

For Christian youth, the giants may be the "everybody's-doing-it" immorality of popular culture. It may be another student who goes out of his way to make life miserable. It may be a teacher who pokes fun at the Christian faith.

God calls us to be courageous and not to retreat in unbelief. We need help to stand for Jesus. We need the support of fellow Christian students. We need group and personal prayer and Bible study.

Concepts for Children

Topic: *Making good choices.*

1. God planned to give His people a wonderful land, but they rebelled against Him.
2. They disobeyed the Lord because they feared giants in the land.
3. God judged their disobedience and one generation died in the desert.
4. Every day we are called to do what God wants us to do, not simply what we want to do.
5. We learn what God wants us to do by studying the Bible, praying, and meeting with other Christians.
6. Jesus gives us His Holy Spirit to guide us in making the right choices.

The Lesson Commentary

I. THE COMMISSION: NUMBERS 13:1-3

The LORD said to Moses, "Send some men to explore the land of Canaan, which I am giving to the Israelites. From each ancestral tribe send one of its leaders." So at the LORD's command Moses sent them out from the Desert of Paran. All of them were leaders of the Israelites.

I YEAR AT
MT SINAI

"On the twentieth day of the second month of the second year, the cloud lifted from above the tabernacle" (Num. 10:11) and Israel "set out, this first time, at the LORD's command through Moses" (10:13). What an exciting day that must have been in camp! What enthusiasm must have gripped their hearts. Everyone was prepared and ready to move. The tabernacle was packed up according to the Lord's instructions. Israel was on the march from Mount Sinai at last!

Moses knew that enemies stood in Israel's path, so he prayed, "Rise up, O LORD! May your enemies be scattered; may your foes flee before you" (10:35). However, Israel's enemies were not limited to pagan tribes. The enemy also lurked within the camp. God sent fire to burn the outskirts of the camp after the people complained about the hardships of the journey (11:1-3).

DISCONTENT

One of the hardships was their plain food, called manna, which they made into porridge and cakes (11:8). So "the Israelites started wailing" for meat (11:4, 13). The Lord was very angry and Moses was so upset he asked God to kill him (11:10-15). God said He would provide so much meat for a whole month that the people would come to loathe it. This was His judgment because Israel had rejected Him (11:19-20). Sickness came over Israel and the people who had craved meat died (11:34).

Another enemy within Israel raised its ugly head. Miriam and Aaron not only criticized Moses for marrying a Cushite (Nubian) woman, but they also were jealous of his leadership, asking, "Has the LORD spoken only through Moses? Hasn't he also spoken through us?" (12:1-2). God reasserted His trust in Moses as His faithful servant, and judged Miriam and Aaron. She was smitten with leprosy, and was healed only when Moses pleaded to God for her (12:4-15).

JEALOUSY

God's leader was not only a faithful prophet, but also the most humble person on the face of the earth (12:3, 6). Having been thus affirmed, Moses set about the task of exploring Canaan. God told him how to do this. Each of Israel's tribes was to send a leader to join the team of explorers. Their names are given in the text, but only two of the 12 achieved greatness in the eyes of God: Caleb (13:6) and Hoshea (vs. 8), whom Moses renamed Joshua (vs. 16).

The expedition was anchored in God's promise that He was giving Canaan to Israel. This team was supposed to bring back a detailed report of what they found. They were to check out the land, the people, the towns, the fertility of the soil, and the produce because it was time for the first grape harvest (vss. 17-20).

II. THE FEARFUL REPORT: NUMBERS 13:32-33

And they spread among the Israelites a bad report about the land they had explored. They said, "The land we explored devours those living in it. All the people we saw there are of great size. We saw the Nephilim there (the descendants of Anak come from the Nephilim). We seemed like grasshoppers in our own eyes, and we looked the same to them."

The team spent 40 days exploring Canaan (13:21-25). (Consult a map in a Bible dictionary to see the ground they covered.) They discovered two things that apparently impressed them the most. The land was a bountiful land, flowing with milk and honey (13:27). To prove it, they carried back to Israel one cluster of grapes that was so big it had to be carried by two men (13:23). The second thing they discovered frightened them. They found some of the descendants of Anak, evidently a race of giants like Goliath.

However, Caleb spoke up and confidently called for an invasion of Canaan (13:30). But the rest of the group said it was useless because "they are stronger than we are" (vs. 31). Thus began a contest between obedience and disobedience, between faith and fear, between those who believed God and those who did not.

The naysayers contradicted Caleb by exaggerating what they had seen in Canaan. That's why it is called a bad or evil report. They said nothing about Canaan's abundance, but charged that "the land . . . devours those living in it" (vs. 32). They were determined to discourage Israel from following God.

They also lied when they said "all the people . . . there are of great size" (vs. 32). Actually, they had found only one village inhabited by the giants (vs. 22), and they named only three of them. Maybe they were most notorious, or possibly they were the only ones.

This contingent of scouts was so overwhelmed by fear of the giants that they could not consider anything else about Canaan. Psychologically, they were wiped out. They compared themselves to grasshoppers (vs. 33). From that standpoint, they were in no condition to invade Canaan. Remember, the spies had been leaders of the tribes, not just ordinary people.

III. THE PEOPLE'S DESPAIR: NUMBERS 14:1-4

A. They Wept: vs. 1

That night all the people of the community raised their voices and wept aloud.

Apparently few Israelites, if any, recalled God's deliverance at the Red Sea. When they heard the frightening news from the scouting team, they dissolved into tears. Israel was in great distress.

Apparently it had been common knowledge that Canaan was ripe for the plucking. The people thought the land would open before them as they marched in. No one thought that the local inhabitants—giants or not—would put up a fight.

So, instead of rejoicing over the bounty of the land, and instead of remembering and trusting in God's promise to give them the land, the people fell into grief, despair, and weeping. To put it very plainly, they were not only scared by giants, but they had also forgotten their Almighty God and His promises.

In the journey of faith, "giants" of various kinds are sure to appear. These seemingly insurmountable difficulties test our faith in God. That's when Christians draw on the resources of Scripture, Christian fellowship, worship, and prayer.

B. They Grumbled: vs. 2

All the Israelites grumbled against Moses and Aaron, and the whole assembly said to them, "If only we had died in Egypt! Or in this desert!"

Soon the weeping turned nasty. The people attacked their leaders, Moses and Aaron. They jumped to the false conclusion that they were as good as dead. Rather than attack Canaan (which they thought meant certain death), they would have preferred to die in Egypt or in the desert.

This turn of events was the result of their having been overwhelmed by fear after hearing about the giants. Their grumbling was based on a completely false assessment of the facts. The convenient targets of their outrage were Moses and Aaron.

With their emotions completely out of control, their minds could not consider the prospects of Canaan rationally. Their fear and grumbling overwhelmed their knowledge of God's past mercies, power, and deliverance. When faith, hope, and trust go out the window, we are at the mercy of all kinds of sinful reactions.

C. They Blamed God: vs. 3

"Why is the LORD bringing us to this land only to let us fall by the sword? Our wives and children will be taken as plunder. Wouldn't it be better for us to go back to Egypt?"

Worst of all, the people turned on God and blamed Him. They accused God of bringing them to the brink of death. They blamed God for the loss of their wives and children. Even slavery in Egypt looked better than this dilemma.

Their accusation revealed the depths of their despair, disobedience, and rebellion. "God, it's all your fault!" is the cry of those who have lost their spiritual compasses. Logic, of course, had no place in their thinking. We marvel that they did not recall what God had done for them in recent years.

Yet, how many times do we turn on the Lord and blame Him for our difficulties? That's why the New Testament writers put such strong emphasis on the power of faith and perseverance in times of trouble. They tell us that our faith is being refined, our character is being developed, and our personalities are being shaped in Christ's image (1 Pet. 1:6-7; Rom. 5:3-4; 8:29).

D. They Wanted to Return to Egypt: vs. 4

And they said to each other, "We should choose a leader and go back to Egypt."

The people decided to take matters into their own hands. They decided to throw out Moses and Aaron and pick new leaders who would take them back to

Egypt. Their rash decision proves how misguided they had become because they had forgotten the Lord.

Very simply, they had grossly miscalculated. In total ignorance, they had decided it was better to be a slave in Egypt than to fight and die in Canaan. This was because their own tribal leaders (ten of them) had distorted what they had seen in Canaan. When the courage and faith of their leaders failed, the people went down the drain spiritually and they disobeyed God.

IV. GOD'S JUDGMENT: NUMBERS 14:20-24

A. No One Will See the Land: vss. 20-23

The LORD replied, "I have forgiven them, as you asked. Nevertheless, as surely as I live and as surely as the glory of the LORD fills the whole earth, not one of the men who saw my glory and the miraculous signs I performed in Egypt and in the desert but who disobeyed me and tested me ten times—not one of them will ever see the land I promised on oath to their forefathers. No one who has treated me with contempt will ever see it."

The rebellion of the people instigated a powerful dialogue. Actually, it was a do-or-die spiritual battle between Moses, Aaron, Joshua, and Caleb and the whole Israelite assembly (vss. 5-12).

While Moses and Aaron fell to the ground in utter grief and disbelief, Joshua and Caleb tore their clothes as a sign of repentance for the people's sins. Then they spoke. They told the truth about Canaan. They did not deny the giants, but said, "We will swallow them up" (vs. 9).

They reminded the people of how wonderful Canaan was. They reminded them of God's promise to give them the land. They urged them not to rebel against God. They told them not to fear the Canaanites because "their protection is gone" (vs. 9). Their final rallying cry was, "The LORD is with us" (vs. 9).

For all their efforts, Joshua and Caleb were almost stoned to death (vs. 10). Then God intervened. He charged the people with rebellion and unbelief "in spite of all the miraculous signs I have performed among them" (vs. 11). He said He would destroy Israel and start a new nation with Moses (vs. 12).

Moses made an exceptional appeal to stay the hand of God's immediate judgment on Israel. He reminded the Lord that the Egyptians and other nations had heard about His deliverance of Israel and His promise to take them to Canaan (vss. 13-16). They had heard that God was with Israel and that He was guiding them by the pillars of cloud and fire. Therefore, if God wiped out Israel, the surrounding pagan nations would say that He was not able to bring them into Canaan.

Moses also addressed God's character, speaking of His love, mercy, and forgiveness, as well as His justice (vss. 17-19). He appealed to God to forgive Israel's sins according to His great love. He also recalled God's previous pardons of Israel's sins.

Moses' appeal brought both forgiveness and judgment. God would not wipe out Israel and start all over again with Moses. Nevertheless, Israel's rebellion was a costly business. This rebellious generation of Israelites would never live to see God's promised land.

Israel was immeasurably blessed and honored above all other peoples on the earth because the people had seen God's glory and His miracles in Egypt and the desert (vs. 22). With that great privilege came the responsibility to trust and obey the Lord. However, they disobeyed the Lord, tested Him, and treated Him with contempt. "Ten times" (vs. 22) is an idiom for "over and over again." Therefore, none of these people would live to see the promised land of Canaan.

God's judgments are true and righteous. The yardstick of God's judgment was clear for all to see—His glory and His miracles. Similarly, in the New Testament Jesus based His appeal for faith on the evidence of His deeds and His words (John 10:25-32; 14:9-12). The apostle Paul said there is abundant evidence in the created world for everyone to believe (Rom. 1:18-20). Just as Israel was without excuse, so are unbelievers today (Rom. 1:20).

The writer of Hebrews used Israel's rebellion against God as a strong warning for those who profess to be Christians to beware of "a sinful, unbelieving heart that turns away from the living God" (Heb. 3:12). Twice he urged, "Today, if you hear his voice, do not harden your hearts as you did in the rebellion" (3:15; 4:7). That's why the story of Israel's rebellion, tragic as it is, carries a powerful lesson to the Church today.

B. Except Caleb and Joshua: vs. 24

"But because my servant Caleb has a different spirit and follows me wholeheartedly, I will bring him into the land he went to, and his descendants will inherit it."

The people had cried that it would have been better to die in Egypt or in the Sinai desert (vs. 2). God heard their desire, and in His judgment granted it (vss. 28-29). Their grumbling against God had invoked His severe punishment. Everyone 20 years old or more who had complained against God would indeed die in the desert.

The only exceptions were Caleb and Joshua (vss. 24, 30). Caleb was singled out because he had "a different spirit" and followed God wholeheartedly. By "different spirit" was meant that he exercised strong faith in God, believed His promises, and knew that Israel would prevail over the Canaanites because God was with them.

The rest of Israel's tribal leaders would perish. Their children—whom they had feared would be stolen from them by the Canaanites—would live to enjoy the land that their elders had rejected. Meanwhile, the nation would wander aimlessly in the desert for 40 years, one year for each day the scouts had explored Canaan. During those four decades one entire generation would perish (vss. 28-35). God called them a "wicked community" that had banded together against Him (vs. 35). The tribal leaders who had brought back the faithless report and thus instigated a national rebellion were struck down at once (vs. 37).

When Moses described God's coming judgment, the people repented and said they would go to Canaan at once. But Moses told them not to go, because God was not with them. Nevertheless, they went anyway and were soundly defeated (vss. 39-45).

It's important to ask why this rebellion happened. One reason is that apparently many people did not internalize their faith. They saw God's power and glory, but did not apply it to their circumstances and challenges. Their faith was so weak that they were easily led astray by false reports about conditions in Canaan.

Another reason is that faith equals courage, and when the challenge came, Israel lacked courage and succumbed to false reports. Faith also means trusting God for all things. Grumbling and complaining have no place among people of faith.

Discussion Questions

1. Why do we sometimes fail to do what God tells us to do?
2. How do you account for Israel's rebellion?
3. What challenges seem hard for Christians to accept? What is the hardest thing God has asked you to do?
4. How would you describe Caleb's character in contemporary terms?
5. What unique stresses were put upon Moses? How did he respond? Why?
6. How can you support your leaders when rebellion occurs in the ranks?

Contemporary Application

The fearful price of disobeying God and rebelling against Him is not a popular subject for discussion. But those corpses in the desert speak to us about the huge risks of saying "No" to God. God takes grumbling, complaining, and disobedience very seriously. God detests the attitude of those who say they believe Him, but refuse to do what He says.

The challenge to enter Canaan reminds us that the walk of faith requires obedience, courage, and hope. Real faith looks the enemy squarely in the eye and says, "We will win because God is with us."

The power of Christ indwells every believer. Therefore, we don't need to be afraid when tests of our faith come. We have to check our emotions. We have to be sure our facts are straight. We have to check human advice against the Word of God. We have to practice obedience in the little things, so that when larger calls to obedience come from the Lord we will be disciplined to obey Him.

The Desert Years

Scripture

Background Scripture: *Deuteronomy 1:41—2:25*
Scripture Lesson: *Deuteronomy 1:41-2:8a*
Key Verse: *The LORD your God has blessed you in all the
work of your hands. He has watched over your journey
through this vast desert. These forty years the LORD your
God has been with you, and you have not lacked anything.* Deuteronomy 2:7.
Key Verse for Children: *These forty years the LORD
your God has been with you, and you have not lacked
anything.* Deuteronomy 2:7.

Lesson Aim

To believe God's warnings about the dangers of
rash disobedience, and to thank Him for providing
all our needs in Christ.

Lesson Setting

Time: *1400 B.C.*
Place: *Wilderness of Sinai*

Lesson Outline

The Desert Years

  I. Israel's Defeat: Deuteronomy 1:41-46
     A. Presumptive Attack: vs. 41
     B. God's Warning: vs. 42
     C. Arrogant Rebellion: vs. 43
     D. Defeat: vs. 44
     E. God's Deaf Ear: vss. 45-46
 II. Desert Journeys: Deuteronomy 2:1-8a
     A. Around the Hill Country: vs. 1
     B. Through the Land of Seir: vss. 2-6
     C. God's Provision: vss. 7-8a

Introduction for Adults

Topic: *In the Wilderness*

Have you ever gotten lost as an adult? It can make you feel a little foolish. Many urban adults take adventure trips to "get away from it all"—but it's not funny when you end up lost in a wilderness swamp in New Jersey along with a canoe guide who doesn't know where he is either. In that particular case, the hapless "adventurers" pulled out their canoe and battled their way through thick azalea bushes and scrub oak toward the road.

That was a mild adventure compared to what Israel suffered in the desert. It was also nothing compared to the spiritual wilderness that many people find themselves in today. In our churches there are many unhappy Christians who can't seem to find their way out of the wilderness. They apparently are unwilling to admit that their struggles are caused by their own disobedience, by their unwillingness to do what they clearly know God wants them to do. Getting lost in the thickets of sin is no accident. We bring it on ourselves.

Introduction for Youths

Topic: *Paying the Price*

At many public high schools, small groups of students gather just off campus for their lunch hour smoke. It's tempting to ask, "Do you know the price you are paying for that cigarette? Cancer is no fun."

Sadly, most young smokers rationalize that they won't get lung cancer. Somehow, they believe they are invincible and will dodge that bullet. They don't want to believe there's a long-term price for short-term indulgence.

This principle of reaping what we sow is firmly embedded in the universe. God put it there. If we go against the grain of the universe, we will get splinters. That's what happened to Israel.

Everyone acquires some splinters along the way. That's part of God's training school. Paying the price for sin needs to be the centerpiece of what we tell young people today—with love, patience, and understanding, of course.

Concepts for Children

Topic: *Obeying God*

1. God's people disobeyed Him and suffered the consequences.
2. Sometimes our short-cuts are not God's will, and we take long detours as a result.
3. We learn from these experiences how to trust and obey God more completely.
4. On the one hand, God turned a deaf ear to Israel, but on the other He gave them all they needed 40 years in the desert.
5. We need prayer, love, and wisdom from fellow Christians so we can stay on the road Jesus wants us to take.
6. We can also help one another to be faithful to Jesus.

The Lesson Commentary

I. ISRAEL'S DEFEAT: DEUTERONOMY 1:41-46

A. Presumptive Attack: vs. 41

Then you replied, "We have sinned against the LORD. We will go up and fight, as the LORD our God commanded us." So every one of you put on his weapons, thinking it easy to go up into the hill country.

Most of the 40 years of wandering in the desert are covered by events in Numbers 13—36. Following the rebellion at Kadesh after the spies came back from Canaan, another rebellion broke out, led by Korah, Dathan, and Abiram (chap. 16). It really was an attack on God, who judged it severely. God reaffirmed Aaron's priestly leadership by producing fruit from his staff (chap. 17). Later, when the Edomites refused Israel safe passage, the people had to make a long detour east around Edom (chap. 20). Miriam and Aaron both died (chap. 20).

As Moses neared the end of his life, he appointed Joshua to be his successor (27:12-23). Just before Israel prepared to enter Canaan, Moses gave a series of farewell addresses. In the book of Deuteronomy he summarized Israel's history and restated the basic laws God had given at Mount Sinai.

Deuteronomy 1—4 is an historical introduction. It was very important for the new generation of Israelites that had grown up in the wilderness to know the stories of God's deliverance and Israel's disobedience. Those who had refused to enter Canaan were buried in the wilderness. Their successors needed to know why this happened. Moses' explanation was the necessary foundation for his explanation of God's laws for His people.

The exact place and date of Moses' first speech are given in verses 1-4. Forty years after the exodus from Egypt Israel was camped in the plains just east of the Jordan River. The distance covered by Israel in 40 years could have been traversed in eleven days, had it not been for their disobedience (vs. 2).

Moses' assignment was to "expound" God's laws (vs. 5). The Hebrew word means to dig, or to hew, and thus to make clear. He first told the Israelites what the laws were, explained those laws, and then exhorted the people to obey them.

Moses began by rehearsing God's wonderful promise to Israel after the giving of the law at Horeb (Mount Sinai). The scope of His gift to Israel was impressive. Their land stretched from the southern desert to the western foothills along the Mediterranean Sea, and up the coast as far as Tyre, to Lebanon, and the Euphrates River. During King David's time this was the extent of Israel's kingdom.

God told His people to take the land because He had promised it to Abraham, Isaac, Jacob, and their descendants. Israel marched through the desert toward the hill country of the Amorites and reached Kadesh Barnea. Again God said, "See, the LORD your God has given you the land. Go up and take possession of it as the LORD, the God of your fathers, told you. Do not be afraid; do not be discouraged" (vs. 21).

When the people rebelled in fear, Moses told them to remember how God had fought for them "as he did for you in Egypt, before your very eyes, and in the desert. There you saw how the LORD your God carried you . . . all the way you went until you reached this place" (1:30-31). He also reminded them that although God directed them day by day with the cloud by day and fire by night, the people did not trust Him. Therefore, God's judgment was fully justified. He sent Israel back into the desert, where the unbelieving generation would die.

The keynotes of Moses' address thus far are the faithfulness of God and the disobedience of His people. Moses himself was not excluded from God's judgment (vs. 37), because a few years previously he had become angry with God at Meribah (Num. 20:1-13; Ps. 106:32-33). However, even in the midst of judgment God provided a future leader, Joshua, to lead Israel into Canaan (v. 38). Their children, whom they feared would be taken captive, would take possession of the land (v. 39).

But, Moses reminded them, the people didn't want to accept God's judgment. They made the presumptuous decision to fight for Canaan after all. They acknowledged their sin. They professed to obey the Lord, and rushed to put on their weapons. They thought they would achieve an easy victory.

Presumption, of course, is a very serious sin. First, the Israelites refused to do what God had commanded; second, they tried to do what He did not command. Both are flagrant violations of God's will. They refused to accept God's judgment. They did not believe that all of the unbelieving adults would perish in the desert. So they rashly decided to go ahead on their own.

B. God's Warning: vs. 42

But the LORD said to me, "Tell them, 'Do not go up and fight, because I will not be with you. You will be defeated by your enemies.'"

God clearly warned Israel not to attack the hill country of the Amorites, even though previously He had told them to do so (vs. 7). They assumed His earlier command was still good.

If they had obeyed the first command, God would have fought for them and defeated the Amorites. Perhaps the Israelites thought victory would be easy because of God's previous promise. Like many others who have disobeyed the Lord, they failed to appreciate the cost of their sin.

Even so, God tried to keep them from disaster. He told the Israelites not to attack. He guaranteed their defeat. It is vitally important to hear and obey the Lord, even when His warnings contradict our rash, well-intentioned plans.

C. Arrogant Rebellion: vs. 43

So I told you, but you would not listen. You rebelled against the LORD's command and in your arrogance you marched up into the hill country.

Moses recalled those bitter days of 38 years ago. What a tragic epitaph: "I told you, but you would not listen." How those words must have penetrated the hearts of the new generation in Israel.

Sin in this case was both presumptive and arrogant. Arrogance, of course, led to rebellion and disobedience. The people paid no attention to God's warning. They could not accept the prospect of wandering and dying in the desert over the course of four decades. Therefore, they struck out on their own.

Part of the basic human condition caused by sin is the stubborn refusal to accept the fact of God's certain judgment. "Not a man of this evil generation shall see the good land," God said (vs. 35). That was God's judgment on Israel's sin.

In the New Testament, the Gospel is accepted by those who first believe God must sentence them to hell because of their sin. They know they will never see heaven because of God's righteous judgment. Therefore, they gladly acknowledge their sin, declare God to be just and true, and receive His forgiveness through faith in Jesus Christ.

"No one comes to the Father except through me," Jesus said (John 14:6). Israel could not get to Canaan without God's intervention. Trying to get there without Him was doomed to failure. Trying to get to heaven on our own, without the blood of Jesus, is also doomed to failure.

D. Defeat: vs. 44

The Amorites who lived in those hills came out against you; they chased you like a swarm of bees and beat you down from Seir all the way to Hormah.

Moses gave the new generation of Israelites a grim, graphic picture of what happened when the people almost 40 years ago rebelliously and presumptively marched against the Amorites, despite God's warning not to do so. Their defeat was guaranteed because God was not with them.

The Amorites gathered in force and attacked the Israelites. The outcome was never in doubt. "They chased you like a swarm of bees" shows how the Israelites fled before the Amorites. The Amorites not only defended their own territory, they routed the Israelites further back into the desert at Hormah; almost all the way back to Kadesh, in fact. (Consult a map in the back of your Bible, or in a Bible atlas.) "Hormah" means "devoted to destruction."

The Amorites, as the most powerful nation of Canaan, gave their name here—and elsewhere—to the Canaanite tribes generally (vss. 7, 19; Num. 14:44-45).

The New Testament makes clear that lost opportunities cannot always be redeemed (Eph. 5:15-17; Col. 4:5; Heb. 3:13-19; 12:16-17). God allows violations of His will by His own people to be judged. God's people today cannot casually dismiss the warnings of defeat because of sin.

E. God's Deaf Ear: vss. 45-46

You came back and wept before the LORD, but he paid no attention to your weeping and turned a deaf ear to you. And so you stayed in Kadesh many days—all the time you spent there.

Israel's calamitous defeat brought tears of remorse and repentance, but to no avail. This is one of the most tragic descriptions of spiritual despair: God paid no attention to their weeping and turned a deaf ear to their cries.

The personal, knowable, Almighty God of Israel refused to make light of their sin. What a powerful example this was to Israel and to the church (1 Cor. 10:11). Read 1 Corinthians 10:1-11 for Paul's application to the church of the events we have been studying in Numbers and Deuteronomy.

There is a principle in Scripture that repentance can come too late (Heb. 6:4-6). This tragic story proves the point. Disobedience not only brought defeat; it triggered the need for discipline. God's heart is always open to the cries of His people, but sometimes they have to learn some hard lessons first.

Of course, rebellion and sin must be confessed, often with weeping. But with the tears must come God-given determination not to repeat the sin. So when God turned a deaf ear to Israel, He gave them time—"many days," Moses recalled, actually close to 40 years—to think things over. Israel's cause was not irrevocably lost, but God's school of obedience was exceedingly tough.

We can only wonder, as Paul did, why the people—and especially their tribal leaders—acted so precipitously and brought this disaster on Israel. Obviously, they had not yet learned what it meant to trust in God (vs. 32). They lacked the faith to attack Canaan when God had told them to do so.

They also lacked the faith to believe God when He warned them not to attack the Amorites. They refused to believe God that only Caleb and Joshua of the older generation would live to see Canaan (vss. 34-36). Everything revolved around their failure to believe God's word was true. They did not believe His power, goodness, love, and wisdom.

II. Desert Journeys: Deuteronomy 2:1-8a

A. Around the Hill Country: vs. 1

Then we turned back and set out toward the desert along the route to the Red Sea, as the Lord had directed me. For a long time we made our way around the hill country of Seir.

Defeat led to a long time of finding another way around the mountains of Seir. In Moses' speech to the new generation, he simply called this journey "a long time." The events of this period are described in Numbers 20—21.

Moses made very clear that their route had been directed by God. He continued to meet with the Lord at the tabernacle. God's presence continued in the cloud by day and fire by night, hovering over the tabernacle. So the people were not abandoned by God while they suffered the consequences of their sins.

B. Through the Land of Seir: vss. 2-6

Then the Lord said to me, "You have made your way around this hill country long enough; now turn north. Give the people these orders: 'You are about to pass through the territory of your brothers the descendants of Esau, who live in Seir. They will be afraid of you, but be very careful. Do not provoke them to war, for I will not give you any of their land, not even enough to put your foot on. I have given Esau the hill country of Seir as his own. You are to pay them in silver for the food you eat and the water you drink.' "

The people were camped at Kadesh in the second year of the Exodus and were still there some 38 years later. They had left Kadesh in a southeasterly direction, but later left the mountains of Seir inhabited by the Edomites and headed north toward Canaan once more.

The command of verses 2-3 relates to the journey from Kadesh to Mount Hor (Num. 20:22; 33:37) and directed their march around the southern extremity of Mount Seir so as to avoid the land of Edom (Num. 21:4; Judges 11:18). From there they headed north toward the Arnon River "among the desert road of Moab" (vs. 8). This circuitous route was demanded because the Edomites refused to allow them to pass through their territory.

God gave explicit details about how to treat the Edomites, the descendants of Esau, Jacob's twin brother. He was a blood relative, but probably the Israelites who lived hundreds of years after Jacob and Esau thought the bitter feud should have evaporated.

From Numbers 20:18-20, it appears that the Edomites had made formidable plans to stop the Israelites from passing through their land. However, they did not intervene to prevent their passage along their eastern frontier, which was open and defenseless.

Israel was told to be very careful to avoid a fight with the Edomites. Israel would not take any of their land, not even walk on it, because God had given this land to Esau's descendants. Israel was even to go so far as to pay for their food and water.

Although the Edomites refused passage to Israel, they did not decline to sell the necessary provisions (vss. 28-29). In fact, they feared the Israelites (vs. 4) and thus allowed them to dig wells for water and provided food.

C. God's Provision: vss. 7-8a

The LORD your God has blessed you in all the work of your hands. He has watched over your journey through this vast desert. These forty years the LORD your God has been with you, and you have not lacked anything. So we went on past our brothers the descendants of Esau, who live in Seir.

Moses made a striking summary of the desert journey. He declared four major truths that they obtained throughout this whole miserable time: (1) God has blessed you and the work you have done; (2) God has watched over you during the entire desert journey; (3) God has been with you the whole time; (4) Consequently, you have not lacked anything.

What an astounding benediction this was. Keep in mind the disasters described in Numbers, the revolts, the complaints, and the steady trips outside the camp to bury an entire generation. Yet, Moses boldly declared God's faithfulness, blessing, love, and power over four decades.

How could he do this? Had not God allowed suffering, pain, and defeat? Yes, but in the big picture God had not given up on His people, even though He had threatened to do so after their rebellious refusal to enter Canaan.

Moses' benediction tells us to look at life from the vantage point of God's perspective. The focus here was on what God had done, not what the people had done. Now it was time for the people to look upward in praise and thanksgiving, because God had not quit on them. Miraculously, they had survived in the desert.

Discussion Questions

1. Why do you think Israel rashly attacked the Amorites?
2. Under what circumstances are Christians tempted to disobey God and do what they choose to do? Why?
3. Why did God say He would not go with Israel?
4. Why did God turn a deaf ear to Israel's remorse?
5. What warnings can Christians take from this story?
6. Why is it good to rehearse God's provisions in times of darkness and perversity?

Contemporary Application

Israel's trip from Egypt to Canaan was beset by sins of complaint and rebellion. God threw up His hands, as it were, but Moses interceded and rather than destroy Israel, God permitted one generation of rebels to die in the desert. He graciously offered a new generation the opportunity to follow His leading to Canaan.

What does this say to us today? In New Testament terms, it means those who choose to follow Christ will be assaulted from within and without by Christ's enemies—the world, the flesh, and the devil. It means we must be fortified by faithful preaching and teaching of God's Word, lest we drift away into indifference and outright disobedience.

We must take up what Paul called "the full armor of God" so we can "stand against the devil's schemes" (Eph. 6:11). Our battle is against "the spiritual forces of evil in the heavenly realms" (Eph. 6:12). God's armor includes truth, righteousness, the Gospel, faith, salvation, and the Holy Spirit.

One crucial duty is "always keep on praying for all the saints" (Eph. 6:18). Do we know when our fellow believers are in trouble? When they are down on God, on the church, even on friends and family? We must develop open, honest friendships with one another, so we can carry on in faithful obedience, even when we are tempted to push God out of the way. That is our best protection against the disaster that befell Israel.

The Great Commandment

Scripture

Background Scripture: *Deuteronomy 6*
Scripture Lesson: *Deuteronomy 6:1-9, 20-24*
Key Verse: *Hear, O Israel: The LORD our God, the LORD
is one. Love the LORD your God with all your heart
and with all your soul and with all your strength.*
Deuteronomy 6:4-5.

Lesson Aim

To love God totally, and to teach, explain, and obey
His commands.

Lesson Setting

Time: *1400 B.C.*
Place: *Desert of Sinai*

Lesson Outline

The Great Commandment

  I. Reasons for the Command: Deuteronomy
     6:1-3
     A. *To Fear the Lord: vss. 1-2*
     B. *To Prosper the Family: vs. 3*
  II. Consistent Teaching: Deuteronomy 6:4-9
     A. *Love God Totally: vss. 4-5*
     B. *Learn the Commands: vs. 6*
     C. *Teach the Commands: vss. 7-9*
 III. Rehearse the Meaning: Deuteronomy 6:20-24
     A. *The Question: vs. 20*
     B. *God's Deliverance: vs. 21*
     C. *God's Miraculous Signs: vs. 22*
     D. *God's Promise: vs. 23*
     E. *God's Plan: vs. 24*

Introduction for Adults

Topic: *Teach Your Children Well*

One day a junior high boy asked his dad a tough question: "What right do you have to make all these rules I'm supposed to keep?" His dad thought for a moment and then said, "John, I'm under authority myself. I didn't take this job for myself. God gave it to me. And one day I will have to stand before Him and give an account of everything I did as your father. That scares me. I want to be able to tell the Lord that I did my very best. That's why I'm trying to give you some good rules to live by."

The fact that his dad was under authority, and not the supreme boss, was a new thought for John. When we teach our children God's rules, we have to be sure not to usurp power that is not ours. God has delegated His authority to fathers and mothers. As wise, faithful stewards, we will want to do everything for our children that Moses taught the parents in Israel.

Introduction for Youths

Topic: *Link in the Chain*

If you wear glasses, you know how frustrating it is to drop your glasses and have the frame snap right at the bridge holding the two lenses together. Glue might work for awhile, but most people realize that glue is not the solution to the problem. The bridge is too vulnerable to stress.

The lives of teenagers are as fragile as glasses frames. Many fractures occur, and some lives are damaged and even ruined. These teens need more than glue to hold the pieces of their lives together. They need the inherent, integrating power of God's love, wisdom, and commands.

Our primary task is to answer the question posed by the son in Israel, "What do these commands mean? What good are they? Why should I listen to them?" As we build trust with our youth, we can explain how each command of the Lord is designed for our spiritual, physical, and emotional wholeness. We must make clear that the issue is trust. Can I really trust God to do better for me than I can do for myself?

Concepts for Children

Topic: *Learning God's Greatest Rule*

1. God desires us to love Him with all of our being.
2. We learn to love God by keeping His commands.
3. We can learn God's commands in our families and churches.
4. Sometimes we disobey the Lord. We can ask Him to forgive us because Jesus died and rose again for us.
5. We can help one another in our families to learn God's commands and to talk about how to keep them in school and with our friends.
6. God desires to bless us far more than we can imagine, so He gave us good rules to live by.

The Lesson Commentary

I. REASONS FOR THE COMMAND: DEUTERONOMY 6:1-3

A. To Fear the Lord: vss. 1-2

These are the commands, decrees and laws the LORD your God directed me to teach you to observe in the land that you are crossing the Jordan to possess, so that you, your children and their children after them may fear the LORD your God as long as you live by keeping all his decrees and commands that I give you, and so that you may enjoy long life.

In the first four chapters of Deuteronomy Moses gave an historical overview of Israel's unbelief following God's deliverance of the nation from slavery in Egypt. The old generation had died in the desert. The new generation was about to enter Canaan, which God had promised to the Israelites. Moses had to expound God's laws and he reiterated the Ten Commandments (5:1-32).

Our lesson is part of Moses' exposition of the first commandment. In 6:1-3 we find the reasons why God's commands are so important, and what obedience will bring for the faithful Israelite.

Moses spoke of three generations: "You, your children and their children." The basic thing they were to learn from God's commands was to obey Him, and thus enjoy His blessings. Moses himself was the inheritor of a great spiritual family ancestry. Physically and spiritually he was descended from Abraham, his great-great-great-great-grandfather. Levi, one of Jacob's sons, was apparently his great -randfather (Exod. 6:16-20).

Moses knew that if God's people were to survive in Canaan, godliness had to penetrate the basic relationships in life. The people could not pick and choose which of the commands to accept. All of God's commands were to be kept— "observe" (vs. 1), "keeping" (vs. 2). This meant doing exactly what God said, neither adding nor subtracting from His laws. There is no large difference between commands, laws, and decrees. God's commands consist of His decrees and laws.

Lest any Israelite should think this was unreasonable, Moses reminded them that they belonged to God. Twice he said, "The Lord your God." He had chosen Israel for His own glorious purposes. By His love and mercy He had redeemed them from Egypt. To be sure, they had rebelled and failed Him, but God was faithful and He would continue to love and lead them.

To fear the Lord in this context meant doing His will and obeying His commands. The root idea of fear is reverential awe and respect, not a traumatic, unsettling, nerve-racking experience. It is very clear that when we do what God tells us to do, we are fearing Him.

B. To Prosper the Family: vs. 3

Hear, O Israel, and be careful to obey so that it may go well with you and that you may increase greatly in a land flowing with milk and honey, just as the LORD, the God of your fathers, promised you.

Moses had two goals in mind. First, he wanted to awaken a holy fear of God in the hearts of His people, that is, a steadfast obedience to the terms of God's revealed covenant. Second, he wanted their temporal prosperity as well, which would result from their obedience. Thus, the glory of God and the welfare of His people were to be seen as the great purposes of Moses' teaching.

This was a glorious vision of what God intended to do for His people. Israel's future in Canaan depended on obedience. The promise of a good life, an abundant life in a very prosperous land depended on obedience. It also depended on God's promise. This is where the element of faith entered the equation. The Israelites would be motivated to obey the Lord if they really believed His promise of a wonderful land and posterity.

God is to be obeyed because He is God, but with obedience comes incomparable blessings. Moses did not issue a blank check for material wealth. Israel's prosperity went far deeper than "milk and honey."

God's promise included prosperity of soul, mental and spiritual health, deep satisfaction in life as a whole, and love and acceptance. Moses gave the Lord's assurance that obedience to Him would spill over into every area of their lives.

II. CONSISTENT TEACHING: DEUTERONOMY 6:4-9

A. Love God Totally: vss. 4-5

Hear, O Israel: The LORD our God, the LORD is one. Love the LORD your God with all your heart and with all your soul and with all your strength.

Before emphasizing the critical need of consistent teaching of God's commands in everyday life, Moses gave the all-encompassing command to love God totally. The command to love God with all your heart, soul, and strength was based on God's singular nature. He was Israel's God and He was the one true God. He was not a multiplicity of pagan deities.

These words are the beginning of the Jewish Shema (meaning "Hear") and are used in the daily morning and evening services. They are often called the creed of the Jews. In Hebrew, the words are terse and forcible, literally, "Yahweh [YAH-weh] our Elohim, Yahweh one." Their very brevity has given rise to many translations. The simplest seems to be, "The LORD our God is one LORD."

This was more than a mere declaration of God's unity as opposed to polytheism. It was more than a declaration of the unique sole authority of the revelation He had made to Israel. Moses asserted that the Lord God of Israel is absolutely God, and none other. He and He alone is Yahweh, the absolute, uncreated God. By His election of them as His people, God made Himself known to Israel.

B. Learn the Commands: vs. 6

These commandments that I give you today are to be upon your hearts.

The question naturally arises, How does one love God totally? Moses gave the answer: learn His commands (vs. 6) and teach his commands (vss. 7-9). God's laws are meant to be kept in our hearts. His laws are not simply for academic speculation. They are not open to debate; they are not optional.

God's commands are fixed eternally. They are absolute and irrevocable. Therefore, we must learn them and saturate our hearts and minds with them. Our attitudes and our actions must be kept in conformity to God's commands. Otherwise, we drift helplessly in a sea of shifting human opinions and philosophies.

Why learn God's commands? To love and obey Him, to worship, honor, and praise Him. Also, we learn His commands for our own well-being. We prosper in proportion as we learn His commands. Our minds and hearts are kept free of sin and law-breaking. Our hearts are purified when they are bathed in God's commands.

We learn God's commands the same way we learn anything else. We take time for disciplined study. We engage in discussions with other believers. We ask the Holy Spirit to be our teacher. Thoughtful Christians will engage in systematic personal Bible study, along with their studies in Sunday school classes and their exposure to Bible teaching from the pulpit.

C. Teach the Commands: vss. 7-9

Impress them on your children. Talk about them when you sit at home and when you walk along the road, when you lie down and when you get up. Tie them as symbols on your hands and bind them on your foreheads.

Moses knew that the family in Israel was the key to the transmission of God's laws. That's why Moses' command was so pervasive and encompassed every waking moment of the day. "Impress them on your children" meant that God's laws had to be repeated over and over again until they were fully integrated into the lives of the Israelites. This had to be a daily exercise, systematically planned and followed.

When you sit, when you walk, when you lie down, when you get up—there was not a moment when parents were not to be teaching God's commands to their children. Every activity was to be permeated with a sense of, "This is God's Word. What does it mean? How does it apply to our lives?"

Consistent teaching ensured the solidarity of family life, as well as the preservation of God's laws in the community. Moses told the people to tie God's commands on their hands and foreheads. He told them to write them on their doorframes and gates. No aspect of everyday life was to be left untouched by the influence of God's commands.

Later on, the Jews inscribed a small piece of parchment with Deuteronomy 6:4-9 and 11:13-21. This was rolled up in a small cylinder of wood or metal and affixed to the right-hand post of every door in a Jewish house. Pious Jews touched the cylinder, or Mezuzah [muh-ZOO-suh], every time they passed it, kissing their finger and reciting, "The LORD shall preserve thy going out" (Ps. 121:8, KJV).

III. REHEARSE THE MEANING: DEUTERONOMY 6:20-24

A. The Question: vs. 20

In the future, when your son asks you, "What is the meaning of the stipulations, decrees and laws the LORD our God has commanded you?"

Having firmly emphasized Israel's primary duty toward God, Moses added a number of warnings and cautions (vss. 10-25). This was necessary because of Israel's unique circumstances. The people were on the verge of leaving a nomadic lifestyle—largely separate from other nations—for a settled life in the midst of pagan people. They would trade the poverty of living on what they carried for "a land with large, flourishing cities . . . houses filled with all kinds of good things . . . wells . . . vineyards and olive groves" (vss. 10-11).

They would be exposed to two dangers: (1) forgetting the Lord; and (2) false tolerance of the idolatries practiced by their neighbors. In 6:10-25, we find his counsel regarding the former danger; in 7:1-11, we find his warnings about idolatry.

Verses 20-25 describe more particularly the basic command of 6:7: "Impress them on your children." The context is the Israeli family: "When your son asks you . . ." The children could be expected to ask about the meaning of God's laws.

Questions, of course, provide ideal teaching opportunities. It was not enough for parents to declare what God's laws were; they had to be able to interpret and apply them to everyday life. "What do they mean?" is the crucial question.

Parents had to be prepared for this tough question. They had to know God's laws backwards and forwards. They had to discuss the meanings among themselves. They had to keep on learning and growing in spiritual wisdom and insight.

B. God's Deliverance: vs. 21

Tell him: "We were slaves of Pharaoh in Egypt, but the LORD brought us out of Egypt with a mighty hand."

The bottom line answer to the son's question is in verses 24 and 25, but Moses knew the importance of laying a proper foundation in Israel's history. God's rightful commands for His people were rooted in His deliverance of them from Egypt.

"Son, just remember who we are and where we came from," the father said. "We were slaves; we were nobodies; we were weak captives in a powerful, ungodly nation. Pharaoh owned us. We had no rights. But God saw our helpless condition and broke the power of Egypt and set us free. That's why we must learn and obey what He tells us to do. It's our duty because God loves us and wants us to love Him completely."

C. God's Miraculous Signs: vs. 22

"Before our eyes the Lord sent miraculous signs and wonders—great and terrible—upon Egypt and Pharaoh and his whole household."

Then the fathers in Israel would go on to describe how God's mighty hand delivered Israel. "God worked miracles before our very eyes, son. He sent great disasters, signs, and warnings against the Egyptians and even Pharaoh himself and his family."

The fathers would recount in great detail each of the ten plagues, culminating with the death of the firstborn and the Passover. They told these stories again and again. Of course, they also told how God led them across the Red Sea on dry ground. How that story must have thrilled the hearts and stirred the minds of Israel's children.

The important thing was that these stories were not myths, but the accounts of people who had lived them. God's power was demonstrated not in a dark corner, but publicly for all Israel, Egypt, and the other nations to see. The children had to know that their ancestors saw God's mighty power firsthand.

D. God's Promise: vs. 23

"But he brought us out from there to bring us in and give us the land that he promised on oath to our forefathers."

Israel's children needed to know that God had brought them out of Egypt to give them a land of their own. That was His fundamental promise and commitment.

"Son, a long, long time ago God promised Abraham, Isaac, and Jacob a land for their descendants. We are their descendants. They faithfully followed the Lord and kept His commands. Over many centuries our people kept hoping and praying for a land of our own. Now God has brought us out of Egypt so He can give us this wonderful land. We keep God's commands as a sign that we belong to Him and that He will keep His promise of an inheritance in Canaan for us."

E. God's Plan: vs. 24

"The Lord commanded us to obey all these decrees and to fear the Lord our God, so that we might always prosper and be kept alive, as is the case today."

Rehearsing the meaning of God's commands included His promises for the future as well as His provisions in the past. Israel's children were to obey God because of past mercies and future promises. God's commands pointed to a wonderful future.

"Son, we are supposed to keep God's commands and fear Him, because that is the only way our people will have a secure future. God has promised to bless us and to protect us from our enemies. We trust in His wise, loving promises.

When we keep His commands, He will take care of all of our needs. Obedience will be for our own good."

In words similar to these, the fathers in Israel would try to make clear their salvation heritage and hope. The former slaves were about to possess their own land. But to survive and prosper they would have to love God totally, consistently teach and keep His commands, and faithfully tell their children their history and their hopes.

Discussion Questions

1. How would you describe the influence of God's commands in Israel's families?
2. What responsibilities fell to parents and their children?
3. Put the great command (vs. 5) in your own words. How would you tell another person what it means to love God totally?
4. What obstacles to total love for God creep up in our lives?
5. Why is knowing God's salvation history important, if we are to love and obey Him?
6. What rights does God have over Christians? Why?

Contemporary Application

Many people confess that their lives lack focus and meaning. If you believe the ads you see on TV, just buy a certain expensive car and your problems will be solved! Envious friends, a sense of well-being, and happiness are yours the moment you slide behind the wheel. If only life were that simple!

God knows that to find meaning and purpose for living we must commit ourselves to something higher than ourselves. The key is to find that one ingredient or secret that will bring everything together. That's exactly what God's great command does for us.

Life has its satisfying center in God and His commands. That's the word people long to hear. Disillusionment hits many people because they don't know where to look for that integrating factor that will make them whole.

We must tell the world, "Love God with everything you've got. Don't hold back. Abandon yourself completely to Him, and your life will come together in a beautiful wholeness." For Israel's ancient people, that meant obeying the commands God gave to Moses. For everyone today, it means obeying the Gospel revealed in Jesus Christ.

The magnificent news of the Gospel is that when we confess our failure to love God totally, we can receive forgiveness through faith in Christ. He comes to live in us and motivates us to do what Moses so beautifully described to the children of Israel.

A Warning

Scripture

Background Scripture: *Deuteronomy 8*
Scripture Lesson: *Deuteronomy 8:7-20*
Key Verse: *Be careful that you do not forget the* LORD *your God, failing to observe his commands, his laws and his decrees that I am giving you this day.* Deuteronomy 8:11.

Lesson Aim

To beware of pride, self-sufficiency, idolatry, and forgetting the Lord.

Lesson Setting

Time: *1400 B.C.*
Place: *Desert of Sinai*

Lesson Outline

A Warning

 I. The promised land: Deuteronomy 8:7-9
   A. *Abundant Water: vs. 7*
   B. *Abundant Food: vss. 8-9*
 II. Don't Forget: Deuteronomy 8:10-14
   A. *Praise the Lord: vs. 10*
   B. *Keep God's Commands: vs. 11*
   C. *Watch Out for Pride: vss. 12-14*
 III. God's Provision: Deuteronomy 8:15-16
   A. *Water in the Desert: vs. 15*
   B. *Manna to Eat: vs. 16*
 IV. Remember the Lord: Deuteronomy 8:17-18
   A. *Temptation to Self-Sufficiency: vs. 17*
   B. *God Gave the Wealth: vs. 18*
 V. The Cost of Disobedience: Deuteronomy 8:19-20
   A. *The Sin of Idolatry: vs. 19*
   B. *God's Judgment: vs. 20*

Introduction for Adults

Topic: *Don't Lose Perspective*

If you're a parent, you probably enjoy school art shows, not just to see what your own children have done, but also to listen to the comments of other parents. Some give enthusiastic praise, even for art that doesn't win prizes. But other parents chastise their children for not doing better.

Giving commendations is an important part of building self-esteem. Our children need to feel good about themselves. However, when we grow up, sometimes we get carried away with self-esteem. Our heads get too big for our hats. Our hearts are filled with self-praise. We love to brag about what we have done.

Moses knew what pride and self-sufficiency would do to God's people, so he warned them to be careful. "Keep God first," he said. "Don't forget the Lord when you are enjoying the good life" (which is exactly the time when we are most prone to forget Him).

Introduction for Youths

Topic: *Don't Forget*

I'm sure teenagers get tired of being reminded, "Don't forget . . ." as they rush out of the house. Then when they get to school and realize they have forgotten their term paper, they wish they had paid attention to mom's warnings.

"Don't forget" suggests we don't have our acts together. It suggests that we are not perfect, that we have some flaw that will get us into trouble. Exactly. We all have those flaws, but our pride keeps us from admitting it.

Moses knew that when Israel relaxed in prosperous times, the key word had to be, "Don't forget the Lord who made all this possible." Parents and elders in Israel had to keep on saying, "Don't forget."

It's a good way to start the day. Don't forget your wallet, your glasses, your gym bag, your term paper. And certainly don't forget the Lord when you crash out the front door for school.

Concepts for Children

Topic: *Remembering God's Goodness*

1. Moses was like a faithful, loving, wise parent to Israel.
2. Therefore, he taught them to remember God's goodness at all times.
3. Sometimes we are too proud to admit that we owe everything to God.
4. When we do something well and receive credit for it, we should say thank You to Jesus.
5. We can think of things to do to help us not forget God.
6. God wants us to love Him alone, and not the things He gives us to enjoy.

71

The Lesson Commentary

I. The Promised Land: Deuteronomy 8:7-9

A. Abundant Water: vs. 7

For the LORD your God is bringing you into a good land—a land with streams and pools of water, with springs flowing in the valleys and hills.

After rehearsing the Ten Commandments and the great commandment, Moses urged Israel to drive out the people inhabiting Canaan and to destroy their idols (Deut. 7). Moses knew the Israelites would be afraid of these people, so he promised, "The LORD your God will deliver them over to you" (Deut. 7:23).

His theme in chapter 8 can be stated in two ways, "Remember" or "Don't forget." He reminded them of the purpose of their travails in the desert. God was testing them to know what was in their hearts, whether they would obey Him or not (8:2). Their hunger was really a spiritual lesson, to show that "man does not live on bread alone but on every word that comes from the mouth of the LORD" (vs. 3). God disciplined Israel as a father disciplines his son (vs. 5).

The significance of these desert lessons is highlighted in the New Testament. When Jesus was tempted by Satan to turn stones into bread, He resisted the temptation by recalling Israel's hunger experience in the wilderness and the truth it was intended to teach (Matt. 4:4).

When the writer of Hebrews explained the purposes of God's discipline of His children, he argued from the principle stated by Moses (Heb. 12:7-10).

Moses anticipated Israel's occupation of Canaan. He sketched both the delights and the perils of the land. He clearly stated the key to finding God's best: "Observe the commands of the LORD your God, walking in his ways and revering him" (Deut. 8:6). Whatever the years would bring, Israel must not stray from the Lord.

God would bring His people into a land of abundant water: streams, pools, and springs flowing everywhere. Having lived in the desert with barely enough water to survive, this must have sounded like an impossible dream to the Israelites. No longer would they have to march from place to place in search of water.

Of course, throughout the eastern Mediterranean, water was a valuable commodity. Clans fought over water. Abraham's servants fought over wells. Flocks depended on water. Without water crops failed to produce. Therefore, this was an astonishing promise for Moses to make.

B. Abundant Food: vss. 8-9

A land with wheat and barley, vines and fig trees, pomegranates, olive oil and honey; a land where bread will not be scarce and you will lack nothing; a land where the rocks are iron and you can dig copper out of the hills.

Moses emphasized that Israel's good fortunes depended on the Lord. "God is bringing you into a good land" (vs. 7). This promise reflected on their desperate need for bread in the wilderness, which God had provided. Now Israel could look forward to the security of having daily bread, and not worrying where the next day's supply of bread would come from.

The promised land would be so good that "you will lack nothing" (vs. 9). Again, this promise surely astounded the people. Only four decades from Egypt, they would soon enjoy their own land and live in the abundance of God's goodness. Great rejoicing must have filled their hearts.

Moses added an interesting promise about future mining (vs. 9b). The Canaanites actively mined the land, but while traces of iron and copper works have been discovered in some places, mining does not seem to have been extensively carried on by the Jews. The fact that both copper and iron could be mined within the confines of Solomon's kingdom was a fulfillment of verse 9.

II. DON'T FORGET: DEUTERONOMY 8:10-14

A. Praise the Lord: vs. 10

When you have eaten and are satisfied, praise the Lord your God for the good land he has given you.

Moses knew very well how easy it would be for Israel to forget the Lord. This is especially true when things are going well. In the good land, they would eat and be satisfied. They would enjoy the fruit of their labors. They might forget that God had given them abundant food and water.

Therefore, he told them to praise the Lord for the good land. Praise is the best antidote to spiritual forgetfulness. Each day is to be marked by praise. It is interesting to think about how this should be done.

Moses said, "When you have eaten and are satisfied, praise the Lord." This means that after each meal the family should pause to say "Thank You" to the Lord. Our custom is to give thanks before we eat. In some families, the custom is to praise the Lord both before and after eating.

Whatever the custom, the principle is the same: Take time to praise God for His abundant blessings. This practice brings God to the center of our attention at the time our bodies crave food.

B. Keep God's Commands: vs. 11

Be careful that you do not forget the Lord your God, failing to observe his commands, his laws and his decrees that I am giving you this day.

Of course, all of life in Israel was to be guarded by God's laws. The faithful teaching of His laws would keep the people from forgetting the Lord. As they remembered and obeyed the Lord's commands, they would be preserved from falling into sin and idolatry.

"Be careful" reminds us that obedience is never easy. It is much easier to forget than to remember. Spiritual discipline is tough. This is why many people memorize God's words.

Faithful study of God's Word, personally and in small groups, serves to promote spiritual growth and resistance to sin. God's commands must be at the heart of church and family life.

C. Watch Out for Pride: vss. 12-14

Otherwise, when you eat and are satisfied, when you build fine houses and settle down, and when your herds and flocks grow large and your silver and gold increase and all you have is multiplied, then your heart will become proud and you will forget the LORD your God, who brought you out of Egypt, out of the land of slavery.

What will happen if Israel fails to keep God's commands? People will fall into pride and forget the Lord (vs. 14). Moses pointed out the alternative to faithful obedience. The people needed to know the consequences of unfaithfulness.

"Otherwise" means other than keeping the Lord's commands. The temptation to disobedience would come with plentiful food, comfortable houses, large flocks and herds, and wealth. When everything is "multiplied," people would become proud and forget the Lord.

God's rich blessings in effect would become a test of their faith and obedience. The abundance of physical blessings would cause them to forget their redemption from Egypt (vs. 14). They would forget their lowly estate as slaves. They would forget how God had delivered them from bondage.

Of course, pride grows in the soil of self-sufficiency. Forgetting the Lord means taking credit for physical and material well-being. Pride says, "We did it. We earned our houses and our treasures. Who needs God?"

Moses told them to watch out for pride because it would bring spiritual impoverishment in the midst of physical plenty. If Israel failed to obey the Lord's commands, the door would be open to the terrors of pride, which God detests.

The prophet Jeremiah warned, "This is what the LORD says: 'Let not the wise man boast of his wisdom or the strong man boast of his strength or the rich man boast of his riches, but let him who boasts boast about this: that he understands and knows me, that I am the LORD, who exercises kindness, justice and righteousness on earth, for in these I delight,' declares the LORD" (Jer. 9:23-24).

There was nothing wrong with Israel's prosperity, but if it led to boasting and forgetting the Lord, then it would bring the country's downfall.

III. GOD'S PROVISION: DEUTERONOMY 8:15-16

A. Water in the Desert: vs. 15

He led you through the vast and dreadful desert, that thirsty and waterless land, with its venomous snakes and scorpions. He brought you water out of hard rock.

To jog Israel's memory, Moses returned to a familiar theme—the events of 40 years in the Sinai Desert. God not only had brought Israel out of Egypt, he had provided water in "the vast and dreadful desert." When there was no water to be found, God produced water "out of hard rock" (Num. 20:6-11). The desert was infested with poisonous snakes, and God delivered those who looked to Him in faith (Num. 21:4-9).

The point is that Israel was completely helpless in the desert. If not for God's provision, the nation would not have survived. Therefore in the good times ahead, the best protection against spiritual disaster would be to recall the miraculous water in the desert.

B. Manna to Eat: vs. 16

He gave you manna to eat in the desert, something your fathers had never known, to humble and to test you so that in the end it might go well with you.

Not only did God provide water for Israel, He also gave them manna to eat in the desert. Interestingly, manna was not only food, but a kind of spiritual checkpoint "to humble and to test you." Severe as the test was, it was for Israel's good.

Of course, the issue in the desert was the same as the theme of Moses' teaching here—Israel's pride. Hunger in the desert was used by God to humble His people (vss. 3, 16). This shows what a pernicious sin pride is. It led to rebellion in the desert and the loss of an entire generation.

Only when pride is defeated will it "go well with you." Israel's well-being in Canaan was not defined by food, houses, flocks, herds, and wealth, but by humble trust in the almighty God.

IV. REMEMBER THE LORD: DEUTERONOMY 8:17-18

A. Temptation to Self-Sufficiency: vs. 17

You may say to yourself, "My power and the strength of my hands have produced this wealth for me."

Moses created a hypothetical saying to show what the spiritual temptation would be. The people might look around at their wealth and say that they themselves had produced it. This was the height of arrogance.

Moses' statement was reaffirmed by the Lord Jesus Christ when He told the story about the wealthy farmer. This man gave no credit to the Lord for his abundant crops. Instead, he built bigger barns to store more grain, so that he could live a life of comfort and ease. When God demanded his life, He called the wealthy man a fool (Luke 12:16-20).

Taking credit for abundant blessings is the height of spiritual folly. It not only breeds self-sufficiency, but discredits and despises the Lord, who gives all good gifts. "Be careful that you do not forget the Lord" is the best protection against the sin of self-sufficiency.

B. God Gave the Wealth: vs. 18

But remember the LORD your God, for it is he who gives you the ability to produce wealth, and so confirms his covenant, which he swore to your forefathers, as it is today.

God is the creator and giver of all wealth. He delegates the work required to produce wealth. The farmers of Israel plowed the soil and planted their seeds. They bred their flocks and fed them. God gave them the ability to do these things. This was part of His promise to Israel's patriarchs, Abraham, Isaac, and Jacob.

Therefore, in the families of Israel, each harvest, each increase in flocks and herds, each gain in silver and gold was to be the occasion of celebrations of praise and thanksgiving to God. God was to be honored in the ordinary workaday world. All of life was to be permeated with praise and honor to God for blessing Israel.

Regular prayer and praise were the keys to protecting Israel from the sins of pride and self-sufficiency. Each material blessing was to spark a hymn of praise to God and a testimony to His goodness.

V. THE COST OF DISOBEDIENCE: DEUTERONOMY 8:19-20

A. The Sin of Idolatry: vs. 19

If you ever forget the LORD your God and follow other gods and worship and bow down to them, I testify against you today that you will surely be destroyed.

Moses returned to another major theme of spiritual life and teaching—the perils of idolatry. The gods of the Canaanites would act like powerful magnets toward the Israelites. They would be drawn into the corrupt worship of these pagan deities.

This warning harks back to the first of the Ten Commandments. Obedience to God's command was the only way to avoid idolatry. Israel's God was the one true God. He alone was to be worshiped. That is why the command to love God totally (Deut. 6:5) was so important. This command had to be drummed into their hearts and minds.

Surrounded as they were by Canaanites, the Israelites would be tempted to worship gods they could see. Idols made of wood and stone were everywhere in the countryside. It would seem to make sense to worship the seen gods rather than the unseen God. But Israel had to learn to walk by faith, not by sight. Israel had to learn to trust the God of salvation from Egypt, not idols made by Canaanites themselves.

B. God's Judgment: vs. 20

Like the nations the LORD destroyed before you, so you will be destroyed for not obeying the LORD your God.

The sin of idolatry would bring God's severe judgment. The people would be destroyed for violating God's command against idolatry. The basic issue in idolatry was disobedience. To love and obey God meant complete separation from foreign gods.

As Moses and the people looked ahead, they could see the attractiveness of

God's promised blessings. They could also see the great risks of displeasing the Lord. The future was filled with potential for enjoying life under God's good hand. It was also filled with potential perils of pride, self-sufficiency, and idolatry.

As Israel's history played out, the nation ultimately was destroyed—as Moses predicted it would be—because of idolatry. The sermons of Isaiah, Jeremiah, and Ezekiel make very clear that forsaking God for foreign deities was the root cause of the nation's destruction.

Discussion Questions

1. How would you summarize Moses' "commencement address"?
2. Why was it important to balance blessings and warnings?
3. Why is it hard to remember God when the good times roll?
4. What are the keys to a sharp spiritual memory?
5. What part should warnings play in the teaching of Christian families and the church?
6. How can Christians encourage one another to stay true to God, and to thank and praise Him for all of life's blessings?

Contemporary Application

"Do not forget the Lord" seems like trite advice until we look around the circles of our families and friends and see how many have done exactly that. In spite of such overwhelming evidence that many people do forget God, some Christians get upset when sermons include warnings about spiritual fallout.

That will never happen to me, we think. But the apostle Paul warned that those who think they are safe should beware of falling (1 Cor. 10:12). That's why regular warnings of spiritual perils are much needed, even if they sound negative.

In Moses' address, he balanced blessings and warnings. We all need to be reminded of Christ's unsearchable riches (Eph. 3:8). But we also need to be reminded of how severely He chastised phony believers and hypocritical religion.

When we study our Bibles and pray together, we need to pray as Jesus did for His disciples, that God would protect them from disunity, deception, and defection (John 17). How great it is to celebrate God's goodness when we enjoy the abundance of His material blessings. We also need to celebrate all we have in Christ—our imperishable spiritual inheritance—so that we will stay true to Him.

Spiritual forgetfulness attacks us especially when everything goes well. Those are the times we must be on guard. We must thank God for those servants like Moses who warn us of our proneness to pride and self-sufficiency.

Joshua Succeeds Moses

DEVOTIONAL READING

Numbers 27:12-23

DAILY BIBLE READINGS

Monday November 1
*Deuteronomy 31:1-6 God
Will Lead Israel across
Jordan*

Tuesday November 2
*Deuteronomy 31:7-13 Read
and Obey the Law*

Wednesday November 3
*Deuteronomy 31:14-23
Joshua Is Commissioned to
Succeed Moses*

Thursday November 4
*Deuteronomy 34:1-7 Death
of Moses in Moab*

Friday November 5
*Deuteronomy 34:8-12
Moses is Mourned and
Remembered*

Saturday November 6
*Joshua 1:1-9 God's Promise
and Command to Joshua*

Sunday November 7
*Joshua 1:10-16 Israel
Prepared to Cross the
Jordan*

Scripture

Background Scripture: *Deuteronomy 31:1-8; 34*
Scripture Lesson: *Deuteronomy 31:1-8; 34:5-9*
Key Verse: *"The LORD himself goes before you and will
be with you; he will never leave you nor forsake you. Do
not be afraid; do not be discouraged."* Deuteronomy
31:8.

Lesson Aim

To trust in God and look for His provision when we
suffer losses in leadership.

Lesson Setting

Time: *1400 B.C.*
Place: *Desert of Sinai, and the plains of Moab, east of
Canaan.*

Lesson Outline

Joshua Succeeds Moses

   I. Moses' Charge to the People: Deuteronomy
      31:1-6
      A. Moses Will Not Cross the Jordan: vss. 1-2
      B. The Lord and Joshua Will Cross Over: vs. 3
      C. The Lord Will Defeat Their Enemies: vss. 4-5
      D. Be Strong, God Will Not Forsake You: vs. 6
  II. Moses' Charge to Joshua: Deuteronomy 31:7-8
      A. Be Strong and Courageous: vs. 7
      B. The Lord Will Go With You: vs. 8
 III. Moses' Death: Deuteronomy 34:5-9
      A. He Died and Was Buried in Moab: vss. 5-6
      B. He Died in Strength: vs. 7
      C. Israel Mourned Him: vs. 8
      D. Israel Followed Joshua: vs. 9

Introduction for Adults

Topic: *Maintaining Continuity*

If you are a board member of an organization, maybe you have sat through this familiar refrain: "We must be sure to maintain things as they are. We have to preserve the good things we have." But many managers say this is a sure recipe for disaster. Changes are inevitable. They key is how to manage change without losing sight of your vision and goals.

In Moses' farewell address, he deserves an A-plus for managing change. His charges to the Israelites and to their anointed leader, Joshua, were superb. He kept the main thing the main thing. God must be obeyed. Canaan must be entered. But you must do it under new leadership. The key to success will be your faith, courage, and obedience to the Lord. Those things never change.

Change brought great pressures on Joshua, as well as the Israelites. Things would be different, but God's promises would not change. If Joshua and the people believed God would continue to go with them, they could handle change in the best possible way.

Introduction for Youths

Topic: *Receiving the Torch*

Every four years the Olympic torch is passed hand-to-hand by runners from all over the world. People all over the world thrill when the last runner arrives at the stadium and ignites the Olympic torch to open the games!

Young people are on the receiving end of something far more precious than the Olympic torch. They receive the Christian faith from their parents. It is their duty to pick up the torch of Jesus Christ and carry it faithfully, until they in turn pass it on to their children. For a grandparent, the most satisfying thing in life is to see one's grandchildren preparing to take up the torch of Christian faith.

Moses gave us the key to a successful transfer of the torch. He handed the torch to the people and to Joshua with the same words, "Be strong and courageous. The Lord will be with you." With the command he gave the promise.

Concepts for Children

Topic: *Following New Leaders*

1. When Israel faced the challenge of entering Canaan, Moses gave words of encouragement.
2. God always draws near to help us when we face unexpected difficulties.
3. We can count on God's promise that He will never leave or forsake us.
4. We can help one another to be bold and brave, and to be faithful to Jesus, even when some others ridicule us.
5. When Moses died, God gave Israel a new leader, Joshua.
6. God takes care of us when friends and respected leaders die.

The Lesson Commentary

I. MOSES' CHARGE TO THE PEOPLE: DEUTERONOMY 31:1-6

A. Moses Will Not Cross the Jordan: vss. 1-2

Then Moses went out and spoke these words to all Israel: "I am now a hundred and twenty years old and I am no longer able to lead you. The LORD has said to me, 'You shall not cross the Jordan.'"

Moses called Israel to faith and obedience (Deut. 7—11). Then he spelled out in great detail various laws covering every aspect of life (Deut. 12—26). This he followed with a powerful pronouncement of curses and blessings (Deut. 27—30).

Next, he gave his charge to the people, in which he revealed that he himself would not cross the Jordan River into the promised land, but Joshua would do so under God's guidance and protection.

How much he must have longed to enter Canaan. But the decision was not his to make, because God had revealed that he would not cross the Jordan. This verdict dated back to the time when Moses smote the rock in anger to get water for the Israelites in the desert (Num. 20:12; Deut. 3:21-29; 32:48-52).

Moses had pleaded with God to "go over and see the good land beyond the Jordan" (Deut. 3:25). But God told him not to bring the matter up anymore. He told him to go to the top of Mount Pisgah and "look at the land with your own eyes" (Deut. 3:27). Apparently, Moses blamed Israel for his disappointment (Deut. 3:26).

On the other hand, Moses did not complain. He accepted God's wisdom in the matter. In fact, he admitted that at 120 years of age he was too old to keep on leading Israel. The days ahead would include grueling marches and hard battles against the Canaanites.

When Moses said, "I am no longer able to lead you," he meant literally, "I can no longer move about as I please." His statement here does not necessarily conflict with Deuteronomy 34:7, "Moses was a hundred and twenty years old when he died, yet his eyes were not weak nor his strength gone." Here, he indicated that his age would disqualify him from the rigors of future national leadership, while the biographer who wrote about Moses' death showed that he was in full possession of his natural faculties and strength.

B. The Lord and Joshua Will Cross Over: vs. 3

"The LORD your God himself will cross over ahead of you. He will destroy these nations before you, and you will take possession of their land. Joshua also will cross over ahead of you, as the LORD said."

Probably the people's hearts sank when they heard Moses say that he would not lead them across the Jordan. How could they make it without him? He had been their conduit to the Lord. He had saved them from extinction. He had been their brave captain through 40 years in the desert.

However, that was not the end of the story. Moses reminded them that God would cross over ahead of them, and that Joshua would be their new leader. "You will take possession of their land," Moses confidently declared. This was his morale builder, because he knew what was going through their minds.

The people's faith was about to be tested again, but God did not leave them in the dark. He did not leave them leaderless. The people stood on the brink of a great leap of faith. Would they trust God once again? Would they put their confidence in Him and follow His leader, Joshua? On the eve of occupying Canaan these were the big questions.

C. The Lord Will Defeat Their Enemies: vss. 4-5

(SIGH hun)   (ahg)

"And the LORD will do to them what he did to Sihon and Og, the kings of the Amorites, whom he destroyed along with their land. The LORD will deliver them to you, and you must do to them all that I have commanded you."

Moses continued his faith-building charge to the people by reminding them that the Lord would defeat their enemies across the Jordan in Canaan.

To bolster Israel's faith, Moses reminded the people of the previous battle with the Amorites (Num. 21:21-35; Deut. 2:24—3:11). God had destroyed them to make way for Israel's passage to the promised land. Moses therefore could make an iron-clad guarantee: "The LORD will deliver them to you" (vs. 5).

Once again the issue before Israel was faith and obedience. The people had to believe God's promise. Then they had to obey him and do everything He had commanded. Faith without obedience and courage is no faith at all.

D. Be Strong, God Will Not Forsake You: vs. 6

"Be strong and courageous. Do not be afraid or terrified because of them, for the LORD your God goes with you; he will never leave you nor forsake you."

Of course, Moses knew the Israelites very well. He remembered how they had quaked in fear before the Red Sea. He remembered how their fear had kept them from entering Canaan in the first place. They needed strength and courage.

Fear was probably uppermost in their minds, because they lacked military skills, and they were invading the homeland of powerful people. Besides, they still had to cross the Jordan River.

The antidote to fear is strength and courage. The Israelites had to get their eyes off the Canaanites and focus on God Himself. If they kept thinking about their enemies, they would never enter the land. They had to enter in full assurance that God was with them. He would never leave or forsake them.

The sweet essence of faith is knowing the personal presence of the Lord. The Israelites had seen God's power manifested in many ways since Egypt. They had to believe that His power would continue to go with them into Canaan.

Today, believers count on Christ's personal presence. The intimacy of faith is what Jesus talked about. "Remain in me, and I will remain in you. . . . I am the vine; you are the branches," He said (John 15:4-5). "Surely I am with you always," He promised (Matt. 28:20). Christ in us is our hope of glory, the apostle Paul declared (Col. 1:27).

II. MOSES' CHARGE TO JOSHUA: DEUTERONOMY 31:7-8

A. Be Strong and Courageous: vs. 7

Then Moses summoned Joshua and said to him in the presence of all Israel, "Be strong and courageous, for you must go with this people into the land that the LORD swore to their forefathers to give them, and you must divide it among them as their inheritance."

After speaking to the congregation of Israel, Moses turned to Joshua and charged him in front of the people. Joshua had served the Lord faithfully under Moses' leadership throughout the 40 years in the desert. After the first scouting mission, he and Caleb had urged the people to move into Canaan at once, but their counsel was rejected.

Nevertheless, he was certainly awed and frightened by the new leadership responsibilities the Lord had given him. Joshua probably thought about all the times the people had complained and rebelled in the desert. Were they really ready to follow him into Canaan? Was he ready to lead them?

Moses gave him the same counsel he had given to the people: "Be strong and courageous." Of course, as the commander-in-chief he had to set the standard for the people to follow. He could not retreat. He had to lead the march.

His strength and courage had to be both physical and spiritual. He had to find new depths of faith and trust in the Lord. He had to draw strength and courage from his walk with God. He had to meet with God day by day in prayer and worship. Strength and courage arise from meetings with God.

B. The Lord Will Go with You: vs. 8

"The LORD himself goes before you and will be with you; he will never leave you nor forsake you. Do not be afraid; do not be discouraged."

Ultimately, of course, Joshua's strength and courage would come from the knowledge that God was with him. Moses sought to allay Joshua's fears and insecurities by reminding him that God would go into Canaan before him.

Fear and discouragement would defeat Joshua and Israel. That's why Moses kept coming back to these two maladies. He knew how easily God's people could retreat, lose faith, and fail to obey the Lord.

Moses boldly stated God's promises. Joshua had to grasp them, believe them, and then act. It would be easy to say, "Yes, I know all that, but I'm still scared."

Of course, fear is a natural protective device against danger, but when fear keeps us from doing what God wants us to do then it is harmful. The whole point of Moses' charge was to be sure that Joshua and the people did not turn back, and refuse to enter Canaan, as the Israelites had done before.

Therefore, he not only told them to be strong and courageous, but to believe God's promises. "He will never leave you" was the foundation promise in which Joshua had to lead the people into Canaan. Our salvation in New Testament terms rests on believing God's promises of forgiveness and eternal life in the Gospel. We take God at His word when He says that because Jesus died for us, our sins cn be forgiven. Our faith in His promises grows stronger in worship, praise, fellowship, prayer, and Bible study. We need the kind of reminders that God gave Israel and Joshua.

III. MOSES' DEATH: DEUTERONOMY 34:5-9

A. He Died and Was Buried in Moab: vss. 5-6

And Moses the servant of the LORD died there in Moab, as the LORD had said. He buried him in Moab, in the valley opposite Beth Peor, but to this day no one knows where his grave is.

Deuteronomy 32 is a wonderful song of praise to the Lord, which Moses recited before the assembly of Israel. At the same time, it was a song of profound warnings to Israel to be faithful to God. At the end he said, "Take to heart all the words I have solemnly declared to you this day. . . . They are not just idle words for you—they are your life" (Deut. 32:46-47). Then he pronounced blessings on each of the tribes (Deut. 33).

As the Lord had instructed him to do, Moses climbed Mount Nebo east of the Jordan River in what is now the western part of the country of Jordan. It was due east of the city of Jericho in Canaan. From his vantage point Moses could see all of the promised land. God reminded him that this was the land He had promised to Abraham, Isaac, and Jacob.

Imagine the great leader's feelings. His eyes may have filled with tears as he recalled God's faithfulness, going back even to his birth. Probably he remembered the 40 years guarding sheep in the desert before God called him to lead Israel out of Egypt. The encounters with Pharaoh, the parting of the Red Sea, and the painful journey in the desert—through all of them God was always there. God had indeed birthed a nation under the leadership of Moses.

But he would not live to set foot on Canaan. He died in Moab overlooking the land. He was buried there. The Bible is right. No one knows where he was buried, although local Jordanian Bedouins claim to know the place. Verse 6 says God buried Moses, but other translations simply say, "He was buried."

Some scholars think the reason Moses' burial site is unknown is because he was translated into God's presence as Enoch and Elijah were. Perhaps so. We meet Moses again in the New Testament, on a mountain talking to Jesus (Mark 9:2-4).

There would be no prophet in Israel to match Moses until Elijah. Looking at his life, it could easily be said that no one surpassed Moses except the Lord Jesus Christ. Yet the amazing thing is that he was simply called "the servant of the LORD" (vs. 5). What a fitting epitaph for Moses, or for any believer for that matter! "Well done, good and faithful servant" is what Jesus told us will be God's criterion of judgment for His people.

B. He Died In Strength: vs. 7

Moses was a hundred and twenty years old when he died, yet his eyes were not weak nor his strength gone.

Moses lived to be 120 years old, quite remarkable in view of the incredible pressures he faced. Even more remarkable was his physical resilience. He did not waste away with a chronic illness; he died a strong man. Even his eyesight was good. God simply decided it was time to take His servant home. He had faithfully done all that God had expected of him.

The record shows that God was faithful to His promises when He called Moses. He not only gave him spiritual authority and strength, but He blessed him with good health as well. The rigors of leadership take a heavy physical and emotional toll, but God preserved Moses through all of the heavy demands of his position.

C. Israel Mourned Him: vs. 8

The Israelites grieved for Moses in the plains of Moab thirty days, until the time of weeping and mourning was over.

Appropriately, Israel mourned the loss of Moses, their great leader. The mourning lasted a full month. The people waited east of the Jordan, no doubt reflecting on the last words of Moses about obeying the Lord and moving into Canaan with faith and courage.

At the same time, changes in leadership also gave rise to speculation about the future. People got nervous because of the uncertainties. Why had God removed Moses at this critical juncture? Why had God not allowed Moses to lead them into Canaan? And so on.

Grieving also allowed time for orderly transfer of leadership. This was a critical time. Probably Joshua spent more time than usual before God in prayer. He probably checked with his tribal leaders, to see how they were adjusting. The people had to get used to their new leader.

Above all, it was a time for people to tell their children the great stories about Moses. The priests could rehearse the laws of God that Moses had delivered. Each person had an important part to play, if they were to show the strength and courage that Moses had urged upon them.

D. Israel Followed Joshua: vs. 9

Now Joshua son of Nun was filled with the spirit of wisdom because Moses had laid his hands on him. So the Israelites listened to him and did what the LORD had commanded Moses.

Apparently Moses had anointed Joshua and laid hands on him, signifying to the people and tribal chiefs that this man truly was his successor. This symbolic act also evidently filled Joshua with the Holy Spirit, which he greatly needed for his future responsibilities.

The people accepted the transfer of authority and followed Joshua. This was no time for tribal rebellions. Unity was critical for the move into Canaan. In political terms, this was a successful transition from one leader to another. In spiritual terms, it meant that the Israelites had decided to obey the Lord and to trust His anointed leader.

Discussion Questions

1. Why are changes in leadership so critical?
2. Why did Moses emphasize, "Be strong and courageous"?
3. Under what circumstances do Christians need strength and courage?
4. What do you think Joshua thought about after Moses died? Why?
5. Why is our faith tested when respected leaders change positions or die?
6. What steps can churches take to ensure the orderly, courageous, and faithful changes in leadership?

Contemporary Application

Changes in leadership can be very traumatic, for example, the sudden death of a president. They can also be very emotional when a beloved pastor leaves, and extremely upsetting when a pastor leaves for moral reasons.

Such sudden changes catch us unprepared. They remind us of Moses' exhortation to be strong and courageous. Many churches have floundered because of a lack of faith in the Lord. Some people think the church belongs to them and to their pastors, but the church really belongs to Christ. He gave Himself for the church; He loves the church; He nourishes His church.

When we realize that Christ is the Head of His Body, the church, we can gain strength and courage. Leaders come and go, but Jesus never leaves His church. We need mature Christians who will stand up at the critical time of leadership change and remind us who really owns us.

After a pastoral change, one such lay leader reminded the people that God would provide a new pastor for them, just as He had provided a ram in the thicket for Abraham to sacrifice instead of Isaac. This man knew his Bible and how to apply God's principles to a change in leadership. The people were greatly encouraged.

Who will be Moses among us and remind us to look to God at all times, especially when we have lost our leader? "God will never leave you nor forsake you" is true when we lose our leaders and when we are expected to fight new battles of faith in the days ahead.

Israel Crosses the Jordan River

DEVOTIONAL READING
Joshua 4:15-24

DAILY BIBLE READINGS
Monday November 8
Joshua 2:1-7 Spies Are Sent to Jericho

Tuesday November 9
Joshua 2:8-14 Rahab Seeks Assurances of God's Protection

Wednesday November 10
Joshua 2:15-24 Rahab Helps the Spies Escape

Thursday November 11
Joshua 3:1-6 Israel Follows Ark of the Covenant

Friday November 12
Joshua 3:7-13 Israel at Jordan's Banks

Saturday November 13
Joshua 3:14—4:3 Israel Crosses the Jordan

Sunday November 14
Joshua 4:4-14 Twelve Memorial Stones Placed in Jordan

Scripture
Background Scripture: *Joshua 3*
Scripture Lesson: *Joshua 3:7-17*
Key Verse: *"Have I not commanded you? Be strong and courageous. Do not be terrified; do not be discouraged, for the LORD your God will be with you wherever you go."*
Joshua 1:9.

Lesson Aim
To grow in confidence in God's promises.

Lesson Setting
Time: *1400 B.C.*
Place: *East bank of Jordan River*

Lesson Outline
Israel Crosses the Jordan River
   I. God's Word to Joshua: Joshua 3:7-8
      A. He Promised His Presence: vs. 7
      B. His Command to the Priests: vs. 8
  II. Joshua's Word to the People: Joshua 3:9-13
      A. God Will Drive Out Their Enemies: vss. 9-10
      B. The Ark Will Go before Them: vss. 11-12
      C. The River Will Dry Up: vs. 13
 III. God's Mighty Miracle: Joshua 3:14-17
      A. The People Obeyed: vs. 14
      B. The Flood Waters Were Held Back: vss. 15-16
      C. Everyone Crossed on Dry Ground: vs. 17

Introduction for Adults

Topic: *Going Forward in Faith*

One of the old hymns of the church goes like this: "When I tread the verge of Jordan, bid my anxious fears subside. Bear me through the swelling current, land me safe on Canaan's side" (William Williams, 1717–1791). Jordan stands for death; Canaan for heaven. But in this lesson we see that Jordan stands for victory and the confirmation of God's promises.

Joshua set out to cross the Jordan River, a formidable barrier in flood season. God met him and reassured him of His presence and gave him a plan for crossing the river. The priests had to take the first dangerous steps into the water and the Israelites had to follow them.

Such a challenge is not likely to happen to many of us today. This story sounds more like a space mission, or a space walk, when the astronaut has to step out of his vehicle into thin air. Not for me, we say.

On the other hand, God confronts the church with obedience to His commands, even when the circumstances are not right, easy, or comfortable. That's the story of a growing, obedient church—looking at closed doors for witness and service and asking God for faith to find His way to open them.

Introduction for Youths

Topic: *Trusting Promises*

Someone has said that youth today lack heroes, or that they follow the wrong kinds of pop music and film stars. The Bible is full of heroes, or models, like Joshua. He accepted a dangerous mission because he knew God personally.

Joshua will not attract youth, however, unless they are convinced that the way of faith, courage, and obedience is much more satisfying. They need to see this kind of advertisement, if you will, in the lives of other youth and adults as well. When adults show that serving God makes a difference, youth will notice.

In this lesson, we find not only a courageous leader, but also courageous followers. The key was an unshakable confidence in God's presence.

Christian youth face a similar impossible assignment when they choose to follow Christ. Moral decisions are tough, and sometimes they stumble, but they need encouragement and guidance to keep growing in their faith.

Concepts for Children

Topic: *Trusting Others*

1. God directs His people when they are faced with difficulties.
2. People can be assured of God's presence.
3. Joshua's example shows how to follow God.
4. Even in life-threatening situations, we can trust God for strength, courage, and hope.
5. We can help our friends trust Jesus when they face hard decisions.
6. Prayer to trust God's promises is a continual need in our lives.

The Lesson Commentary

I. GOD'S WORD TO JOSHUA: JOSHUA 3:7-8

A. He Promised His Presence: vs. 7

And the LORD said to Joshua, "Today I will begin to exalt you in the eyes of all Israel, so they may know that I am with you as I was with Moses."

Excitement gripped the camp of Israel on the east bank of the Jordan River following the favorable report and the great confidence of the men who had returned from reconnoitering Jericho. Perched on the hills of Moab, they could see the fertile city on the west bank. Probably they were eager to attack at once, but they had to wait three days (Josh. 3:2).

They had to be organized and instructed about how to cross the river, which was not very wide, less than 100 feet normally, but now it was at flood stage (vs. 15). Equally important, they had to worship God (vs. 5). They were not moving out on their own strength, but under the leadership and protection of God Himself. They had to be prepared in heart and mind, as well as with military strategies, because God was going to do some great things (vs. 5).

The Israelites were not professional fighters and they were in strange territory. The Jordan River and the walled city of Jericho must have loomed like insurmountable obstacles. But the ark of the covenant represented God's presence, and they were supposed to follow it (vss. 3-4).

Crossing the Jordan was to be the first test of Joshua's leadership. God had told him to be strong and courageous, but now he faced an insurmountable obstacle: how to get the multitude of men, women, and children across a swollen river—40,000 warriors, plus their families and others (Josh. 4:13). Before God revealed how His people were to cross the river, He appeared personally once again to His leader to bolster his confidence for the task.

Moses himself was given divine credentials and performed miracles, so the people would accept his leadership. God had promised the same to Joshua (Josh. 1:5) and the people came to recognize him in the same way they had revered Moses (4:14).

B. His Command to the Priests: vs. 8

"Tell the priests who carry the ark of the covenant: 'When you reach the edge of the Jordan's waters, go and stand in the river.'"

After reassuring Joshua, God gave His first strategy for crossing the river, and it was a strange one indeed: the priests were to take the ark and stand in the river with it. Joshua did not tell us how he felt about this plan. Was he dismayed? Frightened? Or did he think back four decades and recall how God had led Israel across the Red Sea?

There is no record that he debated the plan with God, and in fact he boldly took it to the people (vs. 9). That was his first step in obedience and courage. God's leaders get a clear picture from Him about what they are to do, and they do it. Often, the most courageous act of a leader is to stand before the people and present God's plan, even when it may appear to fly in the face of logic.

II. JOSHUA'S WORD TO THE PEOPLE: JOSHUA 3:9-13

A. God Will Drive Out Their Enemies: vss. 9-10

Joshua said to the Israelites, "Come here and listen to the words of the LORD your God. This is how you will know that the living God is among you and that he will certainly drive out before you the Canaanites, Hittites, Hivites, Perizzites, Girgashites, Amorites and Jebusites."

Joshua went from his private audience with God and convened an assembly of the people. This had been the typical pattern on the way from Egypt. After Moses had met with God, he would call the people together and give them the teaching. They knew Joshua was their intermediary, so they were prepared to listen.

Was God indeed among them? That was the crucial issue, of course. Without Him, they were lost. Joshua promised them they would have the assurance that He was with them as their "living God." This was a pointed reminder that their God was different from all others worshiped by the Egyptians and the Canaanites. The ensuing conquest of Canaan would not be just a military conquest, but a spiritual one as well.

Joshua named all the fearsome enemies who lived across the Jordan. Nominally, these tribes were under the control of Egypt, but they all held their own tribal territories. Sometimes they were grouped under six or seven nations. Basically, they were organized as city-states under a king. Apart from tribal distinctives, they were labeled by Moses as very wicked (Deut. 9:4-5).

Some historians claim that when Joshua arrived at the Jordan, many of the Canaanites were fed up with their leaders and were looking for freedom. Apart from the nobles, there was little prosperity. The artisans, tenant farmers, and slaves lived in villages close to the cities and worked for the king, priests, and nobles.

The gods of the tribes were the deified powers of nature. The most important was Baal the storm god who supposedly brought rain, and his wife who brought fertility to crops, herds, flocks, and people. Temple priestesses and priests, sometimes called cult prostitutes, were part of the religion, as was human sacrifice. The "detestable ways" of the Canaanites (Deut. 18:9) included cultic activities related to sex and the dead.

B. The Ark Will Go before Them: vss. 11-12

"See, the ark of the covenant of the Lord of all the earth will go into the Jordan ahead of you. Now then, choose twelve men from the tribes of Israel, one from each tribe."

Joshua gave the congregation the most reassuring sign possible: the ark of the covenant would go into the river ahead of them. He also reminded them that their God was "the Lord of all the earth," which meant that He not only ruled and controlled history, but also nature itself, since He was the creator of the universe.

The ark of the covenant is mentioned 15 times in the story of crossing the Jordan. Essentially, it was a sacred box containing some objects. In reality, this box symbolized the throne of the invisible God. God was said to be seated on it (Ps. 80:1; 99:1). The ark showed that God was with Israel and was guiding them on their way (Num. 10:33).

The covenant refers to God's Word, the Ten Commandments plus the entire Mosaic teaching (Deut. 10:1-5; 31:24-26). The ark also contained a jar of manna, a reminder of God's grace in the wilderness and of the people's dependence upon Him for both physical and spiritual food.

The ark was the religious, ethical, and social center of the people as they journeyed from Egypt to Canaan. Therefore, it occupied center stage for the crossing of the Jordan. Without it, Israel would have been attempting the conquest on purely human strength. The ark was constantly in sight throughout the whole event, but the people were to stay about six-tenths of a mile from it (Josh. 3:4), as a reminder of God's holiness and unapproachability. Also, only the authorized priests could carry it.

C. The River Will Dry Up: vs. 13

"And as soon as the priests who carry the ark of the LORD—the Lord of all the earth—set foot in the Jordan, its waters flowing downstream will be cut off and stand up in a heap."

Whatever the people may have thought, probably no one dreamed about the possibility of the flooding river's being dammed up to permit them to cross. Here then was another test of their faith, courage, and obedience.

Probably most people thought about delaying the assault on Canaan until later in the summer, when the flood waters would recede. But God's word to Joshua did not seem to allow that possibility. Rather, His plan required brave priests to step into the river and the people to follow them.

The success of the plan hinged on a promise: the flood would be cut off. Right from the opening of Scripture, people are confronted with such challenges and opportunities to believe God. Noah had to believe God's promise, so did Abraham. That's all they had to go on. Moses led the people out of Egypt on the basis of a promise. Is God faithful to His word or not?

III. GOD'S MIGHTY MIRACLE: JOSHUA 3:14-17

A. The People Obeyed: vs. 14

So when the people broke camp to cross the Jordan, the priests carrying the ark of the covenant went ahead of them.

After the three-day wait for instructions and worship, the Israelites moved toward the river. They apparently broke camp without argument, rebellion, or delay, which must have been a tremendous encouragement to Joshua.

Joshua doubtless recalled the bitterness and whining that had afflicted Israel on the way out of Egypt. They had complained against Moses and against God when they were pursued by Pharaoh's army and blocked by the Red Sea. They decided that it would have been better to remain in slavery in Egypt.

Even after being rescued, once they got out of Egypt they continued to grumble about the lack of food and water. Their rebellion culminated in their refusal to go straight for Canaan. Consequently, an entire generation was wiped out for lack of faith and obedience. On the verge of Jordan, however, they were ready to obey the Lord and follow Joshua.

B. The Flood Waters Were Held Back: vss. 15-16

Now the Jordan is at flood stage all during harvest. Yet as soon as the priests who carried the ark reached the Jordan and their feet touched the water's edge, the water from upstream stopped flowing. It piled up in a heap a great distance away, at a town called Adam in the vicinity of Zarethan, while the water flowing down to the Sea of the Arabah (the Salt Sea) was completely cut off. So the people crossed over opposite Jericho. (AIR ah bah)

(ZAHR eh than) The priests probably felt much like the apostle Peter when he stepped out of the boat at Jesus' command. No one feels comfortable about stepping into a flood-swollen river.

Not having witnessed comparable miracles ourselves, we stagger at what happened here. The Jordan ceased to flow from north to south. The blockage occurred at Adam, sixteen miles up river, which left 20 to 30 miles of dry river bed from there to the Salt Sea, called the Dead Sea today.

Scholars sometimes try to find a natural explanation for miracles like this. For instance, in 1927 earth tremors caused a collapse of the high clay riverbanks at the same spot, and the Jordan was dammed up for over twenty-one hours.

However, in this case God controlled the timing precisely. Instantaneously, the Jordan ceased to flow when the priests stepped into it.

C. Everyone Crossed on Dry Ground: vs. 17

The priests who carried the ark of the covenant of the LORD stood firm on dry ground in the middle of the Jordan, while all Israel passed by until the whole nation had completed the crossing on dry ground.

If the people west of Jordan felt safe because of the river, their security was dashed by this miraculous crossing. The news traveled fast to Jericho as the Israelites completed their crossing. The priests held their ground in the middle of the river, as God had told them to, and everyone crossed safely.

"Crossing over" is the central event. In this passage it's mentioned 21 times, showing not only its importance but also the culmination of God's plan from the time He first heard Israel's anguished cries out of slavery in Egypt.

Interestingly, the biblical account does not speak of Israel's "crossing" the Red Sea, but of going through it (Exod. 14:22, 29). The Hebrew word used for crossing the Jordan implies crossing over a boundary.

Walking through the Red Sea brought escape and liberation; crossing the Jordan brought a new kind of life in the promised land. The Israelites were now going to achieve a land of their own.

Down through Christian history "crossing the Jordan" has come to mean death and entrance into heaven, which is not an accurate application of what happened. Canaan turned out to be much less than heaven; it was not an earthly paradise, but a place of conflict, suffering, civil war, idolatry, and eventual banishment of the people into captivity.

The New Testament, while holding firmly to the Christian's inheritance in heaven, makes it clear that in the meantime believers are called to suffer for the sake of Christ. God's gift of salvation to us is both present and future. Jesus Christ offers forgiveness, guidance, and strength each day, while we await His call to live with Him in heaven.

Discussion Questions

1. What were Joshua's responsibilities as a leader?
2. What spiritual frame of mind do you have to be in to discern God's leading?
3. In the face of seemingly overwhelming difficulties, what do you do? Why?
4. How has God given you promises to meet specific needs?
5. How would you have felt as one of the priests asked to step into the Jordan? Why? What would have helped you to obey?
6. What obstacles does the church face today that must be overcome to advance the Gospel and God's kingdom?

Contemporary Application

A life of commitment to Christ and faithfulness to God will be tested. Jesus Himself met and defeated Satan; the apostle Paul served Christ through beatings, impoverishment, shipwreck, hunger, and imprisonment. Many "Jordans" have to be crossed throughout our lives.

However, the important thing is not to waste time worrying about difficulties that may come our way. Most of them never materialize. As Christians, our duty is to walk in the light of the Gospel. Thus we are prepared when challenges to "cross the Jordan" arise in our lives.

Joshua and his followers seized the opportunity because they knew God was with them. It was not without considerable risk, however, because God's plan must have sounded like a suicide mission.

The church today does not follow a physical ark of the covenant. Jesus Christ came to reveal God to us and He sent us his Holy Spirit to be our guide and our strength. Our confidence in God's leading rests on Christ's resurrection. He intercedes for us in heaven. The Holy Spirit produces His fruit in us. We cross our individual "Jordans" because we know Christ is with us and will never forsake us.

The Destruction of Jericho

Scripture

Background Scripture: *Joshua 6*
Scripture Lesson: *Joshua 6:1-5, 15-20*
Key Verse: *The seventh time around, when the priests sounded the trumpet blast, Joshua commanded the people, "Shout! For the LORD has given you the city!"* Joshua 6:16.

Lesson Aim

To trust God's plan to give us victories over sin and Satan through our faith in Christ.

Lesson Setting

Time: *around 1400 B.C.*
Place: *Jericho*

Lesson Outline

The Destruction of Jericho

I. The Lord's Instructions: Joshua 6:1-5
    A. *Victory Promised: vss. 1-2*
    B. *Strategy Explained: vss. 3-5*
II. The People Obeyed: Joshua: 6:15-17
    A. *They Circled the City: vs. 15*
    B. *The People Shouted: vs. 16*
    C. *Rahab Was to Be Spared: vs. 17*
III. Warnings and Victory: Joshua 6:18-20
    A. *Avoid Taking Anything: vss. 18-19*
    B. *The Wall Collapsed: vs. 20*

Introduction for Adults

Topic: *Overcoming Obstacles*

Heroes return from battles basking in glory. Grateful citizens show their appreciation with cheers and confetti. Thanks to television, all of us share the moment, even though we're not on the scene.

Meanwhile, in ordinary lives the battles go on every day. Winners and losers go unnoticed by the media. These are not the battles that warrant major television coverage, but they are extremely significant to the participants: battles against cancer, old age, debts, loneliness, the difficulties faced by one's children, unemployment.

But in the church of Jesus Christ, Christians do not fight these battles on our own. We know that although we are not spared life's struggles, we do have a unique companion and friend who stands with us, even the Lord Jesus Christ. We also know we can count on a committed band of friends who pray, counsel, and encourage one another.

Joshua's victory at Jericho was a great one, accomplished in a remarkable way. The New Testament tells us that prayer breaks down walls as well. As we follow Christ, all the walls may not tumble, but Jesus is stronger than our enemy and He will triumph in and through us.

Introduction for Youths

Topic: *Sticking to the Plan*

Competition excites youth, whether in sports, music, or academics. Tragically, in some situations, competition can turn nasty and violent. Many young people lose their lives in violence caused by recklessness, drugs, and alcohol—all in the name of trying to be bigger or better or more respected than the next guy.

Part of the problem can be traced to following influential leaders that seem glamorous or exciting in the moment. Youth take needless risks to be accepted. A challenge is given, and rather than be humiliated, they take it on.

The task of Christians is to direct the energy and enthusiasm of youth into acceptable channels, and to provide challenges that lead to worthy goals and outcomes. The Bible is packed with stories of men and women who accepted God's call. They obeyed what He told them to do and found more than enough challenges.

Joshua's march against Jericho is one example of this. He succeeded because he knew God personally and knew what God wanted him to do. Even though God's command appeared to be ridiculous, Joshua obeyed and found success.

Concepts for Children

Topic: *Solving Problems*

1. God gave Joshua and Israel a plan to defeat the enemy.
2. The people needed faith and courage to win their battle.
3. Sometimes it appears that God's plan to solve our problems will not work.
4. We need time to pray and to ask God for strength and courage.
5. God honors those who trust Him when they face problems.
6. We can find courage and strength from older, wiser Christians.

The Lesson Commentary

I. THE LORD'S INSTRUCTION: JOSHUA 6:1-5

A. Victory Promised: vss. 1-2

Now Jericho was tightly shut up because of the Israelites. No one went out and no one came in. Then the LORD said to Joshua, "See, I have delivered Jericho into your hands, along with its king and its fighting men."

After the successful crossing of the Jordan River, the Israelites set up their memorial stones as God had directed them to do. As soon as the priests carrying the ark of the covenant left the river, it returned to flood stage. The company moved on to Gilgal for a time of worship and celebration, where Joshua reminded them of the reason for their miraculous crossing. "He [God] did this so that all the peoples of the earth might know that the hand of the LORD is powerful and so that you might always fear the LORD your God" (Josh. 4:24).

The men who had grown up during the 40 years in the desert had to be circumcised. Then the whole group celebrated Passover and had their first taste of food from Canaan. The next day the miraculous manna—the food from heaven that had sustained them in the desert—ceased. (See also Exod. 16:35.)

The story of the fall of Jericho begins with the appearance of a divine visitor, the commander of the Lord's army (Josh. 5:13-14). This messenger of encouragement and instruction accepted Joshua's worship. On this holy site Joshua acknowledged that he was not the commander, but God Himself was.

The writer reminds us, parenthetically, that Jericho was a city under siege. This confirms what the spies had learned from Rahab. As the people saw the advancing Israelites, they decided to bar the gates to the city.

Jericho, which could mean "moon city," was tightly closed (vs. 1), delivered into Joshua's hands (vs. 2), and condemned to remain an uninhabited waste (vs. 26). Jericho's fate struck fear into other kings and cities (Josh. 9:3; 10:1). The outcome of this engagement became a pattern for the fate of other cities (10:28).

The angelic visitor is identified as the Lord. He spoke directly to Joshua about the forthcoming battle for the city of Jericho, which stood in the way of Israel's conquest of Canaan. The capture of Jericho and Ai (chaps. 6—8) would open up the passes into the interior of the country. A wedge would thus divide the northern and southern parts of Canaan. Then Joshua could go south and defeat the tribes there (chaps. 9—10), and then on to the north (chap. 11).

God continued to encourage Joshua at each strategic point. Now that the Jordan river had been crossed, he no doubt wondered how to capture Jericho.

When Christians find themselves at stopping places, wondering what to do next, God reveals himself in Scripture and in prayer, making the next steps clear.

B. Strategy Explained: vss. 3-5

"March around the city once with all the armed men. Do this for six days. Have seven

priests carry trumpets of rams' horns in front of the ark. On the seventh day, march around the city seven times, with the priests blowing the trumpets. When you hear them sound a long blast on the trumpets, have all the people give a loud shout; then the wall of the city will collapse and the people will go up, every man straight in."

God revealed a startling strategy. Rather than attack Jericho directly, the Israelites were to march around the city six days, once each day. On the seventh day they were to march around it seven times, with trumpets blowing. At a special signal, the Israelites were to shout and the city's walls would collapse.

No commander had ever attacked a walled city like this. The usual strategy was to lay a groundwork against the wall and try to get some fighters over it.

On the other hand, there was something to be said for God's strategy. It was psychological warfare, not hand-to-hand combat. This was really a war of nerves against Jericho's army and king. Day after day they had to watch the invaders encircle their city and wonder what they were doing.

The order of the procession would be (1) warriors, (2) the seven priests blowing the trumpets, (3) the ark of the covenant, (4) the rear guard. Jericho was a city of considerable size and population. Each circuit of the city may have taken an hour and a half. Thus, with the necessary timeouts for rest, the evening of the Sabbath day would be at hand when Joshua gave the signal to shout.

There was a spiritual factor in this strategy as well. The priests were involved, carrying the ark of the covenant which symbolized God's presence. Note there were seven priests, seven trumpets, seven days, and seven circuits of the city on the seventh day. All of this pointed to perfection, completeness, and the consummation of God's plan. Once again the issue was trust, courage, and obedience.

II. THE PEOPLE OBEYED: JOSHUA: 6:15-17

A. They Circled the City: vs. 15

On the seventh day, they got up at daybreak and marched around the city seven times in the same manner, except that on that day they circled the city seven times.

Having met the commander of the Lord's army, and heard his strange battle plan, Joshua went to work immediately. If he had any questions about what seemed like a futile way to attack a fortified city, he did not voice them. He had seen God do strange things before, contrary to human wisdom, in his experiences under Moses. He also remembered God's command to be strong and courageous, and the Lord's promise to be with him. That was enough.

He summoned the priests and the people and put them into their unusual battle array. "Advance!" he commanded, and they did so. Apart from the sound of marching feet and the trumpet blasts, there was no sound from the people. Every day for six days, the priests, the fighters, the ark, and the people circled Jericho. However, on the seventh day, following God's plan explicitly, they marched around the city seven times.

By now the king and the army of Jericho no doubt were not only deceived but thoroughly confused. The repetition of the march, without an actual attack, certainly would induce them to lower their guard.

B. The People Shouted: vs. 16

The seventh time around, when the priests sounded the trumpet blast, Joshua commanded the people, "Shout! For the LORD has given you the city!"

Perhaps some of the fighters were grumbling by this time, and maybe some of the people were impatient for a frontal attack, but on the whole, Israel maintained a striking unity and discipline. In any military effort, discipline and unquestioned obedience are the keys to victory.

Joshua's chain of command maintained the necessary order. Finally, the seven rams' horns sounded their long blast. This was like an air raid siren. It was a warning to the people of Jericho and in the whole land of Canaan that God was about to act. A similar "long blast" occurred on Mount Sinai (Exod. 19:13). Later on, the prophets used the trumpet blast as a sign of impending judgment (Amos 3:6; Isa. 18:3).

Armies usually charged into battle with great shouts, as Gideon's band did (Judg. 7:18-21). But there was no fight outside Jericho, so the shout by the marchers was more like a ceremonial shout or a cry of celebration in worship. It was a triumphant cheer for certain victory, such as the one mentioned in Psalm 47:3, 5.

Scripture sometimes speaks of God's people suffering in silence, and then rejoicing at God's deliverance. The prophet Isaiah said that Messiah would not cry out, which turned out to be a remarkable aspect of Christ's judgment at the hands of Pilate. But the assembly gathered around Jericho certainly reminds us of the theme of joy and rejoicing by God's people that runs through Scripture (Psalms 66:1; 98:4, 6; 100:1).

C. Rahab Was to Be Spared: vs. 17

"The city and all that is in it are to be devoted to the LORD. Only Rahab the prostitute and all who are with her in her house shall be spared, because she hid the spies we sent."

Joshua's commands on the critical seventh day covered how the victorious Israelites were supposed to conduct themselves once Jericho fell. Everything in the city was "devoted to the LORD," that is, they were to be totally destroyed.

Second, the prostitute Rahab and her family were to be spared from the all-inclusive destruction. This was the contract she had made with the spies (Josh. 2:12-14). Joshua kept the promise of the spies and reminded the Israelites of what Rahab had done for them.

III. WARNINGS AND VICTORY: JOSHUA 6:18-20

A. Avoid Taking Anything: vss. 18-19

"But keep away from the devoted things, so that you will not bring about your own destruc-

tion by taking any of them. Otherwise you will make the camp of Israel liable to destruction and bring trouble on it. All the silver and gold and the articles of bronze and iron are sacred to the LORD and must go into his treasury."

Joshua's warning had a two-fold purpose: (1) The people were not to act like pagan plunderers and carry off everything for themselves; (2) There was deep spiritual peril in accumulating anything the Lord had designed for destruction.

This spiritual principle was established early on by Moses. Certain things were specifically set aside for distinctive purposes, such as property and harvests. Beyond that, objects or people that posed a threat to Israel's pure monotheistic faith (compared to the surrounding people's pagan idolatry) were to be avoided. Israelites who took such things into their houses were themselves polluted and banned.

Consequently, even whole cities were to be destroyed because of the acute danger of spiritual infection (Deut. 13:12-18). Harsh as it may seem, that law was handed down simply to keep Israel from worshiping false gods. Joshua knew the laws of God very well. As commander, he had to make the restrictions clear. Now, at the gates of Jericho, the obedience of the Israelites was to be tested.

The total destruction of Jericho, as well as personal separation from anything in the city, symbolized the radical break between the faith of God's people and the other nations. Moses warned that the nations had to be destroyed because they would lead future generations away from the Lord and into terrible sins (Deut. 7:2-4; 20:18).

Every living thing in Jericho was put to death, except for Rahab and her family, as a sacrifice to God. The indestructible goods (vs. 19) were brought into the treasury of Israel's sanctuary.

Joshua led the people into compliance with this severe command, not only with regard to Jericho, but also Ai, Makkedah, Eglon, Hebron, Debir, Hazor and the cities of the north, and the Anakim and their cities. Such a radical separation appears strange to modern readers accustomed to mingling different faiths. They do not understand God's requirement of total loyalty and holiness. Tragically, as Israel's history unfolded, God's warning about spiritual pollution was ignored and his people did in fact fall into abominable idolatrous practices.

The first instance of such a departure from the Lord's command occurred in Jericho. One of the fighters, Achan, apparently overcome by greed, took some clothing, silver, and gold from Jericho and buried it inside his tent (Josh. 7:20-21). His disobedience cost Israel a defeat at Ai, as well as the destruction of Achan, his family, and his possessions.

B. The Wall Collapsed: vs. 20

When the trumpets sounded, the people shouted, and at the sound of the trumpet, when the people gave a loud shout, the wall collapsed; so every man charged straight in, and they took the city.

The people obeyed Joshua to the last detail and victory was theirs. Says the writer of Hebrews, "By faith the walls of Jericho fell, after the people had marched around them for seven days" (11:30).

This victory became a powerful object lesson to God's power to overcome seemingly impossible obstacles, and to the absolute necessity of faith in and obedience to God's commands. Isaiah and Ezekiel spoke of God's coming judgments when towers and walls will crumble and fall (Isa. 2:15; Ezek. 38:20).

Rahab's house was located in the city wall (Josh. 2:15). Perhaps that part of the wall did not fall along with the rest. Or, the outer wall could have collapsed, leaving part of her house intact. Enough of it was left for the two spies who had been there to find the scarlet cord, which was the sign they had agreed upon (vs. 17).

The Israelites were true to their word and rescued Rahab and her family. Apparently, they became fully accepted members of Israel's camp (6:22-25).

Discussion Questions

1. What do you think the Israelites thought as they circled the city without attacking it? Why?
2. Why is it often hard to be patient for God to act, and to wait for his will and way to be revealed?
3. What temptations would have awaited the victorious army? How do you think the fighters felt about the ban?
4. How do you feel when you think God has denied you something you deserve? Why?
5. Why is it difficult today to be uncompromising about God's truth and his commands?
6. Why is God's judgment of sin so hard to accept?

Contemporary Application

Joshua's victory at Jericho has been immortalized in an African-American spiritual song. The crumbling walls send a strong signal that the weak and the powerless can win, despite overwhelming obstacles.

The key to such victory, of course, is to know God's commands and to obey them. That is the victory of faith. Faith is not wishful thinking that the walls will collapse. Faith means accepting God's way of living, His righteous principles, and acting courageously in the face of opposition.

All of us face different walls at different times of our lives. Whatever the walls may be, they challenge our faith and our commitment to follow Jesus Christ, regardless of the cost. Thank God for leaders who instruct the church and teach God's people to learn and obey God's Word.

Choosing to Serve the Lord

Scripture

Background Scripture: *Joshua 24*
Scripture Lesson: *Joshua 24:1-2, 14-22, 25*
Key Verse: *And the people said to Joshua, "We will serve
the LORD our God and obey him."* Joshua 24:24.

Lesson Aim

To be certain our commitment to God is total.

Lesson Setting

Time: *slightly after 1200 B.C.*
Place: *City of Shechem.*

Lesson Outline

Choosing to Serve the Lord

   I. Joshua Calls the Assembly: Joshua 24:1-2
  II. Joshua Challenges the Assembly: Joshua:
     24:14-18
     A. He Commits Himself to God: vss. 14-15
     B. The People Promise to Follow God: vss. 16-18
 III. Joshua Demands Commitment: Joshua 24:19-
     22, 25
     A. He Warns of Judgment: vss. 19-22
     B. He Makes a Covenant for the People: vs. 25

Introduction for Adults

Topic: *Making the Right Choice*

     Every time we hear a sermon, listen to the teaching of a Sunday school lesson, and read the Scripture we should think about our response. The Word of God demands decision; choices must be made; courses of action decided.

     Otherwise, we face the danger James described: "Anyone who listens to the word but does not do what it says is like a man who looks at his face in a mirror and, after looking at himself, goes away and immediately forgets what he looks like" (Jas. 1:23-24).

We need to be brought up short on occasion. It is easy to slide into an easy, comfortable Christianity. That is why Peter admonishes us, ". . . make every effort to add to your faith . . ." (2 Pet. 1:5).

We should be glad when the pastor looks us straight in the eye and tells us to make a decision. Every part of our lives—our time, money, work, and family relationships—must come under Christ's control.

Introduction for Youths

Topic: *Making Life's Choices*

The Christian faith sometimes is conceived of as a one-time-only commitment: you make a decision, take the church membership class, get your name on the church roll, and that's it. But the enemy of our souls never stops trying to subvert that decision. He wants us to skirt the tough moral and ethical requirements of Christian commitment. He is delighted when Christian youth live just like non-Christians.

Many youth find it easier to follow the crowd than to make their own decisions. However, when they are challenged to follow a better way, many of them do respond positively.

Joshua's forthright challenge to the people is what youth like to face. They prefer to hear it straight, rather than have the issues blurred by a lot of double-talk. Sadly, instead of issuing clear guidelines, parents and other adults often act like marshmallows.

Concepts for Children

Topic: *Renewing Promises*

1. Children often face hard choices and find it difficult to accept disappointments.
2. They need to have clear guidance from parents and adult leaders.
3. Saying "Yes" to God always means saying "No" to other choices.
4. There is great value in making a public declaration of faith.
5. False gods make appeals to children in various guises.
6. God's people can help us renew our vows to the Lord.

The Lesson Commentary

I. JOSHUA CALLS THE ASSEMBLY: JOSHUA 24:1-2

Then Joshua assembled all the tribes of Israel at Shechem. He summoned the elders, leaders, judges and officials of Israel, and they presented themselves before God. Joshua said to all the people, "This is what the LORD, the God of Israel, says: 'Long ago your forefathers, including Terah the father of Abraham and Nahor, lived beyond the River and worshiped other gods.' "

Joshua, the great captain of the conquest of Canaan, was about to depart. It was a fitting time for him to give praise to God and to challenge the Israelites "to love the LORD your God" (23:11).

Joshua reminded them of God's faithfulness: ". . . not one of all the good promises the LORD your God gave you has failed" (23:14). He rehearsed all the great events by which God had taken them from bondage in Egypt and had given them a home in Canaan and crops to live on (24:6-13).

However, Joshua knew how easy it would be for the Israelites to revert to the old paganism and to adopt the idols of the Canaanites, so he challenged them directly to choose between the false gods and the one true and living God. The people acknowledged God's protection and His provision, and they confessed their desire to serve Him.

After the fall of Jericho, 36 men died at the city of Ai and the whole nation was shamed by the defeat. However, Ai was subsequently conquered and then all the strategic cities of the south fell before Joshua's army (chaps. 7—10). The kings of the north assembled a formidable alliance, but they also were defeated by the Israelites (chap. 11). The tribes of Reuben, Gad, and Manasseh fulfilled their treaty obligations and returned with Joshua's blessing (chap. 22).

Some years have now elapsed since the division of the land. Joshua was nearing the end of his long and distinguished career, but no successor was in sight. Therefore, he counseled the leaders (chap. 23) that it was essential to keep the laws of God and remain faithful to Him.

Joshua called a national assembly at Shechem between Mount Ebal and Mount Gerizim, which already had been the scene of a solemn rehearsal of the covenant soon after the first entry of the people into Canaan (Josh. 8:30-35). This was also the place where their great ancestor Jacob had solemnly sanctified his house to the service of God, giving the same directions that Joshua repeated (see also Josh. 24:23, 26 and Gen. 35:1-4).

At Shechem God made the first recorded promise of the land to the seed of Abraham (Gen. 12:6-7). Here, the bones of Joseph and his brethren were to be laid to rest, as an acknowledgement that the promises of God to the patriarchs had now by the hand of Joshua been fulfilled (Josh. 24:32; Acts 7:16).

There could be no more fitting scene for the people to make a solemn renewal of their covenant with God that had—on His part—been so fully kept. The spot itself suggested the allusions to Abraham, Isaac, and Jacob in Joshua's address. Its associations could not but give special force and moving affect to his appeals.

Perhaps the tabernacle and the ark were brought from Shiloh for this occasion. The people came with awe and reverence to hear, not just from Joshua, but as it were, from God Himself. "All the people" were not there in totality, but in representative form. Elders, leaders, judges, and officials were there, along with as many of the people who cared to come.

II. Joshua Challenges the Assembly: Joshua 24:14-18

A. He Commits Himself to God: vss. 14-15

"Now fear the Lord and serve him with all faithfulness. Throw away the gods your forefathers worshiped beyond the River and in Egypt, and serve the Lord. But if serving the Lord seems undesirable to you, then choose for yourselves this day whom you will serve, whether the gods your forefathers served beyond the River, or the gods of the Amorites, in whose land you are living. But as for me and my household, we will serve the Lord."

Joshua's speech is attributed to God. God speaks directly to the assembly through Joshua (vss. 2-13). God's speech starts with Abraham and continues through the lives of Moses and Aaron and His deliverance of His people from slavery in Egypt. As far as these people were concerned, the main event began with the miraculous crossing of the Jordan River.

Israel could not claim the land by virtue of its own power and strength: "You did not do it with your own sword and bow" (vs. 12). Joshua did not have military superiority, but his army was commanded by the Lord of hosts. The armies of Canaan were numerically superior, but helpless before Israel because of panic and confusion. God said He had "sent the hornet" to give them victory (vs. 12), not the real insect, of course, but a graphic metaphor of how Israel's enemies fled before them.

In that sense, *Israel* did not earn either victory in battle, or the cities, vineyards, and olive groves they enjoyed. All were gifts of God because of His mercy, love, power, and faithfulness. Such a sense of debt to the Lord is the foundation of humility, worship, praise, thanksgiving, and obedience.

At this point Joshua begins to speak for himself. He makes the issue very clear. The choice was between serving idols—old ones from Babylon (beyond the Euphrates River) and new ones in Canaan—and serving God. God had reminded them earlier (vs. 2) that their forefathers had worshiped other gods, called "household gods" in Genesis 31:19, 30, 34.

Joshua made two demands on the people: (1) throw away the false gods; (2) choose to serve the true and living God. Worship of God requires the abandonment of all idols. God cannot tolerate divided loyalties. The Israelites could pretend to be following God, and yet worship idols secretly. Joshua knew they were on thin ice. Any hint of idolatry was deadly. It could not be toyed with or tolerated in the name of getting along with the local people.

As leader with an unblemished record of faithfulness and obedience, Joshua once more declared his total allegiance to God. Come what may, he would remain true. Defectors would arise in Israel; people would make unwise choices and lapse into idolatry, but Joshua would maintain his spiritual integrity.

No doubt such a forceful testimony moved the leaders to follow Joshua's example. What he said wasn't new, but it was a needed reminder of both the risks and of the necessity to take a stand.

B. The People Promise to Follow God: vss. 16-18

Then the people answered, "Far be it from us to forsake the LORD to serve other gods! It was the LORD our God himself who brought us and our fathers up out of Egypt, from that land of slavery, and performed those great signs before our eyes. He protected us on our entire journey and among all the nations through which we traveled. And the LORD drove out before us all the nations, including the Amorites, who lived in the land. We too will serve the LORD, because he is our God."

Joshua's challenging declaration brought the desired response. The people recognized the truth of what he said. They went on to affirm the basic truth of God's sovereign love, His choice of them, and His great miracles (vss. 17-18).

Israel made a solemn promise not to forsake the true and living God for idols. They claimed the Lord as their God and promised to serve Him (vs. 18).

The people rightfully built their commitment on their knowledge of what God had done for them in the past. They celebrated God's deliverance from Egypt with "great signs" (vs. 17). They remembered how He had protected them during the 40 years in the Sinai Desert. They rehearsed God's victory over the Amorites (vss. 17-18).

III. JOSHUA DEMANDS COMMITMENT: JOSHUA 24:19-22, 25

A. He Warns of Judgment: vss. 19-22

Joshua said to the people, "You are not able to serve the LORD. He is a holy God; he is a jealous God. He will not forgive your rebellion and your sins. If you forsake the LORD and serve foreign gods, he will turn and bring disaster on you and make an end of you, after he has been good to you." But the people said to Joshua, "No! We will serve the LORD." Then Joshua said, "You are witnesses against yourselves that you have chosen to serve the LORD." "Yes, we are witnesses," they replied.

Often in the emotion of stirring addresses, people make premature responses. This was an emotion-laden scene. The old warrior-leader was about to die. He had once again set the example of faithfulness to the Lord.

Now the people had made the same declaration. Joshua was constrained to elaborate on what it meant to serve God. The crucial question was the nature of God Himself. Before one can promise to serve Him, one must know His demands.

To make the issue clear, Joshua singled out God's holiness (vs. 19). He is so holy that He cannot overlook sin. He is also "jealous" in the sense that He cannot tolerate mixed loyalties. God's nature requires total allegiance and obedience.

Joshua also warned of impending disaster if the Israelites forsook the Lord (vs. 20). Because God is holy, He cannot blink at sin. God does forgive sin, if we repent and confess our sins. However, the point of Joshua's warning is that if Israel *persists* in rebellion and sin, there will be no forgiveness.

The people persisted in their declaration of obedience to God. It is wise to count the cost and to face the consequences of any decisions or commitment.

There was enthusiasm here, but Joshua gave the people a chance to examine their response in light of God's character. His holiness and His judgment of sin did not deter them from professing allegiance to Him. This is what God expects today: count the cost and then declare openly where you stand.

Joshua could not appeal to any other people or gods as witnesses, so he appealed to the people themselves. He named them as witnesses of the covenant. They agreed to this procedure and accepted the obligation.

Was this a rash decision? Were the people too hasty in answering Joshua's challenge? Perhaps some of them were simply carried along with the enthusiasm of the moment, but others were affirming the true sentiments of their hearts.

Now a specific act was called for. When we promise to do God's will, there will be a corresponding adjustment in behavior. God's holiness demands changes in the way we live. If we don't change, then our profession is a lie and Christian commitment sheer hypocrisy. A covenant with God is like a covenant with anyone: when we sign on the dotted line, we promise to do certain things.

The issue was foreign gods, or idolatry. Something had to be done immediately. "Throw away the foreign gods," Joshua demanded (vs. 23). That was the negative side of commitment. The positive side was: "Yield your hearts to the LORD."

A true response to God always involves both sides, as the apostle Paul makes clear in Colossians 3:5-17. Certain things have to be "put away" and certain things "put on." Sinful practices must be abandoned by an act of the will; our hearts must rest completely in God himself. To "yield" your heart to God means to trust Him personally and obey His commands (see also John 14:21, 23).

B. He Makes a Covenant for the People: vs. 25

On that day Joshua made a covenant for the people, and there at Shechem he drew up for them decrees and laws.

The people again promised to serve and obey the Lord. As far as they could understand, they would not serve the gods of the Canaanites. This was an effective monitor on the Israelites for many years. "Israel served the LORD throughout the lifetime of Joshua and of the elders who outlived him and who had experienced everything the LORD had done for Israel" (vs. 31).

The establishment of the covenant was the climax of Joshua's farewell. It was a solemn moment. The whole nation, as it were, stood in the spotlight before God and the surrounding nations. The Israelites were to be God's light-bearers, the bearers of truth and holiness in a corrupt, depraved society. Therefore, Joshua chose to make both a written and a public record of this momentous occasion.

To make a covenant means to formalize the agreement the people had just made between themselves and God. Their promise was general: "We will serve the LORD our God and obey him." First, this meant throwing out the idols some of them were keeping. Beyond that, however, were other implications. These "decrees and laws" Joshua wrote down in a book that he called "the Law of God" (vs. 26).

There would be a permanent record of the commitment made by the people and the requirements of the Lord in lieu of their promise. This book probably was placed "beside the ark of the covenant," in the same way that Moses had done (see Deut. 31:26).

No Christian need be in the dark about what God requires upon his or her confession of faith. When we trust in Christ for our salvation, we place ourselves under obligation to obey God's written Word. His Word has been preserved for us down through the centuries, despite many attempts to suppress it.

Discussion Questions

1. How can we arrange similar opportunities for God's people to make public affirmations of their promises to Him?
2. Why do you think Joshua tried to get them to rethink their promise?
3. What value was there in Joshua's making the first declaration himself?
4. How can we use our own knowledge of God's past faithfulness to inspire obedience in the future?
5. Should our churches have annual times of reaffirmation of our commitments to Christ and to the churches' membership covenants?
6. Since having secret household idols is not today's problem, what would it mean to throw out your idols today?
7. What things do we have to put away that get in the way of our total commitment to God?

Contemporary Application

There are few opportunities today for the public at large to witness Christian declarations of faith and obedience. However, in some countries where Christians are a tiny minority, they often take to the streets in parades, carrying banners proclaiming their commitment to Jesus Christ.

In effect, our commitment to Christ is based on our word, and yet it is a sign of moral and spiritual courage to take a stand for Christ in a public way. Standing up, raising a hand, or going to the front of a church doesn't make a person a Christian, but if a person professes to believe in Christ, then it is not unreasonable to ask for a public response. Making a public response strengthens the resolve of the person doing so, and encourages others who may be wavering.

We need not worry about making the cost of Christian discipleship too steep. Joshua did not lower the demands to gain a public response. If God is at work in the hearts of people, they will openly confess Christ as Lord and Savior. Rather, we need to worry about people making professions without understanding the full implications of faith in Christ.

Studies in Matthew

Unit I: Beginnings: Birth and Ministry

Unit II: Jesus' Teachings and Ministry

Unit III: Fulfillment of Jesus' Mission

King's Herald and Baptism

DEVOTIONAL READING

Matthew 21:23-27

DAILY BIBLE READINGS

Monday November 29
*Matthew 3:1-6 John
Preaches and Baptizes*

Tuesday November 30
*Matthew 3:7-12 John
Proclaims Jesus' Coming*

Wednesday December 1
*Matthew 3:13-17 Jesus Is
Baptized by John*

Thursday December 2
*Matthew 11:2-6 John
Sends Messengers to
Question Jesus*

Friday December 3
*Matthew 11:7-11 Jesus
Praises John the Baptist*

Saturday December 4
*Matthew 11:12-19 Jesus
Admonishes the Crowd*

Sunday December 5
*Matthew 14:1-12 John the
Baptist Is Executed*

Scripture

Background Scripture: *Matthew 3*
Scripture Lesson: *Matthew 3:1-8, 11-17*
Key Verse: *"I baptize you with water for repentance. But
after me will come one who is more powerful than I,
whose sandals I am not fit to carry. He will baptize you
with the Holy Spirit and with fire."* Matthew 3:11
Background Scripture for Children: *Luke 1:26-56*
Scripture Lesson for Children: *Luke 1:26-35, 38-40*
Key Verse for Children: *"Do not be afraid, Mary, you
have found favor with God."* Luke 1:30

Lesson Aim

To follow the example of John's boldness and
humility.

Lesson Setting

Time: A.D. *26*
Place: *Jordan River east of Jerusalem*

Lesson Outline

King's Herald and Baptism

  I. John's Mission: Matthew 3:1-4
     A. He Preached Repentance: vss. 1-2
     B. He Prepared the Way: vs. 3
     C. He Lived Simply: vs. 4
  II. The People's Response: Matthew 3:5-8
     A. They Repented and Were Baptized: vss. 5-6
     B. Some Were Hypocrites: vss. 7-8
  III. John's Prophecy: Matthew 3:11-12
     A. One More Powerful Is Coming: vs. 11
     B. He Will Act as Judge: vs. 12
  IV. The Baptism of Jesus: Matthew 3:13-17
     A. John First Refused: vss. 13-14
     B. Jesus Insisted: vs. 15
     C. The Dove Descended: vs. 16
     D. The Voice Acclaimed Him: vs. 17

Introduction for Adults

Topic: *Time of Preparing*

Secret Service agents who go to a city to check over all the details for the president's visit do not become as famous as the presidents they work for. John the Baptist's chief purpose was to prepare people spiritually to receive God's Son. By the nature of his role he was not great in the world's eyes. But Jesus said of him, "Among those born of women there has not risen anyone greater than John the Baptist" (Matt. 11:11).

When John had the chance to brag because people were flocking to hear him preach, he said that he was only "a voice of one calling in the desert." In our search for spiritual leaders today, often we are trapped into seeking the world's standards of greatness, rather than those of a person like John. How many are willing to be humble "preparers of the way"?

Introduction for Youths

Topic: *Fire and Water*

Often young people are attracted by strange figures whose dress and life styles drive their parents crazy. Probably, in A.D. 26, if your kids had gone to hear John the Baptist, you would have been equally skeptical, because this man did not look or behave like the "respectable" establishment.

Some 35 years ago the Jesus people and the Jesus movement swept across America. Thousands of long-haired youths, wearing dirty, torn jeans, responded to the simple Gospel of Jesus Christ, again confounding adults and church leaders. Today many of them serve Christ in strategic Christian leadership positions, as well as in their professions.

What counts is not what a person wears or eats, but whether or not his or her life backs up what the person professes to believe. Young people need authentic leaders who refuse to blindly go along with the prevailing world culture, and who instead stand for truth and righteousness. John was like that.

Concepts for Children

Topic: *Jesus' Mother is Chosen*

1. God came to Mary in a special way with a special message.
2. She was willing to trust God when she heard the startling news.
3. God often interrupts our plans by giving us a special task.
4. We can trust Him to enable us to do what we know He wants us to do.
5. Those who seek God's help in prayer and Bible study receive courage to obey the Lord.
6. In Christ, all of us are special to God the Father.

The Lesson Commentary

I. John's Mission: Matthew 3:1-4

A. He Preached Repentance: vss. 1-2

In those days John the Baptist came, preaching in the Desert of Judea and saying, "Repent, for the kingdom of heaven is near."

Matthew summarized John the Baptist's message, the fulfillment of prophecy, his lifestyle, and the response to his ministry. (For additional facts, study Mark 1:3-8; Luke 3:2-17; John 1:6-8, 19-28.) John's unique role was to prepare people spiritually for the life and ministry of the Messiah, Jesus Christ.

John's birth about 5 B.C. came about because of a special intervention of the Lord. Zechariah and Elizabeth, his parents, were both godly people, but they were getting old and had no children. That's why Zechariah the priest was astounded when he received God's message about a son to be born, and the angel made him speechless until John was born.

John's childhood and youth were summarized by Luke this way: "And the child grew and became strong in spirit; and he lived in the desert until he appeared publicly to Israel" (1:80). His godly parents doubtless had a strong influence in his life. But when he retreated to the desert, they probably wondered how he could "make ready a people prepared for the Lord" (Luke 1:17).

Matthew's account of John's life and ministry can be dated about A.D. 26 when John was about 31 years old. He called him "the Baptist" because that was the most auspicious thing he did (Matt. 3:6). The biblical writers gave him a distinguishing name so he would not be confused with the apostle John.

John started to preach in the Desert of Judea, so called because it did not sustain farming, but only grazing. It is a dry, hilly, barren territory between Jerusalem and the Jordan River, overlooking the Dead Sea. One oasis in the desert is the city of Jericho, which is probably where John preached at first, for two reasons: it was the main center for travelers from all over the East, and it was close to the river. When the people in Jericho heard him, the word spread quickly to Jerusalem.

There was no mistaking John's message: "Repent." Repentance was necessary because God's kingdom, in the person of Christ, was near at hand. Repentance meant a change in behavior. John looked for deep and lasting change. Repentant sinners acknowledge that they have broken God's laws and that they deserve His judgment.

B. He Prepared the Way: vs. 3

This is he who was spoken of through the prophet Isaiah: "A voice of one calling in the desert, 'Prepare the way for the Lord, make straight paths for him.'"

Matthew linked John's coming with the prophecy of Isaiah. God's plan for Messiah's coming was revealed seven centuries before John was born.

"Prepare the way for the Lord" means preparation morally and spiritually. The people had to examine themselves in the light of God's breaking into history in the person of Christ.

Isaiah compared John's spiritual ministry to that of a road builder. "The way" and "straight paths" literally are roads. Occasionally a king such as Solomon would have a small part of the road surfaced for his personal use. This became known as the "king's highway."

Such roads were maintained for any trip the king might want to take. Before the king was due to arrive in any area, a message was sent out to the people to get the king's roads fixed up. John the Baptist was telling the people to get the roads of their lives fixed up for the coming of the King of kings, Jesus Christ.

C. He Lived Simply: vs. 4

John's clothes were made of camel's hair, and he had a leather belt around his waist. His food was locusts and wild honey.

John's food and clothing were consistent with his preaching. As a prophet, he followed the pattern set down by earlier prophets, whom the people of Israel would recognize. Elijah was the one most easily identifiable with John's lifestyle (2 Kings 1:8).

Of much greater importance was his spiritual discipline. He separated himself from society so that he could concentrate on God and His message. No doubt his strict physical disciplines contributed to his deep spiritual sensitivities and boldness. Physical deprivation heightens spiritual awareness, which is why the Bible recommends fasting.

II. THE PEOPLE'S RESPONSE: MATTHEW 3:5-8

A. They Repented and Were Baptized: vss. 5-6

People went out to him from Jerusalem and all Judea and the whole region of the Jordan. Confessing their sins, they were baptized by him in the Jordan River.

As a result of John's dynamic preaching, the multitudes confessed their sins and were baptized. They acknowledged the truthfulness of John's call and saw themselves as convicted sinners under God's judgment.

The Gospel of Christ today demands the same response. After hearing of Christ's death and resurrection for their sins, people should repent and confess their sins. Then they are prepared to receive Christ by faith as the one whom God sent to save them from the just punishment they deserve.

To be baptized by John meant that the people had received his message and were changed by repenting. It was an outward act symbolizing an inner spiritual reality. (The use of ceremonial washings as symbols of purification was common among Jews and people of other religions.)

John's baptism was "from heaven" (Matt. 21:25). He had God's authority for it. He baptized so that people could show they had repented. The fact that people received his baptism shows that the Spirit of God was stirring in Israel.

B. Some Were Hypocrites: vss. 7-8

But when he saw many of the Pharisees and Sadducees coming to where he was baptizing, he said to them: "You brood of vipers! Who warned you to flee from the coming wrath? Produce fruit in keeping with repentance."

Among the crowds who came to be baptized were some Pharisees and Sadducees—the former representing rigid law-keepers and ceremonialists, the latter representing religious liberals. Because of John's popularity, they wanted to check him out. They also wanted to be accepted by the people, because they represented religious authority and expertise. They would even go as far as to be baptized by John, to ingratiate themselves with the people.

We know from John's severe rebuke that they were not sincere. Instead of honoring and praising them, he called them "vipers" (poisonous snakes). John wasn't interested in gaining their praise and recognition. He was interested in spiritual integrity, not in outward show and position. He wasn't awed by the Pharisees and Sadducees, even though they represented religious power.

After calling them snakes, John asked them why they were repenting to escape "the coming wrath," that is, God's judgment. This was a very pointed question, to expose their real motives. Did they really confess they were sinners deserving God's wrath?

To show what he meant by repentance, John demanded "fruit," that is, evidence in changed behavior. However, the Pharisees and Sadducees did not understand spiritual truth that way. Their confidence and standing before God depended on their religious ancestry. The patriarch Abraham was their father; therefore, they did not need to repent.

John exposed the folly of such logic. Pouring insult upon insult, he said God could produce children for Abraham out of the stones they were standing on (vs. 9). They had absolutely nothing to be proud of and nothing to commend themselves to God.

III. John's Prophecy: Matthew 3:11-12

A. One More Powerful Is Coming: vs. 11

"I baptize you with water for repentance. But after me will come one who is more powerful than I, whose sandals I am not fit to carry. He will baptize you with the Holy Spirit and with fire."

John's task was to prepare people spiritually for the coming of Christ. He was content with that and humbly confessed that the Messiah was greater than he was. Jesus was superior ("more powerful"). John was completely unworthy to prepare the way for Him. John didn't think he was even fit to carry Christ's sandals.

Such humility was another hallmark of his spiritual power and authenticity. The spectacle of large crowds coming forward could have filled John with pride, but he consistently saw his role as secondary to that of Jesus. Secondary, but of great importance and value because he told people to get ready to believe in their Messiah.

John's sermon in vss. 11 and 12 was preached to the self-righteous Pharisees and the carnal, unspiritual Sadducees. That is why he spoke so harshly of the coming judgment under the Messiah. At this point, John did not specifically refer to Jesus as the Messiah, only as the person who would follow him with much greater power.

John contrasted himself with the Messiah. His baptism was "with water for repentance," Christ's would be "with the Holy Spirit and with fire." John baptized as an indicator that people were repenting of their sins. Jesus baptized with the Holy Spirit—to signify the permanent dwelling of God in believers (John 14:16-17; 1 Cor. 6:19)—and with fire, because He is the judge of all humanity.

B. He Will Act as Judge: vs. 12

"His winnowing fork is in his hand, and he will clear his threshing floor, gathering his wheat into the barn and burning up the chaff with unquenchable fire."

There is a great separation coming under the mighty hand of Christ, a separation of wheat and chaff. When the church proclaims the Gospel, warning of judgment to come is part of the message. We cannot be faithful to Christ, and to the needs of unbelievers, if we dodge the fact of judgment. Jesus came to save people from judgment. If they are to be saved, they must see Christ clearing His "threshing floor" and burning the chaff.

IV. THE BAPTISM OF JESUS: MATTHEW 3:13-17

A. John First Refused: vss. 13-14

Then Jesus came from Galilee to the Jordan to be baptized by John. But John tried to deter him, saying, "I need to be baptized by you, and do you come to me?"

Apart from John's preaching, we are also struck with his humility in relation to Christ. He knew that every knee should bow and every tongue confess that Christ is Lord. Therefore, it was proper for him to confess his own unworthiness contrasted to the Messiah.

John might have been exalted by his successful preaching. Crowds were coming, including the religious authorities, and now Jesus Himself appeared. He could have fallen into pride. But he made it clear that he, too, was a sinner and needed to be baptized by Jesus. He was appalled that Jesus would want to be baptized by him.

B. Jesus Insisted: vs. 15

Jesus replied, "Let it be so now; it is proper for us to do this to fulfill all righteousness." Then John consented.

Jesus did not need to be baptized because He was born sinless and lived a perfect, holy life, always pleasing His Father in everything He did. Why then did He too enter the waters of the Jordan?

Most likely because He wanted to identify Himself fully with fallen humanity. He was the Son of Man as well as the Son of God. He came to bear and take away the sins of the world. The writer of Hebrews makes a special point of the fact that Jesus is not ashamed to be called our brother. He shared our humanity, not in our sinfulness, of course, but in our trials so that He can be faithful and merciful to us (Heb. 2:5-18).

It appears that when Jesus was baptized He was publicly recognizing His role as taking responsibility for human sin. In one sense, He was baptized there for all of us, because we are all sinners. "Christ was innocent of sin, and yet for our sake God made him one with the sinfulness of men" (2 Cor. 5:21, NEB).

C. The Dove Descended: vs. 16

As soon as Jesus was baptized, he went up out of the water. At that moment heaven was opened, and he saw the Spirit of God descending like a dove and lighting on him.

After John agreed to baptize Jesus, he and the crowds were given two powerful signs from heaven about who it was that had just been baptized. The first sign was a dove, which signified the Spirit of God coming on Jesus. This is why the church has used the dove to symbolize the Holy Spirit.

Obviously, the people could not see the Holy Spirit, but they could see the dove, so it reminded them that this was indeed a sign of God's pleasure from heaven. This was no ordinary man who had just come up out of the water with John.

This was not only a special sign to the people, but to Jesus Himself. This was the sign that He had done the right thing in coming to the Jordan to be baptized and to identify Himself with sinners. Now He knew that this was the time His Father had chosen to begin His public ministry.

D. The Voice Acclaimed Him: vs. 17

And a voice from heaven said, "This is my Son, whom I love; with him I am well pleased."

God not only sent the dove, but also He spoke from heaven to acclaim Jesus of Nazareth as His Son. This was the most powerful testimony Jesus could receive. Both Jesus and John were fully assured of God's approval at this precipitous moment in their lives.

Before the birth of Jesus His deity was prophesied by the angel who said He was to be the world's Savior. But a long time had passed since then. Jesus had lived in obscurity in Nazareth. Here at the Jordan River He assumed a public stance, and was recognized by God the Father as His beloved Son with whom He was well pleased.

This means that Jesus had indeed fulfilled all righteousness (vs. 15) in His early life as a carpenter and in His obedience in coming to the river for baptism. He is the only perfect person who has ever lived. He alone among all human beings could merit God the Father's perfect pleasure. That is why we can confidently trust in Him for our eternal salvation.

Discussion Questions

1. How would you have felt in the company of John?
2. Why is it difficult to confront religious people with their need to repent? How can we do this?
3. How can the churches "prepare the way of the Lord" for people today?
4. Does the fact of coming judgment lead people to repent today? Why or why not?
5. How do you account for John's humility in the face of overwhelming crowds?
6. What does it mean to you that Jesus fully pleased His Father?

Contemporary Application

God places contemporary John the Baptists in families, schools, churches, offices, factories, stores, prisons, rehabilitation centers, the military, and so on. They are Christians who seize opportunities to be faithful witnesses to Jesus Christ. They do not need to dress and live like John did, but they do need to be courageous and forthright in standing for the good news of Christ's saving love.

Sometimes Christians think the only place that people can come to faith in Christ is in a church service or evangelistic rally. But many people are reluctant to mix with Christians on their turf. Therefore, it is essential for Christians to prepare the way for these people to investigate Christ for themselves.

Preparing the way is done not only by preaching, as John did, but by conversations with friends and by inviting them to their homes where the Bible can be studied. This requires building friendships of mutual trust, respect, and love. Sometimes we are too eager to preach (this often seems like ramming unpalatable food down someone's throat) instead of being willing to wait for God to make the opening for a clear presentation of the Gospel.

Temptations and Ministry

DEVOTIONAL READING
Luke 4:14-21

DAILY BIBLE READINGS
Monday December 6
Matthew 4:1-11 Jesus Is Tempted by the Devil

Tuesday December 7
Matthew 4:12-17 Jesus Begins His Ministry in Galilee

Wednesday December 8
Luke 4:14-19 Jesus in the Synagogue at Nazareth

Thursday December 9
Luke 4:20-30 Jesus Is Rejected in Nazareth

Friday December 10
Luke 4:31-37 Jesus Casts Out a Demonic Spirit

Saturday December 11
Luke 4:38-44 Jesus Heals and Preaches

Sunday December 12
Luke 5:12-16 Jesus Heals a Man with Leprosy

Scripture
Background Scripture: *Matthew 4:1-17*
Scripture Lesson: *Matthew 4:1-14*
Key Verse: *Jesus said to him, "Away from me, Satan! For it is written: 'Worship the Lord your God, and serve him only.' "* Matthew 4:10
Background Scripture for Children: *Matthew 1:18-25*
Scripture Lesson for Children: *Matthew 1:18-25*
Key Verse for Children: *"Joseph son of David, do not be afraid to take Mary home as your wife."* Matthew 1:20

Lesson Aim
To follow the way of Jesus in defeating temptation and sin.

Lesson Setting
Time: *A.D. 26*
Place: *Desert east of Jerusalem*

Lesson Outline
Temptations and Ministry
  I. The Setting: Matthew 4:1-2
    A. Led by the Spirit to the Desert: vs. 1
    B. Extreme Hunger: vs. 2
  II. His First Temptation: Matthew 4:3-4
    A. Turn the Stones to Bread: vs. 3
    B. Jesus' Answer: Live by the Word: vs. 4
  III. His Second Temptation: Matthew 4:5-7
    A. Throw Yourself Down: vss. 5-6
    B. Jesus' Answer: Do Not Test God: vs. 7
  IV. His Third Temptation: Matthew 4:8-10
    A. Worship the Devil: vss. 8-9
    B. Jesus' Answer: Worship God Only: vs. 10
  V. His Early Preaching: Matthew 4:11-14
    A. The Angels Tended Him: vs. 11
    B. He Fulfilled Prophecy: vss. 12-14

Introduction for Adults

Topic: *Time of Testing*

Medical tests scare us and we worry and pray at the same time, hoping for negative results. Would it not do much to revive our souls and the life of our churches if we took spiritual tests with the same degree of seriousness?

Perhaps we are not as concerned about the health of our souls as we are about the health of our bodies. Jesus was terribly weakened in body during 40 days in the desert, yet His primary concern was for the well-being of His soul and His obedience to His Father.

God brings us to places of moral and spiritual testing so we can grow stronger in faith and obedience. The key, of course, is to know how to pass the test.

Introduction for Youths

Topic: *Temptation!*

When I think I won't have trouble with something, I usually do. Therefore, I ask God to show me where I am weak and vulnerable, so I can build up my protection.

Being tempted is not wrong, but giving in is. The devil keeps after us, poking and probing our weak points. That's why we need God's wisdom and help. He knows our hearts and our failings. But through Christ's indwelling power, we can win.

We need close friends to talk with about our temptations and weaknesses. We all need support and encouragement. We can also learn from each other, because my temptation is usually the same as someone else's. Most of all, we need to walk closely with Jesus every day, so He can keep us from falling into sin.

Concepts for Children

Topic: *An Angel Appears to Joseph*

1. God knew Joseph was afraid, so He encouraged him.
2. God knows our fears and meets us with prayer and encouragement from friends.
3. God's Son, Jesus, was born to a virgin so He could be our sinless Savior.
4. The name given to Jesus by the angel tells us about God's love to save us from our sins.
5. The birth of Jesus was predicted many centuries before He was born.
6. God keeps His word and fulfills His promises to us.

The Lesson Commentary

I. THE SETTING: MATTHEW 4:1-2

A. Led by the Spirit to the Desert: vs. 1

Then Jesus was led by the Spirit into the desert to be tempted by the devil.

There is a dramatic contrast in Matthew's story of Jesus between the exaltation of Jesus by His Father at His baptism (3:17) and His battle with the devil in the desert (4:1). But just as the dove and the voice from heaven confirmed Jesus in His calling, so did the leading of the Holy Spirit to the desert. This was rugged, mountainous country east of Jerusalem above the fertile plain of Jericho.

Jesus hardly had time to catch His breath after hearing God's voice telling of His pleasure in His Son. The Holy Spirit had come upon Him, so we know Jesus was not mistaken to go into the desert. However, it must have seemed an unusual step to take. Was this part of His Father's pleasure in Him?

Jesus was "led" to the place of temptation; he did not seek it Himself. This is an important principle. Jesus did not fall into temptation because He disobeyed His Father. He did not recklessly expose Himself to Satan's tricks. We must avoid the devil at all costs, and not think we are immune to his blandishments.

God did not lead His Son to do evil. We cannot avoid temptation, but we can resist it. In response to the Holy Spirit's leading, Jesus was brought to the place of supreme spiritual testing. God's salvation plan hinged on the outcome. The power of the Holy Spirit was with Jesus throughout this experience. Luke wrote that He returned from it "in the power of the Spirit" (4:14).

The writer of Hebrews said that Jesus was tempted as we are, but without sin (4:15). Jesus suffered this encounter with Satan, as well as many other testings, as part of His obedience to His Father (Heb. 5:8). We can assume that this meeting was typical of other such temptations throughout Jesus' ministry, because the devil kept after him (Luke 4:13).

In God's plan it was necessary for His Son to be subjected to and to overcome temptation. This proved his full identity with human beings, apart from sin. According to Hebrews 2:18 and 4:15, the temptation of Jesus gives us encouragement to come to Him when we are tempted, since we know He has gone through the same things.

B. Extreme Hunger: vs. 2

After fasting forty days and forty nights, he was hungry.

Jesus fasted 40 days in the desert. Perhaps this was a sign to Israel that He remembered the 40 years' wandering in the desert after the exodus from Egypt. To fast does not necessarily mean not eating anything. It may include engaging in intense spiritual discipline to draw close to God by existing on water and a restricted diet. All the while, Satan tempted Him (Luke 4:2), not just at the end of the 40 days.

Satan not only attacked Jesus after His high exhilaration at the Jordan, but also when He was physically weak. This is also part of his strategy toward us. He knows how much we are bothered by our physical weaknesses, so when we suffer, he tries to inspire doubt, disobedience, and unbelief.

II. HIS FIRST TEMPTATION: MATTHEW 4:3-4

A. Turn the Stones to Bread: vs. 3

The tempter came to him and said, "If you are the Son of God, tell these stones to become bread."

The temptation of Jesus did not represent a trial on God's part to see if His Son would pass or fail. Rather, it demonstrated Christ's total commitment to His Father and to His wisdom, love, and care. Jesus fulfilled righteousness at His baptism; in His temptations, His righteousness was tested.

Before Jesus began preaching about the coming of God's kingdom and the overthrow of Satan's, He had to meet and defeat the enemy on the battle-ground of His own life. Since Jesus had dedicated Himself to following His Father's will, even to the cross, the devil tried by every means possible to get Jesus to avoid dying on the cross to set people free from sin and Satan. Only by His subsequent death and resurrection did Jesus defeat Satan.

Knowing that Jesus was extremely tired and hungry, Satan invited Him to turn the stones into bread, implying that this act would prove that He really was the Son of God. In reality, Satan was testing Christ's commitment to His Father's love and care.

What could have been more logical and necessary than to provide bread for Himself? Was this not a legitimate thing for Jesus to do? What was wrong with using His deity to satisfy His physical needs? What kind of trap was this?

The temptation was the implication that Jesus could take things into His own hands and provide for His own needs, without trusting His heavenly Father for these things. Was it right to stop trusting God? No. Even though He was hungry, Jesus could not sell out to the devil on those grounds.

B. Jesus' Answer: Live by the Word: vs. 4

Jesus answered, "It is written: 'Man does not live on bread alone, but on every word that comes from the mouth of God.' "

Jesus resisted the temptation by telling the devil that there are higher priorities in life than eating. Of course, our physical needs are legitimate. We do need bread, but we also need something more valuable—the life-giving Word of God.

We cannot make decisions just because of a physical need or drive. It is possible to misuse our normal physical appetites for selfish purposes, rather than in obedience to God. God's laws outrank our physical needs.

Jesus defeated Satan by quoting Deuteronomy 8:3. Jesus met the test with

Scripture. His quotation referred to Israel's grumbling about the manna God had given to them when they were hungry. The Israelites were dissatisfied with God's provision. His promises were not good enough.

Jesus told Satan that God's Word is sufficient for all our needs. Christians who want to trust God will have to learn again and again to trust the promises found in Scripture, "every word that comes from the mouth of God." The Bible is our reliable, nourishing, life-sustaining spiritual food.

III. HIS SECOND TEMPTATION: MATTHEW 4:5-7

A. Throw Yourself Down: vss. 5-6

Then the devil took him to the holy city and had him stand on the highest point of the temple. "If you are the Son of God," he said, "throw yourself down. For it is written: 'He will command his angels concerning you, and they will lift you up in their hands, so that you will not strike your foot against a stone.' "

The devil next threw at Jesus a subtle test for Him to prove that He enjoyed a unique relation to God. He posed his second temptation in the form of a challenge: "*If you are the Son of God . . .*"

When he tempted Jesus to prove His deity by throwing Himself down from the highest level of the temple, Satan added another clever trick to his arsenal—he quoted a Scripture (Ps. 91:11-12), which Jesus knew very well.

Of course, Satan quoted these verses out of their context, which is what false teachers still do. Historically, the verses applied to Israel's demand for signs to prove God's presence. We do not have to attempt foolish risks to prove that God cares for us.

What was the temptation? Would it have been wrong for Jesus to do this to prove His deity and His Father's care? Yes, because what the devil proposed was not confidence and trust in God, but foolish presumption. Not reliance and faith, but a foolhardy, unnecessary risk. Jesus did not need to do this to prove to Himself and to the devil that He was the Son of God. If Jesus had done what the devil proposed, He would have tempted His Father's loving care. He would have presumed on God's wisdom and love for no good reason at all.

B. Jesus' Answer: Do Not Test God: vs. 7

Jesus answered him, "It is also written: 'Do not put the Lord your God to the test.' "

Jesus answered the devil by quoting Deuteronomy 6:16. This proves that Satan was trying to provoke Him into daring God to save Him, or forcing God to preserve Him from disaster, even though throwing Himself down from the pinnacle of the temple had nothing to do with obedience to His Father's will. The devil really was saying that Jesus could choose the life of a popular miracle worker, if He wanted to, rather than face opposition and death for His obedience to God's will.

Jesus' answer was not directed at the devil for tempting Him. He used the Scripture to support His own refusal to throw Himself off a tall building. This is an instructive example for us—to steer clear of daredevil options. The Lord Jesus used Scripture for specific guidance in His temptations. He obeyed immediately and unequivocally. He did not try to dodge or rationalize Scripture. We can best resist temptation by immediately doing what we know is right and true.

IV. HIS THIRD TEMPTATION: MATTHEW 4:8-10

A. Worship the Devil: vss. 8-9

Again, the devil took him to a very high mountain and showed him all the kingdoms of the world and their splendor. "All this I will give you," he said, "if you will bow down and worship me."

The devil's third temptation was the offer to give Jesus control of the kingdoms of the world if He would worship him. Jesus called him "the prince of this world" (John 16:11). The apostle Paul called him "the ruler of the kingdom of the air" (Eph. 2:2). Therefore, Satan's offer was no idle boast. He could deliver the kingdoms of the world. But his price was extremely high: Jesus had to worship him.

In this temptation we see the clearest evidence of the devil's attempts to sidetrack Jesus from the cross. God's plan is to have His Son rule the world in righteousness. If that is true, the devil reasoned, why go through suffering and death to attain it? Why not align yourself with me and I will put my enormous influence in the world at your disposal? Christ's kingdom would then be established by satanic power.

Ultimately, this was a temptation to what the apostle John called "the boasting of what [one] has and does" (1 John 2:16). It was a temptation again to be dissatisfied with God's plan and to choose an alternative instead. All temptations are attractive, whether for physical needs or for pride, power, and prestige, but they all exact a horrific cost. In this case, the cost was the denial of God and the worship of Satan.

B. Jesus' Answer: Worship God Only: vs. 10

Jesus said to him, "Away from me, Satan! For it is written: 'Worship the Lord your God, and serve him only.'"

Jesus resisted this powerful temptation by establishing the priority of worship and service to God alone. He did it by quoting the commandment of Deuteronomy 6:13. No matter how high the offer, nothing could stand in the way of worshiping God alone. The whole world was not worth selling out to Satan for. Yet how subtle this was—to have this humble village carpenter made world ruler by one act of homage to the devil.

The devil does not need to offer us the kingdoms of the world, because most of us would settle for far less. But the devil's lie is still the same. If he can't convince us that our physical needs and our pride are supreme, perhaps he can convince us that power and authority are—at least part of this world's kingdoms. For what would we sell out to the devil?

Once again Jesus defeated Satan with the Word of God. God's Word clearly taught that He alone is worthy of worship and obedience. Deuteronomy 6:13 came out of Israel's worship of a false god, the golden calf. It was a powerful warning against any kind of false religion and worship, all of which originates with Satan.

The way Jesus conquered temptation by using Scripture bears out the wisdom of the apostle Paul's teaching that we "can extinguish all the flaming arrows of the evil one [by taking] . . . the sword of the Spirit, which is the word of God" (Eph. 6:16-17).

V. His Early Preaching: Matthew 4:11-14

A. The Angels Tended Him: vs. 11

Then the devil left him, and angels came and attended him.

The devil left the mountain in utter defeat. Jesus had not yielded even to his cleverest tricks. The Son of God refused to be taken in. He knew the commands of Scripture that successfully voided Satan's logic. But Satan did not quit; this was a temporary cessation of spiritual warfare.

When the devil left, the angels came. What a refreshing time that must have been! God had not abandoned His Son. His Son had emerged triumphant.

We don't know specifically what the angels did for Jesus, but obviously they provided spiritual comfort and encouragement. Probably they also brought Him food and water. They gave Him tokens of God's love and care.

B. He Fulfilled Prophecy: vss. 12-14

When Jesus heard that John had been put in prison, he returned to Galilee. Leaving Nazareth, he went and lived in Capernaum, which was by the lake in the area of Zebulun and Naphtali—to fulfill what was said through the prophet Isaiah.

Sometime later Jesus left the mountain and went back to the beautiful plain of Galilee to the north. Now He knew it was time to preach, because John had been imprisoned by King Herod. Jesus left His carpenter's shop and His quiet home in Nazareth and moved on to Capernaum. This city on the shore of the Lake of Galilee was to become His home base for ministry.

Matthew's story carefully points out how Jesus fulfilled the specific prophecy of Isaiah 9:1-2. This is very important to prove that Jesus was the Messiah. It was no accident that Jesus chose Capernaum. He went there because seven hundred years before Isaiah had predicted that the Messiah would live in Galilee of the Gentiles (vs. 15).

Isaiah pictured the Messiah's preaching as the giving of a great light (vs. 16).

Jesus would bring spiritual light to people living in darkness; He would bring hope and life to those living in the shadow of death. He truly was the light of the world.

Jesus first brought the light by telling people to repent (vs. 17). They needed to confess and repent because God's kingdom had arrived in the person of Jesus the Messiah.

Discussion Questions

1. How can we tell the difference between faith and presumption? How can we tell if a risk is according to God's will?
2. How are Christians tempted in regard to attaining worldly goods? What forms might the devil's offer take today?
3. What would it mean to worship the devil? How can the world's aspirations and goals divert us from worshiping and serving God?
4. Since we can't turn stones into bread, how might we be tempted in this regard today? What legitimate needs might in fact keep us from growth in faith and obedience?
5. How can the Word of God be an effective weapon against temptation? Why don't Christians use the Bible more effectively this way?
6. How can we use our homes to equip families to resist temptation with the Word of God?

Contemporary Application

Hardly a day passes that we are not tempted to break God's laws and sin. Yet, for the most part, the world makes fun of those who take temptation seriously and try to resist it. The powerful lie of powerful culture is that yielding—not resisting—is the way to have fun.

Therefore, if the church takes Jesus seriously, we have to take temptation seriously as well. We can't pretend to be followers of Christ and take no thought about protecting ourselves from the devil.

Often, the devil outsmarts us because we can't see the traps he lays for us. We get so accustomed to following the world's values that we don't realize we have sold out to him. We follow whatever seems to be the popular thing to do, whether it is God's will or not.

To meet the devil's strategy, we need to keep very close to Jesus and His words. He needed the Scripture to defeat Satan, and so do we. Every hour invested in Bible study and prayer will return huge dividends in victories over Satan.

Birth of Jesus

Scripture

Background Scripture: *Matthew 1*
Scripture Lesson: *Matthew 1:1-6, 18-25*
Key Verse: *"She will give birth to a son, and you are to give him the name Jesus, because he will save his people from their sins."* Matthew 1:21
Background Scripture for Children: *Luke 2:1-20*
Scripture Lesson for Children: *Luke 2:1-20*
Key Verse for Children: *"Today in the town of David a Savior has been born to you; he is Christ the Lord."* Luke 2:11

Lesson Aim

To rejoice and praise God for the birth of Jesus our Savior.

Lesson Setting

Time: *4 B.C.*
Place: *Nazareth of Galilee*

Lesson Outline

Birth of Jesus
   I. The Genealogy of Jesus: Matthew 1:1-6
   II. The Circumstances of Christ's Birth: Matthew 1:18-21
       A. Mary's Pregnancy Was "Through the Holy Spirit": vs. 18
       B. Joseph Planned to Divorce Mary: vs. 19
       C. The Angel Intervened: vss. 20-21
   III. Christ's Birth and Prophecy: Matthew 1:22-23
   IV. Joseph's Obedience: Matthew 1:24-25

Introduction for Adults

Topic: *Time of Rejoicing*

Christians rejoice at Christmas because we celebrate why Christ was born. His name alone tells us the purpose of His life and ministry. He came to save us from the guilt, condemnation, and power of sin. That's why we rejoice.

The Roman historian Tacitus, writing near the end of the first century, said, "The vulgar call them Christians. The author or origin of this denomination, Christus, had, in the reign of Tiberias, been executed by the Procurator, Pontius Pilate." From the second century on, the title Christian was accepted by believers as a badge of honor.

"Christos" is the Greek equivalent of the Hebrew "Messiah," meaning "anointed one." It signifies the nature of Jesus Christ as God's anointed, or promised deliverer and savior. The Lord Jesus Christ was given a divinely appointed name by His parents, the name "Jesus," which means "the Lord saves." That name signified His work. It was given to tell all people that He came on a saving mission from heaven.

Introduction for Youths

Topic: *A King Is Born*

Christmas marks the birthday of King Jesus. But He was not born with all the trappings of royalty. Instead, our King was born into a peasant family living under the shadow of scandal.

Young people today are familiar with babies born out of wedlock. For some, it's an honor, not a shame, to have a baby while unmarried. But it wasn't like that in Mary's time. To show signs of pregnancy before marriage brought terrible shame and even the risk of death by stoning. Mary and Joseph her betrothed faced a horrible dilemma. Even if they obeyed God and did not get a divorce, they could be openly taunted about their situation.

Some teens may feel trapped by unfortunate circumstances, the outcome of unwise decisions. But Jesus knows all about their hurts and dilemmas. Christians must offer hope of a better future to young people who perhaps feel they have thrown their lives away for a momentary sexual gratification.

Concepts for Children

Topic: *Jesus Is Born*

1. The baby Jesus was born into a poor, humble, God-fearing family.
2. God sends us help when we face hard decisions.
3. Shepherds came to worship Jesus, and Christians have proclaimed Him as Lord and Savior ever since.
4. Angels brought good news and praised God. We can follow their example.
5. Our friends may be lonely and disturbed, even at Christmas, so we can look for ways to help and encourage them.
6. At Christmas we thank God for His wonderful love in sending us a Savior.

The Lesson Commentary

I. THE GENEALOGY OF JESUS: MATTHEW 1:1-6

A record of the genealogy of Jesus Christ the son of David, the son of Abraham: Abraham was the father of Isaac, Isaac the father of Jacob, Jacob the father of Judah and his brothers, Judah the father of Perez and Zerah, whose mother was Tamar, Perez the father of Hezron, Hezron the father of Ram, Ram the father of Amminadab, Amminadab the father of Nahshon, Nahshon the father of Salmon, Salmon the father of Boaz, whose mother was Rahab, Boaz the father of Obed, whose mother was Ruth, Obed the father of Jesse, and Jesse the father of King David.

Matthew's story of Jesus begins with the genealogy of Jesus, tracing His ancestry not only to the great hero King David, but all the way back to Abraham, the ancestor of all Israel. Matthew wanted to show Jesus as the Jews' Messiah, descended from the royal line of David. Matthew abbreviated his genealogy to fit his pattern: 14 names from Abraham to David (vss. 1-6); 14 names from David to Jeconiah (vss. 6-11); 14 from Jeconiah to Jesus (vss. 12-16). His pattern of fourteens may have been suggested by the fact that the Hebrew letters in the name "David" add up to that number. The letters of the Hebrew alphabet also served as numbers.

"Son of David" (vs. 1) came first because of God's promise to him of an unfailing succession. However, the nation's monarchy ceased at the time of the exile to Babylon (586 B.C.). Therefore, God's promise to David was understood as the promise of a future Messiah.

Some of the names in the genealogy are familiar, people like Abraham, Isaac, and Jacob. Not until we get to Rahab and Ruth (vs. 5) do we encounter other well-known people.

Scholars have long been fascinated by the names of the women included by Matthew: Tamar (vs. 3), Rahab and Ruth (vs. 5), and Uriah's wife Bathsheba (vs. 6). Perhaps the main point of this is that God's love and purposes have not been limited to decent people of a particular race. In His wisdom, He chose to have His Son identified with both women and men, and with people who had their botches as well as successes. Whatever the reasons, "Jesus is not ashamed to call them brothers" (Heb. 2:11) or sisters.

II. THE CIRCUMSTANCES OF CHRIST'S BIRTH: MATTHEW 1:18-21

A. Mary's Pregnancy Was "Through the Holy Spirit": vs. 18

This is how the birth of Jesus Christ came about: His mother Mary was pledged to be married to Joseph, but before they came together, she was found to be with child through the Holy Spirit.

Does the economy of words in the four Gospels about the birth of Jesus mean His birth is unimportant? Not at all, but it does show that the modern pageantry associated with Christ's birth—and certainly the commercialism and showmanship—are hardly in tune with the simple, factual, unadorned narratives we have in the New Testament.

The single most important emphasis is on Christ's divine origin and the purpose of His coming. The miraculous cannot be avoided in considering Christ's birth. His birth to a virgin mother is an essential foundation stone of Christian faith and doctrine.

In contrast to the miraculous, we also see the simplicity. We are stunned by the fact that the one who made the world chose to enter it by being born into a humble peasant family, in an obscure country village, in a cattle barn, with no publicity and fanfare whatsoever, except for the singing of angels to shepherds.

The angel had revealed to Mary that the Holy Spirit would come upon her. This was in response to her understandable question about how she could become pregnant (Luke 1:34-35).

Matthew simply presented the fact that it became obvious that Mary was "with child" during the time of her engagement to be married to Joseph. The key fact is that this happened "before they came together," that is, prior to sexual intercourse. Mary's virginity is a matter of historical record. That is why her pregnancy is attributed to the Holy Spirit.

This is not a legend, or myth, or fairy tale. It is not the invention of writers, who, after Jesus died, were trying to bolster His claims to deity by saying that He had no human father. There is no point in trying to explain the virgin birth naturally. Christians believe this is what happened, on the authority of solid historical and literary evidence. Plus, they have the remarkable prophecy that God gave 700 years before, which told how the Messiah would be born (vs. 23; see also Isa. 7:14). Mary became pregnant apart from the usual physical process, in a way that can be attributed only to the power of God.

God could have sent Jesus fully grown, like a visitor from another planet. But it pleased God to have Jesus born the same way all other babies are born.

We not only encounter divine mystery with regard to the virgin birth of Jesus, but also with regard to His mother Mary. Who was she? What was she like? The brief New Testament references to her leave many gaps, which over the centuries pious people have tried to fill with countless legends. All we know for sure is that this young woman, possibly even younger than eighteen, was living at Nazareth in Galilee and was engaged to be married to a carpenter named Joseph.

Considering all the facts in the Gospels, we are left with the conviction that our Lord's mother was a woman of genuine faith, tremendous courage, and obedience to the will of God. In contrast to the fictitious embellishments, she was, above all, humble. She was not sinless, but certainly God chose a woman of high moral and spiritual integrity to mother His Son.

B. Joseph Planned to Divorce Mary: vs. 19

Because Joseph her husband was a righteous man and did not want to expose her to public disgrace, he had in mind to divorce her quietly.

Mary was engaged to be married to Joseph. Joseph was her husband officially, but they had not had sexual relations, yet Mary was pregnant. It is helpful to understand the historical context, because engagement and marriage customs then were far different from those in the West now.

First, there was the engagement, often made by parents when the future bride and groom were just children. Marriage was much too serious a matter to be left to falling in love, or passion. Second, there was betrothal. This was the ratification of the engagement. Up to this time, the girl could refuse to go along with the engagement. However, once betrothal took place, it was absolutely binding.

Betrothal lasted for a year, during which the couple was known as man and wife, but they could not enjoy sexual relations. Joseph and Mary were at this stage in their relationship. Legally, Mary was his wife and he could divorce her. The only way a betrothal could be terminated was by divorce. After the year's betrothal, the third and final stage was marriage proper.

Of course, Joseph had a serious and embarrassing problem. Not knowing anything about the angel's announcement to Mary, "The Holy Spirit will come upon you" (Luke 1:35), he assumed Mary's pregnancy was due to unfaithfulness on her part. Today, some critics of Christ's deity and His virgin birth actually say that Jesus was the result of Mary's infidelity. This view fails to account for the revelation of God to Mary, Joseph, and the prophet Isaiah.

Adultery was an acceptable ground for divorce, so Joseph planned to do what was his right. However, he planned to divorce Mary "quietly," without exposing her publicly, so she would not suffer "public disgrace." Usually persons accused of adultery were treated very harshly, ostracized, and even put to death.

According to Matthew, Joseph was a descendant of King David. Although Joseph was not the father of Jesus in the physical sense, he nevertheless acted as His father, taking Him to Jerusalem for purification and fleeing with Him to Egypt to escape Herod. He returned to Nazareth and settled there, and took Jesus to Jerusalem each year for the Passover. Because of the lack of any mention of Joseph thereafter, it is assumed that He died sometime after Jesus was twelve.

Matthew called him a "righteous man." That obviously meant he was a good, hardworking, God-fearing husband and parent. He trusted in the Lord and wanted to obey Him in all that he did. The gracious way he proposed to deal with Mary's condition speaks volumes to us about his character.

The basic commitment of both Mary and Joseph to do God's will is seen in how they responded to the angels. Mary said, after the Holy Spirit told her she would be with child: "I am the Lord's servant. May it be to me as you have said" (Luke 1:38). When the angel told Joseph that Mary's pregnancy was by the Holy Spirit, he did as he was commanded and took her as his wife (Matt. 1:24).

This couple was living in faith, in openness, in trust, so that when God spoke words that were humanly, physically impossible to accept and understand, they believed God and did as they were told. God chose to have His Son born and raised in a family that put obedience to the word of God above everything else.

C. The Angel Intervened: vss. 20-21

But after he had considered this, an angel of the Lord appeared to him in a dream and said, "Joseph son of David, do not be afraid to take Mary home as your wife, because what is conceived in her is from the Holy Spirit. She will give birth to a son, and you are to give him the name Jesus, because he will save his people from their sins."

Joseph was deeply puzzled by what had happened. He knew Mary was not the kind of woman who would betray him, but he could not deny what he saw. However, because of his love and trust, he did not act rashly. Matthew said he first considered the matter.

While Joseph paused for reflection and prayer, the angel of God spoke to him. God was not going to allow Joseph to divorce Mary. She was innocent, and the only way for Joseph to know this was by some direct intervention from the Lord.

God often gave directions in dreams and visions, in response to the pleas of His people for help and wisdom. Because Joseph was determined to do the right thing, and not hurt Mary, God gave him the wisdom he needed.

The angel's message was explicit. God knew the man's feelings. Joseph was afraid to take Mary as his wife because of her condition, so God spoke to his fears. The angel revealed that Mary's pregnancy was "from the Holy Spirit."

Joseph didn't get an explanation of how this had happened. Joseph simply accepted that God was able to do the physically impossible. He was assured that no sin brought about Mary's pregnancy. This was the result of the mighty power of God who, after all, created the world and human beings out of nothing. Therefore, implanting a baby in the virgin's womb was consistent with His original creation.

Joseph learned both the divine origin and the purpose of Mary's pregnancy. This was wrapped up in the name he was told to give the baby: Jesus, which means "the Lord saves." This baby one day would save people from the consequences (divine wrath and judgment) of their sins.

Thus, in the first Christmas story we find not only facts about how the baby was born, but also the fact that everyone has sinned and therefore needs a personal Savior. The core of the Gospel is in the angel's explanation. We do not have to invent reasons why Jesus was born. He was born to save us from our sins.

No one can be good enough to earn God's forgiveness. Our only hope is for

God himself to do something about our condition. Jesus Christ, born of the Holy Spirit, born apart from any taint of the sinful nature that infects every person born of woman and man, is alone qualified and capable of saving us. He Himself was without sin, but He atoned for our sins by His death and resurrection (2 Cor. 5:21).

III. CHRIST'S BIRTH AND PROPHECY: MATTHEW 1:22-23

All this took place to fulfill what the Lord had said through the prophet: "The virgin will be with child and will give birth to a son, and they will call him Immanuel"—which means, "God with us."

New Testament writers consistently interpreted Christ's coming in the light of Old Testament prophecies. The fulfillment of prophecy was the main burden of apostolic proof of the deity of Christ.

Matthew quoted Isaiah 7:14, a prophecy given seven centuries before the birth of Jesus. It dealt with the two main facts revealed to Joseph: Mary was a virgin and her child was the result of God's plan to come to earth in human form.

After the angel's appearance, Joseph saw things in a new light. Even the Old Testament predicted such a miracle, the birth of a child to a virgin. The value of being a faithful student of Scripture is that one can appreciate how all of it relates to the central theme of the coming of Christ.

The prophet said the child's name would be Immanuel, or "God with us." Isaiah spoke of the one who would come as a certain sign that God had not forsaken His people. Jesus Christ is the proof that God truly is with us and provides salvation for all people.

"Jesus" explains what He came to do (save); "Immanuel" explains who He is (God). The effectiveness of Christ's saving work depends on who He is. Many people have died for noble, humanitarian causes, but their deaths are not the means of saving people from their sins. Only Jesus Christ can save us from the guilt, condemnation, and punishment of our sins, because He is "God with us."

IV. JOSEPH'S OBEDIENCE: MATTHEW 1:24-25

When Joseph woke up, he did what the angel of the Lord had commanded him and took Mary home as his wife. But he had no union with her until she gave birth to a son. And he gave him the name Jesus.

God's word changed the course of Joseph's life. He had arrived at a logical decision, one that seemed eminently proper and even kind, but then he was faced with another decision. It was the word of the angel versus his own reason and instincts. Joseph chose to obey God, in the face of certain ridicule and embarrassment. On some occasions, people hear the word of God but refuse to change, especially when God's commands run counter to their own desires and reason. Even Christians sometimes face trouble in this matter.

But Joseph cared for Mary and accepted her as his wife. He refrained from sexual intercourse until Jesus was born. When it came to naming the baby, Joseph recalled the words of the angel. No doubt by this time both he and Mary had compared notes, and had discovered that God had told both of them what the baby's name was to be.

Jesus is the Greek form of the Jewish name Joshua. It means "Yahweh [the LORD] is salvation." Such a name was fitting, for above everything else, Christmas means that God offers salvation freely to all who receive the gift of His Son.

To receive such a gift, people have to make hard choices, like Joseph did. The basic choice is between trying to save yourself and allowing God to save you. Unless we give up our self-dependence, there is no hope of salvation.

Discussion Questions

1. What impresses you about Mary and Joseph in this story? Why?
2. What impresses you about God? Why?
3. How many gifts have come to you as a result of Christ's saving you from your sins?
4. What do you think motivated Joseph to obey the Lord? How would you have reacted?
5. What does "God with us" mean in everyday life?
6. How can you relate the basic salvation story to friends and neighbors at Christmas?

Contemporary Application

During the nineteenth-century potato famine in Ireland people were put to work building roads that had no purpose or destination. One day a boy came home and cried to his father, "They're making roads that lead to nowhere."

Isaiah's prophecy and its fulfillment in Mary prove that God is making a road to somewhere. Our lives have purpose and eternal destiny because Jesus Christ is the road to God, the truth about God, and the life of God (John 14:6).

At Christmastime, people often try to cover their inner hurts and pain with a lot of parties and family get-togethers. They do not know and understand that the baby of Bethlehem can enter and transform their lives. Christians see God's hand in Christmas, and they have a great opportunity to make Christ real to others during the holiday season.

Coming of the Wise Men

DEVOTIONAL READING
Psalm 98

DAILY BIBLE READINGS

Monday December 20
Luke 2:1-7 The Birth of Jesus

Tuesday December 21
Luke 2:8-20 Jesus' Birth Announced to Shepherds

Wednesday December 22
Luke 2:21-27 Jesus Is Presented in the Temple

Thursday December 23
Luke 2:28-38 Simeon and Anna Praise God

Friday December 24
Matthew 2:1-6 Wise Men Inquire about Jesus' Birth

Saturday December 25
Matthew 2:7-12 Wise Men Visit and Honor Jesus

Sunday December 26
Matthew 2:13-18 Herod's Wrath Is Unleashed

Scripture

Background Scripture: *Matthew 2*
Scripture Lesson: *Matthew 2:1-12*
Key Verse: *"Where is the one who has been born king of the Jews? We saw his star in the east and have come to worship him."* Matthew 2:2.
Key Verse for Children: *"Where is the one who has been born king of the Jews?"* Matthew 2:2.

Lesson Aim

To bring our worship and adoration to Jesus our Savior.

Lesson Setting

Time: *About 3 B.C.*
Place: *Jerusalem and Bethlehem*

Lesson Outline

Coming of the Wise Men

    I. The Wise Men's Quest: Matthew 2:1-2
   II. Herod's Inquiry: Matthew 2:3-4
  III. The Prophet's Answer: Matthew 2:5-6
  IV. Herod's Treachery: Matthew 2:7-8
   V. The Wise Men's Worship: Matthew 2:9-12

Introduction for Adults

Topic: *Time of Worshiping*

    The editors of a newspaper decided to find out what their readers remembered most about Christmas. They asked them to write letters describing their most memorable Christmas experiences.

    The more than 300 respondents wrote about joy and thanksgiving, as well as about unhappiness and even disappointments. The editors picked what they thought was the best letter.

As an underprivileged girl of eight, she had been given a doll by the volunteer firemen of her town. But she didn't keep it. Her five-year-old neighbor girl also wanted a doll, so she decided to give away the cherished doll she had just received.

As this week's lesson shows, that's the heart of Christmas—giving, not getting. The wise men persisted and overcame great difficulty, at considerable risk, not to get something for themselves, but to give something away. Why? Because they recognized that it was their privilege to respond to God's great gift to them.

Introduction for Youths

Topic: *Search until You Find*

It's hard to decide if Tchaikovsky's Nutcracker or Charles Dickens's Ebenezer Scrooge captures the most interest today. Those exciting tales, enacted with power and drama, never fail to draw wide interest as Christmas entertainment.

But what about the saga of King Herod and the Magi from the East? Here's a classic story of intrigue and treachery, and in the end bitter tragedy for the people of Bethlehem who lost all their boy babies. Everything ends well for Tchaikovsky's kids and even for the old curmudgeon Scrooge. Not so for Herod and the people of Bethlehem.

However, one brilliant light shines gloriously through the king's wickedness. It's the light that brought the Magi to the feet of Jesus Christ, bowing with full praise and giving the most extraordinary gifts to the child. Once again we have the chance to help young people grasp the essence of divine grace and the human response to it.

The world is still full of treachery and killing, so much so that far too many teenagers take suicide as the way out. Christmas can be a very depressing time for youth today, many of whom have to share the holidays with many different sets of parents and grandparents because of broken families. What a rare opportunity Christians have to bring some hope and meaning to the thousands of youths whose family life does not measure up to the romantic paintings of happy families gathered around the fireplace.

Concepts for Children

Topic: *Wise Men Look for Jesus*

1. People with true wisdom today give honor and praise to Jesus Christ.
2. Jesus still has some enemies like King Herod today.
3. Receiving lots of toys, games, and clothes at Christmas is delightful, but most important is God's supreme gift of His Son.
4. Many children suffer at Christmas because of poverty, unemployment, hunger, and lack of love at home.

The Lesson Commentary

I. THE WISE MEN'S QUEST: MATTHEW 2:1-2

After Jesus was born in Bethlehem in Judea, during the time of King Herod, Magi from the east came to Jerusalem and asked, "Where is the one who has been born king of the Jews? We saw his star in the east and have come to worship him."

Matthew began his account of the life and ministry of Jesus with His ancestry (1:2-17). Then he briefly told about His virgin birth and the fulfillment of the prophecy in Isaiah 7:14 (vss. 18-25). Matthew did not see fit to describe the manger scene and the revelation to the shepherds and their visit to Mary and the baby. He simply told where and when Jesus was born, choosing to focus instead on the visit of the mysterious Magi from the east.

Bethlehem was a small town six miles southwest of Jerusalem. It sits on an elevation just off the main road from Jerusalem to Hebron. Now the place where thousands of pilgrims gather every year, Bethlehem in ancient times had no prominence at all. Naomi, Ruth, and David lived there, but Bethlehem owes its fame to the birth of Jesus Christ.

Palestine was divided into three western divisions: Galilee, Samaria, and Judea. Although Joseph was from Nazareth in Galilee, he was obligated to go to Bethlehem with Mary because the Roman Emperor Augustus had ordered a census to be taken throughout his empire. According to Jewish custom, people were enrolled in their ancestral homes. Since both Joseph and Mary were descended from David, they went to Bethlehem, probably in 5 B.C., since King Herod died in 4 B.C.

"During the time of King Herod" sets the stage for the unfolding drama of the Magi. Herod the Great founded the Herodian dynasty. He was an Idumean (Edomite) by birth and partly Jewish by race. He made an agreement with the Romans under which he was given the title, "King of the Jews."

He conquered Palestine in 37 B.C. and ruled as its undisputed master until he died. A passionate builder, Herod the Great gave Palestine some remarkable monuments, including the temple in Jerusalem and a palace for himself. Above all, as far as the Romans were concerned, he maintained peace and order in this notoriously rebellious province.

In hard times, Herod eased up on taxes. In the famine of 25 B.C., he melted down his own gold plate to buy food for starving people. However, he was a ruthless murderer because he was insanely suspicious.

Herod murdered his wife Mariamne and her mother Alexandra. Three of his sons, including his eldest, Antipater, were assassinated by him. In the most bizarre, blood-thirsty act of all, Herod ordered some of Jerusalem's most distinguished citizens jailed when he realized he was about to die himself. He commanded that when he died, they should all be killed. He knew no one would mourn his passing, but he was determined that tears should flow anyway.

To get the whole story on the Magi [MAY-jeye], or wise men, we have to consult both Matthew's account and some wonderful traditions about them. Matthew did not count them, but according to tradition there were three of them (three gifts are mentioned in vs. 11), named Melchior, Caspar, and Balthasar.

Astronomy as a science was in those days mixed with astrology. These men probably came from Babylon in Persia, where many people were fascinated by the constellations and tried to predict the future by reading the stars.

As the legends about the Magi grew, they became kings ("We three kings of Orient are"). The legends say that Melchior was an old man with a long beard. He brought the gift of gold. Caspar was young and beardless with a ruddy complexion. He brought the frankincense. Balthasar was swarthy with a sprouting beard. He brought the myrrh.

The Magi intended to find the recently-born king of the Jews, so that they could worship Him. They had sighted a special star, which they called the king's star. Among the explanations of this heavenly phenomenon are these:
• It was Halley's Comet (11 B.C.), or another comet seen in 4 B.C.
• It was a planetary conjunction of Jupiter, Saturn, and Venus early in 7 B.C.
• It was a supernova, a sudden, unpredictable brightening of a faint star that temporarily dominated the sky. A supernova produces more light than all the other stars put together.

We may not know for sure what the Magi really saw, nor why they associated this sudden appearance in the sky with the birth of the king of the Jews. The Bethlehem star, however, does things that even unusual heavenly objects don't do.

Historians say there was an almost eager expectation for a world deliverer. Of course, the Jews had been dispersed throughout the Roman and eastern worlds, taking with them their fervent hopes and prayers for the Messiah. They believed the prophets and no doubt influenced others to believe too, as these quotes from Roman writers and other factors reveal:
• "There had spread all over the Orient an old and established belief, that it was fated at that time for men coming from Judea to rule the world" (Suetonius).
• "There was a firm persuasion . . . that at this very time the East was to grow powerful, and rulers from Judea were to acquire universal empire" (Tacitus).
• The Roman poet Virgil wrote what is known as the Messianic Eclogue, about a future golden era. About the time Jesus was born, Augustus, the Roman emperor, was hailed as the savior of the world.
• Jewish believers associated the Messiah's coming with a special star, according to Numbers 24:17 ("A star will come out of Jacob; a scepter will rise out of Jacob"), a prophecy probably known to the surrounding cultures.

So, the Magi came to Jerusalem on a special mission. The Christmas story tells us much more than the birth of an ordinary child. The kingship of Jesus runs from His birth to His death (see also Matt. 27:11, 29, 37) and beyond. He came as both King of the Jews and King of all kings (1 Tim. 6:15; Rev. 17:14). He is Head and Lord of the Church and the rightful ruler of our lives.

II. HEROD'S INQUIRY: MATTHEW 2:3-4

When King Herod heard this he was disturbed, and all Jerusalem with him. When he had called together all the people's chief priests and teachers of the law, he asked them where the Christ was to be born.

We don't know who the Magi initially asked for directions, but their appearance in town (were they strangely dressed?) set the grapevine to work. It wasn't long before the news reached the court. Knowing Herod's character as we do, his response was predictable. He wanted to know what the Jewish Scriptures said about Messiah's birth. He was probably well aware of the Jews' Messianic hopes, but he didn't know how to interpret the prophets.

What could Herod do? Were the Magi really on to something? If the public found out and clamored for a new king, the Messiah, he would be in serious trouble with Rome. The emperor, if he wished, could unseat Herod if he failed to maintain peace.

We must observe the sharp contrast between the panic and fear of Herod and "all Jerusalem with him" and the peace of the shepherds and the wise men who came to worship the Christ child. When strange, unforeseen things happen, people who have no inner peace quickly panic. When they reject God's rule and choose to go their own way, they are victimized by their circumstances.

Christ is preached today, yet the world is still gripped by vexation and turmoil, just as Jerusalem was when He was born. People refuse His offer of forgiveness and salvation, choosing to tremble in their own uncertainties.

III. THE PROPHET'S ANSWER: MATTHEW 2:5-6

"In Bethlehem in Judea," they replied, "for this is what the prophet has written: 'But you, Bethlehem, in the land of Judah, are by no means least among the rulers of Judah; for out of you will come a ruler who will be the shepherd of my people Israel.'"

Although Herod was mystified, he got his answer quickly, because the Jewish scholars were well aware of what was recorded in Micah 5:2. "Bethlehem . . . of Judah" means that it was located in the territory assigned to Jacob's son Judah. There was another Bethlehem in Zebulun (Josh. 19:15). "Rulers of Judah" refers to the elders, or heads of families.

Micah's prophecy not only foretold where the Messiah was to be born, but it also predicted His coming reign. The prophecy combines the compassion of Christ ("the shepherd") with his power ("a ruler").

Matthew's record stresses the fulfillment of Old Testament prophecies about Jesus. First, His virgin birth (Matt. 1:22-23 and Isaiah 7:14), and then His birthplace and coming reign. Of course, the people He came to rule ended up rejecting Him (John 1:11), but one day "every knee [shall] bow, in heaven and on earth and under the earth, and every tongue confess that Jesus Christ is Lord, to the glory of God the Father" (Phil. 2:10-11).

IV. HEROD'S TREACHERY: MATTHEW 2:7-8

Then Herod called the Magi secretly and found out from them the exact time the star had appeared. He sent them to Bethlehem and said, "Go and make a careful search for the child. As soon as you find him, report to me, so that I too may go and worship him."

Herod's sheer and murderous duplicity surfaces in his plan to use the Magi to report their findings to him. He didn't want to worship the child; he wanted to kill Him. Of course, he could not trust anyone in his court with this plot, so he invited the Magi for a secret interview.

Herod had to know the age of the baby, so he could kill all the children of that age in Bethlehem and be sure to eliminate all possible rivals to his throne. That's why he wanted to know when the star had first appeared to the Magi. As a result, all male babies under two years of age were killed (vs. 16). This gives us an important clue about how old Jesus was when the Magi came to visit him.

V. THE WISE MEN'S WORSHIP: MATTHEW 2:9-12

After they had heard the king, they went on their way, and the star they had seen in the east went ahead of them until it stopped over the place where the child was. When they saw the star, they were overjoyed. On coming to the house, they saw the child with his mother Mary, and they bowed down and worshiped him. Then they opened their treasures and presented him with gifts of gold and of incense and of myrrh. And having been warned in a dream not to go back to Herod, they returned to their country by another route.

Whatever special star the Magi saw, they followed it straight to the house (not the stable) where Mary, Joseph, and the baby were living. Perhaps they had lost sight of their heavenly guide while they were in Jerusalem. But, having found their way again and their desired destination, they broke into great rejoicing.

Seeing the child and His mother, the Magi prostrated themselves in worship. How ironic that the representatives of the Gentiles, rather than the Jewish religious leaders, were so quick to worship the baby. How paradoxical, also, that although the wise men came to see and worship a royal child, they saw nothing unusual about Him. Quite the opposite. This king was born in utter poverty among the poor people of the land, not among the mighty in Jerusalem

Nevertheless, the Magi knew. "They bowed down and worshiped him" (vs. 11). They did not worship Joseph and Mary. Joseph isn't even mentioned here.

Their worship proves that their quest was much more than an inquisitive scientific adventure. God, who had given them clear signs in heaven, evidently had also shined a light in their hearts, to give them some knowledge of who this baby was. Otherwise, why would they have worshiped Him?

Next, the Magi gave their gifts to the child. Of course, sacrificial giving is the essence of worship, and their gifts represented enormous sacrifices. Christian tradition has attached spiritually symbolic importance to their gifts:

- Gold was the gift for a king, and it represents Christ as king. It tells us that our response to Jesus should be complete submission to His lordship.
- Frankincense was a gift for a priest. It was used in the temple worship as a sweet perfume. Jesus is the Christian's merciful, sympathetic, high priest (Heb. 2:17-18; 4:14-16; 7:11-28). He opened the way to God.
- Myrrh was the gift for a person about to die. It was used in embalming. It was used on the body of Jesus (John 19:39). Thus, the wise men showed by this gift that Jesus Christ came into the world to die for sinners. Myrrh depicts our suffering Savior.

At their audience with Herod, the wise men had had no way of knowing that he did not intend to worship the baby but was planning to kill him. They were unaware that they, too, might have been executed, if they reported their findings to him as he had ordered (vs. 8).

Their ecstasy and thanksgiving in worship was shattered by God's warning for them not to go back to Jerusalem. They had to find a safe escape route back to the East, probably wondering what the king was planning to do.

Discussion Questions

1. What kind of searches are people on today? What do they find?
2. How does God guide people to find and worship Jesus today?
3. Why do you think the chief priests and teachers of the law were so uninterested in finding their newborn king?
4. What keeps people from discovering the real Jesus?
5. What causes people to pretend to be worshipers of Jesus, especially on religious holidays?
6. Since worship means sacrifice, what sacrifices can Christians bring to Jesus?

Contemporary Application

The birth of Jesus produced a wide spectrum of reactions—some threatened; some uncaring; some joyful and eager—that we still see today. Like Herod, some people are openly hostile to Jesus. They see Him as a threat to the way they want to run their lives.

Then there are some like the chief priests and teachers of the law. They know the religious routine, but are unmoved by it. They even have some Bible knowledge, but they couldn't care less. Jesus simply isn't for them in any life-changing way. They are content to be religious, but not converted.

However, the Magi gave adoring worship to Jesus. When they got information about Him, they acted on it. They were not the same. It took their time and persistence, but they found Christ. They gave Him the noblest gifts they could bring. Can we afford to do anything less? When we realize God's love at Christmas, shouldn't we respond with wonder, love, and praise?

The Twelve Disciples

Scripture

Background Scripture: *Matthew 4:18-22; 9:9-12; 10:1-4*

Scripture Lesson: *Matthew 4:18-22; 9:9-12; 10:1-4*

Key Verse: *"Come, follow me," Jesus said, "and I will make you fishers of men."* Matthew 4:19

Background Scripture for Children: *Matthew 4:18-22; 9:9-12; 10:1-4, 7*

Scripture Lesson for Children: *Matthew 4:18-22; 9:9-12; 10:1-4, 7*

Lesson Aim

To discover and fulfill our calling as Christ's disciples.

Lesson Setting

Time: *A.D. 28*
Place: *Sea of Galilee*

Lesson Outline

The Twelve Disciples

   I. The Call of the Fishermen: Matthew 4:18-22
      A. Peter and Andrew: vs. 18
      B. The Challenge and Response: vss. 19-20
      C. James and John: vs. 21
      D. Their Obedience: vs. 22
  II. The Call of Matthew: Matthew 9:9-12
      A. The Tax Collector: vs. 9
      B. The Dinner Party: vss. 10-11
      C. Christ's Challenge: vs. 12
 III. The Sending of the Twelve: Matthew 10:1-4

Introduction for Adults

Topic: *Thinking about Commitment*

Commitment has gone out of style. Marriages fail because vows are not kept. Families fall apart. Careers suffer. Public confidence ebbs when leaders don't keep their word.

Yet, the heart of Christian faith is life-long commitment. The apostle Paul prayed that the Corinthians would not "be led astray from your sincere and pure devotion to Christ" (2 Cor. 11:3). Defection is always a possibility, because "Satan himself masquerades as an angel of light" (2 Cor. 11:14).

Jesus reminds us that we are committed to Him first and foremost, not to some religious routine that costs us only one hour a week. When we fall in love with Jesus, our commitment will remain strong.

Introduction for Youths

Topic: *Follow Me*

Jesus asked the disciples to follow Him, to be with Him, to be His helpers and companions. Too often, it seems, we make the Christian faith into something esoteric, mystical, and complicated. Young people can easily grasp the concept of Christian discipleship when we show them how clear Jesus made it.

Being Christ's follower sets Christian teenagers apart. To follow Him like the disciples did means making decisions by His will, not ours. It means being a loyal, dedicated servant, willing to take risks. It does not mean abandoning your brains; it means using them for God's glory. What is especially beneficial is knowing the relief Christ's guidance and peace can bring, of having a sure hope in a confusing world.

Concepts for Children

Topic: *Jesus Calls Twelve Disciples*

1. Jesus invites us to be His friends and companions.
2. To be a disciple means to be a learner and follower.
3. Those who follow Jesus obey His words and trust Him for salvation.
4. It is valuable to be able to tell others that Jesus is God's Son.
5. God gives us many chances to show what it means to follow Jesus.
6. Jesus keeps on loving, helping, and teaching us.

The Lesson Commentary

I. THE CALL OF THE FISHERMEN: MATTHEW 4:18-22

A. Peter and Andrew: vs. 18

As Jesus was walking beside the Sea of Galilee, he saw two brothers, Simon called Peter and his brother Andrew. They were casting a net into the lake, for they were fishermen.

Peter occupied center stage during the life and ministry of Jesus, and he was the premier evangelist until the apostle Paul came along. In effect, the early church in Jerusalem was built on his fearless preaching. He also wrote two letters in the New Testament, and probably was the source of Mark's Gospel.

Matthew's account of the calling of Peter and Andrew appears to be abrupt, because he did not tell what happened prior to this encounter. To get the full story, we have to look at additional facts from both John and Luke. Apparently Peter's first contact with Jesus came through the testimony of his brother Andrew, who had been impressed by the witness of John the baptizer (John 1:40-42). At their first meeting Jesus told Simon (which means "hearing") that He would get a new name, Cephas, or "rock." Cephas is the Aramaic and Peter is the Greek and Latin form. Andrew, Peter, and Philip came from the town of Bethsaida on the northern shore of the lake of Galilee.

Luke told about a fascinating encounter between Jesus and Peter during which Jesus gave the veteran fisherman a lesson in how to catch fish (Luke 5:1-11). Peter recognized something special about Jesus, not just from the huge catch of fish but also from His teaching. He confessed his own sinfulness to Jesus on the spot, but Jesus allayed his fears and called him to be one of His disciples.

Peter was an impulsive, warm-hearted, aggressive man and probably the oldest of the twelve disciples and their natural leader.

B. The Challenge and Response: vss. 19-20

"Come, follow me," Jesus said, "and I will make you fishers of men." At once they left their nets and followed him.

Jesus spoke both a command and a promise. His command was simple and clear, but very demanding. He asked Peter and Andrew to follow Him, that is, to be His learners and disciples. Mark added the significant fact that Jesus first of all wanted these people to be His friends and companions—"that they might be with him" (Mark 3:14).

But this kind of friendship was so radical that it required a change of vocation. Instead of fishing for a living, Jesus promised them a new kind of career, "fishing" for people. Peter and Andrew could not have grasped the implications of that statement on the spot. We read back into it and understand that it was a call to the work of evangelism. Not until after the Holy Spirit came upon Peter and the others on the day of Pentecost did they realize their commission.

Whatever Peter and Andrew may have understood about their new careers, they did realize that they had to quit their old ones. They traded security, income, and comfortable homes for the lives of itinerant preachers and healers.

What makes their obedience even more astounding is that apparently Jesus gave them no details about what was coming. He did not reveal a daily schedule, or discuss a vision statement, or tell them what their specific duties would be. They were to follow and learn from their companionship with Him.

Ever since, "leaving your nets" has become a metaphor for those who have sensed God's call to a full-time ministry in Christian service. But the call to discipleship is much broader than that. Christ's call is first of all to be His follower, His learner, His disciple, His friend and companion. Once that is settled, He issues new directions for life, whether in a new vocation or in the same one.

C. James and John: vs. 21

Going on from there, he saw two other brothers, James son of Zebedee and his brother John. They were in a boat with their father Zebedee, preparing their nets. Jesus called them . . .

The shores of Galilee bustled with fishermen. Jesus had found Simon and his brother Andrew throwing their net into the lake (vs. 18). Next, He found two other brothers, James and John, working in their father's boat, preparing to head into the lake for the day's catch. He also "called them," that is, invited them to follow Him and fish for people (vs. 19).

Later on, James and John—plus Peter—became Christ's inner circle. They saw Him raise Jairus's daughter and witnessed Christ's transfiguration. They were close to Him in the garden of Gethsemane.

Jesus gave James and John an illuminating nickname, "sons of thunder" (Mark 3:17). Jesus rebuked them for their impetuousness and for failing to understand His mission. At one point they wanted Him to destroy a Samaritan village which rejected Him. Another time, James and John asked for special places of honor in Christ's kingdom. Jesus told James that he would "drink the same cup" that He was going to drink. This prophecy was fulfilled when King Herod Agrippa I killed James with the sword (Acts 12:2).

Scholars think John was younger than James. They were cousins of Jesus on his mother's side. Zebedee was a person of some means, because he had hired servants (Mark 1:20).

John is not mentioned by name in the Gospel of John, although the sons of Zebedee are referred to in John 21:2. However, almost surely John was "the disciple whom Jesus loved" (John 21:20). Jesus entrusted his mother Mary to John's care at the cross.

In Acts, we find that Peter and John bore the main brunt of Jewish opposition to the early church. Both men showed outstanding boldness and courage. According to tradition, John took Mary to live in Ephesus. From there he was eventually banished to Patmos, where he wrote the Book of Revelation.

D. Their Obedience: vs. 22

. . . and immediately they left the boat and their father and followed him.

James and John acted immediately, just as Peter and Andrew had done. They dropped their work on their nets, left the boat and their father, and followed Jesus. Zebedee must have been astonished when he saw them leave.

Their quick obedience assumes they had heard Jesus preach (4:17; Mark 1:14-15). Also, in Luke's account we learn that Jesus had also begun to heal many people (Luke 4:38-44). Therefore, people in Capernaum and throughout Galilee had been alerted that a new prophet had arisen. Many had responded to John the Baptist's preaching to get ready for the Messiah's coming. Peter, Andrew, James, and John had been spiritually prepared for this moment when their lives took on a new direction.

II. THE CALL OF MATTHEW: MATTHEW 9:9-12

A. The Tax Collector: vs. 9

As Jesus went on from there, he saw a man named Matthew sitting at the tax collector's booth. "Follow me," he told him, and Matthew got up and followed him.

Matthew, also called Levi, is never identified (inside the book) as the writer of the Gospel bearing his name, but the early church attributed it to him without dispute. Practically nothing is known about him, except his name, occupation, and that he was a member of the original 12 called by Jesus. After the listing of his name in Acts 1:13, he disappears from the record of the early church, although there are some legends about him.

The story of his call by Jesus is also recorded in Mark 2:13-17 and Luke 5:27-32. They emphasize his obedience and his willingness to reach others for Jesus.

His call occurred in Capernaum (9:1) just after Jesus healed the paralytic. On the surface it looks as if Jesus more or less accidentally laid His eyes on Matthew and called him on the spur of the moment. However, Jesus had been teaching and healing in and around Capernaum for some time. He had had many chances to see Matthew at work in his conspicuous tax collector's "office"—which was more like a roadside stand than a modern office. Capernaum was in the territory of Herod Antipas, so Matthew was not collecting taxes directly for the Romans. He served Herod.

Capernaum was a great meeting place of roads. The great road from Egypt to Damascus led through Capernaum. People went there for business. Matthew probably was a customs officer who collected duty on trade goods leaving or entering Herod's territory.

People generally despised tax collectors, because the system was abused. We don't know if Matthew cheated people. But typically, a tax collector often added a "tax" to the tax owed to the government, which he put in his own pocket.

The call of the tax collector proves what the apostle Paul declared later on: "He [God] chose the lowly things of this world and the despised things . . . so that no one may boast before him" (1 Cor. 1:28-29). Matthew's call encourages people who feel they are beyond God's help.

As simply and directly as Jesus had called him, Matthew obeyed. The implication here is that he did much more than go for a walk with Him. He left his lucrative job and abandoned everything for the sake of following Jesus. He gave up the security of his position for the insecurity he shared with Jesus (Luke 9:58).

How do we account for his obedience? Possibly Matthew was impressed that Jesus accepted despised people like himself. For whatever reasons, Matthew did what Jesus asked. He lost income and security, but gained honor and purpose.

B. The Dinner Party: vss. 10-11

While Jesus was having dinner at Matthew's house, many tax collectors and "sinners" came and ate with him and his disciples. When the Pharisees saw this, they asked his disciples, "Why does your teacher eat with tax collectors and 'sinners'?"

The first thing Matthew did as a disciple was to serve as a go-between between his old friends and his new friend and leader. He did this very simply: he arranged a dinner party at his house. Luke called it a great feast (Luke 5:29).

Of course, he invited Jesus and His disciples. But he also invited the "wrong" people—tax collectors and sinners like himself. Probably this made the other disciples quite uncomfortable. It certainly stirred up the self-righteous Pharisees. They disdained any association with these people, so they questioned why Jesus allowed Himself to be contaminated by them. Such a role did not befit their concept of a holy prophet, and certainly not the Messiah.

However, Matthew thought this was the best way for his friends to meet Jesus. Matthew did not wait until he had received some training. He just did what he knew how to do, throw a party. And in so doing, he gave us a wonderful example of how Christ's disciples can serve Him in the ordinary events of life.

The party also tells us what kind of a person Matthew was. He was outgoing and willing to take risks, even if it meant offending the religious establishment.

C. Christ's Challenge: vs. 12

On hearing this, Jesus said, "It is not the healthy who need a doctor, but the sick."

Of course, Jesus heard the question by the Pharisees. Their question hit the heart of His mission. He tried to clarify the issue by dividing people into the healthy and the sick. These were metaphorical terms for the self-righteous Pharisees and the tax collectors and "sinners."

The "healthy" Pharisees really were sick, of course, but they did not know they needed a doctor. The "sick" sinners at least knew they needed a doctor. Jesus said He came to heal those who knew they were sick and needed a doctor—people like Matthew.

III. THE SENDING OF THE TWELVE: MATTHEW 10:1-4

He called his twelve disciples to him and gave them authority to drive out evil spirits and to heal every disease and sickness. These are the names of the twelve apostles: first, Simon (who is called Peter) and his brother Andrew; James son of Zebedee, and his brother John; Philip and Bartholomew; Thomas and Matthew the tax collector; James son of Alphaeus, and Thaddaeus; Simon the Zealot and Judas Iscariot, who betrayed him.

Jesus was not a leader who demanded more of His followers than He was willing to do Himself. Matthew gave a summary of His work (9:35-38), then described how He sent out His twelve disciples.

Jesus taught, preached, and healed. That was also the mission He gave His disciples. His main purpose was to prepare people for repentance and faith in Him as Israel's Messiah. Whatever He did, He was filled with compassion (9:36).

What Jesus did, why He did it, and how He did it were intended to be models for His disciples to follow. Before He commissioned them, He told them they were entering a plentiful harvest field with few workers. Then He commanded them to pray for more workers (9:38).

Would-be disciples must not be misled into thinking there are some easy secrets to success. Jesus called discipleship hard work; prayer is hard work. Having made that clear, Jesus sent out the twelve with spiritual authority over evil spirits, disease, and sickness. He also commanded them to preach (10:7).

Discussion Questions

1. Why do you think Jesus called humble, uneducated fishermen rather than educated theologians?
2. What consequences faced Peter, Andrew, James, and John for following Jesus?
3. What does it cost to follow Jesus?
4. What factors did Matthew probably weigh before deciding to follow Jesus?
5. How many things can you do with your resources to be a disciple of Jesus?
6. Into what harvest fields does Jesus send His disciples today?

Contemporary Application

Discipleship leads to mission. Jesus came to seek and to save the lost (Luke 19:10). Therefore, His disciples do the same. As His Father sent Him, so He sends us (John 20:21).

However, over the years too many Christians have assumed that mission is the job of professional clergy and missionaries. They are highly trained people, called by God to work in His harvest. Therefore, other Christians have counted themselves out of this responsibility.

Jesus told His disciples that He would make them fish for people. Then He sent them out to fish. If Christians are not doing that, they and their churches are failing in their divine calling.

The church must recapture the vision of Jesus. When we enlist to be His disciples, we also enlist in hard work and prayer, so that "harassed and helpless [people], like sheep without a shepherd" (Matt. 9:36) will be loved and brought into God's kingdom.

Teachings on Prayer

Scripture

Background Scripture: *Matthew 6:1-15*
Scripture Lesson: *Matthew 6:1-15*
Key Verse: *"But when you pray, go into your room, close the door and pray to your Father, who is unseen. Then your Father, who sees what is done in secret, will reward you."* Matthew 6:6.

Lesson Aim

To beware of pitfalls in prayer and learn to follow Christ's model prayer.

Lesson Setting

Time: A.D. *28*
Place: *The Horns of Hattin, a hill in Galilee*

Lesson Outline

Teachings on Prayer
   I. The Practice of Piety: Matthew 6:1-4
      A. The Wrong Way: vss. 1-2
      B. The Right Way: vss. 3-4
  II. The Practice of Prayer: Matthew 6:5-8
      A. Do Not Show Off: vss. 5-6
      B. Do Not Use Many Words: vss. 7-8
 III. The Model Prayer: Matthew 6:9-13
      A. God's Name: vs. 9
      B. God's Will: vs. 10
      C. Daily Needs: vs. 11
      D. Forgiveness: vs. 12
      E. Protection: vs. 13
 IV. Prerequisite for Prayer: Matthew 6:14-15

Introduction for Adults

Topic: *Thinking about Prayer*

People learn new skills all the time. People like to talk about how they learned to use a computer. We laugh about the mistakes we made and how we inadvertently wiped out some important material. We keep taking refresher courses to upgrade our computer skills.

Learning to pray is like that, because praying is a new skill. It's not something you fall into. Prayer is a developed discipline. Prayer takes the same kind of training and discipline. While we pray, we learn more about it and find new pleasure in it, but it requires time and concentration.

Prayer is not like technology, however, because anyone can pray. That's because prayer is having a talk with God. But for the conversation to be satisfying, we have to think about what we say and how we say it. We have to use our best thoughts and skills, conditioned by a proper attitude.

Introduction for Youths

Topic: *Private Conversation*

The concept of prayer as conversation with God has tremendous appeal. We have to take prayer out of the realm of stuffy, pious jargon. We have to show teenagers that prayer is not limited to the people who do the praying in public services. Rather, prayer pleases God because it shows that we love Him and His fellowship.

Many times Christian teens pray for the first time on retreats, or in small campus and church groups. They touch levels of intimacy in prayer because they are vulnerable to each other, more so than many adults. Therefore, our concern is not with the right words and tone of voice, but with honesty and integrity. That's what Jesus talked about.

Our goals for youth are to develop strong daily prayer habits, as well as quality prayer in fellowship groups. Then as they pray, they can develop the needed spiritual muscles for standing up in spiritual battles.

Concepts for Children

Topic: *Jesus Teaches about Prayer*

1. Jesus said that make-believe prayers are useless because we can't fool God.
2. God loves to hear His children talk to Him in prayer.
3. God wants us to talk to Him about all of our fears and needs.
4. When we ask God to forgive our sins, we must also forgive those who have wronged or hurt us.
5. It is helpful to pray with our parents and friends.
6. By setting aside a special time to pray every day, we grow stronger in our faith.

The Lesson Commentary

I. THE PRACTICE OF PIETY: MATTHEW 6:1-4

A. The Wrong Way: vss. 1-2

"Be careful not to do your 'acts of righteousness' before men, to be seen by them. If you do, you will have no reward from your Father in heaven. So when you give to the needy, do not announce it with trumpets, as the hypocrites do in the synagogues and on the streets, to be honored by men. I tell you the truth, they have received their reward in full."

Jesus began this section of His Sermon on the Mount by giving a general warning against doing good deeds simply for the sake of earning public approval. This, of course, is what the religious leaders loved to do, especially in their giving (vss. 2-4) and in their praying (vss. 5-8).

"To be seen by men" (vs. 1) exposed the motives of the Pharisees and teachers of the law, but the danger was not limited to them. From the Galilean hillside, Jesus warned His disciples and the crowds of ordinary people as well.

Jesus knew that even the best of deeds can be tarnished by the human desire to show off. The desire to elevate oneself before others is so deeply ingrained that it permeates both our worship and our deeds of charity.

Jesus warned against giving for the sake of earning the approval of onlookers. Those who set out to impress others with their charity and piety will get what they want—the notice and praise of people. That is their reward; it goes no further. Their piety does not impress God.

B. The Right Way: vss. 3-4

"But when you give to the needy, do not let your left hand know what your right hand is doing, so that your giving may be in secret. Then your Father, who sees what is done in secret, will reward you."

Jesus commanded that gifts should be given privately. The motivation for giving should be to obey and please God. God not only sees our acts of giving and praying, He knows what inspires them. God knows what is in our hearts when we make our offerings and when we pray.

God "sees what is done in secret" and He rewards God-honoring gifts and prayers. His reward is not specified, but it was promised by Jesus (vss. 4, 6).

II. THE PRACTICE OF PRAYER: MATTHEW 6:5-8

A. Do Not Show Off: vss. 5-6

"And when you pray, do not be like the hypocrites, for they love to pray standing in the synagogues and on the street corners to be seen by men. I tell you the truth, they have received their reward in full. But when you pray, go into your room, close the door and pray to your Father, who is unseen. Then your Father, who sees what is done in secret, will reward you."

First, Jesus spoke against praying to impress people. The word "hypocrites" means play-actors or show-offs. The public could immediately identify these religious figures. They knew the people who loved to make an impression of piety on their peers. They made sure that people noticed them praying, both in the synagogues and on the streets.

Jesus described the appropriate attitude and setting for prayer. In effect, the hypocrites prayed to the public, not to God. The crucial issue is not where you pray, but to whom you pray. To guard against praying for one's reputation, it is much better to pray alone in secret where no one can see you.

This wise counsel is not a directive against public prayers, but against hypocrisy. Jesus did not address corporate Christian worship, but the motivation of those who paraded their piety for public acclamation. Public prayers are numerous in Scripture. The risk Jesus addressed was praying for outward show.

Jesus contrasted being seen by people in public with being seen by God in private. "Pray to your Father, who is unseen," He said. Although we can't see God, He can see us. The reward for such praying is not the Father's dispensing favors to us. The reward is meeting God Himself. Prayer is its own reward. Such a reward far surpasses any temporary adulation from one's peers.

B. Do Not Use Many Words: vss. 7-8

"And when you pray, do not keep on babbling like pagans, for they think they will be heard because of their many words. Do not be like them, for your Father knows what you need before you ask him."

Jesus first warned against being hypocritical in prayer, then He warned against vain repetition. God does not answer prayer in proportion to how long we pray. Long, repetitious prayers are based on the faulty assumption that this is how to gain God's attention or favor. That was how the pagans prayed.

In praying to their idols, the pagans heaped up empty phrases, saying the same words over and over again. In reality, their words went nowhere and achieved nothing. (See also 1 Kings 18:25-29.)

Of course, the apostle Paul taught that Christians are to pray constantly (1 Thess. 5:17). But that does not mean using the same words and phrases. Prayer is hard work, requiring intense concentration. Prayer is not the routine mouthing of pious phrases and generalities. It must be specific and personal.

Another reason not to emulate the pagans is that God knows our needs. Pagan idol worshipers made repeated requests for what they wanted, but this is unnecessary because God knows our needs. As a wise, loving heavenly Father, He knows our circumstances precisely.

III. THE MODEL PRAYER: MATTHEW 6:9-13

A. God's Name: vs. 9

"This, then, is how you should pray: 'Our Father in heaven, hallowed be your name . . .'"

After telling the people how not to pray, Jesus gave them a model prayer to follow, the so-called Lord's Prayer, which, incidentally, can easily become the kind of vain habit Jesus warned against. He said, "This is how to pray," not, "This is exactly what I want you to say every time you pray."

First, Jesus said, we are to address our prayers to God the Father. God is the Father of all by creation, but also Father in a unique way to those born again by faith in His Son. True prayer grows out of this special Father-child relationship. Through Christ, we become His sons and daughters and God welcomes us into His family. Our great privilege is to know and address Him as our Father.

God's children are to keep His name holy ("hallowed"). God's name represents the essence of His nature and character. In prayer, we can refresh our minds with thoughts about God's love, majesty, power, and wisdom. In prayer, we can give Him the praise He alone is worthy of receiving (Rev. 4:11). Our prayers must begin with a focus on God, to keep us from being filled with our own requests.

B. God's Will: vs. 10

"*. . . your kingdom come, your will be done on earth as it is in heaven.*"

After addressing God and giving Him our praise and glory, our first requests should center on the coming of His kingdom and the accomplishment of His will on earth. All prayer must come under the authority of God's good and perfect will, not our own desires.

Because God's will must be the supreme desire of all of His children, it must be our chief concern in prayer. The kind of prayer that pleases Him answers the basic question: Whose will are we really seeking? Ours or His? "Your will be done" is the basic confession of God's control of our lives.

At the same time, the scope of His control must extend to the entire world that Jesus died to redeem. Therefore, we pray for God's will to be done in our families, schools, businesses, government, and throughout all countries of the globe.

Looking at eternity through the book of Revelation, we know what God's will is in heaven: obedience, praise, glory, honor, and blessing given to the King of kings and Lord of lords. That is what all Christians desire to see done on earth as well.

C. Daily Needs: vs. 11

"*Give us today our daily bread.*"

Proper prayer, according to Jesus, does not begin with requests but with a humble confession of God's great name and the control of His will. Only then are requests appropriate, such as a prayer for God to provide our daily necessities (represented by bread).

The word "daily" is a tough one for Bible translators. They aren't sure if it means "give us bread for today," or "give us bread for tomorrow." Regardless, it's a confession that we depend on God for all of our bodily, material needs. These needs arise every day. We can't eat today and quit. Every day we depend on food that God provides, even though we may think it comes from the super-market.

Of course, according to this model, we can rightfully ask God for much more than our food. This request confirms that vs. 8 does not rule out our asking God for our necessities, even though He knows all our needs. "Bread," however, cannot be expanded to include all of our luxuries and desires. Very simply, Jesus said it's all right to ask for enough to live on one day at a time. This rule wipes out selfish praying for all kinds of things we don't really need.

Actually, when we begin by worshiping God's great name, and yield our wills to His, we will lose much of what could be considered selfish desires.

D. Forgiveness: vs. 12

"Forgive us our debts, as we also have forgiven our debtors."

Jesus moved from asking God to give us our basic physical necessities to a request for forgiveness. The clear implication is that everyone needs forgiveness because everyone has offended a holy, righteous, just God. The request has been translated, "Forgive us the wrong we have done" (NEB). In the context, these wrongs, sins, or transgressions have been committed against other people, but the ultimate offense is against God. The Jews thought of these sins as debts on one's moral balance sheet.

Rarely, if ever, do we enjoy the pleasure of having a debt forgiven. Banks do not forgive mortgages, and credit card companies do not forgive our accumulated balances. But Jesus opened a vast new realm of spiritual pleasure when He taught that we can ask God to lift the load of our accumulated transgressions.

He added the important fact that forgiven "debtors" (sinners) must forgive their own debtors (people who sin against us). This aspect of prayer requires us to examine the balance sheet we keep of offenses committed against us. When we ask God to clear our debts, we must also wipe out the "accounts receivable," so to speak—our record of wounds and hurts that we would like to be compensated for. (See further discussion below under vss. 14-15.)

"Forgive us our debts" requires an inward focus of prayer. How have we lived today? Was my record perfect? If not, what went wrong? How did we fail God? Not only how did we break His laws, but how did we fail to do what we should have done?

Prayer forces us to examine our lives in the light of God's holiness and His commands, such as the Ten Commandments and the Sermon on the Mount. The wrongs must be straightened out, first with God and then with others.

This part of prayer really amounts to confession. Christians believe the promise, "If we confess our sins, he is faithful and just and will forgive us our sins and purify us from all unrighteousness" (1 John 1:9). Confession means telling God specifically what sins we have committed. Christians believe they are forgiven on the basis of Christ's death for their sins and His resurrection. When people turn to Christ in faith, He forgives all their sins. As they live as Christians, they find and enjoy daily experiential forgiveness. Prayer includes confession and rejoicing in God's forgiveness.

E. Protection: vs. 13

"And lead us not into temptation, but deliver us from the evil one."

Another general category of prayer requests covers the many potential risks and dangers we face every day, both physical and spiritual. Here Jesus seemed to emphasize the priority of prayer for one's spiritual integrity, the kind of faith emphasized in Hebrews 3 and 4.

The danger of falling into temptation was vividly illustrated by the fate of the Israelites in the wilderness: "Do not harden your hearts as you did in the rebellion, during the time of testing in the desert" (Heb. 3:8). The antidote is clear: "Let us then approach the throne of grace with confidence, so that we may receive mercy and find grace to help us in our time of need" (Heb. 4:16).

That's the kind of prayer Jesus talked about, fleeing to God's throne when temptation—originated by the devil—assaults us. Christians concerned about their holiness will ask God to take them safely through or away from Satan's enticements to sin. The Bible teaches that Satan seeks to deceive, trap, and devour Christians, so they will mess up their lives.

Left to our own strength, Christians are no match for him. Therefore, prayer is needed to stay away from both the obvious and the hidden snares of the devil. It is hypocritical to make this prayer if we are trying to see how close we can get to sin without being caught.

IV. PREREQUISITE FOR PRAYER: MATTHEW 6:14-15

"For if you forgive men when they sin against you, your heavenly Father will also forgive you. But if you do not forgive men their sins, your Father will not forgive your sins."

In vs. 12, the pattern for prayer follows the basic principle of asking God for forgiveness. That's the Godward aspect of prayer. On the other hand, Jesus taught that it is essential to forgive those who have sinned against us. This is the logic:

If we accept God's forgiveness of our sins through Christ, how can we fail to forgive those who have hurt us? The answer is we can't. Even the thought of not extending forgiveness to others is preposterous. God's great love moved Him to forgive us. How can our love be so small as to fail to forgive others?

To be forgiven by Jesus means we must reach out to others and forgive them. In prayer, this means thinking how we have treated other people and how they have treated us. Did someone do us wrong, cheat us, malign us, gossip about us? How do we feel about these offenses?

Valid prayer is the way to forgive. This should be done every day, so the wounds do not fester. In prayer, we confess our need for God's forgiveness and at the same time we forgive others. Jesus laid down the rule of prayer that asking God for forgiveness is useless unless we have forgiven others.

Discussion Questions

1. How would you put Jesus' rules of prayer in your own words?
2. What are the important principles to follow?
3. Is there a time limit to how long you should pray for something?
4. Should every request be ended with "If it be Your will"?
5. What kinds of prayers would fit "hallowed be Your name"? Give specific examples of prayers of praise in this regard.
6. Why is it harder to worship God in prayer and easier to ask for things for ourselves?

Contemporary Application

In His teaching about prayer, Jesus gave negative and positive examples. Christians have to evaluate our prayer lives according to His standards. Do we pray to be seen as spiritual people? Do we go on praying the same pious phrases? Do we honor God and seek His will first? Do we forgive as we ask God's forgiveness?

These are all-important questions, but a prior question must be raised: Do we pray at all? That is not a silly question, because surveys show that professing Christians on the whole pray very little. In small group discussions, Christians admit it is hard to find time to pray, either by themselves or as families. Invariably, time pressures crowd out prayer.

Looking at the church, it is obvious that prayer meetings have virtually vanished. Even many large churches draw only 20 to 50 people for midweek prayer services. On the other hand, some cities have successfully had "concerts of prayer" where hundreds and sometimes thousands of people gather for a united prayer service.

Today we have to challenge the opening statement by Jesus, "And when you pray . . . ." More likely, it should be, "And if you pray . . . ." That is a tragic indictment of Christian spirituality, especially against the rising tide of religious revival in other religions such as Islam, where praying five times daily is the accepted routine. Let's renew our commitment to pray as Jesus taught.

Miracles of Compassion

Scripture

Background Scripture: *Matthew 9:18-38*
Scripture Lesson: *Matthew 9:18-31, 35-36*
Key Verse: *When [Jesus] saw the crowds, he had compas-
sion on them, because they were harassed and helpless,
like sheep without a shepherd.* Matthew 9:36
Scripture Lesson for Children: *Matthew 9:18-34*
Key Verse for Children: *When [Jesus] saw the crowds,
he had compassion on them.* Matthew 9:36

Lesson Aim

To share the compassion of Jesus for those in need.

Lesson Setting

Time: A.D. *28*
Place: *Capernaum in Galilee*

Lesson Outline

Miracles of Compassion
I. Jesus Raised Jairus's Daughter: Matthew
   9:18-19, 23-26
   A. *Jairus Came to Him: vs. 18*
   B. *Jesus Responded: vs. 19*
   C. *He Encountered Death: vss. 23-24*
   D. *He Raised the Girl: vss. 25-26*
II. Jesus Healed the Woman with a Hemorrhage:
   Matthew 9:20-22
   A. *The Woman's Need and Faith: vss. 20-21*
   B. *Jesus Healed Her: vs. 22*
III. Jesus Healed the Blind Men: Matthew
   9:27-31
   A. *Their Appeal: vss. 27-28*
   B. *Jesus' Response: vss. 29-31*
IV. Jesus' Example: Matthew 9:35-36
   A. *He Taught, Preached, and Healed: vs. 35*
   B. *He Was Compassionate: vs. 36*

Introduction for Adults

Topic: *Thinking about Wholeness*

Sickness and death confront us on every hand. Even though we try to hide the realities, we cannot escape them. The battle against aging, disease, and death occupies our greatest minds and consumes vast resources.

Jesus constantly encountered people who were sick, blind, crippled, and dying. He did not dodge them but went out of His way to help them. Since then, His followers have done likewise. Filled with compassion as He was, they have been at the forefront in ministries of healing and caring.

However, each of us in our own circle must claim in fresh ways our responsibilities. Jesus heals today. He touches people through Christians who demonstrate His compassion, love, and power.

Introduction for Youths

Topic: *Healing Touch*

Jesus loves to heal. That's the word we must spread among teenagers. Many of them hurt very painfully—not always because of their own misdeeds, but also because of the misdeeds of others, including their own parents.

Jesus can heal body, soul, and spirit. He brings wholeness to those who seek Him. He responds to rugged faith, no matter how desperate our needs. No one's case is beyond the love and help of Jesus.

Our greatest task is to keep Jesus the center of our appeal to youth. Not rules, not dogma, not religious organization. We have to strip away all the arguments and tangents, so people will be brought face-to-face with Him.

Concepts for Children

Topic: *Jesus Performs Miracles*

1. Jesus responded to the crisis in one family.
2. He loves to answer our cries for help.
3. When our friends are sick, we can pray for them and tell them about Jesus.
4. In our families, we are drawn together in faith with other Christians, to find help and strength.
5. Jesus wants us to be as loving and as compassionate as He was.
6. Our faith grows when we allow Jesus to take care of us.

The Lesson Commentary

I. Jesus Raised Jairus's Daughter: Matthew 9:18-19, 23-26

A. Jairus Came to Him: vs. 18

While he was saying this, a ruler came and knelt before him and said, "My daughter has just died. But come and put your hand on her, and she will live."

After preaching His great sermon (Matt. 5—7), Jesus came down from the hilltop and was met by surging crowds of hurting people. He healed a leper, the paralyzed servant of a Roman centurion, Peter's mother-in-law, and another paralytic. He also cast out demons. Also, Jairus, a ruler of the synagogue in Capernaum, came to Jesus for his daughter.

Matthew did not cite the synagogue ruler's name, which we learn from Mark 5:21-43 and Luke 8:41-56. Jairus is the Greek form of the Hebrew Jair (Num. 32:41), meaning "[The Lord] enlightens." Generally, the synagogue had only one ruler. He conducted the worship and selected those who were to lead the prayer, read the Scriptures, and preach. The synagogue in Capernaum was quite impressive, as even such ruins show us today.

It was highly unusual for a person of such high stature to come to Jesus. Why did he do so? He had heard of Jesus' healings or possibly seen someone healed. At any rate, Jairus's coming shows the high regard he had for Jesus.

He came first as a worshiper, kneeling before Jesus in homage. He was sure Jesus could help him. He told Jesus about the terrible tragedy in his family and urged Him to come and touch his daughter. If Jesus complied, he knew his dead daughter would live again.

Jairus came with the proper attitude to Jesus and gave an honest report of his need. He made a simple, uncomplicated request. He had faith in Christ's power to raise his daughter. His despair drove him to Jesus.

B. Jesus Responded: vs. 19

Jesus got up and went with him, and so did his disciples.

Jesus did not put off Jairus. Instead, He went with him. What seems like the worst news to us does not fall on deaf ears when we bring it to Jesus. We know He hears and gives Himself to our needs. Supremely, He gave Himself for us on the cross (Rom. 8:32). Therefore, nothing—not even death in the family—cuts us off from His love (Rom. 8:38-39).

C. He Encountered Death: vss. 23-24

When Jesus entered the ruler's house and saw the flute players and the noisy crowd, he said, "Go away. The girl is not dead but asleep." But they laughed at him.

Thronged by people on the way to Jairus's house, Jesus nevertheless healed a sick woman (vss. 20-22). When He got to the house, He encountered all the signs of death itself—hired mourners and musicians. Being a person of considerable social stature, Jairus would be expected to pull out all the stops.

However, Jesus flouted all of these customs and banished the mourners, explaining that the girl was not dead, but only sleeping. He would not tolerate the signs of death because He knew the outcome. He was about to do something that would make mourning unnecessary.

Jesus' interruption broke all the rules of social behavior. He also violated common sense, so the people laughed at Him. They knew death when they saw it. Here was a case of clear, visible, physical evidence. Perhaps we can excuse them, because they did not know that Jesus could defeat death and raise the dead.

D. He Raised the Girl: vss. 25-26

After the crowd had been put outside, he went in and took the girl by the hand, and she got up. News of this spread through all that region.

Jesus shut Himself in with the girl's parents and three of His disciples (Mark 5:21-43; Luke 8:40-56). Jesus did not prostrate Himself on the girl's body as Elisha had done in 2 Kings 4:34. He did not plead with God in long, agonizing prayers. Instead, He did His mighty work without a struggle. He simply took the dead girl by the hand and restored her to life. This was not a public spectacle, but a quiet demonstration of His divine power.

This was the tone of Jesus' healing ministry. He was not a showman out to attract crowds and gain public approval. Instead, He went to great lengths to discourage miracle-seekers who would misconstrue His mission.

Since then, Christ's miracles of raising the dead have been seriously criticized and rejected. Three times He raised the dead. These were the mightiest displays of His power. Because they defy reason and the physical laws of life and death as we know them, many people have stumbled over these miracles.

II. Jesus Healed the Woman with a Hemorrhage: Matthew 9:20-22

A. The Woman's Need and Faith: vss. 20-21

Just then a woman who had been subject to bleeding for twelve years came up behind him and touched the edge of his cloak. She said to herself, "If I only touch his cloak, I will be healed."

There are marked differences between this unidentified woman and Jairus. Whereas he was a ruler of the synagogue and a person of considerable means, she was a nobody. She had no claims to prominence. However, they were also remarkably similar. Both of them faced seemingly hopeless circumstances: death in the family and an incurable illness. They were also alike in that both threw themselves on Jesus for relief.

This woman had suffered from a hemorrhage for 12 years. Luke, the physician, added that no one could heal her (Luke 8:43). Mark wrote that she was not only getting worse, but also that many doctors were plunging her into poverty (Mark 5:25-26).

Of course, she was also a social outcast. By Levitical law she was to be kept apart, and whoever touched her also would be unclean (Lev. 15:19, 25).

However, because Jesus was surrounded by a throng of people on the street, it was easy for the woman to sneak up behind him and touch the fringe of His garment. She had amazing trust in the love and power of Jesus. Matthew emphasized her deep conviction: "I will be healed."

However, according to Mark and Luke, Jesus drew out her faith. She had to identify herself in the crowd. She had committed a serious offense by Jewish standards by touching Jesus, because that transmitted her ceremonial uncleanness to Him. But her faith was strong enough for the test, and she came forward and fell down before Jesus.

B. Jesus Healed Her: vs. 22

Jesus turned and saw her. "Take heart, daughter," he said, "your faith has healed you." And the woman was healed from that moment.

Jesus spoke to the woman's discouragement: "Take heart, daughter." He expressed great tenderness by calling her "daughter." In the Gospel accounts, this is the only time Jesus used this term. He knew she needed emotional uplift as well as physical healing.

How strongly He reassured her. Jesus did not rebuke her for her audacity, but commended her faith. She would not be judged; she would be healed. Her healing was instantaneous. Jesus attributed it to her faith.

III. JESUS HEALED THE BLIND MEN: MATTHEW 9:27-31

A. Their Appeal: vss. 27-28

As Jesus went on from there, two blind men followed him, calling out, "Have mercy on us, Son of David!" When he had gone indoors, the blind men came to him, and he asked them, "Do you believe that I am able to do this?" "Yes, Lord," they replied.

Stories about healing the blind abound in the Gospels. This one is reported by Matthew alone. Each of these healings by Jesus fulfilled the prophecy of the Messiah in Isaiah 35:5: "Then will the eyes of the blind be opened."

One reason for the many such healings is that eye diseases were rampant in Jesus' time. In this case, two unnamed blind men followed Jesus after He left Jairus's house. They called Him "Son of David," which shows that they believed He was the promised Messiah. They were willing to declare their faith in their quest for healing.

However, Jesus did not respond to them immediately in the street. Somehow, the blind men were able to get into a house with Him. Their faith had to grow beyond their public acclamation of Him. It had to be tested. They were not healed immediately, but were interviewed by Jesus.

The earnestness of their desires and the depth of their faith were thus revealed, and Jesus gave them the healing they sought.

B. Jesus' Response: vss. 29-31

Then he touched their eyes and said, "According to your faith will it be done to you"; and their sight was restored. Jesus warned them sternly, "See that no one knows about this." But they went out and spread the news about him all over that region.

Jesus touched their eyes and they were healed. Jesus attributed their healing to their faith. Faith is the instrument that links us to God's blessings.

Jesus told the healed men not to spread the word about His healing, but they did it anyway. Obviously, Jesus did not intend to hide His own good deeds. He did try to forestall false hopes among the people, that is, a premature rush to make Him king of the Jews, which would only bring down the wrath of Rome.

IV. Jesus' Example: Matthew 9:35-36

A. He Taught, Preached, and Healed: vs. 35

Jesus went through all the towns and villages, teaching in their synagogues, preaching the good news of the kingdom and healing every disease and sickness.

This walk through the streets of Capernaum culminated in Jesus driving out a demon and the startling accusation of the Pharisees that Jesus Himself had demonic power (vss. 32-34). Such incredible unbelief came in the face of all that Jesus had done, proving how stubbornly the Pharisees clung to their outworn traditions and power.

Then Matthew summarized how Jesus spent His time in Galilee between A.D. 27 and 29. His ministry was itinerant rather than settled. He traveled constantly. He visited large towns and small villages. Jesus described His lifestyle this way: "Foxes have holes and birds of the air have nests, but the Son of Man has no place to lay his head" (Luke 9:58).

Jesus refused to accept the usual amenities and rewards of the traveling teacher. He was content with the hospitality of friends. He did not seek personal honor and gain. He did not seek a great reputation. He accepted the risks and uncertainties of travel. He cultivated no congregation. He was at the mercy of what local people could provide.

Jesus' healing also witnessed to His deity and His special relationship to God the Father. When His disciple Philip demanded, "Show us the Father," Jesus pointed to both His teachings and His miracles (John 14:8-11).

B. He Was Compassionate: vs. 36

When he saw the crowds, he had compassion on them, because they were harassed and helpless, like sheep without a shepherd.

Teaching, preaching, and healing have to do with the works of Jesus; compassion has to do with His motivation. Jesus was not turned off by the unceasing demands of harassed, helpless people. When He saw the crowds, He felt their needs keenly. He compared them to sheep without a shepherd.

Today, mental health professionals use almost the same words Jesus did to describe many of the people in their care. They say they are helpless, hopeless, and hapless. Christians have many opportunities to introduce these same people to Jesus, who said, "I am the good shepherd. The good shepherd lays down his life for the sheep. . . . I am the good shepherd; I know my sheep and my sheep know me" (John 10:11, 14).

Jesus then directed His disciples to the crowds (Matt. 9:37-38). He compared them to a plentiful harvest field that lacks workers. He told them to pray for workers to be sent into the harvest fields. Compassion includes prayer. If we are to respond to people's needs with the kind of compassion Jesus had, Christlike actions will emanate from us.

Discussion Questions

1. What compelled Jairus to go to Jesus? What obstacles to faith did he overcome?
2. What compelled the chronically ill woman to touch Jesus? What obstacles to faith did she overcome?
3. What compelled the blind men to cry out to Jesus? What obstacles to faith did they overcome?
4. If you had witnessed these events, how would you have reacted? Why? Would you have felt like the Pharisees, the most outwardly zealous religious people of the day?
5. How do you define compassion? How can Christians show compassion?
6. How can Christians be like Jesus to people suffering from death, illness, and long-term disabilities?

Contemporary Application

Jaded, technologically equipped people respond to stories about Jesus' healings with a yawn, and go about their business as usual. They rarely stop to examine the implications of what Jesus did. However, when God interrupts their plans they start looking for answers.

Jesus raised the dead, healed the sick, cured the blind, and cast out demons. He also taught people what it means to become a child of God and enter His kingdom. Those are the facts Christians are familiar with.

But in contemporary culture Christians often must first establish their credentials as trustworthy, loving friends. People aren't ready to hear about Jesus until they first see some compassion. They seek acceptance from Christians who confess they also are vulnerable to sickness and death.

No one escapes what is common to all people. But when we cast our lot with Jesus, we find hope, strength, peace, and healing. So when Christians go through the valleys, so to speak, they do so not alone but with Jesus who cares for them and enables them. That is the experience they can share with those who do not know Jesus.

Opposition to Jesus

Scripture
Background Scripture: *Matthew 12:22-45*
Scripture Lesson: *Matthew 12:22-32, 38-40*
Key Verse: *"He who is not with me is against me, and he who does not gather with me scatters."* Matthew 12:30.
Scripture Lesson for Children: *Matthew 12:22-32, 35-37*
Key Verse for Children: *[Jesus said,] "He who is not with me is against me."* Matthew 12:30.

Lesson Aim
To beware of the perils of unbelief

Lesson Setting
Time: *A.D. 28*
Place: *Galilee*

Lesson Outline
Opposition to Jesus
  I. The Pharisees' Unbelief: Matthew 12:22-24
     A. Jesus Healed: vss. 22-23
     B. The Pharisees Rejected Him: vs. 24
  II. The Lord's Answer: Matthew 12:25-30
     A. His Appeal to Logic: vss. 25-26
     B. His Direct Challenge: vs. 27
     C. His Announcement: vs. 28
     D. His Illustration: vs. 29
     E. His Warning: vs. 30
  III. Blasphemy against the Holy Spirit: Matthew 12:31-32
  IV. The Sign of Jonah: Matthew 12:38-40
     A. The Pharisees Demanded a Miracle: vs. 38
     B. Jesus Refused: vs. 39
     C. He Predicted His Death and Resurrection: vs. 40

Introduction for Adults

Topic: *Thinking about Jesus' Power*

Uncle Ed was a great one with parlor tricks. Kids were mystified by his sleight of hand. After he died, Ed's wife received a card from one of her nieces, telling what fun she always had watching Uncle Ed's disappearing and reappearing quarters. "How do you do that?" they always asked after a performance, but Uncle Ed's secret power stayed with him.

When people saw Jesus at work, their natural question was, "How does he do that?" They could not imagine that the carpenter's son from Nazareth could heal the sick and raise the dead. Some of them thought He was crazy; others, that He was in league with the devil. Relatively few acknowledged that He was the Messiah, God's Son in the flesh.

Whenever we hear stories about the deeds of Jesus, we are forced to think about His power. His place in history is not in doubt. What people have to decide is whether He came from God and thus drew upon His deity.

Introduction for Youths

Topic: *Trouble!*

Trouble for teenagers grows like dandelions in a spring lawn. It seems to sprout everywhere. Some teens admit their troubles are their own fault. They didn't study very much, so they flunked the test. Others like to blame their troubles on other people, rather than face their own responsibilities.

Troubles are not reserved for bad kids. Some very tough things happen for no apparent reason. In some cases, troubles fall on kids precisely because they try to stay out of trouble by living conscientiously according to Christian values.

Those kinds of trouble are hard to explain, but even harder to explain are the troubles suffered by the Lord Jesus Christ, who lived a perfect life. The story of how people rejected Him, even after He healed the sick and raised the dead, shows how explosive unbelief can be.

When we stand up for Jesus, we can expect the same kind of rejection He faced. However, like Him, we continue to do God's will in faith, knowing that our heavenly Father takes care of us.

Concepts for Children

Topic: *Jesus Meets Opposition*

1. Many people refused to believe in Jesus, even after they saw Him heal the sick and raise the dead.
2. Jesus challenged unbelief and gave people the chance to follow Him.
3. When people see that we love Jesus, they may give us the cold shoulder.
4. Each day gives opportunities to show Christ's love to those who have not yet received Him.
5. When we are hurt by opposition, we can pray and seek the support of Christian friends.
6. Jesus is with us, even when we are ridiculed for our faith.

The Lesson Commentary

I. THE PHARISEES' UNBELIEF: MATTHEW 12:22-24

A. Jesus Healed: vss. 22-23

Then they brought him a demon-possessed man who was blind and mute, and Jesus healed him, so that he could both talk and see. All the people were astonished and said, "Could this be the Son of David?"

After commissioning His disciples (Matt. 10), Jesus continued to teach, preach, and heal throughout Galilee (Matt. 11:1). Crowds flocked after Him and He healed their sick (Matt. 12:15).

On one occasion, they brought to Him a demon-possessed man who was blind and mute. After Jesus healed the man, the people raised the question of His identity. Naturally, they wondered if He was the Messiah, the Son of David.

This was their necessary first step toward salvation and the kingdom of heaven. They had to confess who Jesus was before they could be saved. This was not easy. Other false messiahs had come and gone. How could they be sure Jesus was really the true Messiah?

B. The Pharisees Rejected Him: vs. 24

A heathen god considered by the Jews to be the supreme evil spirit.

But when the Pharisees heard this, they said, "It is only by Beelzebub, the prince of demons, that this fellow drives out demons."

[bee EL zih bub]

However, all was not serene in the halls of religious power. Leaders of the most prestigious and zealous party—the Pharisees—hounded Jesus everywhere He went. Apparently, they did not even consider the possibility that He could be the Messiah. In spite of the evidence, they dismissed Him out of hand.

On this occasion they went much further than refusing to repent. They took the offensive against Him with a nasty attack on the source of His power. They charged him with the basest insult. They said he was driving out demons by the power of the prince of demons, Beelzebub. The name means "lord of the flies." He was an idol worshiped in Ekron. By New Testament times, he was identified as "the prince of demons." When Jesus answered this scurrilous attack, He identified Beelzebub with Satan (vs. 26).

II. THE LORD'S ANSWER: MATTHEW 12:25-30

A. His Appeal to Logic: vss. 25-26

Jesus knew their thoughts and said to them, "Every kingdom divided against itself will be ruined, and every city or household divided against itself will not stand. If Satan drives out Satan, he is divided against himself. How then can his kingdom stand?"

Jesus did not let the Pharisees' accusation stand unchallenged. The issue of His identity and the source of His healing power were so important that the Pharisees—and the crowd of onlookers—needed to hear what He had to say in response. Could the people actually believe what the Pharisees said? Apparently so.

Jesus began by appealing to logic and exposing the foolishness of what the Pharisees had just said. Jesus used common sense in building His defense. He cited three cases that people could easily understand: (1) Countries are torn apart by civil war. (2) Cities fall when people are not united in their defense. (3) Families come to ruin when disputes flare. In each case, internal fighting guarantees defeat. Unity must be maintained for survival.

Jesus appealed to simple logic. If Satan drives out Satan (that is, if it was Satan's power that enabled Jesus to deliver the demon-possessed man), then Satan is fighting against himself and his kingdom will be brought down.

Jesus stated this principle as a rhetorical question. He demanded that the people and the Pharisees think about how ridiculous the charge was.

B. His Direct Challenge: vs. 27

"And if I drive out demons by Beelzebub, by whom do your people drive them out? So then, they will be your judges."

Next, Jesus challenged their own experience with casting out demons. Their society was permeated with fear of evil spirits. Demon possession was a common phenomenon, as we see by the number of times Jesus cast them out.

Exorcism of demons was practiced by many pious men. They invoked God's name, prayed, and fasted. Therefore, Jesus rightly asked why He should be accused of being Satan's tool, when the Pharisees' own followers ("your people," or "your children," that is, people under their teaching) were doing the same.

Another rhetorical question. The Pharisees were hung up. They could not possibly charge their own people with casting out demons by Satan's power. Therefore, Jesus concluded that the Pharisees would be judged by their own followers for making such a charge against Him.

C. His Announcement: vs. 28

"But if I drive out demons by the Spirit of God, then the kingdom of God has come upon you."

Jesus then forthrightly declared that God's kingdom had come in His own person, and the proof of His claim was to be seen in the fact that He cast out demons by God's Spirit, not by Beelzebub. This announcement forced the people to make a choice. Was it Beelzebub or God's Spirit working in Jesus?

The great sign of the kingdom of God was the presence and power of the Holy Spirit. The most conspicuous sign of the power of Satan over people was possession by evil spirits. The surest sign, therefore, of God's kingdom was Jesus revealing the power of the Holy Spirit over evil spirits.

God's kingdom offers release from the powers of darkness. This is why people brought demon-possessed people to Jesus (vs. 22). He knew what was at stake. Deliverance was important for those possessed. Jesus used it to announce God's kingdom. If the people could see beyond the healed man, they could enter God's kingdom.

D. His Illustration: vs. 29

"Or again, how can anyone enter a strong man's house and carry off his possessions unless he first ties up the strong man? Then he can rob his house."

Once again Jesus appealed His case by using an illustration the people could easily understand. He did not give them a theological lecture, but He asked a question that had an obvious answer.

You cannot enter a strong or well-armed person's house and take things unless you first tie up the victim. The "strong man" in this story is Satan. Jesus had plundered his house by delivering the demon-possessed man. To do that, Jesus first had to "tie up" the strong man (make him powerless).

Jesus was not working by Beelzebub's power; He was fighting against him. He was stronger; He could tie him up. Then He could release those he held.

E. His Warning: vs. 30

"He who is not with me is against me, and he who does not gather with me scatters."

Jesus then warned of the serious consequences of being against Him. Again, He appealed to simple logic. If people did not believe in Him, they were against Him. If they did not work with Him, they were frustrating His work.

The primary lesson is that it is impossible to be a fence-sitter about Jesus. There is no middle ground. People are either with Him or against Him. In other words, if we do not say "Yes" to Jesus, we are not being neutral. Unresponsiveness to Jesus puts us in the enemy's camp.

III. Blasphemy against the Holy Spirit: Matthew 12:31-32

"And so I tell you, every sin and blasphemy will be forgiven men, but the blasphemy against the Spirit will not be forgiven. Anyone who speaks a word against the Son of Man will be forgiven, but anyone who speaks against the Holy Spirit will not be forgiven, either in this age or in the age to come."

Not only were the Pharisees and their followers working against Jesus, they were blaspheming the Holy Spirit. By accusing Jesus of using Beelzebub's power, the Pharisees had attributed to Satan the work of the Holy Spirit. This is why Jesus declared that their accusation was unforgivable.

These people were not playing theological games. They had fallen to such a low state that they failed to realize the heinousness of their charge against Jesus. Their attack was not just against Jesus of Nazareth, but against God's Spirit.

The sin which cannot be forgiven must be a diabolical sin. This is what put the Pharisees in mortal danger. Knowing what they did, they chose evil and refused good, and deliberately called good evil. This is not a sin of passion, as when someone utters curse words against God. Neither is it falling into some worldly or sensual lust. The sin against the Holy Spirit seems to be the hatred of what is good and righteous simply because it is good and righteous. Jesus is the ultimate in good and righteousness.

Jesus escalated the stakes with His revelation. The Pharisees had to understand where they were spiritually. If they persisted in rejecting Jesus, they lost all hope of salvation.

IV. THE SIGN OF JONAH: MATTHEW 12:38-40

A. The Pharisees Demanded a Miracle: vs. 38

Then some of the Pharisees and teachers of the law said to him, "Teacher, we want to see a miraculous sign from you."

After warning the Pharisees about blaspheming the Holy Spirit, Jesus called them to repent (12:22-37). He especially wanted them to repent of sinning by their words (vss. 36-37). This was probably a reference to their charge against Him.

Incredibly, they asked for a miracle. Of course, they had seen His miracles for themselves, so why did they ask for another one? Perhaps they wanted to dodge the very personal appeal Jesus had made to them to get their hearts right. Jesus had called them a "brood of vipers" (vs. 34), so they were in no mood to respond with a confession of their sins.

Or, perhaps they were looking for a different kind of "sign" than the healing of the sick and demon-possessed. By "sign" they meant something conspicuous from heaven, as if a portent in the clouds carried more weight than a healing miracle. Maybe they could have wanted something like the fire that came down from heaven after Elijah's prayer on Mount Carmel.

B. Jesus Refused: vs. 39

He answered, "A wicked and adulterous generation asks for a miraculous sign! But none will be given it except the sign of the prophet Jonah."

Jesus minced no words in responding to this ridiculous request. He exposed their hypocrisy by calling them a "wicked" and "adulterous" generation. Despite their outward show of religious zeal, their hearts were far from God. Religious orthodoxy did not save them. They were trying to hide behind their religious masks when they asked for a sign.

Their spiritual ears were stopped and their spiritual eyes blinded. Of course, there were notable exceptions in Israel, such as godly Elizabeth and Zechariah, Joseph and Mary, and Simeon and Anna (Luke 1—2). When John the Baptist appeared, he awakened the hearts of those looking for the Messiah (Luke 3:15).

C. He Predicted His Death and Resurrection: vs. 40

"For as Jonah was three days and three nights in the belly of a huge fish, so the Son of Man will be three days and three nights in the heart of the earth."

Jesus refused to work a miracle for the Pharisees, but He did give them another sign: Jonah's experience in the belly of the great fish. They all knew this story, of course, but how was Jonah a sign of Jesus?

Jonah spent three days and nights in the fish's belly. Jesus said He would spend three days and nights "in the heart of the earth." This was an obvious reference to His suffering and death.

Could they get the point? Probably not. But this was a noteworthy sign because it showed that opposition to Jesus would continue to mount until the rulers of the Jews demanded that the Romans execute him.

Perhaps if the Pharisees read Jonah's story again, they would see the outpouring of God's Spirit on a wicked city. Perhaps they would respond to Messiah's call to repentance. After Christ's resurrection thousands turned to Christ, among them a large number of priests (Acts 6:7). Were some Pharisees among those who repented?

Discussion Questions

1. How would you describe the Pharisees? What were their spiritual maladies?
2. What are some obstacles to belief in Christ today? How can Christians help to overcome them?
3. From what you observe, why do some people oppose Jesus?
4. How can Christians use opposition as opportunities to help people come to faith?
5. Why was Jesus so confrontational with the Pharisees?
6. What is the best "sign" you can give a person to believe in Christ?

Contemporary Application

Opposition to Jesus and His church breaks out somewhere every day. Even in a country where religious freedom is a constitutional right, some communities are openly hostile to Christians.

Of course, this should not surprise us, because Jesus said persecution would come upon His followers. He told His disciples, "A time is coming when anyone who kills you will think he is offering a service to God" (John 16:2). He said, "In this world you will have trouble. But take heart! I have overcome the world" (John 16:33).

However, we can learn much from how Jesus handled opposition and criticism. He did not back away from it. He was courageous, forthright, and true. He exposed falsehood; He warned about the dangers of unbelief; He called people to repent; He never retaliated in kind against His enemies.

When people attack the church, we can make reasonable defenses without becoming contentious and obnoxious. Above all, we can pray for our persecutors. We can ask God to help us show love to unbelievers. We cannot lose sight of our primary mission, which is to win them to faith in Christ.

Laborers in the Vineyard

Scripture

Background Scripture: *Matthew 19:16—20:16*
Scripture Lesson: *Matthew 20:1-16*
Key Verse: *"So the last will be first, and the first will be last."* Matthew 20:16

Lesson Aim

To beware of greed in kingdom service.

Lesson Setting

Time: A.D. *28*
Place: *Galilee.*

Lesson Outline

Laborers in the Vineyard

  I. The Employer Hired Workers: Matthew 20:1-7
     A. Some Were Hired Early in the Morning: vss. 1-2
     B. Some Were Hired at 9 A.M.: vss. 3-5a.
     C. Some Were Hired Later in the Day: vss. 5b-7.
  II. The Employer Paid His Workers: Matthew 20:8-16
     A. Those Hired Last: vss. 8-9
     B. Those Hired First: vss. 10-12
     C. The Moral of the Story: vss. 13-16

Introduction for Adults

Topic: *Thinking about Rewards*

      What intrigued people, and irritated some, was the way Jesus reversed the commonly accepted values and standards. He really was counter-cultural. For instance, He told people not to accumulate wealth on earth but in heaven. Rather than focus our energies on our health, food, clothing, and jobs, we should focus on God's kingdom. Instead of seeking how to get even with our enemies, we should love them and bless them.

Jesus saw hypocrisy and pride as the mortal enemies of our souls. He was forever trying to get people to look beneath the surface and find out what really motivated them. Even religious pride was bad news.

So, when He explained to His disciples that the first would be last, and the last first, He was contradicting everything they believed. That's just not the way it is in the real world. But in God's kingdom things are quite different.

Looking at the story about how a vineyard owner paid all of his workers fairly, despite how long they had worked, we have to probe our internal motivations. Are we thankful for grace? Or are we angry because God hasn't paid us more?

Introduction for Youths

Topic: *Turn It Around*

The late Leo Durocher, who achieved remarkable success as both a fiery baseball player and manager, coined the phrase, "Nice guys finish last." The concept has been applied not only to sports, but also to the business and professional worlds. According to this perspective, the way to get ahead in life is to use the people under you as steps up the ladder to success.

Young people absorb this philosophy of life because it figures so prominently in what they see, hear, talk about, and read. It's hard for them to believe that another way of life is far superior, especially if they do not see Christ's values demonstrated by their parents.

Therefore, Christian youth face tough choices. What counts most is not how much you accumulate, or how much you are admired by your peers, but in receiving God's grace and His generosity. Can we really trust God to take care of us if we don't behave the way non-Christians do? The central question is what kind of a God we serve.

The story Jesus told helps us to see God as eminently fair. When we follow Him wholeheartedly, He will surprise us by how well He takes care of us.

Concepts for Children

Topic: *Jesus Teaches about Service*

1. God loves to call us to serve Him.
2. In God's kingdom there are many jobs we can do, so we must look for ways to work for Him.
3. Sometimes it seems to us that God is unfair, but we have to trust His goodness and generosity.
4. God loves to give good gifts to His children.
5. When people complain about God, we need to remain cheerful and thankful.
6. When obeying God seems to go against what other people think and do, we can ask Jesus to help us remain true to God.

The Lesson Commentary

I. THE EMPLOYER HIRED WORKERS: MATTHEW 20:1-7

A. Some Were Hired Early in the Morning: vss. 1-2

"For the kingdom of heaven is like a landowner who went out early in the morning to hire men to work in his vineyard. He agreed to pay them a denarius for the day and sent them into his vineyard."

In Matthew's story of Jesus, after His fierce encounter with the Pharisees He told several parables to the large crowds of people (Matt. 13:1-3). After hearing about the beheading of John the Baptist, Jesus went off by Himself to meditate and pray. The crowds followed Him and He healed the sick and fed a crowd of over 5,000 hungry people (14:13-21).

After that, He sent the disciples away in a boat while He prayed by Himself. Then He rejoined them by walking on the water. On the other side, He continued to heal the sick (14:22-36). The Pharisees attacked Him again, this time for ceremonial uncleanness (15:1-2), and once again they demanded "a sign from heaven" (16:1). Drawing apart with His disciples, He elicited Peter's confession that He was the Christ (16:16). This was a major turning point, because from that time on Jesus began to tell His disciples that He would suffer and die in Jerusalem, and be raised from the dead (16:21).

Then came His transfiguration, the healing of a boy afflicted by a demon, and more teachings about the kingdom of heaven. He answered a question about divorce (19:1-12), welcomed little children, and sought to bring a rich young man to eternal life (19:16-30).

Unfortunately, the chapter division after 19:30 breaks the connection between the parable of the vineyard workers and Jesus' answer to Peter's question, "What then will there be for us?" (19:27). Peter and the other disciples obviously were moved by the man's inability to let go of his great wealth. Trying to show how much better he and the disciples were, Peter reminded Jesus that they had left everything to follow Him (vs. 27). So, Peter in effect demanded, "What's in it for us?"

Were the 12 disciples following Jesus so crass as to suggest that their aim was material gain? Their question calls us to examine our own motives. It's entirely possible that some people seek Jesus because they want a better deal in life.

The Gospel is not a magic wand that guarantees success, fortune, and prosperity. Quite the opposite. One thing faith does guarantee is suffering. "For it has been granted to you on behalf of Christ not only to believe on him, but also to suffer for him," the apostle Paul wrote (Phil. 1:29).

On the other hand, faith in Christ guarantees the kind of wealth that transcends what Peter asked Jesus about. God "has blessed us in the heavenly realms with every spiritual blessing in Christ" (Eph. 1:3). We "have been given fullness in Christ" (Col. 2:10).

Peter's question exposed the tendency to put Christian obedience on a tit-for-tat basis—so much work for so much pay. Of course, Jesus knew the carnal spirit underlying Peter's question, so He told the story about the vineyard workers to nip in the bud this wicked spirit of the mercenary. Salvation "is the gift of God—not by works, so that no one can boast" (Eph. 2:8-9). This parable came as a warning of what might happen to the disciples if they were not careful.

It is important to note that before Jesus told this parable He did promise significant rewards to His followers who sacrificed for Him (Matt. 19:28-29). He followed that promise with a warning against self-seeking and jealousy (19:30). The parable was sandwiched between warnings, showing that it was intended to expose the serious danger of pride and self-aggrandizement.

Jesus began His story by comparing the kingdom of heaven to a landowner who went out early in the morning to hire workers for his vineyard. The workers agreed to work all day for one denarius, a Roman silver coin, which was the usual wage for a full day's work from 6 A.M. to 6 P.M. It was also the daily pay of a Roman legionnaire.

This scene illustrated a principle later taught by Jesus in John 15:16: "You did not choose me, but I chose you and appointed you to go and bear fruit." The call to work in the spiritual vineyard comes from God.

B. Some Were Hired at 9 A.M.: vss. 3-5a

"About the third hour he went out and saw others standing in the marketplace doing nothing. He told them, 'You also go and work in my vineyard, and I will pay you whatever is right.' So they went."

The pool of farm workers gathered in the village market square, which resembled today's central hiring hall for day laborers. Of course, most of the men would be called to work at 6 A.M., but in this case the landowner found some still unemployed at 9 o'clock. (The Jews, as well as the Greeks and Romans, divided the time between sunrise and sunset into 12 equal parts. During the summer, of course, some parts would have been longer. In this story, the day was divided into four larger parts.)

The first group was offered the standard wage and accepted it, but the second group agreed to the landowner's promise, not of a specific wage but of a fair wage: "whatever is right." It is important to note this fact, because it became the key to the outcome of the story. By agreeing to his terms, the workers demonstrated their trust in their employer.

Here Jesus gave a slight hint of what was to develop when the day ended and all the workers came to collect their day's pay. The first group saw their work as a contract to fulfill, while the second group apparently was grateful for any work they could get and demonstrated a simple, humble spirit.

Already we see a subtle reflection on Peter's question, "What's in it for us?"

C. Some Were Hired Later in the Day: vss. 5b-7.

"He went out again about the sixth hour and the ninth hour and did the same thing. About the eleventh hour he went out and found still others standing around. He asked them, 'Why have you been standing here all day long doing nothing?' 'Because no one has hired us,' they answered. He said to them, 'You also go and work in my vineyard.' "

Jesus' story took a strange twist. It was highly unusual for a vineyard owner to hire people at noon, 3 P.M., and 5 P.M., just an hour before quitting time. He was surprised to see the men standing around with nothing to do, but he accepted their explanation. No wages were specified, so we can assume that these groups were hired on the same basis as the 9 A.M. group: "I will pay you whatever is right."

Perhaps these men had been out of work so long that they jumped at the chance to work for just a few hours. Perhaps the employer had so much work to do in his vineyard that he needed all the help he could get. If his grapes were ripe, he had to get them harvested immediately.

Of course, in His kingdom, God keeps on calling people to His work all of the time. This story illustrates the principle that some people serve Him a lifetime, while others engage in God's kingdom work at mid-life or later on.

II. The Employer Paid His Workers: Matthew 20:8-16

A. Those Hired Last: vss. 8-9

"When evening came, the owner of the vineyard said to his foreman, 'Call the workers and pay them their wages, beginning with the last ones hired and going on to the first.' The workers who were hired about the eleventh hour came and each received a denarius."

The owner assembled the workers at "evening," that is, 6 o'clock, the traditional time for getting paid. The law of Moses stipulated, "Pay him his wages each day before sunset, because he is poor and counting on it. Otherwise he may cry to the LORD against you, and you will be guilty of sin" (Deut. 24:15).

But in this case the owner did a strange thing. He instructed his foreman to pay first those who had been hired last. Ordinarily, those who had been hired first would be paid first, and so on down the line. This was a clue that Jesus was about to drive home the main point of His story.

Imagine the grumbling among the tired men who had worked all day. Now they had to stand in line for their pay, while those who had worked only one hour got paid first. But that was nothing compared to the shock that followed when they saw the latecomers receive the same amount they had been promised. The men who had worked only one hour received a full day's pay. Probably that was also true for those who had worked three and six hours.

While the first hired workers got angry, the last hired were overjoyed by the employer's generosity. Their trust in him to pay them whatever was right was amply rewarded. What they received felt more like a gift than a wage.

The Lord Jesus Christ is the foreman set over all God's house (Heb. 3:6). The entire administration of God's plan of salvation is in His hands, including the distribution of rewards (Rev. 2:7, 10, 17, 28).

In God's kingdom vineyard, all workers likewise will be called to stand before Him. The apostle Paul labored under the truth that his work for God would be scrutinized (1 Cor. 3:10-15). This motivated him to devote his full energies to advancing the Kingdom by reaching people with the Gospel of Christ. Although this is a sobering reality, all workers for Christ can be sure that He will reward them fairly and generously. This truth applies not only to missionaries and pastors, but to every Christian, no matter what his or her occupation.

B. Those Hired First: vss. 10-12

"So when those came who were hired first, they expected to receive more. But each one of them also received a denarius. When they received it, they began to grumble against the landowner. 'These men who were hired last worked only one hour,' they said, 'and you have made them equal to us who have borne the burden of the work and the heat of the day.' "

As the parade of workers progressed, those who had waited longest realized that the vineyard owner was indeed quite generous. Their mood changed. Rather than thinking him unfair to give those last hired a full day's pay, they began to dream about how much they would get from him.

Obviously, if a man got one denarius for only an hour's work, they might get 12! But they were handed the same single coin, and they were outraged by the seeming unfairness of it all. Rather than feel good about his generosity to those last hired, they complained because they had not been paid more.

Working in God's kingdom vineyard, Christians sometimes think God is unfair. Competitiveness arises in the church and causes great harm. Christians think they do not serve God for pay, but when a fellow Christian gets a higher recognition—or the same recognition for less work—then hard feelings and bitterness cause trouble. Or, if they carry a heavier workload, or work in the "scorching heat," and are not sufficiently praised, they can fall into complaining.

C. The Moral of the Story: vss. 13-16

"But he answered one of them, 'Friend, I am not being unfair to you. Didn't you agree to work for a denarius? Take your pay and go. I want to give the man who was hired last the same as I gave you. Don't I have the right to do what I want with my own money? Or are you envious because I am generous?' So the last will be first, and the first will be last."

Jesus brought the scene to a surprising conclusion. In His story, the vineyard owner responded to his workers' complaint. First, he did not cheat them. They had agreed to work a full day for one denarius and that was what they had received. He was within his rights when he gave all of the workers the same pay. After all, the money was his and he could do with it what he wished.

The owner made his point with questions. Although the answers are not given, we know the workers had to agree with him. Yes, they had agreed to work for one denarius. Of course, he had the right to give the last hired as much as the first hired.

His third question drove to the heart of the matter. Did they envy his generosity? Sadly, yes, which shows how much they misunderstood the character of the one who had called them to work.

However, Jesus took the story to a different conclusion. He showed Peter and the other disciples that by His reckoning, what seems to be unfair becomes fair. "The last will be first." Those hired last were paid first. "The first will be last." Those hired first were paid last. Plus, they all got the same pay.

No, the owner was not unfair, but he was extremely generous. He turned the tables on every worker's expectations. Jesus said that's the way it is in God's kingdom. Human pride and self-seeking go unrewarded. Instead, every worker is treated fairly—more than fairly!—because God's generosity knows no bounds. Trusting God to be fair, workers in His kingdom can rest assured that their labors are not in vain.

Discussion Questions

1. How do you account for Peter's "What's in it for us?" attitude?
2. How does that attitude show up in the church today?
3. What examples do you have of God's calling people to work in His kingdom vineyard?
4. What kinds of things keep people from going to work for Him?
5. Do you think God's rewards are worth the effort of serving Him? Why?
6. In what situations have you been forced to grow spiritually by being treated in a way that seems unfair? By being treated last instead of first?

Contemporary Application

If we're honest with ourselves, probably most of us sympathize with the workers in the vineyard who worked all day and got paid the same as those who had worked only one hour.

We all demand fairness. We find it hard to accept the fact that generosity is not unfairness. Some wealthy person dies and leaves millions to one school, but not to another equally worthy institution.

The same spirit carries over into the church. What's the problem? Pride, envy, self-seeking. When we put price tags on our service for God, we totally misunderstand His nature.

For one thing, God can do as He pleases. He is not accountable to us for how He dispenses His grace. If we really grasped His grace, we would never utter a word, or feel envious, when someone else who seems less deserving also receives a full measure of His grace.

Coming to Jerusalem

DEVOTIONAL READING

Luke 19:29-44

DAILY BIBLE READINGS

Monday January 31
*Luke 9:51-56 Jesus Sets
His Face toward Jerusalem*

Tuesday February 1
*Matthew 21:1-11 Jesus
Enters Jerusalem amid
Hosannas*

Wednesday February 2
*Matthew 21:12-17 Jesus
Cleanses the Temple*

Thursday February 3
*Matthew 21:23-27 Chief
Priests and Elders Resist
Jesus*

Friday February 4
*Matthew 21:33-46 Parable
of the Wicked Tenants*

Saturday February 5
*Matthew 22:23-33 A
Question about the Resur-
rection*

Sunday February 6
*Matthew 22:34-46 The
Greatest Commandment of
All*

Scripture

Background Scripture: *Matthew 21:1-17*
Scripture Lesson: *Matthew 21:1-13*
Key Verse: *"Say to the Daughter of Zion, 'See, your king
comes to you, gentle and riding on a donkey, on a colt,
the foal of a donkey.' "* Matthew 21:5

Lesson Aim

To show more praise to Jesus and to acknowledge
Him publicly as Lord and Savior.

Lesson Setting

Time: *A.D. 30*
Place: *Jerusalem and nearby villages*

Lesson Outline

Coming to Jerusalem

   I. Messiah's Triumphal Entry: Matthew 21:1-11
     A. *His Instructions: vss. 1-3*
     B. *His Humility: vss. 4-5*
     C. *The Crowd's Response: vss. 6-9*
     D. *The City's Response: vss. 10-11*
  II. Messiah's Cleansing of the Temple: Matthew
     21:12-13
     A. *He Drove Out the Buyers and Sellers: vs. 12*
     B. *He Gave His Reasons: vs. 13*

Introduction for Adults

Topic: *The Guidance of the Word*

Pageantry excites people, whether it's a sports event, a political rally, an art or music fair, or even a religious event. In Christendom, Christmas, Easter, and Palm Sunday call for pageantry, including processions, music, and colorful banners. For many years, until politics intervened, the Palm Sunday procession leading from the Mount of Olives into Jerusalem was one of the most exciting religious processions anywhere.

Jesus did not avoid a wild public demonstration when the time was right according to his purposes. His triumphal entry, what we now call Palm Sunday, signified that He threw down the gauntlet to the nation of Israel. Would the people accept His coming as from heaven, from God above? Or would they see Him simply as another imposter, a false messiah?

This lesson forces us to examine our motives in coming to Jesus. If we join the crowd in hailing Jesus, we must accept all He has to offer and the changes He wants to make in our lives.

Introduction for Youths

Topic: *Greatness through Humility*

At first the airline crew thought they were witnessing a hostage-taking event. Three teenagers were guiding a fourth one, who was blindfolded, toward the entrance ramp of the aircraft. The crew was relieved to learn that these fellows actually were celebrating by taking their friend to a surprise destination for the weekend.

It's hard to find creative ways to celebrate, but youth will find them somehow. When the Lord Jesus Christ chose to enter Jerusalem, to make His claim to be the Lord's Messiah as king of Israel, He planned a distinctive public celebration. But He also cut across the grain of accepted ways of achieving military and political popularity. He did not enter riding a stallion accompanied by a retinue of flag-waving, spear-wielding soldiers.

Humility, not pomp and power, was Christ's strength. He chose to identify with the hopes of the common people, gladly accepting their praise and the shouts of little children. The gentleness of Jesus was stronger than the power of weapons and popularity.

Concepts for Children

Topic: *Honoring Jesus*

1. Children love Palm Sunday because of its high drama and pageantry.
2. Jesus loved and encouraged the praise of children.
3. God keeps His promises, even after hundreds of years.
4. Jesus was both gentle and courageous.
5. Jesus did not come as a conquering warrior, but as a suffering Savior.
6. Even some leaders who saw Jesus' love in action refused to worship Him.

The Lesson Commentary

I. MESSIAH'S TRIUMPHAL ENTRY: MATTHEW 21:1-11

A. His Instructions: vss. 1-3

As they approached Jerusalem and came to Bethphage on the Mount of Olives, Jesus sent two disciples, saying to them, "Go to the village ahead of you, and at once you will find a donkey tied there, with her colt by her. Untie them and bring them to me. If anyone says anything to you, tell him that the Lord needs them, and he will send them right away."

According to Matthew's account of the life of Jesus, after His transfiguration He continued to teach His disciples as He moved toward Jerusalem. A number of explosive questions came up about such things as paying taxes, who would be greatest in the kingdom of heaven, what to do if you are sinned against, and divorce. Jesus also encountered a rich young man seeking eternal life and told him to sell all his possessions and follow Him. All the while he told the disciples what was coming: betrayal, condemnation, death, and resurrection.

In Matthew 21:1-5 we have one of the most specific fulfillments of Old Testament prophecy. Matthew's Jewish readers would undoubtedly be struck by the fact that Isaiah and Zechariah had given such a remarkable picture of this incident in the life of the Messiah. This would give the kind of confirmation they needed to show that Jesus of Nazareth really was the promised Messiah.

The triumphal entry began the last week of our Lord's life before His crucifixion. "As they approached Jerusalem" (vs. 1) includes the entire trip from Jericho to Bethany (John 12:1). They arrived Friday evening, had supper at the close of the Sabbath, and left Bethany on Sunday morning.

The immediate walk began from Bethany about two miles east of Jerusalem and led through Bethphage [BETH-fah-jee], a tiny village on the northern road over the Mount of Olives. This four-peaked hill stands 2,723 feet above sea level at its highest rising east of Jerusalem. It is separated from the city by the deep valley of the Kidron. It was named for olive orchards that formerly covered it.

The two disciples sent by Jesus are not identified by Matthew, so we guess they were Peter and John, who seem to have gone together on such errands. Their assignment was a strange one. Nothing like this had been requested before by Jesus.

The disciples could sense impending doom as they approached Jerusalem, based on what Jesus had told them, but we know from later events that they still were not prepared to accept His death. So they were probably trying to fit His request for the donkey and her colt into the melange of ideas accumulated over the past three years.

B. His Humility: vss. 4-5

This took place to fulfill what was spoken through the prophet: "Say to the Daughter of Zion, 'See, your king comes to you, gentle and riding on a donkey, on a colt, the foal of a donkey.'"

At this point Matthew explained that this event was the fulfillment of the prophecy of Zechariah 9:9. Israel's king would not come as a mounted warrior, but as a humble servant of the people. This was quite contrary to the popular expectations of the day. The people were looking for a military conqueror to overthrow their Roman overlords. They had failed to understand what their Scriptures taught about the Messiah.

Zion was the part of Jerusalem were David and the kings after him lived. "The Daughter of Zion" represented the people of the city. Jesus was indeed their king, and far more: He was the king of the universe.

Jesus taught and practiced humility. Gentleness was not the traditional quality of earthly rulers, who showed their power by ruthless vindictiveness. They often killed hundreds, even thousands, of innocent people to bring countries to fearful subjection. If they didn't kill them, they hauled them off into slavery.

Jesus was unmistakably different from human conquerors. His claim to sovereignty did not rest on political and military subjugation, but on strength of character and obedience to God's will. Nowhere did His distinctiveness become more apparent than when He rode into Jerusalem.

C. The Crowd's Response: vss. 6-9

The disciples went and did as Jesus had instructed them. They brought the donkey and the colt, placed their cloaks on them, and Jesus sat on them. A very large crowd spread their cloaks on the road, while others cut branches from the trees and spread them on the road. The crowds that went ahead of him and those that followed shouted, "Hosanna to the Son of David!" "Blessed is he who comes in the name of the Lord!" "Hosanna in the highest!"

The disciples did as Jesus had told them and found the donkey and the colt tied with her. No one had ever ridden the colt. The mare may have been brought along to keep her colt at ease.

Some of the disciples put their outer garments on the colt as a makeshift saddle. Jesus mounted the animal and started the steep ascent into the valley, a route that for years was jammed with thousands of pilgrims coming to Jerusalem for Passover. The climb from the valley into the city gate is more gradual.

His ride was a living parable, setting forth His claim to be King, God's Messiah. His kingdom was at hand, but what a different kingdom it was!—a kingdom of peace, love, humility, and gentleness. This king was gentle and peaceful, doing good to His enemies, bearing their persecutions with a gentle, forgiving spirit, even on the cross.

Somehow, a large crowd gathered at the Mount of Olives, sensing that something dramatic was about to happen. Of course, it included critics as well (Luke 19:39-40), but generally this was an emotionally charged multitude, full of high hopes as they came from all over Israel and the world to celebrate the Passover. According to a census taken by the Roman emperor Nero, nearly three million Jews came to Jerusalem for the Passover.

A spontaneous outburst of adulation, welcome, and praise filled the air. People tore off their garments and threw them on the path. Others cut branches off the trees to cover the road. Spreading garments in front of an approaching king was a customary sign of tribute and allegiance. This was an ancient practice long before Sir Walter Raleigh took off his rich mantle and threw it into the mud for Queen Elizabeth to walk on.

Our practice of using palm branches on the anniversary of the triumphal entry comes from John's description of the event (John 12:13). Matthew, Mark, and Luke use different words: A young slip, a shoot, or twig (Matthew); a litter of branches and leaves (Mark); a mass of straw, rushes, or leaves beaten together or thrown loosely about, to form a bed or carpet (Luke).

The uproar soon focused on the shouts of "Hosanna!" This is a rendering into Greek letters of the Hebrew words, "Save, we pray" (Ps. 118:25). This did not mean "Save us," but "God save the king." This cry reflected the deepest aspirations of the Jewish people, who, except for a brief interlude during the Maccabean rebellion, had been a subject people for 600 years. To have their own king and be set free was their centuries-old dream. Now it appeared that God had indeed heard their ancient cry.

"Hosanna in the highest!" means in the highest degree, in the highest strains, in the highest heavens. These were the manifold shouts of triumph, taken mostly from the 118th Psalm.

They saw the Son of David as the natural heir to the throne, the one who would inherit all of those glorious promises made to King David (2 Sam. 7:12-16; 1 Chron. 17:10-14). These people had a strong sense of history, which is still true in the Middle East today. They saw their King coming "in the name of the Lord," that is, sent by God and endorsed by Him as His representative.

D. The City's Response: vss. 10-11

When Jesus entered Jerusalem, the whole city was stirred and asked, "Who is this?" The crowds answered, "This is Jesus, the prophet from Nazareth in Galilee."

This stunning scene stirred up the whole city. This was a profound change for this city, used to pretenders, but not having a clear picture about Jesus of Nazareth. Of course, some of them recalled His earlier visit, and many would have heard tales of His wonderful miracles in Galilee. But generally, in an age without media coverage, this event brought a huge uproar.

The word translated "stirred" means shaken as by an earthquake or a storm. It was used by Matthew to describe the effect of a violent storm on the waters of the Sea of Galilee (8:24).

The casual onlookers naturally wanted to know who was riding into the city with such a tremendous commotion. Most people did not recognize Jesus by sight, so the crowds had to identify Him. They called Him a prophet from Galilee.

For Jesus to enter Jerusalem like this required consummate courage. He was entering hostile territory as a rival King to the entrenched political and religious leaders. He was hated by the authorities, who, as we have seen, had long been plotting how to get rid of Him.

To make a dramatic appearance in such a way showed that Jesus was determined to make one last appeal against the indifference and incomprehension of the Jews. When His words and His miracles made little impact, He put His message and His Messianic claim into a dramatic public act.

Jesus did not sneak into Jerusalem under cover of darkness, but deliberately put Himself at center stage, forcing all eyes to be riveted on Him. He showed magnificent, sublime defiance to unbelief, unabashedly claiming to be the Lord's Messiah in the very minute details of the way He entered the city.

His courageous claim, however, was undergirded by love. His appeal was always to the heart. He blended perfectly boldness and gentleness as He provoked the city to answer the fundamental question, "Who is this?"

II. MESSIAH'S CLEANSING OF THE TEMPLE: MATTHEW 21:12-13

A. He Drove Out Buyers and Sellers: vs. 12

Jesus entered the temple area and drove out all who were buying and selling there. He overturned the tables of the money changers and the benches of those selling doves.

The gentle prophet from Nazareth soon began acting quite differently. He made a dramatic appearance in the temple in Jerusalem, obviously being followed by the tremendous crowds that had accompanied Him into the city.

They probably were expecting Him to assault the Roman authorities first, certainly not their own place of worship. This was a great time of preparation for the Passover, so the temple was filled not just with worshipers, but with those whose business it was to provide sacrifices—animals as well as doves—for them to offer. It was required that visitors to the feast purchase their sacrifices in Jerusalem.

Visitors came to Jerusalem with their own local money, so moneychangers had also become necessary. This was a profitable business, too, although apparently those working the temple precincts did not take exorbitant cuts.

In effect, Jesus claimed the temple as His own. He drove out those who had polluted it by commercializing it. No one stood in His way. This was the day of His triumph. This is how He showed what He had come to do, even in Jerusalem.

B. He Gave His Reasons: vs. 13

"It is written," he said to them, 'My house will be called a house of prayer,' but you are making it a 'den of robbers.' "

Jesus explained why He had taken such drastic action, by quoting Isaiah 56:7 and Jeremiah 7:11. Very simply, God's house of prayer had taken on the appearance of a den of robbers. Some of the business transactions were necessary for visiting worshipers, so what Jesus condemned was not the provision of sacrificial animals and local currency, but where all of this was taking place.

Apart from the temptations to exploit people economically, the whole character of the operation had radically changed what was supposed to be a spirit of penitence and prayer into something like a noisy flea market, where business rather than prayer prevailed.

Discussion Questions

1. What do you think the disciples thought about Jesus' plan to enter Jerusalem? Why?
2. Why is it sometimes hard to understand and obey God's instructions?
3. What would you have done, had you been at the Mount of Olives that day? Why?
4. How can Christians show their exuberant, uninhibited praise of the Lord Jesus?
5. What impresses you most about Jesus on this occasion? Why?
6. When Christians are called upon to identify Jesus in a hostile environment, what should they say?

Contemporary Application

Parades in honor of Jesus are out in most places today, but Christians still face the obligation to cry "Hosanna" whenever they can. Sometimes bringing praise to Jesus requires overt public action, even though it might be embarrassing. At such moments we have to recall the admirable courage Jesus exhibited.

On other occasions, however, our praise to Jesus might be inspired by our gentleness in the face of provocation. The church, rather than show its power and influence, might be more concerned about accepting the humility of Christ, even if it means being ridiculed.

The church has to reject political influence and the praise of the media, and follow the model of Jesus riding a donkey's colt, without a handsome saddle or a spear in His hand. What picture of Jesus do Christians paint in their everyday encounters with the world?

We also can bring praise to Jesus by the way we treat children and people with handicaps. He invited praise because of His outgoing love and care. He did not look down on the disabled, but healed them. He did not despise the cries of little children, but encouraged them. Perhaps if the church worked more at following Christ in these matters, He would receive more praise.

Watching for Christ's Return

DEVOTIONAL READING

Matthew 24:36-44

DAILY BIBLE READINGS

Monday February 7
Matthew 24:1-8 Signs of the End

Tuesday February 8
Matthew 24:9-14 Jesus' Followers Will Be Persecuted

Wednesday February 9
Matthew 24:15-28 Beware of False Messiahs

Thursday February 10
Matthew 24:29-35 Coming of the Son of Man

Friday February 11
Matthew 24:36-44 Be Watchful and Expectant

Saturday February 12
Matthew 24:45-51 Call to Be Faithful Servants

Sunday February 13
Matthew 25:1-13 Parable of the Ten Bridesmaids

Scripture

Background *Scripture: Matthew 24:1—25:13*
Scripture Lesson: *Matthew 24:45—25:13*
Key Verse: *"Therefore keep watch, because you do not know the day or the hour."* Matthew 25:13.
Key Verse for Children: *"We will do everything the LORD has said; we will obey."* Exodus 24:7.

Lesson Aim

To be fully prepared for Christ's return by faithfully serving Him now.

Lesson Setting

Time: *A.D. 30*
Place: *Jerusalem*

Lesson Outline

Watching for Christ's Return

   I. Faithfulness to the Master: Matthew 24:45-51
       A. *The Faithful, Wise Servant: vss. 45-47*
       B. *The Wicked Servant: vss. 48-51*
  II. The Bridegroom's Delay: Matthew 25:1-5
       A. *The Foolish Virgins: vss. 1-3*
       B. *The Wise Virgins: vss. 4-5*
 III. The Bridegroom's Arrival: Matthew 25:6-12
       A. *Those Who Were Ready: vss. 6-10*
       B. *Those Who Were Unprepared: vss. 11-12*
  IV. The Lord's Warning: Matthew 25:13

Introduction for Adults

Topic: *The Joy of Being Prepared*

As a seminary student, Joe and his wife lived in a small apartment with a tiny yard, to which he paid very little attention, given the fact that he was overwhelmed with Greek, Hebrew, and theology. But when graduation approached, he tore into that yard with a vengeance. Why? Because his father and mother were coming, and this was their first visit to his place. His dad was a consummate gardener, and so Joe did not want to disappoint him when he appeared. Joe knew the joy of being prepared.

That's something of what it's like to be prepared for the coming of Jesus. Because He is the most special friend we have, we want to be sure to welcome Him properly. We can only anticipate what it will be like to see Him face to face.

However, our meeting will not be joyful unless we are prepared. We have to trim the sinful edges of our lives, and pull out the weeds of sin that sap our holiness. That's a constant battle. Fortunately, Joe knew the date of his dad's arrival, so he could be prepared in advance. However, Jesus won't tell us ahead of time when He's coming, so we can't slack off. We have to be prepared all the time.

Introduction for Youths   ,

Topic: *Be Ready!*

Nothing knocks the starch out of a student more than walking into an exam unprepared. Some kids just can't get ready. Or, they flip through a few pages and hope for the best.

Hoping for the best won't make it with Jesus. He told about five foolish young women who hoped they could borrow some oil when the bridegroom appeared. But their friends sent them off to town instead, and they missed the party.

Young people hate to miss parties, but unless they come to know and love Jesus, they will be locked out of the greatest party of all—the wedding feast of the Lord Jesus Christ. Tragically, the attractions of the here-and-now seem to block out the attraction of being in heaven with Jesus. If we're not ready when Jesus comes, He will not know us at all. That's the saddest destiny we can think about.

Concepts for Children

Topic: *Do Good at All Times*

1. Jesus came to die for our sins and to give us eternal life.
2. He went back to heaven, but He promised that He would come back again for all who love Him.
3. In the meantime, He told us to watch and be ready for His coming.
4. "Watching" does not mean stargazing, but doing good things to help our friends come to know Jesus.
5. We can anticipate His coming by reading His stories and doing His commands.
6. Some of our friends may mock Jesus, but we can be confident that He will use our faith to help them.

The Lesson Commentary

I. FAITHFULNESS TO THE MASTER: MATTHEW 24:45-51

A. The Faithful, Wise Servant: vss. 45-47

"Who then is the faithful and wise servant, whom the master has put in charge of the servants in his household to give them their food at the proper time? It will be good for that servant whose master finds him doing so when he returns. I tell you the truth, he will put him in charge of all his possessions.

After denouncing the teachers of the law and the Pharisees (Matt. 23), Jesus foretold the destruction of Jerusalem and the end of the age (chaps. 24—25). This is called His Olivet Discourse, because He gave it on the Mount of Olives near Jerusalem (24:3). The day was Tuesday of His Passion week.

This was Jesus' answer to three questions asked by His disciples about the future (vs. 3). Their questions were aroused by dramatic statements He had made when they reflected on the temple's beauty (vss. 1-2). When Jesus predicted that the temple itself would be destroyed (and, by implication, the city of Jerusalem as well), they were dismayed.

They could not imagine such a thing happening. So Jesus gave them a broad outline of God's plan for the future: (1) the characteristics of this age (vss. 4-8); (2) the beginning of the time of tribulation with its signs (vss. 9-14); (3) the details of the troubles and sorrows to come (vss. 15-22); and (4) the assurance of His own return (vss. 23-31).

His key points were: no one knows when He will come (vs. 36); it will be a surprise, as in Noah's time (vss. 37-39); it will be a time of separation and judgment (vss. 40-41); and watchfulness is required, because we don't know the time (vss. 42-44).

His story in verses 45-51 is a simple telling of what happened in many households. The master went away and entrusted his affairs to a servant. He earned the description "faithful and wise" because he obeyed his master. When his master returned, he was carrying out his responsibilities.

The present interval of time in God's plan compares to Jesus (the master of the household) being away on a trip. While away, He has given His servants some things to do, namely, obey His commands and watch for His return.

B. The Wicked Servant: vss. 48-51

"But suppose that servant is wicked and says to himself, 'My master is staying away a long time,' and he then begins to beat his fellow servants and to eat and drink with drunkards. The master of that servant will come on a day when he does not expect him and at an hour he is not aware of. He will cut him to pieces and assign him a place with the hypocrites, where there will be weeping and gnashing of teeth."

The wicked servant's disobedience was based on a terrible miscalculation: he thought his master was delayed. Therefore, he wasn't ready and his master came when he least expected him.

185

We see in this story how Jesus preserved the main idea of the whole Olivet Discourse. His one teaching was watchfulness so we will be ready for His return. Primarily, we are not to be searching for signs, but doing our duties. We will be asked to give an account of our faithful obedience.

Watchful obedience is the best evidence of Christian faith. In the story, those who beat their fellow servants and ate and drank with drunkards did so because they ignored the certainty of the master's return. The time of reckoning is far off, they thought. This is a certain recipe for spiritual disaster.

The servant who fulfilled his duties while his master was away was given a still greater place. But the servant who failed was dealt with severely.

II. THE BRIDEGROOM'S DELAY: MATTHEW 25:1-5

A. The Foolish Virgins: vss. 1-3

"At that time the kingdom of heaven will be like ten virgins who took their lamps and went out to meet the bridegroom. Five of them were foolish and five were wise. The foolish ones took their lamps but did not take any oil with them."

The story of the wise and foolish virgins (or bridesmaids) was at the heart of Christ's concern. There is no mistaking that He equated Himself with the delayed bridegroom. He is absent now, but He will come back, and in the meantime? Well, He said, it's like this wedding.

Ten virgins went out to meet the bridegroom on his arrival. Jesus explained that five of them were "foolish" and five were "wise." Why? The rest of His story gives the answer.

It was night and the bridegroom was traveling from a distance, so no one knew the exact time of his arrival. The guests and wedding party only knew it would be sometime during the night.

The first difference between the wise and foolish virgins is that the foolish ones did not carry a supply of oil. Their lamps consisted of a round receptacle for oil for the wick. This was placed in a deep saucer which was mounted on the end of a long wooden pole. The custom was to have ten such lamps for the wedding party.

B. The Wise Virgins: vss. 4-5

"The wise [virgins], however, took oil in jars along with their lamps. The bridegroom was a long time in coming, and they all became drowsy and fell asleep."

The distinguishing note about the five wise virgins is that they were prepared for the bridegroom's coming. They took flasks of oil with their lamps. Whatever it cost them to get ready, they did.

Applying the story thus far to Christ's return, it is clear: (1) that His coming is delayed and (2) that preparation must be made for His coming. Some will make adequate preparations and some will not.

The immediacy of Christ's return is not of high importance among some Christians, so they don't care about being prepared. Of course, the world at large goes on its merry way without a thought of Christ's return.

III. THE BRIDEGROOM'S ARRIVAL: MATTHEW 25:6-12

A. Those Who Were Ready: vss. 6-10

"At midnight the cry rang out: 'Here's the bridegroom! Come out to meet him!' Then all the virgins woke up and trimmed their lamps. The foolish ones said to the wise, 'Give us some of your oil; our lamps are going out.' 'No,' they replied, 'there may not be enough for both us and you. Instead, go to those who sell oil and buy some for yourselves.' But while they were on their way to buy the oil, the bridegroom arrived. The virgins who were ready went in with him to the wedding banquet. And the door was shut."

Suddenly the time for sleeping was over. The shout went up. The bridegroom was coming. The virgins were urged to go out and meet him. Now the consequences of preparation—or lack of preparation—were revealed.

The wise virgins had taken the thoughtfulness and care to get ready. They had sufficient oil for their lamps, but wisely refused to give some to the foolish virgins, for fear that they would not have enough for themselves. They told the foolish virgins to go buy some oil.

When the bridegroom arrived for the marriage feast, the wise virgins were admitted with him. They had done what they were supposed to do, had prepared for it, and so enjoyed the rewards of the wedding banquet.

B. Those Who Were Unprepared: vss. 11-12

"Later the others also came. 'Sir! Sir!' they said. 'Open the door for us!' But he replied, 'I tell you the truth, I don't know you.' "

The foolish virgins got up with the rest and trimmed their lamps, but the results were disastrous. Their lamps went out for lack of oil. They asked the wise virgins for some of their oil, but were sent to town to buy some.

While they were at the oil dealer, the bridegroom came, and when they returned, the door to the marriage feast was shut. The foolish virgins asked to be allowed in for the festivities, but they were barred. "I don't know you," said the lord of the feast. They were turned away and rejected.

The difference between being prepared and not being ready was tragic. It was the difference between wisdom and folly, care and indifference, thoughtfulness and laziness. In the end, the wise virgins enjoyed the fellowship of the wedding feast, while the foolish ones were left outside.

As far as Christ's return is concerned, the point is best summarized in the statement: "The virgins who were ready went in with him to the wedding banquet" (vs. 10). There is a solid foundation for the appeal to be ready for Jesus Christ, but what does that mean?

For starters, it means being convinced of the reality of His coming. No one will be ready who disbelieves that the same Jesus who suffered and died and rose again one day will come back to earth once more. There are certain proofs of this fact, but none more convincing that the words of Christ Himself: "So you also must be ready, because the Son of Man will come at an hour when you do not expect him" (Matt. 24:44).

At Christ's ascension the angels said, "This same Jesus, who has been taken from you into heaven, will come back in the same way you have seen him go into heaven" (Acts 1:11). The apostles Paul, Peter, and John asserted throughout their writings that Jesus Christ will come again. The Old Testament prophets clearly foretold both His first and second advent.

In the second place, to be ready means acknowledging Jesus as your Savior. He came the first time to accomplish personal salvation from sin by His death and resurrection, but He must be received into one's life by a definite transaction of faith. No one will be ready for Jesus who has not passed from death to life by virtue of the new birth.

Third, to be ready means that a Christian will develop a growing personal relationship to Jesus throughout life. How awkward it is to have an old friend drop in by surprise when you haven't kept in touch over the years. What can you say? "I don't care for you anymore." (See 1 John 2:28.)

IV. THE LORD'S WARNING: MATTHEW 25:13

"Therefore keep watch, because you do not know the day or the hour."

At the end of the story, after both the happy and sad developments were revealed, Jesus made His application and warning. His command was simple and direct: "Therefore keep watch." The reason for His command was clear: "You do not know the day or the hour" when He will come.

From this story it is clear that one of two fates awaits each person at Christ's return—either joyful acceptance, or sorrowful rejection. There is no middle ground. It's a terrible thing to attempt entrance to His wedding feast, only to be turned away because of inadequate preparations.

Yet how difficult it is to wait when the bridegroom is a long time in coming. This is the real test of our faith. Is Jesus really coming? Why doesn't He come now to do something about the world's wickedness? And so we often talk ourselves out of careful, prepared watchfulness.

His disciples had the same problem. Immediately after Christ's resurrection they wanted Him to intervene for them and restore the kingdom to Israel. They were not prepared for His ascension, or for an indeterminate time of waiting. Jesus told them, "It is not for you to know the times or dates the Father has set by his own authority" (Acts 1:7).

It is very easy to fall into the trap of fixing dates rather than watching for Jesus. What does it mean to watch for His return?

First, it means being alert for its surprising suddenness. He made that point very clear throughout Matthew 24 and 25. Christ's return will not only be unexpected, but He will come when least expected. Therefore, we must watch at all times. Our preparation must be constant, not intermittent.

Second, watching does not mean inactivity or idleness. There is no sitting back at ease in Christ's kingdom. On the contrary, watching means active service for the King. It means watchful care over His concerns; alertness for opportunities to serve Him; sensitivity to the needs of others. As we make our own spiritual preparations for His return, we will be used by Him for advancing His work.

Third, watching means looking at what's happening in the world in the light of His coming. Christians can see through the struggles of the world toward the day of Christ's triumphal return. We need not be pessimists, because we know the end of the story. We know who wins! Christians know that all of history is moving toward a consummation and climax at the return of Jesus.

Discussion Questions

1. What temptations do Christians face in regard to putting off obeying Jesus while He is away? What are our duties in His absence?
2. Why is it hard to think about giving an account to Jesus when He returns?
3. How can Christ's return be used to help bring someone to faith in Him?
4. How can we fulfill our responsibilities to be ready?
5. How can we avoid the tendency to set dates and times for Christ's return?
6. What reasons are there for neglecting a growing faith in Christ?
7. Why do some Christians seem to grow stale in their walk with Jesus?

Contemporary Application

Most people are unconcerned about the return of Jesus Christ. They do not begin the day looking for Him. They have too many more important, urgent things to do. They focus on their present duties, not on the possibility that Jesus will come today.

For whatever reasons, in a scientific age where technology is everything, it's hard for Christians to help people face the facts about Christ's return. We do have our share of doomsday prophets, and many people are fascinated by the end of the world. Just look at the headlines in the supermarket tabloids.

The church's main task is to insist that Jesus is coming, while avoiding unnecessary speculation and date setting. While we shouldn't say He will come tomorrow, next week, or next year, we must keep on saying that Jesus *will* return.

These are the truths Jesus Himself emphasized, so we are foolish if we ignore them. If we claim to be obedient followers of Christ, then we will study what He said about His Second Coming, and tell others as well. We must encourage all Christians to do this, even though we may not agree on certain details.

Death of Jesus

DEVOTIONAL READING

John 19:16-30

DAILY BIBLE READINGS

Monday February 14
Matthew 27:1-10 Jesus Delivered to Pilate; Judas's Suicide

Tuesday February 15
Matthew 27:11-18 Jesus before Pilate

Wednesday February 16
Matthew 27:19-23 The Crowd Agitates for Barabbas's Release

Thursday February 17
Matthew 27:24-31 Jesus Is Handed Over for Crucifixion

Friday February 18
Matthew 27:32-44 Jesus Is Crucified

Saturday February 19
Matthew 27:45-56 Jesus Dies

Sunday February 20
Matthew 27:57-61 Jesus Is Buried

Scripture

Background Scripture: *Matthew 27:32-61*
Scripture Lesson: *Matthew 27:38-54*
Key Verse: *"Surely he was the Son of God!"* Matthew 27:54b
Key Verse for Children: *The Father has sent his Son to be the Savior of the world.* 1 John 4:14

Lesson Aim

To thank Jesus for dying for our sins.

Lesson Setting

Time: *A.D. 30*
Place: *Jerusalem*

Lesson Outline

Death of Jesus

   I. The Mocking of Jesus: Matthew 27:38-44
      A. *By the Crowd of Ordinary People: vss. 38-40*
      B. *By the Chief Priests, Teachers, and Elders: vss. 41-43*
      C. *By the Robbers: vs. 44*
  II. The Last Cry of Jesus: Matthew 27:45-50
      A. *"Why Have You Forsaken Me?": vss. 45-47*
      B. *He Gave Up His Spirit: vss. 48-50*
 III. Repercussions of His Death: Matthew 27:51-54
      A. *The Temple Curtain Was Torn and the Earth Shook: vs. 51*
      B. *The Dead Were Raised: vss. 52-53*
      C. *The Soldiers Confessed: vs. 54*

Introduction for Adults

Topic: *The Death in Our Behalf*

The crucifixion of the Lord Jesus Christ has long intrigued the best minds. The heart of the problem is simple from a human standpoint: Why was such a good man put to death? Even those who have not acknowledged His deity have not found any flaws in his character. Therefore, the end of the drama stands as stark tragedy, if not gross injustice.

But reasons for it are not hard to find. You can easily see the stubbornness of entrenched religious power, the political pressure that was brought to bear on the Romans, and the corruption among leaders and followers alike.

The crucifixion reveals the worst that mankind can do, regardless of how you try to explain it. It makes no sense, unless we look at it in the light of our sin and God's holiness and love. "Christ died for our sins" (1 Cor. 15:3) is still the best explanation for what happened at Golgotha.

Introduction for Youths

Topic: *Darkness before Dawn*

The media are drawn to executions like bees to honey. The television cameras of today take the place of the hordes that used to jam the hill outside the Tower of London to watch criminals, political prisoners, and cast-off queens be hanged or beheaded.

Two thousand years ago, when Jesus was executed, the same public atmosphere prevailed. He was treated just like any other prisoner sentenced for His crimes. His executioners saw Him in the same light. No special treatment for God's Son.

At least Jesus was spared the ordeal of the ghoulish media flak. But He felt the pain, the shock, the humiliation that anyone else would. But He also felt something no one else has ever felt: the crushing weight of taking the world's sin and guilt and judgment, thus being cut off from God, not for His own crimes, but for the crimes of others.

Teenagers want to know not only why Jesus died, but why He died for them. Until they answer that question, they will just be counted among the morbid curiosity seekers who flocked to Golgotha to watch Him die.

Concepts for Children

Topic: *Jesus, the Son of God*

1. Wicked people humiliated and tortured the Lord Jesus.
2. Jesus willingly suffered because He obeyed his heavenly Father.
3. Because Jesus died for us, by believing Him we can have our sins forgiven.
4. Sometimes people who do not believe in Jesus hurt those who do.
5. We can find hope and courage to follow Jesus, even though it is hard to do.
6. Following crowds who seem to be in the majority can be a dangerous thing to do.

The Lesson Commentary

I. THE MOCKING OF JESUS: MATTHEW 27:38-44

A. By the Crowd of Ordinary People: vss. 38-40

Two robbers were crucified with him, one on his right and one on his left. Those who passed by hurled insults at him, shaking their heads and saying, "You who are going to destroy the temple and build it in three days, save yourself! Come down from the cross, if you are the Son of God!"

The last week of our Lord's life occupies about one-fourth of the record in the four Gospels, showing us how significant these events were regarded by the writers. At the same time, they did not dwell at length on Christ's physical sufferings unduly. They simply stated in brief, terse sentences what He endured.

But we must study and meditate on these facts, so we can better understand the meaning of Christ's death and grow in our own appreciation of His suffering on our behalf. Christians make much of the cross, not because they take pleasure in reciting unpleasant details, but because the cross represents the outpouring of the Savior's love for them.

Jesus was arrested in Gethsemane and placed on trial before the Sanhedrin, the Jewish high court (26:47-68). After consulting among themselves, they delivered Him to Pilate, the Roman governor, and accused Him of many things. Jesus did not respond to their accusations (27:14)

Pilate bowed to the uproar of the crowd instigated by the chief priests and elders, freed Barabbas, and signed the Jesus' death warrant (vss. 15-26).

When Pilate saw that he could not prevail against the crowd, he tried to make public his own innocence of all that was to follow. In this strange, tragic scene, he washed his hands according to Jewish custom and placed responsibility for Christ's blood on the hands of others (vs. 24). It was a futile gesture. He could not escape his responsibility that way, even though the crowd willingly accepted the burden of Christ's blood.

Pilate then took the fateful step and turned over Jesus to be crucified. The preliminaries were every bit as dreadful as the act itself. The first step was scourging (vs. 26). The victim was stripped, tied to a post, and lashed with a long leather thong perhaps tipped with pieces of bone and lead pellets. Some victims died during this ordeal; most simply passed out.

After this the soldiers took Jesus to the barracks in the governor's headquarters. These soldiers were Pilate's personal bodyguard; they had no idea what was happening or why. For them, Jesus was simply another criminal to be executed, and they did to Him what they felt they were entitled to do. ("The whole company," or battalion, numbered 600 men.)

Stripping Jesus of His own clothes, they put a scarlet robe on Him, probably belonging to one of the soldiers. They fashioned a crown to mock and punish Him. It was made of a common plant that had many small, sharp spines and soft, pliable branches. The leaves resembled a deep green ivy, an imitation of the victor's crown.

For a scepter they handed Him a small piece of native papyrus bulrush that grew along the roadsides. Then they knelt before Him and shouted in false honor to the man they had heard identified as "King of the Jews." This means that they thought He was a self-deluded lunatic.

Our Lord's suffering at this point was both physical and emotional. It is hard to imagine the Lord of glory allowing Himself to be so humiliated, but this is exactly what happened. He took the form of a servant and "humbled himself and became obedient to death—even death on a cross!" (Phil. 2:8).

There was a triple execution on this day. The cross occupied by Jesus stood between crosses holding two robbers. In one sense this was the completion of our Lord's identification with sinners. Unknowingly, the pagan Roman officials were the means of fulfilling a Messianic prophecy given seven centuries earlier: the Messiah would be "numbered with the transgressors" (Isa. 53:12).

Throughout His ministry Jesus attracted throngs of people. His teachings and His miracles were not done in obscurity, but in full public view. Therefore, when His enemies succeeded in having Him killed, there were plenty of citizens ready to join the powerful, influential people.

The city had been jammed for the Passover, and there was no shortage of rabble-rousers to be inflamed against Jesus. When it came to making a choice between Jesus and Barabbas, Pilate was swayed by the tumultuous voices of the people.

The crowds followed the procession to Golgotha, and when they got there they hooted at Jesus. This was no time to take the stand in His defense. People were easily stampeded by blood lust. What better time to yell in derision than when the victim was helpless.

They hurled His own sayings back on Jesus, of course completely misunderstanding the words. The one about destroying and rebuilding the temple had been used against Him at His trial (26:61). The temple was the most sacred spot for the Jews and any thought of destroying it aroused their fury. But Jesus did not mean the temple building in Jerusalem. The saying was a prophecy of His own death and resurrection (see also John 2:19-22).

The people knew Jesus claimed to have come from God, so they challenged Him to prove it by coming down from the cross. Their demand only further revealed their unbelief. They had had ample chances to witness His divine power.

Their taunt was one more strong temptation for Jesus to resist. He had faced this in Gethsemane, asking the Father for some way to avoid execution at Golgotha, but there was no way.

B. By the Chief Priests, Teachers, and Elders: vss. 41-43

In the same way the chief priests, the teachers of the law and the elders mocked him. "He saved others," they said, "but he can't save himself! He's the King of Israel! Let him come down now from the cross, and we will believe in him. He trusts in God. Let God rescue him now if he wants him, for he said, 'I am the Son of God.' "

The common people might have had some small excuse for being carried away at the execution of Jesus, but they deserved better from their spiritual leaders. The chief priests, teachers, and elders mocked Jesus because of the apparent inconsistency between His claim to be the Son of God and His helplessness on the cross. By their reasoning, if He were indeed the King of the Jews, the promised Messiah, He certainly would not be suffering humiliation and death.

Therefore, they also challenged Him to save Himself and come down from the cross. They promised to believe in Him, if He would do that. No such miracle would happen, because they had already turned their backs on the light given to them by God. They had rejected God's Son at the very outset of His work, and they had been planning His demise all along. Therefore, their cry was outrageous hypocrisy, showing once again the wickedness of unbelief.

Christ's obedience to His Father's will became the source of His torment. He obeyed without exception. At His trial no fault could be found against Him. Yet His critics sought to prove that God had deserted Him. By their logic, if Jesus were God's Son, the Father would rescue Him.

God could not save Jesus from the cross that day and still be the holy, righteous, just God of the universe who forgives sinners. If Jesus had been rescued, sinners would have to die eternally as the just condemnation for their offense against God's righteousness and breaking His laws.

C. By the Robbers: vs. 44

In the same way the robbers who were crucified with him also heaped insults on him.

They were bandits, possibly members of the gang of Barabbas. They were crucified with Jesus undoubtedly to add insult to His death and insult the Jews. The Romans implied that the King of the Jews deserved no better company than robbers.

At first, both of the robbers joined in assailing Jesus. But as the day wore on, one of them—moved by the sublime attitude of Jesus and possibly by recalling His teachings and miracles—was actually converted (Luke 23:39-43). He rebuked the other robber for the abuse he was heaping on Jesus. Jesus assured the repentant robber that He would find forgiveness and a place with Him in Paradise.

II. The Last Cry of Jesus: Matthew 27:45-50

A. "Why Have You Forsaken Me?": vss. 45-47

From the sixth hour until the ninth hour darkness came over all the land. About the ninth hour Jesus cried out in a loud voice, "Eloi, Eloi, lama sabachthani?"—which means, "My God, my God, why have you forsaken me?" When some of those standing there heard this, they said, "He's calling Elijah."

At noon, darkness enveloped Jerusalem for three hours. After six hours of excruciating pain, Jesus cried to God and asked why He had forsaken Him. Matthew recorded His words in Aramaic, the common language of the day.

What did our Lord's cry mean? Had God the Father really abandoned His Son in this hour of His darkest trial? Because of the unique relationship between the Father and the Son, we may never be able to grasp the depth of feeling behind Jesus' cry.

However, we can be certain that His cry reflected the feeling that He was being forsaken on the cross. His cry also proves the terrible reality that at the moment—as Jesus bore the sins of the world in His own body—God actually turned His back on His Son and abandoned Him.

Why? The answer lies in the heart of the Christian doctrine of atonement for our sins. We call it Christ's substitutionary atonement because Jesus died in our place and on our behalf.

It was necessary for Jesus to be abandoned by God on the cross. Since God by His nature cannot look upon sin (Hab. 1:13), He hid His face when our sins were placed on His sinless Son. Jesus was forsaken so that we might never be. "Never will I forsake you" (Heb. 13:5).

This is what caused such an anguished cry from our Savior on the cross. Our sins caused Him to suffer not only the nails and the spear, but also the abandonment by His Father.

B. He Gave Up His Spirit: vss. 48-50

Immediately one of them ran and got a sponge. He filled it with wine vinegar, put it on a stick, and offered it to Jesus to drink. The rest said, "Now leave him alone. Let's see if Elijah comes to save him." And when Jesus had cried out again in a loud voice, he gave up his spirit.

Hearing His cry, some of the people thought Jesus was calling for Elijah (vs. 47). But one man ran, filled a sponge with wine vinegar, put it on a stick, and offered it to Jesus to drink. Then the people waited to see if Elijah would rescue Him.

It was commonly believed that Elijah would one day return to Israel. What better time for him to come than when the man who claimed to be God's Son was dying on the cross. "Let's see if Elijah comes to save him" was not a reflection of faith, but a callous call for another thrill. Because of the hardness of their hearts, they did not want any divine interference.

Jesus' cry—called the greatest single word ever spoken—is one word in Greek, but three in English: "It is finished" (John 19:30). To this Jesus added His prayer of dedication to His Father: "Into your hands I commit my spirit" (Luke 23:46).

None of the Gospel writers very directly say that Jesus died. Rather, His loud cry (vs. 50) showed that He did not die as a result of being crucified. His death was voluntary. He actually gave up His life, as He said He would. "I lay down my life for the sheep. The reason my Father loves me is that I lay down my life—only to take it up again. No one takes it from me, but I lay it down of my own accord. I have authority to lay it down and authority to take it up again. This command I received from my Father" (John 10:15, 17-18).

Jesus "gave up His spirit" before physical causes brought about His death. He did it at the moment of His own choosing. Most victims of crucifixion lingered for a day or more. That's what made the execution so horrible. That's why Pilate was surprised that Jesus had died so soon (Mark 15:44).

III. REPERCUSSIONS OF HIS DEATH: MATTHEW 27:51-54

A. The Temple Curtain Was Torn and the Earth Shook: vs. 51

At that moment the curtain of the temple was torn in two from top to bottom. The earth shook and the rocks split.

God signified the meaning of Christ's death on the cross by tearing the temple curtain from top to bottom. After centuries of worship in the tabernacle and the temple, during which the Holy of Holies had been closed to everyone except the high priest on the Day of Atonement, now the way to God's presence was open to everybody.

The writer of Hebrews called this "a new and living way opened for us through the curtain" (10:20). It was opened by the blood of Jesus (10:19). The amazing application of this is that those who place their faith in Jesus can "draw near to God with a sincere heart in full assurance of faith" (10:22).

B. The Dead Were Raised: vss. 52-53

The tombs broke open and the bodies of many holy people who had died were raised to life. They came out of the tombs, and after Jesus' resurrection they went into the holy city and appeared to many people.

Because of a powerful earthquake, graves split apart and some people in them were raised to life. They were called "holy people," that is, people of faith and obedience to God.

Of course, in Israel's history other believers had been raised. Their resuscitation did not mean they would not die again. It pointed to their anticipated final resurrection, when the dead would be raised never to die again.

Matthew added the fascinating detail (vs. 53) that those who had been raised on Good Friday went into Jerusalem after Easter Sunday "and appeared to many people." Probably they prepared the way for many people to believe in Jesus, after they learned that He, too, had been raised from the dead. It's also conceivable that those who came to believe formed the heart of the first church in Jerusalem.

C. The Soldiers Confessed: vs. 54

When the centurion and those with him who were guarding Jesus saw the earthquake and all that had happened, they were terrified, and exclaimed, "Surely he was the Son of God!"

Not all of the people mocked and derided Jesus. The Roman centurion, other guards, and a number of faithful, courageous women (vss. 55-56) stood apart from the mockery. The soldiers, of course, had seen everything. They were significantly impressed by how Jesus had faced torture and death.

The outcome was a strange confession for a Roman officer. According to Mark 15:39, he was the main one who spoke. He recognized that God was present in Jesus Christ. He did not possess full-blown theological understanding of Christ's relation to God, but at least he saw God's hand at work in the way Jesus died. Here was an unsolicited testimony to God's Son.

Discussion Questions

1. What emotions do you feel at the thought of the rejected King and Savior being tortured?
2. How does the cross of Christ become central in your worship, meditation, and daily conduct in the world?
3. How do you explain the intense hatred against Jesus, in view of all the words of love and deeds of mercy He had done for the people?
4. How do you account for the centurion's confession?
5. How do unbelievers mock Jesus? Why?
6. How should Christians react when they are ridiculed for their faith?

Contemporary Application

We don't sing "The Old Rugged Cross" much any more, perhaps because it is an "emblem of suffering and shame." We've become so enamored with ideas of self-fulfillment and pleasure that we instinctively resist connecting suffering and shame with successful Christian living.

How unlike the Savior whom we profess to love and obey. Jesus willingly accepted the worst that sinful humanity could hurl at Him, even though He had legions of angels at His disposal to wipe them out. Today's popular psychology suggests that you are a fool if you do not use power to get ahead and to stick it to your foes.

Christians easily fall before the temptation to use power, to resist being tramped on or taken advantage of. Stick up for your rights and don't be a doormat, we are told. If the suffering of Jesus Christ before and during His crucifixion means anything, it is that we cannot, as Christians, follow the world's way of doing things. The church needs to recapture the spirit of "The Old Rugged Cross," if not the words and the music.

Resurrection and Commission

DEVOTIONAL READING

John 20:19-31

DAILY BIBLE READINGS

Monday February 21
*Matthew 27:62-66 Pilate's
Soldiers Guard Jesus' Tomb*

Tuesday February 22
*Matthew 28:1-10 The
Resurrection of Jesus*

Wednesday February 23
*Matthew 28:11-20 Jesus
Commissions His Disciples*

Thursday February 24
*Luke 24:13-27 Jesus and
Travelers on the Emmaus
Road*

Friday February 25
*Luke 24:28-35 The
Travelers Recognize Jesus at
Table*

Saturday February 26
*Luke 24:36-43 Jesus
Appears to His Disciples*

Sunday February 27
*Luke 24:44-53 Jesus
Blesses the Disciples and
Ascends*

Scripture

Background Scripture: *Matthew 27:62—28:20*
Scripture Lesson: *Matthew 28:1-10, 16-20*
Key Verse: *"Therefore go and make disciples of all nations,
baptizing them in the name of the Father and of the Son and
of the Holy Spirit, and teaching them to obey everything I
have commanded you. And surely I am with you always, to
the very end of the age."* Matthew 28:19-20.
Key Verse for Children: *"Therefore go and make
disciples of all nations, . . . teaching them to obey everything I have commanded you."* Matthew 28:19-20.

Lesson Aim

To serve the risen Christ in His worldwide mission.

Lesson Setting

Time: *A.D. 30*
Place: *Jerusalem*

Lesson Outline

Resurrection and Commission

   I. The Empty Tomb: Matthew 28:1-10
      *A. The Angel of the Lord Rolled Back the Stone:
         vss. 1-4*
      B. The Angel Instructed the Women: vss. 5-7
      C. The Women Met Jesus: vss. 8-10
  II. The Risen Christ's Command: Matthew
      28:16-20
      A. The Disciples Went to Galilee: vs. 16
      B. They Worshiped, But Some Doubted: vs. 17
      C. Jesus Told Them His Authority: vs. 18
      *D. He Commanded Them to Disciple the Nations:
         vss. 19-20a*
      E. He Promised His Presence: vs. 20b

Introduction for Adults

Topic: *The Basis of Our Authority*

Resurrection and the Great Commission; Easter and world missions. Has your church ever had a world missions conference in connection with Easter? Probably not, despite the fact that the New Testament makes an unequivocal connection between the two.

World missions programs have to fight for visibility in the churches, as if Christ's commission was just one of a host of things the church ought to be doing, like Sunday school, camps, youth groups, and choir. But after He rose from the grave, Jesus gave His disciples only one thing to do: Go and make disciples of people of all nations.

Somehow, His single purpose gets lost in the shuffle. Jesus rose from the grave to defeat sin and to accomplish our salvation. But He also rose to give His followers a specific task, a reason for their existence in the world.

We have to face what to do with the gift of Christ's resurrection. How do we account for the millions who do not have the same Easter hope that we have? What are the churches really doing to obey His commission?

Introduction for Youths

Topic: *Being a Winner*

One of the most exciting things that has ever happened in the lives of thousands of Christian young people is the chance to do missionary work overseas during summer breaks from school. They have found that it can be eminently satisfying to do something worthwhile for people in other countries who do not share their affluence and comforts.

Many churches recruit and train their own short-term youth teams. If they can't do this, they send their youth overseas with specialized youth mission agencies, or with their own denominational and independent boards as well.

The world is packed with many worthwhile things that teenagers can do. This lesson gives us the biblical foundation for doing mission work. It shows that regardless of age, one can be a fellow disciple-maker for Jesus.

Concepts for Children

Topic: *Telling Others About Jesus*

1. Jesus rose from the grave so that we can worship, love, and serve Him.
2. Jesus lovingly brought His disciples to Himself, and gave them a job to do.
3. We can help people all over the world to love Jesus by praying for missionaries and giving money to support them.
4. We can learn valuable lessons from Christians in other countries.
5. We can grow in our understanding of world missions by having missionaries stay in our homes.
6. We can find pen-pals among children of missionaries.

The Lesson Commentary

I. THE EMPTY TOMB: MATTHEW 28:1-10

A. The Angel of the Lord Rolled Back the Stone: vss. 1-4

After the Sabbath, at dawn on the first day of the week, Mary Magdalene and the other Mary went to look at the tomb. There was a violent earthquake, for an angel of the Lord came down from heaven and, going to the tomb, rolled back the stone and sat on it. His appearance was like lightning, and his clothes were white as snow. The guards were so afraid of him that they shook and became like dead men.

No one in the crowds at Golgotha the day Jesus Christ was crucified expected Him to come back to life. If this story were a novel, readers would not expect such an amazing conclusion. Even in fiction, dead heroes and leaders of revolutionary movements do not experience resurrection. In that sense, the Gospel story has the strangest twist in all of the world's literature.

The friends of Jesus were overwhelmed by fear, because they assumed that the high priest and the Sanhedrin would ask the Romans to arrest them, too, and possibly have them executed. On the other hand, Jesus had plainly told them on many occasions that after He had been crucified He would be raised from the dead. Apparently His words seemed like a fairy tale to them.

Besides, Pilate had posted guards at the tomb of Jesus. The alliance of political and religious leaders wanted to make sure that the crucifixion was the final blow to this popular movement of Galileans. Of course, high hopes had risen in the hearts of Christ's followers, but now they were all smashed, stained in the blood of Golgotha. A brilliant dream had been shattered.

Against such a dark backdrop we read the startling words of Matthew 28. (For additional details about Christ's resurrection, see Mark 16, Luke 24, and John 20—21. Consult a Bible dictionary for suggestions about how these accounts can be harmonized. For example, after Matthew 28:1-8, read Luke 24:9-12 and Mark 16:9-11. After Matthew 28:9-15, read Luke 24:13-43 and John 20:26-31 and 21:1-25. After Matthew 28:16-20, read Luke 24:44-53 and Acts 1:3-12.)

Matthew began his account with the predawn visit of Mary Magdalene and "the other Mary," the mother of James and Joseph (Matt. 27:56). The days of the week, except the Sabbath or seventh day, were distinguished only by their order, as first day, second day, and so on. The Jews counted a part of a day as a whole day. Since Jesus died on the afternoon of Friday and arose on Sunday morning, he was in the tomb three days according to their reckoning.

In those days people were buried outside the city. Public burial places were simple plots, but the rich could afford to buy private burial places in caves surrounded by gardens. Through the boldness and generosity of Joseph of Arimathea, a prominent member of the Council, Jesus was spared the final indignity of burial in a mass grave.

These rock-hewn sepulchres consisted of a room with a lower cave in which the bodies were placed in hewn-out niches. The door of the tomb might be a circular piece of solid stone, with a flange fitting in a groove to the right or left of the opening. Or the stone door might be supported by hinges against which a stone was rolled for further protection.

The women went to the tomb with spices to complete the embalming of Jesus' body, which was left unfinished by Nicodemus and Joseph because of the Sabbath work ban. These two women had been at the crucifixion site. Mary of Magdala had devoted her strength and possessions to the ministry of Jesus ever since He had cast out seven demons from her (Luke 8:2).

No one saw the actual initial rising of Jesus. None of the New Testament writers described it. For the future of the church, the crucial fact was the empty tomb. Of course, some other major events accompanied the resurrection: an earthquake and the appearance of an angel.

These unusual signs were seen by the Roman guards that had been posted as extra security by Pilate (27:65). They were so terrified that they "became like dead men" (28:4).

The angels had appeared at Christ's birth and they had comforted Him in Gethsemane. Now the angel spokesperson appeared as God's answer to the women's concern about who would roll away the stone for them (Mark 16:3).

B. The Angel Instructed the Women: vss. 5-7

The angel said to the women, "Do not be afraid, for I know that you are looking for Jesus, who was crucified. He is not here; he has risen, just as he said. Come and see the place where he lay. Then go quickly and tell his disciples: 'He has risen from the dead and is going ahead of you into Galilee. There you will see him.' Now I have told you."

The Roman guards may have crumpled before the angel, but God in His goodness took care of the friends who were seeking Jesus. With good reason, they were frightened and perplexed. The angel recognized their fear and urged them to be calm. The angel first ministered to their personal needs in this tension-filled moment.

Naturally, the immediate concern of the two Marys was the whereabouts of the body of Jesus. The angel knew why they were there and gave them the staggering news: "He is not here; he is risen." These are the greatest words of hope ever uttered. These simple words have formed the foundation of the Church's Easter hope ever since.

To prove the truth of what he had said, the angel invited the women to inspect the empty tomb. This was the unmistakable evidence of Jesus' resurrection.

"Come and see where he lay" was not what the two Marys expected to hear. They certainly did not suspect that Jesus had risen from His grave. The angel invited them into the tomb not to let Jesus out, but to show the women that it was empty. The angel not only said that the tomb was empty, he said it was empty because Jesus had risen.

All of the critical attempts to explain away Christ's bodily resurrection fail to account for this fact. The empty tomb is the strongest evidence for His bodily resurrection. It cannot be reasoned away.

C. The Women Met Jesus: vss. 8-10

So the women hurried away from the tomb, afraid yet filled with joy, and ran to tell his disciples. Suddenly Jesus met them. "Greetings," he said. They came to him, clasped his feet and worshiped him. Then Jesus said to them, "Do not be afraid. Go and tell my brothers to go to Galilee; there they will see me."

Possibly half believing and half doubting, half overcome with fright and half overcome with joy, the women obeyed the angel and rushed back to the city. It would be hard to describe their feelings.

Then they met Jesus Himself, and He spoke to them. "Greetings" literally means to rejoice. They were to celebrate His resurrection with rejoicing. Then and there the women poured out their hearts to Jesus. He repeated what the angel had said. He comforted their fears and told them to send his "brothers," the disciples, to meet him in Galilee. The ones who had forsaken Him were still His brothers.

II. THE RISEN CHRIST'S COMMAND: MATTHEW 28:16-20

A. The Disciples Went to Galilee: vs. 16

Then the eleven disciples went to Galilee, to the mountain where Jesus had told them to go.

The authorities tried to cover up Christ's resurrection by bribing the guards to say that His body had been stolen while they slept (Matt. 28:11-15). This was a remarkable confession of dereliction of duty, but despite this their story was widely believed.

However, the disciples went to Galilee as Jesus had told them to do. Amazingly, they agreed to this word from the women. Why? First, it would be good to escape the terror in Jerusalem. Second, what else could they do? They could not stay in hiding forever.

Previously, Jesus had given His disciples directions about what they were to do after He was gone (John 14—16). They were concerned about the reality of His presence and about how He would manifest Himself to the world (14:22).

Jesus had made clear that His mission had a world-wide focus by saying, as He left the Upper Room for Gethsemane, "The world must learn that I love the Father and that I do exactly what my Father has commanded me" (vs. 31).

However, it was not until after His resurrection that He gave His disciples and the church a clear command to take the Gospel to the ends of the earth. (Each of the four Gospels closes with His command in some form, and the Book of Acts begins with it. See also Matt. 28:19-20; Mark 16:15; Luke 24:47; John 20:21; Acts 1:8.)

B. They Worshiped, but Some Doubted: vs. 17

When they saw him, they worshiped him; but some doubted.

There was a mixed response to the appearance of Jesus in Galilee. Of course, worship was the fitting response. Now they were confronted with the fulfillment of Christ's own words that after three days He would rise from the grave.

On the other hand, "some doubted." We know about the specific doubt of Thomas, but did others doubt as well? If so, why? Perhaps the emotional impact was too overwhelming. Intellectually, they could not comprehend a resurrection. So perhaps they thought they were in a trance or were seeing a vision.

C. Jesus Told Them His Authority: vs. 18

Then Jesus came to them and said, "All authority in heaven and on earth has been given to me."

Regardless of the doubters, Jesus pressed ahead and issued what has become known as the church's Great Commission (vss. 19-20), its missionary purpose and calling. But before doing that, He assured them of His universal power, granted to Him by His Father in heaven.

There are three important facts to note about Christ's power: (1) it is all-inclusive ("all authority"), meaning that there is nothing that can withstand His exercise of it; (2) it is universal in scope ("in heaven and on earth"), so that there is no realm of any power beyond His control; (3) it is personal ("given to me"), not blind, irrational, or simply let loose to run its course.

The word translated "authority" includes both power and authority. Jesus has both the ability and the right to rule. He did not hesitate to say that all nations were to come under His dominion. He had to make this tremendous claim before He could send His disciples on their mission.

D. He Commanded Them to Disciple the Nations: vss. 19-20a

"Therefore go and make disciples of all nations, baptizing them in the name of the Father and of the Son and of the Holy Spirit, and teaching them to obey everything I have commanded you."

Jesus gave His disciples a staggering responsibility: disciple all nations. They were Jewish patriots, looking for the restoration of Israel's kingdom (Acts 1:6). Suddenly, Jesus propelled their thoughts beyond the confines of Palestine to the ends of the earth. Jesus Christ was not the King of the Jews only, but the King of all the earth. They had to take His good news beyond the Jewish people to all tribes, tongues, and nationalities.

Jesus gave His command first in general terms. They were to "make disciples." Disciples are learners, followers, obedient subjects. Jesus did not say, "Go and make converts," or "Go and make church members," or "Go and get decisions." His purpose was to bring people into subjection to Himself.

After giving them His general purpose for their worldwide mission, Jesus told the disciples how to do it: (1) baptize converts; (2) teach them to obey all His commands. The disciples followed these steps in making disciples. Both crowds and individual converts were baptized (Acts 2:41; 8:38; 9:18). Then they engaged in consistent teaching of their converts (Acts 2:42).

E. He Promised His Presence: vs. 20b

"And surely I am with you always, to the very end of the age."

The hallmarks of Christ's missionary plan for His church are His authority, His commission, and His presence.

Jesus gave His disciples, and His church, the greatest promise of all time: His personal presence forever. These words of Jesus to His disciples are like those God gave to Joshua when he was given the leadership of Israel to conquer Canaan: "As I was with Moses, so I will be with you; I will never leave you nor forsake you. . . . Do not be terrified; do not be discouraged, for the LORD your God will be with you wherever you go" (Josh. 1:5, 9).

So, when Jesus sent His own into the world to proclaim His saving message, He said He would go with them. Of course, previously in His ministry Jesus had warned the disciples that they would face many opponents. Many people would resist them and their message. They would be persecuted, but He would be with them; His own presence would cheer and guide them.

Discussion Questions

1. How would you have felt at the tomb? Why?
2. Would you have gone to Galilee to see Jesus? Why?
3. How do you think the disciples felt about their worldwide commission?
4. Describe what a Christian disciple looks like. How can you tell one?
5. How should Christians, and their churches, obey Christ's commission?
6. What things get in the way of our giving priority to mission work?

Contemporary Application

Comparing world needs with the church's activities, mission experts tell us that we are falling behind in keeping Christ's commission to make disciples of all nations. Yes, the church is growing in many parts of the world. Many people respond gladly to Jesus when they hear the Gospel. Perhaps up to eighty thousand Protestants from the United States are doing mission work, either full-time or part-time.

So why are we falling behind? Simply because we aren't keeping up with population growth among huge segments of the nations that are not yet Christian. Also, because the task is becoming more difficult and more expensive. Some countries where most of the people are not Christians do not welcome Christian missionaries. In fact, some non-Christian religions are sending out money and missionaries of their own to win the world to their faith.

The only answer is for Christians and their churches to accept Christ's commission, dig deeper and make more sacrifices, so that millions who have yet to hear the Gospel will have the opportunity to do so.

Continuing Jesus' Work

Unit I: Christ the Basis of Unity

Unit II: Unity in Human Relationships

Unit III: The Glory of Christian Ministry

Helping a Church Confront Crisis

Scripture

Background Scripture: *1 Corinthians 1:1-17*
Scripture Lesson: *1 Corinthians 1:2-17*
Key Verse: *I appeal to you, brothers, in the name of our
Lord Jesus Christ, that all of you agree with one another
so that there may be no divisions among you and that you
may be perfectly united in mind and thought.*
1 Corinthians 1:10.
Scripture Lesson for Children: *Acts 18:1-4, 8;
1 Corinthians 1:10-15, 17*
Key Verse for Children: *I appeal to you . . . that all of
you agree with one another.* 1 Corinthians 1:10.

Lesson Aim

To forsake our quarrels and follow Jesus in Christian unity.

Lesson Setting

Time: *A.D. 55*
Place: *Written to Corinth from Ephesus*

Lesson Outline

Helping a Church Confront Crisis
  I. Paul and His Readers: 1 Corinthians 1:2-3
      A. *The Church at Corinth: vs. 2*
      B. *Paul's Greeting: vs. 3*
  II. The Apostle's Confidence: 1 Corinthians 1:4-9
      A. *Thanksgiving for Grace: vs. 4*
      B. *Enrichment in Christ: vss. 5-6*
      C. *Eager Waiting: vs. 7*
      D. *Consummation in Christ: vs. 8*
      E. *God's Faithfulness: vs. 9*
  III. The Church's Strife: 1 Corinthians 1:10-17
      A. *The Demand for Unity: vs. 10*
      B. *The Report of Quarrels: vss. 11-12*
      C. *The Quarrels Ridiculed: vs. 13*
      D. *The Mission Defined: vss. 14-17*

Introduction for Adults

Topic: *Appeal for Unity*

In a small rural church in America's heartland, all of the Sunday school classes met in the sanctuary, separated by one or two rows of pews. Teachers had to speak loudly, and students had to strain to listen. One Sunday the superintendent announced that the classes were supposed to move forward a couple of rows. Everyone moved together in unison, except for one couple. They stayed put in their regular row. They refused to move and never came back.

Many times, it seems, Christians get their noses out of joint over the silliest things. Feelings get hurt, grudges develop, and believers don't talk to each other. What a travesty of how the church is supposed to work.

All of us are susceptible to the sins of disunity. Having been saved by faith in Christ, we somehow fail to accept unity as our high calling in Him. He takes a back seat while we fight. Perhaps we need a time for prayer, confession, and repentance.

Introduction for Youths

Topic: *What Unites?*

A young man who played for his high school baseball team gave it everything he had. When the baseball team reached a critical playoff game, he assumed that the whole team wanted to win this game more than anything else. But he was wrong. Some of the players spent the night before carousing on the town. They lost the game because of disunity.

Followers of Jesus are supposed to be on the same team. Every Christian supposedly wants to win victories of faith and obedience. Sadly, there are some weak links, and too often not everyone in the church pulls together. People sometimes fight for their own agendas, not Christ's.

I would like to think that Christian youth can set a strong example of what it means to work together for the sake of Jesus and His Gospel.

Concepts for Children

Topic: *Live Peacefully*

1. Jesus wants His followers to work to get along with each other.
2. The church is to be a place of love, acceptance, and unity.
3. Sometimes Christians get into fights with one another.
4. We need to cultivate a spirit of humility.
5. The apostle Paul encouraged unity by telling us to center our thoughts on Jesus.
6. We can pray for one another and forgive one another.

The Lesson Commentary

I. PAUL AND HIS READERS: 1 CORINTHIANS 1:2-3

A. The Church at Corinth: vs. 2

To the church of God in Corinth, to those sanctified in Christ Jesus and called to be holy, together with all those everywhere who call on the name of our Lord Jesus Christ—their Lord and ours:

Paul's letters to the church at Corinth deal with matters that also confront the contemporary church. His first letter began with the problem of Christian unity. Corinth, Greece, was a Roman colony founded by Julius Caesar in 46 B.C. It was both a government center and a business hub. Its population included Jews, Greeks, Romans, Asians, and Phoenicians. It was so well known for debauchery of every kind that the name "Corinthian" was synonymous with wickedness.

The apostle Paul founded a church during his eighteen months' sojourn in Corinth, A.D. 52–53 (Acts 18:1-17). Later on, while Paul was at Ephesus (A.D. 54–57) he wrote this letter.

The occasion of Paul's first letter was simply the deteriorating quality of church life at Corinth, including divisions and disorders among them, domestic and social troubles, and certain doctrinal issues. Paul's purpose in writing was to rebuke the disorders and resolve the difficulties.

The opening verses are important because of the facts revealed about the writer and his readers. Paul did not describe himself personally, but he did give his life's calling, "an apostle of Christ Jesus." Paul's readers were the Christians who comprised the church at Corinth. They were "sanctified in Christ Jesus," which means they had believed the Gospel message, repented, and trusted in Christ as Lord and Savior. In Christ they were also "called to be holy."

As we shall see later on, they did not always act sanctified and holy. Nevertheless, Paul's subsequent appeals and instructions were based on what these believers had become in Christ. To be sanctified meant to be set apart for holy purposes; holiness described what Christ had done for them through His death. Therefore, they could rightfully be expected to live consistently with their high calling in Christ.

B. Paul's Greeting: vs. 3

Grace and peace to you from God our Father and the Lord Jesus Christ.

Paul concluded his preface with a typical Christian greeting: a wish for spiritual grace and peace. These spiritual gifts belong to those who have committed themselves to God through faith in His Son.

Grace is God's gift that enables us to be forgiven, to have Christ's righteousness, and to receive eternal life. No one can be good enough to earn God's grace. It is unmerited favor.

Peace is the assurance that all who are in Christ share because of their justification (Rom. 5:1). God's Spirit testifies to their relationship (Rom. 8:16).

II. The Apostle's Confidence: 1 Corinthians 1:4-9

A. Thanksgiving for Grace: vs. 4

I always thank God for you because of his grace given you in Christ Jesus.

Before launching into a discussion of his concerns about the church, Paul wisely reviewed the foundations of his confidence in the believers. He started with the fact that he could be thankful for the Corinthians because of the work of God's grace in their hearts. The fullest demonstration of God's grace was the sending of His Son to die for the sins of the world. If anyone doubts God's grace, the cross proves otherwise.

In the midst of an utterly pagan society, God's grace had appeared at Corinth when the apostle Paul brought the good news of the Gospel. His grace had radically transformed them from pagan idolaters to worshipers of the one true God. Paul could truly be thankful for the remarkable changes wrought by the grace of God in Christ.

B. Enrichment in Christ: vss. 5-6

For in him you have been enriched in every way—in all your speaking and in all your knowledge—because our testimony about Christ was confirmed in you.

The Corinthians had to be reminded of all that God had given to them when they first believed the Gospel. Their lives had "been enriched in every way."

Paul selected just two ways their lives had been enriched, in their "speaking" and in their "knowledge." They had not only grasped the truth in Christ, they had also learned how to express it. Interestingly, these two gifts were highly prized by all cultured Greeks, and the Corinthians were in danger of being carried away by their giftedness. Later in his letter, Paul dealt with the abuse of these gifts.

However, here Paul thanked God for the fact that his witness to Christ had been accepted and "confirmed" in the Corinthians. They were living proof of the power of the Gospel.

C. Eager Waiting: vs. 7

Therefore you do not lack any spiritual gift as you eagerly wait for our Lord Jesus Christ to be revealed.

Because the Corinthians had been enriched in every way (vs. 5), they did not lack any spiritual gifts. Paul will later on give a full discussion of spiritual gifts. Here, his purpose was just to remind the Corinthians of his thankfulness for spiritual giftedness in the church.

At the same time, he reminded them of the certain hope of Christ's return. He was confident that Jesus would soon be revealed, so he encouraged the Corinthians to eagerly look for Jesus, too.

The Lord's return was always central in Paul's experience. It was an anchor for his soul as he waged spiritual warfare for the cause of Christ. Consequently, when persecution set in, the early church adapted Paul's stance of eager anticipation for Jesus to come. Uniformly, they expected His return. This hope purified and strengthened their faith.

D. Consummation in Christ: vs. 8

He will keep you strong to the end, so that you will be blameless on the day of our Lord Jesus Christ.

Paul anticipated Christ's return with confidence because he knew Christ would keep His own safe to the end. The implication was that being a Christian is a battle, and believers need Christ's strength to prevail. "He will keep you" is the Christian's stronghold in the midst of life's struggles.

Paul claimed Christ's power to keep us strong and to keep us blameless. The crucial thing is to stand blameless before Jesus when He returns. "The day of our Lord Jesus Christ" is the time of His appearing again. At that time, all things will be consummated in Him and He will assume His rightful place as Lord of lords and King of kings. God's purpose is "to bring all things in heaven and on earth together under one head, even Christ" (Eph. 1:10).

"Blameless" does not mean perfect, or without sin. Rather, it means unimpeachable. No charges can be brought against us, because of our forgiveness and perfection in Christ. "Who will bring any charge against those whom God has chosen? It is God who justifies. Who is he that condemns? Christ Jesus . . . is at the right hand of God and is also interceding for us" (Rom. 8:33-34).

E. God's Faithfulness: vs. 9

God, who has called you into fellowship with his Son Jesus Christ our Lord, is faithful.

Just to be absolutely sure that his confidence is not misplaced, Paul declared that God is faithful. His promises are true. We can utterly depend on God's faithfulness, love, and mercy. The church is a fellowship of those who belong to Christ. Therefore, every believer can live in the assurance of God's promises.

God's faithfulness is anchored in Christ. Therefore, growth in Christian love and unity depends on our walk with Christ. In Christ we have all the spiritual gifts we need. In Christ we have the hope of His return and the hope of standing before Him in worship and praise. In Christ we have the assurance of God's faithfulness, that He will indeed keep us strong and safe.

III. THE CHURCH'S STRIFE: 1 CORINTHIANS 1:10-17

A. The Demand for Unity: vs. 10

I appeal to you, brothers, in the name of our Lord Jesus Christ, that all of you agree with one another so that there may be no divisions among you and that you may be perfectly united in mind and thought.

In 1 Corinthians 1—6 Paul deals vigorously with reports of scandals in the church. One of these was quarreling among believers (1:10—4:21) that led to divisions in the church. The Christians were "acting like mere men" (3:3), not like sisters and brothers in Christ.

Therefore, Paul demanded that they be "perfectly united in mind and thought." He based his appeal on Jesus, not his own authority or friendship. The demand for unity among believers was Christ's command (John 13:34-35). Christians should act as one in the church because this is what Christ wants. To permit strife and divisions is disobedience to Christ.

Because the church belongs to Jesus, we must do away with disagreements that divide us. Of course, Paul knew that unity in the church must come out of personal commitment to Christ. The deeper we know and love Him, the less we are going to engage in church strife and insist on having our own way.

Paul demanded mutual agreement, an end to dissension, and unity of mind and judgment. To agree with one another literally means to say the same thing. The Greek word translated "united" was used for mending fishing nets, or mending your ways.

Paul did not mean that Christians have to be clones of one another. We do have different opinions about a great many things, but when we allow these differences to cause conflict and dissension, we harm our unity in Christ. When it comes to the basic teachings and purposes of the church, we are to be of one mind.

B. The Report of Quarrels: vss. 11-12

My brothers, some from Chloe's household have informed me that there are quarrels among you. What I mean is this: One of you says, "I follow Paul"; another, "I follow Apollos"; another, "I follow Cephas"; still another, "I follow Christ."

Instead of unity at Corinth there was quarreling. The news had come to Paul from "Chloe's household." We have little information on this group, but obviously, they were disinterested critics outside the church parties mentioned.

Paul was shocked by the idea of Christians quarreling. We learn the nature of the quarrels, but the reasons are unclear. Obviously, the church was split into personality parties, but why? The people named could not be faulted.

Some said they belonged to Paul. Probably they were his converts. Apollos succeeded Paul at Corinth (Acts 18:24; 19:1). His eloquence probably appealed to Greeks and his Bible knowledge to Jews. Cephas is Aramaic for Peter. Perhaps he had visited Corinth (1 Cor. 9:5), or perhaps this party simply honored him because he was a leader in the church in Jerusalem. What about those who said they follow Christ? Perhaps they were the super-spiritual ones who claimed to be above all the others.

Whatever the reasons for these parties in the church, the believers were using different names to cover their deep-seated differences in other matters.

C. The Quarrels Ridiculed: vs. 13

Is Christ divided? Was Paul crucified for you? Were you baptized into the name of Paul?

Paul exposed the foolishness of these quarrels at Corinth by asking three questions about Jesus. Of course, Jesus was not divided. In fact, Jesus had taught that His own oneness with His Father was the model for the unity of His followers (John 17:21). Therefore, how could those who professed to follow Christ be divided?

No apostle, teacher, or evangelist had been crucified for the believers. Only Jesus had died for them. They were all sinners, all saved by the same grace, all the recipients of the benefits of Christ's death. Therefore, they should join together in unity rather than promoting human parties.

The believers had been baptized in Christ's name, not in the name of some other person. Their baptism had identified them with Jesus. They were members of His body. The church belonged to Christ, not to others.

D. The Mission Defined: vss. 14-17

I am thankful that I did not baptize any of you except Crispus and Gaius, so no one can say that you were baptized into my name. (Yes, I also baptized the household of Stephanas; beyond that, I don't remember if I baptized anyone else.) For Christ did not send me to baptize, but to preach the gospel—not with words of human wisdom, lest the cross of Christ be emptied of its power.

Baptizing could possibly lead some to accuse Paul of trying to rally a group of his own followers. In response, Paul said that although he did baptize some, they were not baptized in his name, but in the name of Christ.

Paul laid that issue to rest by stating his primary mission, which was to preach the Gospel. He was also concerned lest anyone think he was drawing people to himself with his eloquence. If that were true, listeners would miss the power of the cross of Christ.

The Gospel is the message of the cross. Everything else is secondary. Therefore, the key to Christian unity is to focus on proclaiming the Gospel of the cross. If we do that, we will not be sidetracked by lesser issues that destroy our unity.

Discussion Questions

1. If you had to choose two adjectives to describe the body of believers in your church, what would they be? Why?
2. How do our lives change when we are given a new identity in Christ?
3. Of what value is it to be assured of our spiritual giftedness and security we have in Christ?

4. How does the hope of Christ's return serve to promote unity among Christians?

5. What potential causes of disunity do you see in your church?

6. How can we help to pull one another together around the basics of what Jesus has done for us?

Contemporary Application

If the apostle Paul were to write to your church, how would he rate your church unity on a scale of one to ten? One thing we can be sure of is that the apostle took seriously the problem of disunity at Corinth. He did not ignore it, or sweep it under the rug. He knew that strife in the church disgraced the name of Christ, and hindered unbelievers from coming to Him.

Sadly, some churches do not take unity as seriously as Paul did. We cannot disregard unity and accept church fights as the norm. One of the reasons for our spiritual impotence is that we do not give high priority to being "perfectly united in mind and thought." We say we follow Christ, but we disobey Him when we fall into divisions. He said the world would believe when Christians live in unity (John 17:21).

The Holy Spirit as Teacher

DEVOTIONAL READING

1 Corinthians 3:1-9

DAILY BIBLE READINGS

Monday March 6
1 Corinthians 2:1-5
Proclaiming Christ Crucified

Tuesday March 7
1 Corinthians 2:6-16 The
True Wisdom of God

Wednesday March 8
1 Corinthians 3:1-9 Put
Away Quarrels and
Jealousies

Thursday March 9
1 Corinthians 3:10-15
Build on the Foundation of
Jesus Christ

Friday March 10
1 Corinthians 3:16-23 We
Belong to God through
Jesus Christ

Saturday March 11
Romans 8:1-8 Life in the
Spirit

Sunday March 12
Romans 8:9-17 We Are
Children of God

Scripture

Background Scripture: *1 Corinthians 2—3*
Scripture Lesson: *1 Corinthians 2:1-2, 4-13, 15-16*
Key Verse: *We have not received the spirit of the world*
but the Spirit who is from God, that we may understand
what God has freely given us. 1 Corinthians 2:12
Scripture Lesson for Children: *1 Corinthians 3:10-*
11; Matthew 7:24-27
Key Verse for Children: *"If you love me, you will obey*
what I command." John 14:15.

Lesson Aim

To appreciate and apply the values of God's
wisdom.

Lesson Setting

Time: *A.D. 55*
Place: *Written to Corinth from Ephesus*

Lesson Outline

The Holy Spirit as Teacher
   I. God's Power in Christ: 1 Corinthians 2:1-2, 4-5
       A. *Human Wisdom Rejected: vs. 1*
       B. *Singleness of Purpose: vs. 2*
       C. *Demonstration of God's Power: vs. 4*
       D. *Faith in God Alone: vs. 5*
  II. God's Wisdom: 1 Corinthians 2:6-8
       A. *Is Not of This Age: vs. 6*
       B. *Is Concealed: vs. 7*
       C. *In Christ's Crucifixion: vs. 8*
 III. Wisdom Received: 1 Corinthians 2:9-13, 15-16
       A. *Not by Natural Means: vs. 9*
       B. *Revealed by the Holy Spirit: vss. 10-11*
       C. *Understanding God's Gifts: vs. 12*
       D. *Teaching by the Holy Spirit: vs. 13*
       E. *The Mind of Christ: vss. 15-16*

Introduction for Adults

Topic: *True Wisdom: A Basis for Unity*

Probably in few areas of church life is there more need for God's wisdom than in achieving spiritual unity. Sadly, when differences of opinion erupt, too often they are debated according to the world's wisdom, not God's. We forget that as believers in Christ we are supposed to use the mind of Christ, not purely human standards.

Of course, this is not always easy. Take the church budget, for example. Recently one of the elders of a local church was fuming because he thought the elders had made a serious mistake on a budget item. His was a minority opinion, however, and he lost the vote on this issue. He had a point. He wanted to be more generous, while the others thought the church could not afford this particular expenditure.

Which side had a corner on God's wisdom? What principles of the Gospel apply in cases like this? Were the elders deciding the issue strictly by human standards? In many cases, the answer is Yes. We look at projected income and expenses, and vote accordingly. The question is, How can and should church leaders be led by the Holy Spirit in making their decisions? Of course, we must look at the balance sheets, but we must also seek God's wisdom.

Introduction for Youths

Topic: *In the Know*

Several years ago at a well-known college, one of the students told the dean that Christians would make better grades than the unbelievers, just because they were Christians. His claim embarrassed a lot of his fellow Christians, who knew very well that some of the unbelievers were smarter than they were and got better grades.

The Bible clearly teaches that the Holy Spirit can supply believers with divine wisdom. But does the Holy Spirit's presence guarantee an "A" in biology if you don't study? No. Every Christian student must work hard, pray faithfully, and trust God for the results. The Holy Spirit may not produce an "A," but He will give unusual peace and courage.

The Spirit's teaching brings Jesus to our hearts and minds. If we learn Jesus, as well as biology, then we are being faithful disciples. That is our primary objective, not making the dean's list.

Concepts for Children

Topic: *Be Good Builders*

1. We can build our lives on Jesus because He loves us and cares for us.
2. Having Jesus as our strong foundation gives us hope and courage.
3. We can help our friends to trust in Jesus.
4. Jesus warned us about the dangers of disobeying His words.
5. For a truly secure life, we can trust what Jesus tells us to do.
6. When difficulties assail us, we can go to Jesus for hope and strength.

The Lesson Commentary

I. GOD'S POWER IN CHRIST: 1 CORINTHIANS 2:1-2, 4-5

A. Human Wisdom Rejected: vs. 1

When I came to you, brothers, I did not come with eloquence or superior wisdom as I proclaimed to you the testimony about God.

In 1 Corinthians 1—3 the apostle Paul drew a clear line between man's wisdom and God's. Many of the Corinthian believers had been raised in the glories of Greek philosophy and learning. Such wisdom was their highest goal in life. Serious intellectual debates were not limited to the universities.

What did Paul mean when he said he rejected human wisdom? To the Greeks, "wisdom" meant careful intellectual and philosophical reasoning (content), plus great oratorical ability to teach it skillfully.

For Paul, however, the issue went much deeper. On the one hand, his teaching about Christ's death and resurrection was completely foreign to the Greek philosophical concepts. On the other hand, Paul's teaching was far superior to Greek philosophy because it revealed God's power and wisdom.

But what about the Greeks' highly polished oratory? Paul admitted he did not measure up to their expectations. In fact, Paul had deliberately rejected what he called "eloquence and superior wisdom," the foundations of Greek philosophy. He preached the plain truth about God and the cross of Jesus Christ. (See 1 Cor. 15:3-8.)

We cannot infer from Paul's statement here that the Christian faith lacks a sound intellectual basis. The Gospel is not irrational. Paul did not preach out of ignorance. He was an accomplished scholar himself, and appreciated sound logic.

Paul emphasized that the Gospel's claim to truth did not rest on his speaking skills or following the accepted Greek philosophical values and methods. He did not avoid the challenges of human wisdom, but grappled with them.

B. Singleness of Purpose: vs. 2

For I resolved to know nothing while I was with you except Jesus Christ and him crucified.

Christ crucified was Paul's challenge to Greek philosophy and eloquence. He refused to be drawn into endless debates about religion and philosophy, even though he was well-versed in those subjects. By focusing on the cross, Paul made a clear distinction between the Christian message and the ideas of the philosophers.

Paul's singleness of purpose and preaching made it clear that human wisdom was not the highest authority. Rather, God's revelation in Christ was ultimate truth. Therefore, the Corinthians had to decide, because they were under considerable pressure to conform to human wisdom. Paul sought to reinforce their conviction that Christ and His death for their sins was far superior to any Greek philosophical system.

C. Demonstration of God's Power: vs. 4

My message and my preaching were not with wise and persuasive words, but with a demonstration of the Spirit's power, . . .

Paul was keenly aware of his human limitations (vs. 3), but he refused to rely on "wise and persuasive words." Of course, in public debates the Greek orators tried to demonstrate their intellectual superiority. But Paul did not try to meet the Greeks on their terms. Instead, he relied on the power of the Holy Spirit. Corinth was full of brilliant speakers, with scintillating ideas, but none of them possessed the power of the Holy Spirit.

Greek philosophers changed "truth" from generation to generation. Paul, however, taught the truth of the Holy Spirit, which is eternal and unchangeable. This is an important difference between human wisdom and God's wisdom.

D. Faith in God Alone: vs. 5

. . . so that your faith might not rest on men's wisdom, but on God's power.

Paul gave a powerful reason for rejecting human wisdom and eloquence in favor of God's wisdom and the Holy Spirit's power. He did not want to win philosophical debates with the Greeks; he wanted to win people to faith in Christ.

There was great competition among the Greek teachers for converts. The philosopher with the most converts won great public acclaim. Likewise, Paul wanted to win converts, but not to himself and his philosophy. He wanted to lead people to Christ.

Paul saw only two possibilities for converts. Their faith could rest either on human wisdom or on God's power. If the former, then it could be swayed and changed by a more brilliant speaker. If the latter, then it was secure. The Corinthians' faith was firm because it rested in God's power revealed in Jesus Christ.

II. GOD'S WISDOM: 1 CORINTHIANS 2:6-8

A. Is Not of This Age: vs. 6

We do, however, speak a message of wisdom among the mature, but not the wisdom of this age or of the rulers of this age, who are coming to nothing.

Paul knew there was a strong possibility the believers would misunderstand his either-or statement about human wisdom and God's wisdom. He did not want their faith to rest in his own cleverness and persuasiveness; he wanted it to rest in God alone. Therefore, he had to contrast God's wisdom and man's.

"The wisdom of this age" centered in human philosophy. It originated with and belonged to human beings. The world's rulers, both religious and political, propagated it. Human wisdom has many starting points, it changes, and it has no unifying center.

Of course, Paul did not mean that Christians should denigrate human learning and knowledge. God has demonstrated His common grace in giving us the benefits of research, education, art, music, medicine, and literature. But in some instances, human knowledge can be an obstacle to faith in Christ. In any case, human wisdom can never be a substitute for knowing and obeying God's wisdom.

B. Is Concealed: vs. 7

No, we speak of God's secret wisdom, a wisdom that has been hidden and that God destined for our glory before time began.

After describing what God's wisdom is not (vs. 6), Paul told what it is: a secret hidden from human understanding, but now revealed through him. It is a "secret," not in the sense of a puzzle or mystery, but in the sense that it was previously unknown. God planned it "before time began" for the "glory" of His church. God's secret was framed in eternity past, to restore people to Himself through Jesus Christ.

Paul produced another sharp contrast between human wisdom and God's. The former leads to frustration because each succeeding generation of philosophers brings a new teaching, supplanting the old. However, God revealed His wisdom "for our glory," that is for the glory of His church.

God's wisdom produces glory through forgiveness and salvation in Christ. God's wisdom heals humanity's fundamental dilemma: the problem of sin and its consequences. Because God's wisdom solves that dilemma, it far surpasses any human philosophy or religious system of thought.

C. In Christ's Crucifixion: vs. 8

None of the rulers of this age understood it, for if they had, they would not have crucified the Lord of glory.

Christ's crucifixion exposes the foolishness of human wisdom. Jesus did not conform to human religion and philosophy. From a purely human standpoint, He was beyond understanding. He brought God's wisdom from above, not only by teaching it but by living it. His wisdom was so holy and pure that He exposed hypocrisy even among the most dedicated religious people. They could not stand His exposure of their corrupt hearts. Because the political and religious leaders could not understand God's wisdom in Christ, they put Him to death.

III. WISDOM RECEIVED: 1 CORINTHIANS 2:9-13, 15-16

A. Not by Natural Means: vs. 9

However, as it is written: "No eye has seen, no ear has heard, no mind has conceived what God has prepared for those who love him."

Paul outlined two approaches to wisdom, the one earthly (human) and the other heavenly (spiritual). Human wisdom is attained by years of study, but God's wisdom is given to people who place their faith in Christ and study His Word.

Paul knew how human wisdom is discovered: first, by observation ("eye has seen . . . ear has heard"); second, by deduction ("mind has conceived"). Sometimes researchers stumble on truth by accident, or by a hunch, but most of the time they do painstaking observation, interpretation, and application.

But God reveals His wisdom in a totally different way. He has "prepared (it) for those who love him." His truth is reserved for those who commit themselves to Him in faith, trust, and obedience. We must commit our wills to Christ before we can receive and understand God's wisdom.

B. Revealed by the Holy Spirit: vss. 10-11

But God has revealed it to us by his Spirit. The Spirit searches all things, even the deep things of God. For who among men knows the thoughts of a man except the man's spirit within him? In the same way no one knows the thoughts of God except the Spirit of God.

Once we receive God's love, a wonderful spiritual program unfolds. Suddenly what once seemed like foolishness begins to make sense. Everything fits; it's perfectly logical. The blinders to our spiritual eyes and ears are removed, so we can understand Jesus and the Gospel.

Paul described the Holy Spirit as both the searcher and revealer of God's wisdom. "The deep things of God" can be known by anyone, regardless of age or education. God's "deep things" are not esoteric philosophical mysteries, but the simple truths of the Gospel.

God's wisdom cannot be discovered by human reason, because only God's Spirit knows God's thoughts. He makes them known to those who have experienced the new birth, which Jesus described as the work of the Holy Spirit (John 3:5-8).

C. Understanding God's Gifts: vs. 12

We have not received the spirit of the world but the Spirit who is from God, that we may understand what God has freely given us.

The Greek philosophers possessed "the spirit of the world," but they did not possess "the Spirit who is from God." Therefore, Paul's message was foolishness to them. Without God's Spirit, no one can understand the Gospel. It doesn't make sense that salvation should be a gift. Such an idea is contrary to human wisdom. Acceptance in the world's religions insists that salvation is earned by good deeds.

Christians, on the other hand, have received the Holy Spirit so they can understand God's gifts. Even the humblest, poorest, least educated believer at Corinth possessed God's Spirit and thus could enter into God's wisdom.

D. Teaching by the Holy Spirit: vs. 13

This is what we speak, not in words taught us by human wisdom but in words taught by the Spirit, expressing spiritual truths in spiritual words.

Paul himself taught God's wisdom by the Holy Spirit. He did not come to Corinth with a new human philosophy, but with "spiritual truths" taught "in spiritual words." He taught divinely revealed wisdom to those who possessed the Holy Spirit.

E. The Mind of Christ: vss. 15-16

The spiritual man makes judgments about all things, but he himself is not subject to any man's judgment: "For who has known the mind of the Lord that he may instruct him?" But we have the mind of Christ.

In contrast to the person who does not have the Holy Spirit, Christians have spiritual discernment, the ability to make "judgments about all things." We can grow in wisdom and knowledge, if we use the Word of God properly and open ourselves to the Spirit's teaching. However, sin in our lives cuts our spiritual vision and hinders our spiritual receptivity.

The answer to Paul's question in verse 16 is obvious: No one instructs the Lord. Christians get their instructions from the Lord because they have a price-less possession: the mind of Christ. All of His wisdom, love, and humility are available to every believer. It is possible to grow in Christlikeness. Christians gain God's wisdom, not for intellectual speculation, but so they can live fully pleasing to Him in all things.

Discussion Questions

1. What kinds of human wisdom represent challenges to the Gospel?
2. How can we prepare ourselves to meet these challenges?
3. Why is it sometimes hard to explain the simple truths of the Gospel?
4. What encouragement do you take from Paul's example?
5. Why is it necessary to confess faith in Christ before receiving God's wisdom?
6. How does the Holy Spirit make God's truths clear to Christians?

Contemporary Application

Our hearts and minds are battlegrounds for truth. The classic struggle is waged when we hear the Gospel and decide it's either foolishness or the great-est news we have ever heard. So much of our secular education tells us it's foolishness. We have to take a monumental step of faith to believe.

The battle never stops, as the apostle Paul well knew. We need the constant reinforcement that God's wisdom is far superior to any human system or reli-gion. When people waver in their faith commitment, it's largely because they have not immersed themselves in Scripture and in prayer.

The church has a tremendous responsibility to teach believers how to build on their faith. Faith is not an irrational leap in the dark. Jesus really lived and died for us, He ascended into heaven, He sent His Holy Spirit to teach us, and He is coming again.

Basically, we have to choose God's wisdom over earthly wisdom, because human wisdom is bereft of what we need for God's forgiveness and eternal life.

The Church and Its Leaders

Scripture

Background Scripture: *1 Corinthians 4:1-13*
Scripture Lesson: *1 Corinthians 4:1-13*
Key Verse: *So then, men ought to regard us as servants of Christ and as those entrusted with the secret things of God.* 1 Corinthians 4:1.
Scripture Lesson for Children: *1 Corinthians 4:1-2; Matthew 25:14-23, 28-29*
Key Verse: *You have been faithful with a few things; I will put you in charge of many things.* Matthew 25:21.

Lesson Aim

To respect and pray for our Christian leaders.

Lesson Setting

Time: *A.D. 55*
Place: *Written to Corinth from Ephesus*

Lesson Outline

The Church and Its Leaders
  I Faithful Leaders: 1 Corinthians 4:1-2
    A. *Entrusted with God's Secrets: vs. 1*
    B. *Required to Be Faithful: vs. 2*
  II. Judgment of Leaders: 1 Corinthians 4:3-5
    A. *God Is the Judge: vss. 3- 4*
    B. *Motives Will Be tested: vs. 5*
  III The Cost of Faithfulness: 1 Corinthians 4:6-13
    A. *Humility: vss. 6-7*
    B. *Hostility: vs. 8*
    C. *Contempt: vss. 9-10*
    D. *Suffering: vs. 11*
    E. *Patient Love: vss. 12-13a*
    F. *Rejection: vs. 13b*

Introduction for Adults

Topic: *Mature Leaders Bring Unity*

David the psalmist sang, "How good and pleasant it is when brothers live together in unity!" (Ps. 133:1). Israel's king was well acquainted with the perils of disunity. He saw the tragedies of strife under King Saul. Later on, he suffered rebellion in his own family. Sadly, in some churches unity is hard to come by, and the witness to Jesus suffers great harm.

However, God has blessed His church with mature leaders. When they teach and preach God's Word and love God's people, the outcome is spiritual maturity. However, as the apostle Paul discovered, achieving unity is not without considerable pain and suffering. We are astounded when we read what he had to endure.

Paul's story should alert us to spiritual discipline. If our leaders are to bless us and help us to grow, we need to lay aside our differences and focus on our worship and the tasks God has given us. When Jesus Christ is central, our differences seem inconsequential. When we support and encourage our leaders, God gives them zeal and wisdom to lead His people in the right way.

Introduction for Youths

Topic: *Lead, but Serve*

One of the social changes that has baffled observers of youth culture is the apparent lack of interest in leadership. For example, leaders of youth organizations on campuses and in churches find it hard to develop leaders. There does not seem to be a natural appetite for the responsibilities of leadership.

Perhaps one reason is that failures of leaders are well publicized. On the highest levels of business, education, and government, leaders have been found guilty of various wrongs. Of course, another reason might be that many youth are more interested in themselves than in organized group activities.

Whatever the case, we recognize that God calls leaders, not to be dictators, but to be servants. Perhaps we have drawn a false picture of what true leadership is. In God's eyes, it entails love, patience, wisdom, and even suffering. The church is an ideal proving ground for leadership. We can encourage youth to strive for leadership, because both church and society in the future will need leaders with Christian values and qualities.

Concepts for Children

Topic: *Be Good Caretakers*

1. We can thank God for the faithful leaders in our churches.
2. God helps us grow and worship Him through the teaching of our leaders.
3. Jesus can help us serve Him in our homes, schools, and churches.
4. He expects us to be faithful in using all of His good gifts,
5. Occasionally we are afraid to risk our Christian faith for the sake of others.
6. We can pray and ask God for wisdom, strength, and courage to give our lives to Him.

The Lesson Commentary

I. FAITHFUL LEADERS: 1 CORINTHIANS 4:1-2

A. Entrusted with God's Secrets: vs. 1

So then, men ought to regard us as servants of Christ and as those entrusted with the secret things of God.

One of the worst problems in the church at Corinth was bickering and division. People really got nasty with each other. The church at Corinth was like the city itself, a volatile racial and social mixture. Very few of the church members were wealthy, influential people. Most of the converts came from the lower classes.

They had little to brag about, but they had the Greek proclivity to brag about how much they knew. This was another irritant that blew the church apart.

Paul began his letter with greetings and prayer (1:1-9), and then plunged into the issue of rival cliques that were destroying the church (1:10—4:21). He reminded them that their human cleverness was a far cry from God's wisdom (1:18—2:16). There was no room for pride. In fact, Paul testified that being a faithful Christian leader meant facing all kinds of persecution and suffering (4:1-13). The Corinthian believers must follow his example instead of exalting themselves at the expense of their fellow Christians.

The apostles who were their leaders saw themselves as servants. If the Corinthians wanted to see a picture of a true Christian leader, it would be that of a servant, not a dictator, military conqueror, or professor of philosophy. Many of the early Christians were slaves, or household servants, so they well knew the model Paul was identifying.

Paul considered himself totally at the command of Jesus Christ. That was his calling. It was also his freedom. In the Christian view of life, servanthood is the highest calling because it frees us from ourselves to serve Christ.

Because he was Christ's servant, he had been entrusted with God's secrets. His secrets are not revealed to an inner circle of erudite scholars, but to all who confess Jesus as Lord and Savior. The Gospel is God's secret because it's so contrary to the best the world has to offer: Christ's death as payment for our sins, and His resurrection so that we can become alive with Him, not only in this world but for eternity.

In Paul's case, he first met Christ when he was traveling to Damascus to imprison Christians. When he said yes to Jesus, he went first to Arabia and then to Damascus for three years (Gal. 1:17-18). That's where the Holy Spirit taught him God's secrets, which he later preached and then wrote in his letters.

Despite all these advantages, Paul was still a servant. His approach to leadership in the church is the best one to follow.

B. Required to Be Faithful: vs. 2

Now it is required that those who have been given a trust must prove faithful.

Paul had been entrusted with the Gospel; therefore, a heavy responsibility fell upon him. He was accountable as a leader for how he discharged his sacred trust. Paul continually served with a sense of divine obligation (Rom. 1:14-15).

He had to prove as faithful to his trust as the executor of an estate is. The executor is accountable for how he or she carries out the terms of the will of the deceased. That is faithfulness to a specific calling. The Gospel had been given to Paul as a trust. He could not ignore the terms of the trust. Since he was a leader, he had to carry it out.

Proving faithful meant staying true to the good news of Christ's death and resurrection. Paul could not change the message he had been given by God. He could not quit as an evangelist, teacher, and leader, no matter how tough the opposition might be (1 Cor. 4:9-13).

Being faithful meant enduring hardships and staying on the job, even when he got criticism, stoning, and imprisonment. Paul knew that one day he would stand before Christ his judge. He would have to give an account for how faithful he had been with his stewardship of the Gospel (3:10-15).

II. JUDGMENT OF LEADERS: 1 CORINTHIANS 4:3-5

A. God Is the Judge: vss. 3-4

I care very little if I am judged by you or by any human court; indeed, I do not even judge myself. My conscience is clear, but that does not make me innocent. It is the Lord who judges me.

Leaders may be judged by other people, by courts, by their own consciences, and by the Lord. The apostle Paul knew the Corinthians were judging him and his leadership very severely. But he reminded them that he was, in the final reckoning, not going to be judged by them, or by any human court of law.

This does not mean he was unresponsive to their concerns. He loved them deeply. But as a servant of Christ he was accountable to a higher power. It would have been easy to judge himself. However, when we do that, we usually pass. No leader judges himself to be a failure.

Of course, conscience is a severe judge, given by God to keep us on track with His will. But we can turn off conscience. Paul said his conscience was clear. He had no regrets for how he had exercised his apostolic leadership. But then he pointed to the only judge who counts—the Lord.

Leaders are accountable to God. They are judged by people, the courts, and their consciences, and they may pass those tests, but ultimately every leader answers to God. When leaders recognize that God judges them, they will act responsibly according to the principles of the Gospel and the Word of God.

B. Motives Will Be Tested: vs. 5

Therefore judge nothing before the appointed time; wait till the Lord comes. He will bring to light what is hidden in darkness and will expose the motives of men's hearts. At that time each will receive his praise from God.

> Paul warned the Corinthians against making premature judgments according to human standards. Judgment awaits the Lord's coming, so we cannot jump to conclusions. Rather than hastily judge our leaders, we must patiently wait until God's judgment is revealed.
>
> The reason human judgments often are wrong is that we cannot see inner motives. We cannot probe and find the real reasons behind the conduct of our leaders. Only God can do that. God's searchlight of truth will prove and expose "the motives of men's hearts."
>
> That's a frightening prospect if our motives are evil and self-centered. But Paul was confident of passing the test and receiving God's approval. Therefore, it is quite encouraging to know that if our leaders are following the Lord, and doing His will, they will gain God's praise. This is a heartening prospect. This truth guards against our making hasty, erroneous judgments, and it also assures us that God will reward faithful leaders.

III. THE COST OF FAITHFULNESS: 1 CORINTHIANS 4:6-13

A. Humility: vss. 6-7

Now, brothers, I have applied these things to myself and Apollos for your benefit, so that you may learn from us the meaning of the saying, "Do not go beyond what is written." Then you will not take pride in one man over against another. For who makes you different from anyone else? What do you have that you did not receive? And if you did receive it, why do you boast as though you did not?

> The church leaders in Corinth who were bragging were the various party leaders mentioned in 1:10-12. During his first visit to Corinth Paul could not speak to them as mature spiritual leaders (3:1; compare Eph. 4:13-16). They were young in the faith and had not grown significantly since then. That's why Paul said they were "acting like mere men" (1 Cor. 3:3).
>
> Trying to rid the church of divisions based on party loyalties, Paul told them that the same standards applied to them as to himself and Apollos. He blamed their pride and used himself and Apollos as examples to follow ("so that you may learn from us"). They were all under the same standards of judgment, the Scripture ("what is written").
>
> These leaders needed a good dose of humility. Paul fingered their root problem: taking "pride in one man over against another." If they really understood God's Word, they would appreciate the destructiveness of the party spirit. Time and again, Paul rebuked them for their lack of humility, which showed itself in their conceit and arrogance (4:18-19; 5:2; 8:8; 13:4).
>
> Paul reminded them that they could not brag about their own accomplishments, because everything they were had been given to them by God. Their

claims to preeminence were unfounded. They were not above ("different from") other people, because all were gifted.

Paul used the word "receive" to show that the giver was God Himself. Their superiority was self-assumed. Their boasting was inappropriate because they owed everything to God's grace.

B. Hostility: vs. 8

Already you have all you want! Already you have become rich! You have become kings—and that without us! How I wish that you really had become kings so that we might be kings with you!

Faithful leaders will face hostility from those who think they have arrived. Paul and Apollos confronted a group of people suffering from delusions of grandeur. According to their self-delusion, they were filled, they were rich, they were reigning like kings. They had reached these lofty heights without Paul and Apollos, implying that they had left them behind on a much lower level. They had even achieved the final triumphant state.

Paul addressed their hostility with bitter irony and perhaps sarcasm. He exposed their unreasonableness and foolishness. Paul tried to make them face up to their dangerous spiritual peril because of their smug self-satisfaction. The self-sufficient often belittle their leaders.

C. Contempt: vss. 9-10

For it seems to me that God has put us apostles on display at the end of the procession, like men condemned to die in the arena. We have been made a spectacle to the whole universe, to angels as well as to men. We are fools for Christ, but you are so wise in Christ! We are weak, but you are strong! You are honored, we are dishonored!

Faithful leaders often face public contempt. "For" introduces the reason for Paul's wish at the end of verse 8. Rather than reigning as kings with the proud party leaders, the apostles were treated like common criminals on their way to execution. Convicted criminals were paraded in public.

In Paul's thinking their humiliation stretched beyond the streets of the Roman Empire; it extended to the ends of the universe and to angels. However, to Paul, this was not bad luck. It was a God-given circumstance. He had put them on display as a public spectacle.

Therefore, the apostles were those who truly showed what it meant to be Christ's disciples, not the full, rich "kings" at Corinth. Being "condemned to die" was what Jesus said His followers should be ready to face. They had to bear the cross for His sake (Matt. 16:24). Public contempt did not humiliate these leaders because their "spectacle" really demonstrated what it meant to be a follower of Christ.

In verse 10 we see more of Paul's irony. How different his experience was from that of the party leaders. Not only were they full, rich, and royal, they were wise, strong, and honored. On the other hand, Paul and Apollos were paraded like criminals, and were considered fools, weak, and dishonorable. In effect, Paul said sarcastically, "How you are to be envied, while we are treated with contempt."

D. Suffering: vs. 11

To this very hour we go hungry and thirsty, we are in rags, we are brutally treated, we are homeless.

Paul enlarged on the cost of true spiritual leadership. In addition to hostility and contempt, the apostles endured physical suffering. Paul did not write of these sufferings in the past tense, but in the present ("to this very hour"), showing that there was no letup.

Hunger, thirst, brutality, homelessness, and lack of decent clothes were the lot of the apostles. They were treated like tramps, like the dregs of society. This was a far cry from the life of the self-sufficient, proud leaders.

E. Patient Love: vss. 12-13a

We work hard with our own hands. When we are cursed, we bless; when we are persecuted, we endure it; when we are slandered, we answer kindly.

Despite such harsh treatment, faithful leaders turn the other cheek with patient love. Paul also added that he did not back off from hard work. Manual labor was despised by the Greeks, but Paul gloried in it (1 Cor. 9:6; 1 Thess. 2:9). Paul mentioned work to highlight the failure of the exalted party leaders in the church to appreciate work as a true Christian virtue.

Also foreign to the haughty Greeks was the attitude commended by Jesus (Matt. 5:9-12, 38-42) which we call "turning the other cheek." Paul gave three examples of how godly leaders respond. When they are cursed, they say a blessing; when they are persecuted, they endure it without taking revenge; when they are slandered, they say a kind word. Such Christian qualities meant nothing to the proud party leaders at Corinth.

F. Rejection: vs. 13b

Up to this moment we have become the scum of the earth, the refuse of the world.

Faithful leaders sometimes face rejection. Paul's picture of rejection was a powerful culmination of his attack on the party leaders. Rather than ruling as kings (vs. 8), the apostles were being treated like garbage. The Greek word translated "scum" is much worse. It refers to human sacrifices. Only totally worthless people were chosen for sacrifice.

Perhaps Christian leaders find this hard to accept. Perhaps they will not be treated like Paul was. However, even though we are joint heirs with Christ, we are subject to suffering and rejection because of our faithfulness (Phil. 1:29).

Discussion Questions

1. How would you describe a faithful leader?
2. Since we are entrusted with the Gospel, how can we meet our obligation to "share the wealth" with others?
3. Describe in your own words the party leaders at Corinth. Why do you think they acted as they did?
4. How do you react to Paul's ironic or sarcastic response to the party leaders? What kind of spiritual leadership was he exercising?
5. What was the key to Paul's endurance of suffering, contempt, and rejection?
6. How can we help our leaders measure up to Paul's standards?

Contemporary Application

Leadership has a high cost. After reading what happened to Paul and Apollos, perhaps we say, "No thanks." But unless we face the high costs, and ask God to help us the way he helped Paul and Apollos, the church will suffer serious weaknesses.

The Holy Spirit calls people to leadership and we respond out of obedience to Christ. The church is enriched by godly leaders, who bless not only believers, but also show how Christ can meet the needs of those on the way to faith in him.

"Scum of the earth"? Perhaps in the eyes of some. But despite the risks, we know that the rewards of serving Christ far surpass any difficulties we may face. Leaders move ahead triumphantly, as Paul did, because they know that as they follow Jesus, He will meet all their needs.

Jesus told His people to pray for workers. Persevering prayer will do much to bring the right people to leadership in our churches.

The Need for Discipline in the Church

Scripture

Background Scripture: *1 Corinthians 5—6:11*
Scripture Lesson: *1 Corinthians 5:1-13*
Key Verse: *Therefore let us keep the Festival, not with the old yeast, the yeast of malice and wickedness, but with bread without yeast, the bread of sincerity and truth.* 1 Corinthians 5:8.
Scripture Lesson for Children: *1 Corinthians 6:12, 19-20; Daniel 1:8, 11-15*
Key Verse for Children: *Do you not know that your body is a temple of the Holy Spirit, who is in you?* 1 Corinthians 6:19.

Lesson Aim

To apply God's standards of holiness to church life.

Lesson Setting

Time: *A.D. 55*
Place: *Written to Corinth from Ephesus*

Lesson Outline

The Need for Discipline in the Church
  I. Sexual Immorality: 1 Corinthians 5:1-5
    A. *Case History: vss. 1-2*
    B. *Judgment: vs. 3*
    C. *Salvation: vss. 4-5*
  II. Purity: 1 Corinthians 5:6-8
    A. *Infection: vs. 6*
    B. *Prescription: vss. 7-8*
  III. Maintaining Holiness: 1 Corinthians 5:9-13
    A. *Standards: vss. 9-10*
    B. *Fellowship: vs. 11*
    C. *Expulsion: vss. 12-13*

Introduction for Adults

Topic: *Discipline Brings Unity*

After a missionary finished his sermon about living a holy life, one of his converts said, "I thought I was saved by grace alone. Now it looks as though I have to walk to heaven on the edge of a razor." The man had a keen way of expressing biblical truth. Sadly, Christians sometimes miss the biblical razor of holiness and its importance in personal and church life.

Christ's forgiveness is a free gift; salvation is by grace alone. But as Paul made clear to the church at Corinth, those who have received God's grace march to a different drummer. To maintain personal and corporate holiness and unity, the church must be a self-policing body.

The church is a body of fellow believers. It is knit together in Christ, its Head. Therefore, personal behavior affects common church life. The body gets sick when one member sins.

Introduction for Youths

Topic: *Who Enforces*

During basic training in the army, recruits are drilled in more than marching and firing a rifle. They are drilled in the principle that the behavior of every soldier in uniform reflects on the entire Army. Even one soldier who gets drunk in town reflects badly on his fellow soldiers, and tarnishes the public's image of the army.

The youth culture is something like that. We see one picture on television of a group of out-of-control high school kids, and we assume that all teenagers act that way. True, some of their habits and fads sweep through schools like a plague. At the same time, however, many do not conform.

Christians have a great opportunity to show what being a follower of Christ really means. The sad episode at Corinth proved that one bad apple can spoil the whole barrel. However, it is up to us to see that that does not happen in our churches. We have to help and encourage one another to stand true to Christ in our moral conduct. People will say of us, "So that's what a Christian looks like."

Concepts for Children

Topic: *Choose Wisely*

1. Jesus died for us and sends His Holy Spirit to live in us when we believe in Jesus.
2. Because our bodies are God's temple, we are called to obey Him and stay away from sin.
3. We can help one another to find ways to please God in our conduct.
4. God will give us the courage to do what is right.
5. We build our courage as we grow in faith, prayer, and knowledge of God's Word.

The Lesson Commentary

I. SEXUAL IMMORALITY: 1 CORINTHIANS 5:1-5

A. Case History: vss. 1-2

It is actually reported that there is sexual immorality among you, and of a kind that does not occur even among pagans: A man has his father's wife. And you are proud! Shouldn't you rather have been filled with grief and have put out of your fellowship the man who did this?

Chapters 5 and 6 of 1 Corinthians show the apostle Paul's strong concern about moral disorder in the church and the need for discipline. He has previously addressed the debilitating problems of worldly wisdom and the consequent divisions in the church caused by various cliques. He has exposed the dangers of following false apostles and defended his own calling and ministry.

"You are still worldly . . . acting like mere men," he had charged in connection with the previous problems (3:3). Although born again by faith in Christ, the believers at Corinth were "mere infants in Christ" (3:1). Nowhere was this more clearly seen than in the case of sexual immorality that was so upsetting.

This case of sexual immorality was so shocking that Paul said it was unknown among the pagans. "Corinth" was synonymous with immorality of all kinds. Even in this licentious, wicked city there was no commonly known relationship like the one Paul described. This does not mean there were no comparable cases. It means that even to the average Corinthian, this behavior was shocking.

What exactly was going on here? "A man has his father's wife" does not necessarily mean they were married, but it indicates they were living together. The wife in this case was presumably not the man's mother, but his stepmother, possibly divorced from his father. Whatever the case, it was a flagrant violation of Christian morality that no doubt even shocked the unbelievers.

Paul himself was outraged not only by the immorality of the case, but also by the fact that the people in the church were proud rather than overcome by grief because of this gross sin. "Grief" here means mourning.

Paul was astonished that "you (emphasizing the Christians) are proud!" It is hard to imagine such a reaction in the church. Were some of them actually bragging about this case? Perhaps so, but we find it hard to understand why. Maybe they were proud of their "tolerance." Whatever the reason, it shows the depth and power of sin in the Christian community.

In addition to calling for mourning for this sin, Paul said the offender should have been put out of the church. Instead of pride, there should have been public humiliation. Sin cannot be excused, tolerated, and boasted about.

B. Judgment: vs. 3

Even though I am not physically present, I am with you in spirit. And I have already passed judgment on the one who did this, just as if I were present.

Paul recognized that he was in no position to clean up the sexual immorality in person, since he was at Ephesus. However, that did not deter him from expressing the strongest possible feelings about the situation. He was at Corinth "in spirit," and so would tell them what to do.

The apostle's conclusion, on hearing about the immorality, was to judge the perpetrator. Even though he was not at Corinth, Paul acted just as forcibly as if he had been there. He was certain of the facts. He was sure he was not reacting to gossip or slander. Apparently no one at Corinth disputed the case. Therefore, Paul felt compelled to judge the man for his sins.

C. Salvation: vss. 4-5

When you are assembled in the name of our Lord Jesus and I am with you in spirit, and the power of our Lord Jesus is present, hand this man over to Satan, so that the sinful nature may be destroyed and his spirit saved on the day of the Lord.

Paul called for some drastic measures to protect the purity and unity of the church. First, he ordered the church to gather in the name of the Lord Jesus. The Christians could not continue to ignore, or even boast about, this intolerable immorality. They had to act at once.

When the believers met, some amazing things would happen. They could be sure that the apostle himself would be there, "in spirit," to be sure. Also, the power of the Lord Jesus Christ would be among them as well. Christ is head of the church and Paul was His anointed apostle. Spiritual authority rested with Jesus, who had delegated it to Paul.

The body of believers is not just another social club with a religious purpose. The church belongs to Christ and is accountable to Him. Therefore, when we read about unity and discipline in the church, we are not talking about Robert's Rules of Order. We stand in the presence of Christ, who is holy and pure.

The will of God in this offender's case was clear. The Christians gathered were to act as judge in the presence of Christ and deliver the man to Satan. This was the most awesome responsibility the believers had to carry out. The man's spiritual welfare was at stake.

The purpose of this severe discipline was that ultimately the man would be saved "on the day of the Lord," that is, the final judgment day. Not only were the purity and unity of the church at stake, so was the man's condition. Redemption was the ultimate goal, not eternal judgment. Later on, Paul urged that the restored man be given ample evidence of Christian love (2 Cor. 2:4-8).

To turn the man over to Satan (1 Tim. 1:20) shows that he was to be removed from the fellowship of the church and delivered to Satan's sphere of control, the kingdom of darkness (Eph. 2:11-12; Col. 1:13; 1 John 5:19). "Sinful nature" may mean the root of his sinful behavior. Since "destroyed" implies physical consequences, the result would be some kind of physical suffering.

Although we may not know exactly what the consequences would be, Paul's language shows that the most powerful spiritual elements were involved. The church at Corinth was to be aware that this was no trifling matter, because Paul invoked the presence of Christ and the power of Satan. Being turned over to Satan is a fearful prospect.

II. PURITY: 1 CORINTHIANS 5:6-8

A. Infection: vs. 6

Your boasting is not good. Don't you know that a little yeast works through the whole batch of dough?

Rather than brag about what was happening in their church, the Corinthians should have been alarmed by the danger of spiritual infection from the sinning brother. To prove his point that they were fooling around with fire, Paul used an analogy from the bakery that they all would recognize.

It takes only a small amount of yeast to "infect" a whole batch of dough. Yeast is a powerful fermenting agent. It spreads silently, quickly. Before you know it, the dough begins to rise.

If the church at Corinth was to maintain its purity, the believers could not risk the working of dangerous spiritual yeast in the form of this man who had broken God's laws of holiness in marriage. The believers had to see that they were exposing themselves to considerable risk and harm. If something were not done, other Christians would also fall into sin.

B. Prescription: vss. 7-8

Get rid of the old yeast that you may be a new batch without yeast—as you really are. For Christ, our Passover lamb, has been sacrificed. Therefore let us keep the Festival, not with the old yeast, the yeast of malice and wickedness, but with bread without yeast, the bread of sincerity and truth.

In this individual's case, Paul prescribed surgery. His old, sinful yeast had to be removed. The dough represented the church. It had been infected by sin. The new batch of dough had to be made without the old yeast.

To show how important it was to preserve the church from pollution, Paul referred to the sacrifice of Christ, the Passover Lamb. His sacrifice demands that the church conform to God's standards of purity. His standards were seen in the rooting out of all leaven in the ancient Jewish Passover festival (Exod. 12:15). The Jews were so scrupulous about this that they searched their houses for the tiniest crumbs of leavened bread.

In Christ, the church was totally pure "without yeast." Paul urged the believers to act accordingly. Their conduct had to conform to their standing in Christ. Since Christ was sacrificed to atone for their sins and to make them holy, the Christians were urged to "keep the Festival." Paul did not mean they were to revert to the Jewish Passover celebration. Rather, the Christians were to keep the Passover symbolically every day as a sign that they had been cleansed. To do so they would have to get rid of the old sinfulness and start afresh with sincerity and truth.

III. Maintaining Holiness: 1 Corinthians 5:9-13

A. Standards: vss. 9-10

I have written you in my letter not to associate with sexually immoral people—not at all meaning the people of this world who are immoral, or the greedy and swindlers, or idolaters. In that case you would have to leave this world.

Immorality is inconsistent with Christian fellowship because it violates God's standards of holiness in the church. Paul had to state this principle again, having written about it once before. The believers were not to fellowship with sexually immoral members of the church, such as the man referred to here.

Paul was talking about associations within the church family, not with people outside the church. His command applies only to professing Christians who have fallen into habitual sin.

How had the church at Corinth fallen into this condition? Paul's Gospel was a Gospel of grace, not of good works (Eph. 2:8-9). Perhaps some of his converts had presumed that grace meant they could go on living in their old ways. Paul spoke to this problem in 1 Corinthians 6:12-20; 10:23, and Romans 6:1, showing that grace meant living according to the highest standards of godliness.

B. Fellowship: vs. 11

But now I am writing you that you must not associate with anyone who calls himself a brother but is sexually immoral or greedy, an idolater or a slanderer, a drunkard or a swindler. With such a man do not even eat.

Fellowship is not to be granted to those who continue in sin. Paul took the one case of sin that apparently everyone knew about and expanded it to a general principle. The context is definitely Christian ("calls himself a brother"), and not pagan society outside the church.

His command was first general ("must not associate with") and then specific ("with such a man do not even eat"). There was to be a clear line of demarcation, because God's people bear the name of Jesus, and He has called them to be holy (1 Pet. 1:15-16; 2:9).

Paul broadened the scope of his principle to include other sins besides sexual immorality, some of which we may not take very seriously. For example, greed and slander. Slanderers engage in personal, malicious abuse to discredit, embarrass, or diminish the influence of another person. Surely such people destroy Christian unity. Or the swindlers, people who squeeze their neighbors for personal gain. Money disputes often wreck church unity.

C. Expulsion: vss. 12-13

What business is it of mine to judge those outside the church? Are you not to judge those inside? God will judge those outside. "Expel the wicked man from among you."

Expulsion from the church body is sometimes required. The open, severe disciplinary action demanded by Paul seems forbidding. We have to confess that for the most part churches do not follow the apostolic teaching in this regard. When it has been applied, feelings have been hurt so badly that churches and families have been split. However, in other cases it has been extremely beneficial, and sinning sisters and brothers have been restored to Christ and His church.

In addition to being denied social fellowship, the sinning brother was also to be denied church fellowship. Paul's concluding command, "Expel the wicked man from among you," culminates his previous orders: "Put [this man] out of your fellowship" (vs. 2); "hand this man over to Satan" (vs. 5); "get rid of the old yeast" (vs. 7). The church was not to worry about the conduct of unbelievers, but it was to handle the sins of its members.

Perhaps Paul's counsel seems inconsistent with love and grace. However, discipline is a function of God's grace, because it is intended to produce holiness.

"Expel the wicked man" is the last option the church has. How that is done requires great wisdom and care. However, the main point is that Christians need to be aware that sin is a serious offense against God and it taints Christ's body, the Church. Christians cannot do as they please and disregard the effects their lives have on the entire company of God's people.

Discussion Questions

1. How would you define the problems in the church at Corinth (ch. 5)?
2. Do you see similar situations in churches today?
3. How did the Corinthians feel about the situation? How should they have felt?
4. How does sin by Christians affect other Christians? Why?
5. What are the weakness of a church that disregards sin among its members? The strengths of a church that strives for purity and unity?
6. Why is church discipline so hard to achieve?

Contemporary Application

In the old story of Achan and his sin against the camp of Israel (Joshua 7), discipline meant his death by stoning. Under the covenant of the Gospel, Christ's church is commanded to exercise loving, compassionate discipline so that sinning Christians can be restored to fellowship with God and with their fellow believers (Gal. 6:1). Perhaps one reason we are shy about applying discipline is that we have not taken the prior steps of trying to help our sisters and brothers overcome their sinful habits.

While churches may differ on how to exercise discipline, there can be no disagreement on Paul's main points. Churches are in danger if they are lulled to sleep by complacent attitudes toward sin in the camp.

Counsel Concerning Marriage

Scripture

Background Scripture: *1 Corinthians 6:12—7:16*
Scripture Lesson: *1 Corinthians 7:1-5, 8-16*
Key Verse: *Do you not know that your body is a temple of the Holy Spirit, who is in you, whom you have received from God? You are not your own.* 1 Corinthians 6:19.
Background Scripture for Children: *Genesis 2:7—3:24; 4:1-7*
Scripture Lesson for Children: *Genesis 2:7, 18, 21-24; 4:1-2*
Key Verse for Children: *"Be at peace with each other."* Mark 9:50.

Lesson Aim

To apply God's standards of holiness to marriage and singleness.

Lesson Setting

Time: *A.D. 55*
Place: *Written to Corinth from Ephesus*

Lesson Outline

Counsel Concerning Marriage

   I. Mutual Responsibilities in Marriage: 1 Corinthians 7:1-5
      A. *Temptation outside Marriage: vss. 1-2*
      B. *Equal Sexual Rights: vss. 3-4*
      C. *Temporary Abstention: vs. 5*
  II. To the Unmarried: 1 Corinthians 7:8-9
 III. To the Married: 1 Corinthians 7:10-11
 IV. Mixed Marriages: 1 Corinthians 7:12-16
      A. *Do Not Divorce: vss. 12-13*
      B. *Mutual Sanctification: vs. 14*
      C. *Hope of Salvation: vss. 15-16*

Introduction for Adults

Topic: *Responsibility in Marriage and Singleness*

Marriage counselors know that in many cases the lack of sexual satisfaction is a major cause of unhappy relationships and even divorce. Christian married couples must find sexual satisfaction or they will be subject to frustration, dissatisfaction, and the temptation to adultery and divorce.

This is why it is so important for Christian husbands and wives to sit down together and discuss a passage like 1 Corinthians 7. Engaged couples should also be very honest in discussing these principles.

Of course, Paul did not limit his counsel to the married. He wished for the gift of singleness for others, but he realized the acceptable role of marriage in God's plan. Our churches need great wisdom and love to help those never married, the widows, the separated, and the divorced. "Singleness" covers a wide gamut of people.

Introduction for Youths

Topic: *Sex and Marriage*

Sexual promiscuity gets many teenagers into trouble, but we have to remember that no generation is sinless. Today's teens may witness immorality purveyed on a wider scale than ever before, which means Christians must be sensitive and courageous when it comes to their witness and conduct.

"Thou shalt not" rarely cuts the mustard with youth. They want to see how someone can actually live a pure life. Those who choose chastity will be on the spot, and perhaps ridiculed as well.

Therefore, Christian teens need strong encouragement and support from their parents, youth leaders, and pastors. This includes honest and frank discussions about the dangers of sexual immorality lurking on virtually every corner. They need the reinforcement of knowing what God says, and how their faith in Christ determines their behavior.

They also need to see authentic Christian marriages in action. If there is conflict at home and the breaking of God's rules regarding marriage, then teenagers will tend to mistrust the advice given by their elders.

Concepts for Children

Topic: *Living in My Family*

1. God created male and female in His image.
2. God gave woman to man to be a suitable helper.
3. God instituted human marriage as a permanent bond, making husband and wife "one flesh."
4. Jesus shows us how to get along together to make our families strong.
5. Because God forgave us, we have to confess our wrongs and forgive one another, especially in our families.
6. When marriages fall apart, we have to ask God for faith and strength to cope.

The Lesson Commentary

I. MUTUAL RESPONSIBILITIES IN MARRIAGE: 1 CORINTHIANS 7:1-5

A. Temptation outside Marriage: vss. 1-2

Now for the matters you wrote about: It is good for a man not to marry. But since there is so much immorality, each man should have his own wife, and each woman her own husband.

The apostle Paul's first letter to the church at Corinth was partly in response to certain questions, as well as problems that had arisen among the believers. Some of their questions pertained to Christian standards of marriage. Chapter 7 is Paul's answer.

To understand what was behind their questions, we have to look at society as a whole in Corinth. The word "Corinthianize" was synonymous with the city's reputation for gross sexual immorality. So we can understand how puzzled the new converts might be. Their basic question was, "Are couples to continue having sexual relations after their conversion?"

Perhaps the statement, "It is good for a man not to marry," or not to have sexual relations with a woman, was Paul's quotation from an actual question. This would seem to be the case, because from vss. 1-7 it is clear that Paul does not agree with the statement. Instead, he says that sexual relations in marriage are a mutual duty.

Perhaps some Christians were urging an end to sexual relations, but Paul said this was not right. In 6:13-20 he strongly condemned sexual license; in 7:1-7, however, he made it clear that sexual intercourse is a legitimate, necessary part of the marriage bond.

Paul recognized the temptation to sex outside of marriage. He understood the tremendous pressure that would arise if married Christians tried to live without sexual intercourse. Therefore, "each man should have his own wife, and each woman her own husband."

"Should have" means "must." Sex in marriage is both right and necessary. It was part of God's plan from the beginning when He established the institution of marriage. The limitation of sex to the marriage union is clear in the words "his own" and "her own."

B. Equal Sexual Rights: vss. 3-4

The husband should fulfill his marital duty to his wife, and likewise the wife to her husband. The wife's body does not belong to her alone but also to her husband. In the same way, the husband's body does not belong to him alone but also to his wife.

Paul then stated a concept that was revolutionary in the ancient world: husband and wife have equal sexual rights. This challenged the prevailing attitude, which was summarized by the famous Greek orator, Demosthenes: "We keep prostitutes for pleasure; we keep mistresses for the day to day needs of the body; we keep wives for the begetting of children and for the faithful guardianship of our homes."

"Should fulfill" is the word used for paying a debt, not conferring a favor. Husbands and wives have rights to the other's body. In fact, Paul went so far as to say that marriage partners should not consider their bodies their exclusive possession ("body does not belong to her . . . him alone"). The wife's body belongs to her husband, and the husband's body belongs to his wife.

C. Temporary Abstention: vs. 5

Do not deprive each other except by mutual consent and for a time, so that you may devote yourselves to prayer. Then come together again so that Satan will not tempt you because of your lack of self-control.

After stating the principle that each partner has the rights to the other's body, Paul said that the only reason a couple might temporarily refrain from intercourse is if both agreed to do so for spiritually useful purposes, for example, prayer. He emphasized that abstention must not be unilateral: "Do not deprive each other." The word means to defraud, to withhold what is owed.

Abstention from sex must be temporary—"for a time." It must have a spiritual goal. Sexual relations must be resumed because otherwise one partner could easily be tempted to have sex with someone else. "Lack of self-control" has brought more than one marriage to ruin.

Paul added that temporary abstention is not a command, but a "concession" (vs. 6). This is evidence of a wise practical balance, because obviously some couples would find it harder to abstain than others.

II. TO THE UNMARRIED: 1 CORINTHIANS 7:8-9

Now to the unmarried and the widows I say: It is good for them to stay unmarried, as I am. But if they cannot control themselves, they should marry, for it is better to marry than to burn with passion.

Paul himself was not married. Some scholars think he was a widower (vs. 8). Regardless, he saw advantages in being single. He said that married and single people have special gifts from God (vs. 7). He said he did not need a marriage partner, but other women and men do. He did not put himself on a higher spiritual plane. His main point was that each Christian must find God's will in the matter.

Paul addressed three groups: (1) unmarried and widows (vss. 8-9); (2) married (vss. 10-11); (3) "the rest," meaning Christians married to unbelieving spouses (vss. 12-16). His commands were very specific, and especially helpful to the confused people in the church at Corinth. They are also applicable to us today.

Paul's first choice for the unmarried and the widows was that they should not marry. Later in this chapter he gave his reasons (vss. 25-35). First, "because of the present crisis" (vs. 26). Scholars have debated what Paul meant. Apparently he felt the current political, social, and economic conditions were unsettled. He explained "that the time is short" (vs. 29), and "this world in its present form is passing away" (vs. 31). Some see this as a reference to Christ's second coming.

Second, married people "will face many troubles in this life" (vs. 28). Not that single persons are free of troubles, but marriage enlarges the potential for a wider range of troubles, which he wanted to spare them.

Third, singleness provides opportunities to be "concerned about the Lord's affairs" (vss. 32, 34), while marriage brings mutual responsibilities to be concerned about the affairs of one's spouse. Marriage brings "divided interests" (vs. 34), which means single persons are freer to devote themselves to spiritual concerns. Paul's goal was "undivided devotion to the Lord" (vs. 35).

Paul did not mean that single persons are spiritually superior to married persons. He simply stated an obvious truth that when one is free of marriage responsibilities, there are more opportunities for spiritual service.

Paul also recognized that his first choice was not possible for all unmarried people. So, he said they should marry if their sexual desires overwhelm them (vs. 9). "If you do marry, you have not sinned" (vs. 28). Of course, he recognized that "burning with passion" could easily lead to sin on the part of the unmarried.

III. To the Married: 1 Corinthians 7:10-11

To the married I give this command (not I, but the Lord): A wife must not separate from her husband. But if she does, she must remain unmarried or else be reconciled to her husband. And a husband must not divorce his wife.

The sanctity of the marriage bond was wholeheartedly endorsed by Paul in his counsel to the married. His rule prohibited separation and divorce. If separation occurs, the parties must not remarry. Rather, they should be reconciled. Actually, Paul's command came from the Lord. Paul knew what God had said at the union of Adam and Eve. He knew that Jesus had reaffirmed what God had given to Adam and Eve. Therefore, he was on solid ground when he said his command came from the Lord. Adam and Eve became one flesh (Gen. 2:24). Paul himself quoted this in Ephesians 5:31. When Jesus quoted this, He added, "Therefore what God has joined together, let man not separate" (Matt. 19:6). The Christian view of marriage, seemingly ignored by many, is not a human invention. It is rooted in creation and in the teachings of Christ and the apostles. Therefore, the church makes no apology for exhorting believers to solve their marital problems, rather than resort to separation and divorce. Faithfulness to our marriage vows is not optional; it is demanded by our commitment to Christ.

IV. MIXED MARRIAGES: 1 CORINTHIANS 7:12-16

A. Do Not Divorce: vss. 12-13

To the rest I say this (I, not the Lord): If any brother has a wife who is not a believer and she is willing to live with him, he must not divorce her. And if a woman has a husband who is not a believer and he is willing to live with her, she must not divorce him.

Paul knew that many marriages are far from perfect. In fact, many are quite messy. We know this from experience. Our churches suffer because of infidelity, desertion, separation, and divorce. The reasons for marital breakdowns are many. Paul did not write a definitive encyclopedia of how to solve every marital problem. Rather, he addressed the major problem in Corinth—mixed marriages—because obviously there were many cases in which either the wife or husband had become a believer, while the partner had not. What to do in such cases?

He spoke from his own God-given insights, not from the Lord, because (the Lord) Jesus had not specifically given a command to cover such situations in marriage. This does not mean Paul's rules are invalid. He was instructed by the Holy Spirit, so we must pay attention and obey.

Paul's basic command was, "Do not divorce, no matter what." He covered both possibilities. The man who had an unbelieving wife, and the woman who had an unbelieving husband. Obviously, in some cases the unbelieving partner simply packed up and left. Paul spoke to cases where the unbeliever was content to live in marriage with the believer.

Contrary to the popular notion that divorce is the quick and easy way out, Paul said we should stay together, even if one partner is an unbeliever. This is not easy to do, but there are valid reasons for doing so. These reasons (vss. 14-16) should be studied and believed by Christians who are married to unbelievers.

B. Mutual Sanctification: vs. 14

For the unbelieving husband has been sanctified through his wife, and the unbelieving wife has been sanctified through her believing husband. Otherwise your children would be unclean, but as it is, they are holy.

Paul's first reason for staying together in a mixed marriage is that the unbelieving partner has been sanctified by the believing partner. Paul's teaching probably was addressed to the concern among Christians at Corinth that somehow their marriage relations with an unbeliever were sinful. Paul had been very strict about fornication with prostitutes (6:15-16), and some believers perhaps thought they were guilty of a similar sin.

Not so, said Paul. There is nothing unholy or defiling about being married to an unbeliever. If so, the children would be "unclean," that is, tainted by sin. As far as the marriage is concerned, the children are "holy."

"Sanctification" in this context does not refer to the normal usage of the word in relation to the Christian's saving faith and dedication to God. Being married to a believer does not automatically confer salvation on the unbelieving spouse. Paul's use of the word here refers to the holiness of the marriage union.

Therefore, the Christian partner in a mixed marriage could rest assured that it would be best to stay married. God's basic principle of "one flesh" applied in these cases as well. This does not mean such marriages are trouble free. To the contrary, often they are quite painful. Nevertheless, there is no sin inherently involved in marriages where one partner is an unbeliever.

Of course, Paul's teaching in this case must not be used as an excuse for a Christian to knowingly enter into a marriage with an unbeliever. Paul's instructions are for the already married, not the unmarried. Unmarried believers are not to be "yoked together with unbelievers" (2 Cor. 6:14).

C. Hope of Salvation: vss. 15-16

But if the unbeliever leaves, let him do so. A believing man or woman is not bound in such circumstances; God has called us to live in peace. How do you know, wife, whether you will save your husband? Or, how do you know, husband, whether you will save your wife?

Of course, Paul knew that some unbelievers would quit their marriages. Therefore, the Christian partner is no longer "bound in such circumstances." This seems to imply that they are free to remarry—keeping in mind, of course, the apostle's first choice (vss. 8-9).

Paul's principle was, "God has called us to live in peace." The opposite of peace is contention, wrangling, bitterness, and so on, even after the unbelieving partner leaves. Any separation brings pain and hurt feelings.

"Live in peace" encompasses all of the problems that arise in mixed marriages. Christians are not to get involved in the turmoil associated with terminating such a marriage, nor are they to sink into the conflicts involved with preserving the marriage against the will of the unbeliever.

Living in peace is also a powerful witness to God's grace available to believers through Christ's indwelling power. Paul seems to offer the possibility that the believing partner's faith and conduct could be the means of the unbelieving partner's salvation.

Some scholars think Paul tried to demolish the idea that clinging to a marriage in spite of the unbeliever's determination to end it could have some saving benefits. However, others interpret his questions as encouragement to hope for the partner's salvation. They translate his question, "How do you know that you will not save your husband?"

Peter tackled the same question and held out the hope that unbelieving husbands could be won to faith in Christ "by the behavior of their wives, when they see the purity and reverence of your lives" (1 Pet. 3:1-2). This seems to be more in tune with what Paul said. Living in peace, rather than in contention, is bound to have a winsome effect.

Discussion Questions

1. How does Paul's teaching contradict some popular notions about the roles of men and women in sexual relationships?
2. How would you describe the elements in a Christian marriage that would have to be true before a couple could achieve what Paul had in mind?
3. Why is singleness sometimes looked down on as an inferior condition?
4. What advantages does singleness have in terms of church and mission work?
5. How can the church stand against our culture's acceptance of divorce?
6. What practical help can we give to believing spouses living with unbelieving partners?

Contemporary Application

If Christians chose to live by the apostle Paul's rules for marriage, the church would be revolutionized. As it is, too many Christians have bought into society's acceptance of misconceptions about marriage, and of quick and easy divorces. Sadly, our pain thresholds are so low that Christian couples often split at the slightest provocation, explaining that personal happiness is more important than saving the marriage.

If personal happiness and fulfillment stand at the top of our desires, then there's little chance for making our marriages work. There must be a higher commitment to obey God's will, and to follow the Word of God. Prevailing cultural values make it very difficult to be truly Christian in our marriages. We must stand against erroneous popular ideas, and stand for the spiritual values enunciated by the apostle Paul.

The incredible pressures to go along with the crowd in matters of sex and marriage make it imperative that we review God's word consistently. We also need to support and pray for one another when tensions arise, so that Christian concern and help can be applied before it's too late.

None of what the apostle Paul said makes any sense to people brought up on television comedies based on fornication, adultery, and marital breakdowns. The church stands out like a sore thumb when Christians insist that certain things are right and certain things are wrong in sex and marriage. While TV shows may not change for the better, our own marriages can not only survive, but can be more meaningful and pleasing as we seek God's grace and wisdom.

Concerning Love and Knowledge

DEVOTIONAL READING

1 Corinthians 10:23—11:1

DAILY BIBLE READINGS

Monday April 3
*1 Corinthians 8:1-6
Knowledge Puffs Up; Love
Builds Up*

Tuesday April 4
*1 Corinthians 8:7-13 Don't
Cause Another to Stumble*

Wednesday April 5
*1 Corinthians 9:1-12 Love
Has Priority over "Rights"*

Thursday April 6
*1 Corinthians 9:13-18
Preaching the Gospel Is
Reward Enough*

Friday April 7
*1 Corinthians 9:19-27 Do
Whatever It Takes*

Saturday April 8
*1 Corinthians 10:1-13
Learn from Lessons of the
Past*

Sunday April 9
*1 Corinthians 10:14-22
Flee from the Worship of
Idols*

Scripture

Background Scripture: *1 Corinthians 8*
Scripture Lesson: *1 Corinthians 8*
Key Verse: *The man who thinks he knows something
does not yet know as he ought to know. But the man who
loves God is known by God.* 1 Corinthians 8:2-3.
Scripture Lesson for Children: *1 Corinthians 8:1;
Luke 10:25-37*
Key Verse for Children: *"Love your neighbor as
yourself."* Romans 13:9.

Lesson Aim

To learn how to appreciate and love those with
whom we differ.

Lesson Setting

Time: *A.D. 55*
Place: *Written to Corinth from Ephesus*

Lesson Outline

Concerning Love and Knowledge
 I. The Truth about Idols: 1 Corinthians 8:1-6
   A. *Knowledge vs. Love: vss. 1-3*
   B. *One God and One Christ: vss. 4-6*
 II. The Truth about Relationships:
   1 Corinthians 8:7-13
   A. *Some Are Defiled: vs. 7*
   B. *Food Was Not Really the Issue: vs. 8*
   C. *Restrain Your Freedom: vss. 9-10*
   D. *Sin against Christ: vss. 11-12*
   E. *The Reason for Abstaining: vs. 13*

Introduction for Adults

Topic: *Let Love Lead*

We may think that the problems in the church at Corinth are far removed from church life today. However, one Christian organization split because a small group decided to show their spiritual "maturity" ("We are the 'stronger brothers,' " they said) by flaunting some practices they knew offended other members. Eventually, they were asked to leave and the ensuing bitterness lasted many years. Their superior knowledge did nothing to advance the cause of Christ. Just the opposite. The work in their area was weakened for years thereafter.

How easy it is to forget the importance of considering the feelings of others. "Do nothing out of selfish ambition or vain conceit, but in humility consider others better than yourselves," Paul taught (Phil. 2:3). When disputes arise, we may think we have the last word. But our last words will be self-defeating if they drive others from Christ and His Church.

Introduction for Youths

Topic: *You Can, But Don't*

Personal influence and example can be a powerful force for good or evil. This principle is the driving force behind advertising that uses famous people to push various products. In a day when personal rights are glorified, it is unusual to see examples of people who refuse to do something because of the ill effects their behavior might cause in others. Younger kids are especially vulnerable to what they see in older kids.

The biblical principle for Christians is simple: Don't do anything that could possibly lead someone astray, or into a habit they will later regret. When we live by that principle, we will be going against the tide of popular opinion. In some cases, people deliberately set out to get others into trouble.

Therefore, we need considerable courage and faith to do the right and honorable thing. The price is high for following such a high standard. But if we can help to keep just one person from wasting his or her life, it will be more than worth it.

Concepts for Children

Topic: *Accepting Differences in Others*

1. Love is the key to accepting those with whom we have differences.
2. Sometimes our pride keeps us from admitting that others are right and we are wrong.
3. The Good Samaritan helped a hurting person who had been rejected by others.
4. God often brings people to us who need our love and care.
5. Sometimes our religious activities keep us from being alert to others in need.
6. Because God forgave us in Christ, we can show His love to others.

The Lesson Commentary

I. THE TRUTH ABOUT IDOLS: 1 CORINTHIANS 8:1-6

A. Knowledge vs. Love: vss. 1-3

Now about food sacrificed to idols: We know that we all possess knowledge. Knowledge puffs up, but love builds up. The man who thinks he knows something does not yet know as he ought to know. But the man who loves God is known by God.

To understand the apostle Paul's teaching in this chapter, we have to look at how people lived in Corinth. Food was a common sacrifice offered to idols. The priests could not eat all of these offerings, so much of the food was sold later on in the market. This means that if you were a Christian, you risked eating food that had been offered to idols. If you were a Jew, you faced serious problems of conscience. That's because the Jews considered all sacrifices to idols to be unclean, hateful to God, and destructive to their faith.

Earlier, Jesus had told the Jews that eating food was not a spiritual issue, because food was not the cause of one's spiritual pollution (Mark 7:18-23). However, most of the Jews who had become Christians still held strongly to their old scruples about not eating food that had been offered to pagan idols. Probably some of the Gentiles were also concerned about discarding their old practices associated with idolatry.

The Christians at Corinth were divided over this issue. Should they, or should they not, eat food offered to idols? Feelings ran so high that they had appealed to Paul for his counsel.

Eating meat that had been offered to idols was a matter of opinion because there was no specific command from God about this. God had spoken clearly about such things as stealing, murder, adultery, and bearing false witness. However, what about other things that were not specifically prohibited?

Paul did not respond with a categorical yes or no. Rather, he emphasized that because of their differences on this issue they were losing sight of a much more basic truth: love builds up the church, while the argument over sacrificial meat was tearing it down. Therefore, they needed to put the argument in a much larger perspective and get their priorities straight.

Of course, both sides claimed to have true knowledge on the matter. Paul did not discount "knowledge" as such, but he attacked the spiritual pride that went with their claim to superior wisdom: ". . . we all possess knowledge. Knowledge puffs up . . . The man who thinks he knows something does not yet know as he ought to know." Paul's warnings in 1 Corinthians 4:6, 18, and 5:2 also show his concern about their arrogance and pride.

The believers who claimed that their views were the only correct ones still lacked knowledge. What had they missed? Love and unity in the church are far more important than winning arguments. True knowledge does not lead to pride, but to love and humility. Love does not produce boasting that divides people. Love produces harmony and strength among Christians. Building up one another should be their first concern, not winning an argument based on supposed superior knowledge. Yet, how often churches have split, not because of wrong knowledge, but because of the way some believers have displayed their knowledge.

All of our knowledge is at best partial (1 Cor. 13:8). Therefore, it's not only arrogant but also risky to claim exclusive insight and higher wisdom. For example, in their differences over food offered to idols, love would preclude spiritual one-upmanship.

B. One God and One Christ: vss. 4-6

So then, about eating food sacrificed to idols: We know that an idol is nothing at all in the world and that there is no God but one. For even if there are so-called gods, whether in heaven or on earth (as indeed there are many "gods" and many "lords"), yet for us there is but one God, the Father, from whom all things came and for whom we live; and there is but one Lord, Jesus Christ, through whom all things came and through whom we live.

Two facts paved the way for Paul's discussion: Idols are not real, and there is only one true and living God and one Lord, Jesus Christ. He thus agreed with one party in the church. However, in his day and ours many people did in fact believe in many "so-called gods."

Paul carefully delineated the biblical doctrine of God, just in case people thought that all religions worship the same God, and therefore all were equally true. The one true God is "God, the Father." He is the one from whom all things come. He is the source of all things, as well as the goal and purpose of our existence.

Further, there is "one Lord, Jesus Christ," the one through whom everything and everyone comes into existence. Of course, people of other religions worship many gods, but not God the Father revealed in His Son, Jesus Christ. Jesus Christ is the only way to God (John 14:6). He is the only mediator between sinners and God. This is the fundamental, irreconcilable difference between Christianity and other religions.

What about the many other "gods" and "lords"? The word translated "idol" simply means a copy. The word is used for the image itself (wood, stone, or whatever) as well as for the deity being worshiped.

Isaiah the prophet declared, "All who make idols are nothing, and the things they treasure are worthless. Those who would speak up for them are blind; they are ignorant, to their own shame" (44:9). Idolatry is devoid of spiritual reality.

However, spiritual forces called demons, or evil spirits, stand behind the idols (Deut. 32:17). Therefore, although "an idol is nothing," the worship of idols engages the powers of darkness arrayed against God and Christ. "The sacrifices of pagans are offered to demons," Paul said (1 Cor. 10:20).

II. THE TRUTH ABOUT RELATIONSHIPS: 1 CORINTHIANS 8:7-13

A. Some Are Defiled: vs. 7

But not everyone knows this. Some people are still so accustomed to idols that when they eat such food they think of it as having been sacrificed to an idol, and since their conscience is weak, it is defiled.

Paul moved from theology to relationships in the church. We will use his categories from Romans 14:2: Christians whose faith allowed them to eat anything, and Christians "whose faith is weak" and ate only vegetables. What should those who eat meat do if their behavior causes fellow believers to violate their consciences and principles? Should the believers keep on eating meat because they were free to do so, or should they abstain for the sake of the other Christians?

Defiling one's conscience was the crucial matter. Some had no problems with conscience, while others did. Those who were "accustomed to idols" found that their consciences were harmed when they ate meat that had been offered as part of pagan worship. They had a keen sense of the idolatrous consecration of the food. Because of their past habits with idols, they could not free themselves from the idea that their meat really was a pagan sacrifice. In such cases, even though their consciences were "weak," they should not have eaten such meat.

The apostle Paul held such a high view of the value of one's conscience that it was better to listen to it than to pollute it. This value outweighed the possibility that one's conscience might be oversensitive in some matters.

B. Food Was Not Really the Issue: vs. 8

But food does not bring us near to God; we are no worse if we do not eat, and no better if we do.

Although it appeared to the church at Corinth that food was the issue, Paul insisted otherwise. Therefore, while he plunged into the dispute about eating meat that had been offered to idols, he wanted to establish basic Christian doctrine, regardless of conscience. The truth was that neither eating nor abstaining would help a person to know God. Neither food nor the lack of it makes any difference in being accepted by God.

People come to God only by faith in Jesus Christ. He alone is the way to God. No religious scruples can achieve anything when it comes to personal salvation. In fact, in many cases people who are the most rigidly scrupulous have the hardest time confessing their sins and admitting their need of God's saving grace in Christ. Strict religious scruples often are a barrier to faith in Christ.

C. Restrain Your Freedom: vss. 9-10

Be careful, however, that the exercise of your freedom does not become a stumbling block to the weak. For if anyone with a weak conscience sees you who have this knowledge eating in an idol's temple, won't he be emboldened to eat what has been sacrificed to idols?

Having established theological truth, Paul issued a word of caution to those who held the true knowledge that idols are worthless and not real. "Restrain your freedom," he said. They were free to eat meat that had been offered to idols. However, "Be careful," Paul warned, because your liberty could pose a problem to those who did not have the freedom of conscience to eat such meat.

Liberty could be a pitfall to weaker brothers and sisters. Therefore, the stronger believers must exercise care, lest their freedom in some way hinder those whose faith was not so robust. Verse 10 explains how this could happen.

The people of "knowledge" were the stronger Christians with freedom to eat the disputed meat. In fact, they had liberty even to sit down at a meal in an idol's temple. But Paul urged them to think about the possible consequences for the weaker Christians. They might be tempted to eat some of the same food, going against their consciences. Nothing must be done that would encourage the weaker Christians with their sensitive consciences to violate their principles.

D. Sin against Christ: vss. 11-12

So this weak brother, for whom Christ died, is destroyed by your knowledge. When you sin against your brothers in this way and wound their weak conscience, you sin against Christ.

In Paul's hypothetical case, weaker believers, emboldened by the stronger Christians eating in the temple, had eaten food against the voice of their consciences. Therefore, their liberty, or "knowledge," had brought spiritual disaster for the others. The sensitive Christians, even though their consciences operated on false premises about idols, must be protected. Superior knowledge and the freedom to eat anything must never be used against those who still have strong feelings about their old associations with idolatry.

Paul described the outcome in three different ways. Weaker sisters and brothers were destroyed; their consciences were wounded; they were sinned against. Above all, however, to sin against fellow believers by encouraging them to violate their consciences really was a sin against Christ. The weaker Christians were placed in an unnecessary quandary.

Paul made the highest appeal possible when he compared fellow believers to Christ. Even though they lacked spiritual insight, knowledge, and maturity, they had to be respected as Christ Himself. Their overzealous consciences had to be respected. They were not to be encouraged to go against their consciences and go back to a pagan temple.

E. The Reason for Abstaining: vs. 13

Therefore, if what I eat causes my brother to fall into sin, I will never eat meat again, so that I will not cause him to fall.

Paul reached an emphatic conclusion that governs our relationships in the church. He was willing to restrain his own liberty for the sake of his fellow believers. Even though he was more robust in faith, even though eating meat that had been offered to idols did not bother him, he voluntarily refrained from eating this meat for the sake of his fellow Christians.

Paul's cardinal concern was the welfare of fellow Christians: "I will not cause him to fall." Paul's liberty gave way to the weaker consciences of his fellow believers. He would do nothing to bring them spiritual harm. Paul's Greek text emphasized his vows with a triple negative. In effect, he said, "I will never, never, never eat meat again."

The two requirements for love and knowledge to work in the church were: (1) All parties, weak and strong alike, must be welcomed; (2) Those who are strong must relinquish certain things they are free to do, lest they harm the weaker believers.

Discussion Questions

1. Over what kinds of issues do Christians differ today?
2. Do you think Christian "liberty" has gotten out of hand? Why?
3. Why is it so hard to put my fellow believer's spiritual welfare ahead of my own freedom?
4. Should stronger Christians try to talk weaker Christians out of their scruples?
5. Why is superior knowledge so difficult to exercise in the context of love?
6. Should the conduct of Christians be determined by the criticisms of other Christians?

Contemporary Application

Meat offered to idols will not be the subject of a seminar near you anytime soon. Nor will you find books, tapes, videos, and conferences on how to avoid being a stumbling block to your fellow Christian. That's because our culture is dominated by self-fulfillment, not by giving up my rights for the sake of someone else's tender conscience.

My rights come first, period. That's the prevailing view today. Yet the apostolic banner of truth was just the opposite. The apostle Paul said he would relinquish his liberty in the larger interest of not offending a fellow believer.

When our churches are dominated by Christians who yield their rights for the sake of others, then they will be known as centers of love and sacrifice. Superior knowledge does not give Christians the right to lord it over others. Jesus said the world will know we are His disciples when we show how much we love each other. Perhaps the supreme test of our love is our willingness to give up our rights for the greater good and upbuilding of the church.

Spiritual Gifts

Scripture

Background Scripture: *1 Corinthians 12:1-30*
Scripture Lesson: *1 Corinthians 12:4-20, 26*
Key Verse: *There are different kinds of gifts, but the same Spirit. There are different kinds of working, but the same God works all of them in all men.* 1 Corinthians 12:4, 6.
Scripture Lesson for Children: *1 Corinthians 12:4-6; Acts 9:36-41*
Key Verse: *Let us not love with words or tongue but with actions and in truth.* 1 John 3:18.

Lesson Aim

To thank God for His gifts to the Church, and to use them for His glory.

Lesson Setting

Time: *A.D. 55*
Place: *Written to Corinth from Ephesus*

Lesson Outline

Spiritual Gifts

   I. Differences in the Body: 1 Corinthians 12:4-7
      A. *Different Gifts: vs. 4*
      B. *Different Services: vs. 5*
      C. *Different Works: vs. 6*
      D. *The Same Purpose: vs. 7*
  II. The Holy Spirit's Gifts: 1 Corinthians 12:8-11
 III. The Church: One Body: 1 Corinthians 12:12-20, 26
      A. *Unity in the Body: vs. 12*
      B. *Placement in the Body: vs. 13*
      C. *Many Parts in the Body: vs. 14*
      D. *No Separation from the Body: vss. 15-16*
      E. *The Human Body Is One: vs. 17*
      F. *God Controls the Body: vss. 18-20*
      G. *Suffering and Rejoicing in the Body: vs. 26*

Introduction for Adults

Topic: *Work Together*

Too often today a discussion about spiritual gifts ends up in arguments and division, not in spiritual unity. We don't have to agree on the precise meaning of the gifts mentioned by the apostle Paul to find common ground in a larger purpose. But many times our larger purpose and our common bond in Christ get lost in our debates.

Meanwhile, some churches are weakened because of a false dichotomy between so-called gifted Christians and the rest of ordinary believers. We have to make room for all believers to exercise their gifts for the common good. We cannot afford to let some Christians think they are second-class because they do not have some of the more publicly recognized gifts.

Paul emphasized oneness, unity, and harmony. He did not glorify the gifts. He would not tolerate fighting over the gifts, which are intended to build Christ's Body. The whole point of his letter was to produce a vital, loving, growing, unified fellowship, not one shattered by arguments and bickering.

Introduction for Youths

Topic: *Many Parts, One Body*

Youth are early introduced to the values of working together. They work on class projects, participate in musical groups and plays, and join athletic teams. They all know that if any member slacks off, the team suffers. They also know that if any player tries to steal the whole show, the team is weakened.

These are the kinds of illustrations teenagers can understand when applied to the church, which is Christ's team. The beauty of the Church is that faith in Jesus is the only requirement to be on the team. It doesn't depend on skill or experience; it only requires faith.

Faith is also required to accept the contributions of all other team members. Perhaps the final production will not be as professional as we would like it to be, but we have to remember that the church is not for professionals. The church is for life-long learners and followers of Christ. We all need to coach each other, so that our team will be as strong as possible.

Concepts for Children

Topic: *Sharing with Others*

1. It is important how we can appreciate and love one another in the church.
2. Christ's Body, the Church, includes believers from all ranks of society and from all races and countries.
3. In the Church we can also learn from different styles of worship.
4. God gives us His spiritual gifts, so He can use us to love, encourage, and strengthen one another.
5. Dorcas was a gifted believer who blessed many people.
6. We can find good things to do for others, and try to help those who hurt.

The Lesson Commentary

I. DIFFERENCES IN THE BODY: 1 CORINTHIANS 12:4-7

A. Different Gifts: vs. 4

There are different kinds of gifts, but the same Spirit.

Here Paul responds to questions from the church at Corinth about spiritual gifts (vs. 1). God had intended that the church at Corinth should be strengthened by spiritual gifts. But jealousy and pride over spiritual gifts were causing dissension. Christians, regardless of their gifts, have to work together as one body.

First, Paul made it clear that the Holy Spirit works within all Christians. "No one can say, 'Jesus is Lord,' except by the Holy Spirit" (vs. 3). However, the Holy Spirit does not clone Christians. Quite the contrary. Christians differ in at least three ways in regard to their gifts: (1) Different kinds of gifts (vs. 4); (2) Different kinds of service (vs. 5); (3) Different kinds of working (vs. 6).

A spiritual gift is an ability given by God. Paul named some of these gifts in verses 8-11 and in Romans 12:6-8. However, Paul's lists did not include all of the spiritual gifts. His main point in verse 4 was that not all Christians have the same spiritual gifts, even though they possess the same Holy Spirit.

B. Different Services: vs. 5

There are different kinds of service, but the same Lord.

Paul emphasized that the point of our having spiritual gifts is to serve the Lord Jesus Christ and His people in the church. Different kinds of service are listed in verses 28-30 and in Ephesians 4:11. Because God in His grace bestows different gifts, service for Christ is possible and is expected of all believers.

Spiritual gifts and Christian service are not limited to the clergy. All Christians have the same Holy Spirit and the same Lord. The church therefore should be a place of coordinated, not competitive or dictatorial service.

C. Different Works: vs. 6

There are different kinds of working, but the same God works all of them in all men.

It is easy to judge different kinds of work, but in God's eyes preaching is not more important or more valuable that ushering or washing dishes after the church supper. It takes all believers and all kinds of gifts and service to do "God's work."

We are called to trust the sovereign Holy Spirit to use us in whatever way to do what is best for the church as a whole. (The word rendered "men" in verse 6 is to be understood as "people.") God is at work, Paul said, which means He gives the wisdom and strength we all need to complete our God-given tasks.

D. The Same Purpose: vs. 7

Now to each one the manifestation of the Spirit is given for the common good.

Why did God give such diversity in His church? Not for our personal glory, but so that the church might be strengthened ("the common good"). Every believer has some "manifestation" of the Holy Spirit. The word means "open to sight, visible, manifest." Spiritual gifts are seen in the way Christians serve one another.

Unity in diversity was Paul's theme. This is the beauty of the church. Because God is the same, and the Holy Spirit is the same, church members can build on what they have in common. That is how the church grows.

II. THE HOLY SPIRIT'S GIFTS: 1 CORINTHIANS 12:8-11

To one there is given through the Spirit the message of wisdom, to another the message of knowledge by means of the same Spirit, to another faith by the same Spirit, to another gifts of healing by that one Spirit, to another miraculous powers, to another prophecy, to another distinguishing between spirits, to another speaking in different kinds of tongues, and to still another the interpretation of tongues. All these are the work of one and the same Spirit, and he gives them to each one, just as he determines.

Paul listed nine spiritual gifts. The "message of wisdom" (see 1 Cor. 2:6-10) was the gift of communicating insightful help to others. Paul associated "knowledge" with mysteries, revelations and prophecies (1 Cor. 13:2; 14:6). This knowledge was supernaturally given, as, for example, to Peter (Acts 5:3).

The gift of "faith" does not mean our initial saving faith (Eph. 2:8). Rather, it refers to exceptional convictions given to Christians to claim God's promises. "Gifts of healing" suggests different gifts for different diseases.

"Miraculous powers" are distinguished from acts of healing. (See Mark 16:17-18; Acts 5:5, 10; 13:11.) The gift of "prophecy" includes predicting future events (Acts 11:27-28), and also preaching God's message with timely words (Luke 1:67; Acts 19:6; 21:9). Such gifted people Paul called "prophets" (1 Cor. 12:28).

"Distinguishing between spirits," that is, between good and evil spirits, was a much needed gift at Corinth because of overwhelming idolatry. Christians were charged by Paul to be alert in this constant battle (Eph. 6:12; 2 Thess. 2:2). All Christians are commanded to test the truth of spiritual messages (1 John 4:1).

The gifts of "speaking in different kinds of tongues" and "the interpretation of tongues" have been difficult to identify because scholars differ on the meaning of "tongues." Some Christians at Corinth were praying privately and speaking publicly in unintelligible words (1 Cor. 14:9). This does not seem to fit the known languages spoken on the day of Pentecost (Acts 2:6). Therefore, it is assumed by some scholars that at Corinth at least "tongues" were ecstatic utterances. Paul emphasized that it was useless to exercise this gift in public if no one had the gift of interpretation (1 Cor. 14:6-17).

III. THE CHURCH: ONE BODY: 1 CORINTHIANS 12:12-20, 26

A. Unity in the Body: vs. 12

The body is a unit, though it is made up of many parts; and though all its parts are many, they form one body. So it is with Christ.

Paul moved on from differences in the church to oneness. To illustrate this point, Paul chose the human body. The body is one, even though it has various parts, or members. Each part fulfills its function jointly with every other part. The result is unity and harmony.

So it is with Christ's body, the Church, made up of many different members with different gifts. In Christ there is one spiritual body, not many bodies. His body includes all those who have confessed their faith in Him.

All Christians are different. Not only do they have varieties of gifts, service, and working, they also have different personalities, skills, emotions, and cultural backgrounds. Christ's body includes men and women, boys and girls, young and old, poor and rich, educated and uneducated, and people of all races and nationalities.

Out of all these different members Christ has made one body. Different churches and different denominations are not different bodies of Christ. Of course, the Church has been organized according to doctrinal, historical, and national differences, but Christ's body transcends all of these human distinctions. The glue holding the body together is commitment to Jesus Christ as Lord and Savior.

B. Placement in the Body: vs. 13

For we were all baptized by one Spirit into one body—whether Jews or Greeks, slave or free—and we were all given the one Spirit to drink.

How can people with so many differences be made one body? That is the work of the Holy Spirit. He makes one body out of all believers, even those from such widely different backgrounds as Jews and Gentiles, slaves and free people. Paul called this Holy Spirit baptism.

This is not the same as water baptism. Spirit baptism binds individual believers into one body. The Holy Spirit does this when people confess their faith in Christ, at which time they are "given the one Spirit to drink."

Jesus promised that the Holy Spirit would come and live in Christians (John 14:16-17, 26). Because all Christians have the same Holy Spirit, they can live in unity with all other Christians.

C. Many Parts in the Body: vs. 14

Now the body is not made up of one part but of many.

The "body" in verse 14 is the physical body, not the spiritual body of Christ (vs. 13). From observing how our human bodies work, we can learn basic lessons about how we relate to each other in Christ's body, the Church.

The human body is a solitary unit, but it has many parts. This fact heads off any ideas of self-importance or preeminence held by the various party leaders in the church at Corinth. No Christian is "the" part of Christ's body. All Christians are important and valuable. All Christians have functions that are essential to the unity and health of Christ's body.

D. No Separation from the Body: vss. 15-16

If the foot should say, "Because I am not a hand, I do not belong to the body," it would not for that reason cease to be part of the body. And if the ear should say, "Because I am not an eye, I do not belong to the body," it would not for that reason cease to be part of the body.

The very idea that one part of the human body could declare itself *not* part of the body sounds ridiculous. But suppose this happened? If it did, the foot or the ear, for example, would still be part of the body.

However, what was ridiculous physically was not ridiculous spiritually. At Corinth, some Christians acted like the foot or the ear in Paul's hypothetical illustration. They didn't feel as important, or as needed as some other members, so in effect they had cut themselves off from the rest of the body.

Nothing that Christians feel can make them "cease to be part of the body." Believers have been joined to Christ and they belong to Him. They may find it hard to relate to some fellow believers, but they belong to those believers nevertheless, because they too are joined to Christ.

E. The Human Body Is One: vs. 17

If the whole body were an eye, where would the sense of hearing be? If the whole body were an ear, where would the sense of smell be?

Paul presented another ridiculous hypothetical illustration. What if the whole body was one big eye and could only see, but not feel or taste or hear? What use would a body like that be? Likewise, neither can an ear be "the whole body." The very word "body" conveys a variety of functions that work together.

Pastors are not "the whole body." If they try to be, they have misunderstood their role and function as builders of all the members of the body (Eph. 4:11-13). All Christians must get the chance to grow, develop, and use their gifts.

F. God Controls the Body: vss. 18-20

But in fact God has arranged the parts in the body, every one of them, just as he wanted them to be. If they were all one part, where would the body be? As it is, there are many parts, but one body.

The human body represents diversity and differences in oneness. God designed our bodies to function in perfect harmony. Each part plays a distinctive role, not on its own, but in concert with all the other parts.

The Corinthians needed to observe this principle in action and then apply it to their relationships in the church. If they chose to ignore these basic facts about how God Himself planned the church to work, they were headed for interminable squabbles. The stronger members would crush and ignore the weaker ones.

G. Suffering and Rejoicing in the Body: vs. 26

If one part suffers, every part suffers with it; if one part is honored, every part rejoices with it.

Paul's hypothetical illustration became real when he showed how it was supposed to work in the church. If you have a headache, you feel lousy all over. Emotional stress can be draining physically. Pain often brings depression. The human body is a unit. It "suffers" and "rejoices" together because it is one.

Likewise, in the church Christians in Christ's body find the encouragement and support they need when they hurt. They also share good news and rejoice with their fellow believers. When Christians carry out the ministries of mutual support and cheering, the whole body grows stronger and Christ receives praise, glory, and honor.

Discussion Questions

1. What are some different kinds of gifts, service, and working you see in the church?
2. What can we learn about our fellow Christians from diversity in the body of Christ?
3. What evidence do you see that your church works according to God's plan?
4. Using Paul's hypothetical illustration of the human body, how would you characterize your church?
5. How can we help Christians appreciate their need of each other?
6. How can we better accept, love, and learn from "different" members of Christ's body?

Contemporary Application

Many people yearn for the kind of human companionship, support, and fellowship offered in Christ's body, the Church. Sadly, many times they don't find it because the church seems to be marked by disunity, party spirit, and self-centeredness. That's why many of these people look elsewhere. They join service clubs, community groups, and sports clubs, or spend a lot of time hanging out at bars.

Because the church does not offer the kind of acceptance they are looking for, they do not seek Christ in the church. The church is supposed to be the one social group that transcends all of our differences. It's supposed to bear witness to people that Jesus can meet their needs. Our witness is only as valid and strong as our visible unity. Our message is heard when we sublimate our differences and work together peacefully in common purpose and love.

Christ's Resurrection and Ours

DEVOTIONAL READING

1 Corinthians 15:12-19, 50-57

DAILY BIBLE READINGS

Monday April 17
1 Corinthians 15:1-11 The Resurrection of Christ the Lord

Tuesday April 18
1 Corinthians 15:12-19 How Can You Deny the Resurrection?

Wednesday April 19
1 Corinthians 15:20-28 The Resurrected Christ Destroys Death

Thursday April 20
1 Corinthians 15:29-34 The Dead Are Raised: Believe It!

Friday April 21
1 Corinthians 15:35-41 God Will Give the Glory

Saturday April 22
1 Corinthians 15:42-49 Raised a Spiritual Body

Sunday April 23
1 Corinthians 15:50-58 We Have Victory through Jesus Christ!

Scripture

Background Scripture: *1 Corinthians 15*
Scripture Lesson: *1 Corinthians 15:20-27, 35-44*
Key Verse: *But Christ has indeed been raised from the dead, the firstfruits of those who have fallen asleep. For since death came through a man, the resurrection of the dead comes also through a man.* 1 Corinthians 15:20-21.
Scripture Lesson for Children: *1 Corinthians 15:20; Luke 24:1-10*
Key Verse for Children: *Christ has indeed been raised from the dead.* 1 Corinthians 15:20.

Lesson Aim

To grasp the hope of our resurrection because Jesus was raised from the dead.

Lesson Setting

Time: *A.D. 55*
Place: *Written to Corinth from Ephesus*

Lesson Outline

Christ's Resurrection and Ours

  I. Our Coming Resurrection: 1 Corinthians 15:20-23
    A. *Christ's Resurrection: vs. 20*
    B. *Adam and Christ: vss. 21-22*
    C. *The Order of Things to Come: vs. 23*
  II. Christ's Triumph: 1 Corinthians 15:24-27
    A. *Enemies Destroyed: vss. 24-25*
    B. *Death Destroyed: vs. 26*
    C. *He Rules over All: vs. 27*
  III. Our Resurrection Bodies: 1 Corinthians 15:35-44
    A. *Illustrated by Nature: vss. 35-41*
    B. *Contrasted to Our Physical Bodies: vss. 42-44*

Introduction for Adults

Topic: *What about the Resurrection?*

Easter celebrates the resurrection of our Lord Jesus Christ. It also guarantees the resurrection of our bodies. The two cannot be separated. Yet many people are resigned to the mistaken idea that when they die, they will cease to exist.

Even brilliant, well-educated people assume that one day they will "die like a dog." They cannot conceive of life beyond the grave. They assume that we are no different than the animals, and to claim immortality is foolishness. They cannot see beyond the physical realm of existence.

Consequently, although we are surrounded by news about death, we try to blot it out of our minds and postpone it as long as possible. We don't like to read the obituaries in the newspaper because that's it. Life is over and done. Life has no meaning beyond the here and now, so why not "eat, drink, and be merry" while we have the chance? If your life is full of poverty, suffering, or regrets, "that's all there is." That's the way so many people think.

But the Christian hope of the resurrection gives meaning to every life. Because He lives, we shall also live. More than ever, Christians need to share the certainty of eternal life in Jesus Christ with hopeless people.

Introduction for Youths

Topic: *What's the Last Word?*

The "last word" about our future is not wishful thinking. Consider these facts about the resurrection. The Lord Jesus Himself said that He would rise from the dead. Eyewitnesses who had seen Him alive after His death and burial wrote the New Testament stories about Him. After His resurrection Jesus appeared to people singly and in groups under many different conditions.

Christ's resurrection was the foundation of early Christian preaching. The Gospel spread and the church was established because Jesus was alive. Of all religions, Christianity alone claims that its founder was raised from the dead. This claim has been disputed, but never refuted.

I once talked to a scientist about the Christian faith. He was not impressed by my arguments. Then I asked him, "What do you make of Christ's resurrection?" He paused for awhile and then said, "I don't know. I've never thought about it." Our assignment this Easter is to help our unbelieving friends think about the meaning of Christ's resurrection.

Concepts for Children

Topic: *What Jesus Did for Me*

1. We celebrate Easter because Jesus was raised from the dead.
2. Jesus lives in heaven and He also lives in all of us who believe in Him.
3. Because Jesus was raised from the dead, we can be sure our sins are forgiven.
4. Christ's resurrection guarantees that one day we shall be raised to new life.
5. We can help people to faith by telling them the good news that Jesus lives.
6. Because Jesus lives, we can pray to, worship, love, and serve Him.

The Lesson Commentary

I. OUR COMING RESURRECTION: 1 CORINTHIANS 15:20-23

A. Christ's Resurrection: vs. 20

But Christ has indeed been raised from the dead, the firstfruits of those who have fallen asleep.

The apostle Paul wrote his first letter to the church at Corinth to answer specific questions about the Christian faith. One of the disputes in the church concerned the resurrection. Some were saying there is no resurrection (vs. 12). This chapter is the most complete defense of the Christian doctrine of Christ's resurrection and ours.

Christ has been raised from the dead. The emphatic truth is that Jesus of Nazareth came back from the tomb. This is the historic keystone of the Christian faith. Paul proved this fact by citing certain eyewitnesses of the risen Christ (vss. 5-8).

The consequences of Christ's resurrection are crucial. Our personal faith rests on it; God's forgiveness of our sins is based on it; our eternal life is guaranteed by it. Without Christ's resurrection, there is no Christian faith (vs. 14).

Christ's resurrection is the guarantee of ours. "The firstfruits" is the reference to the Feast of Firstfruits in the Old Testament (Lev. 23:10-11), when a sheaf of the first grain was waved by the priest as a promise of more grain in the field, and as a sample of the harvest to come. Likewise, Christ's resurrection is a pledge of more resurrections to follow, and a sample of ours.

"Those who have fallen asleep" are believers who have died. Because of Christ's victory over sin, death, and the grave, the sting of death has been removed for Christians. Death is no more than falling asleep for a time. Jesus tasted death (Heb. 2:9), so He knows what it is like. He entered fully into our condition and earned the right to be the firstfruit of those who die in faith.

B. Adam and Christ: vss. 21-22

For since death came through a man, the resurrection of the dead comes also through a man. For as in Adam all die, so in Christ all will be made alive.

Adam's sin brought death for all, while Christ brought victory over death. These verses present the basic truth of the headship of Adam and Christ over two groups of people. Adam's sin brought physical and spiritual death into the world. Thus, it was necessary for Christ to bring life and resurrection. Jesus, who brings life, became a member of the human race. (This basic Christian doctrine was treated by Paul more fully in Romans 5:12-21.)

Adam was the representative head of all humanity. All people inherit a sin nature that produces sinful deeds. Therefore, they incur God's righteous judgment—the death penalty. "In Adam all die" states the consequences of his sin.

The whole New Testament appeal for our salvation is based on the fact that we are dead in our trespasses and sin (Eph. 2:1).

However, everyone who is "in Christ," that is, those who by faith belong to Christ (vs. 23), are now saved and will be made alive. "In Christ" is the apostle Paul's favorite description of believers. To be "made alive" in Christ includes the resurrection of our bodies; it also includes abundant spiritual life now.

There is no life without Jesus Christ. All people today are either dead in Adam or alive in Christ. This is the crucial issue. It is a matter of life and death. Until people commit themselves by faith to Jesus Christ as Lord and Savior, they are totally dead.

C. The Order of Things to Come: vs. 23

But each in his own turn: Christ, the firstfruits; then, when he comes, those who belong to him.

There is a chronological order in the resurrection. "In his own turn" means rank. Jesus ranks first in being raised from the dead (Col. 1:18). Next to be raised are believers who have died in Christ (1 Thess. 4:16). The remainder of the dead, that is, unbelievers, will be raised—not to life—but to everlasting punishment (2 Thess. 1:6-10; Rev. 20:11-15).

Paul explained that believers would be raised at Christ's coming. This is called the rapture (because of the Latin word for "caught up" in 1 Thess. 4:17), when the dead in Christ will meet Him in the air, and living believers will be transformed (vs. 52).

II. CHRIST'S TRIUMPH: 1 CORINTHIANS 15:24-27

A. Enemies Destroyed: vss. 24-25

Then the end will come, when he hands over the kingdom to God the Father after he has destroyed all dominion, authority and power. For he must reign until he has put all his enemies under his feet.

All of Christ's enemies, including death, will be destroyed and the kingdom will be delivered to the Father. Paul's teaching about our resurrection led him to outline the consummation of all things. Christ's resurrection from the dead assures His final triumph over all His enemies. What we celebrate at Easter is not just an important event in the past, but also the promise of the future restoration of all things to God the Father.

Christ will conquer all His enemies. Jesus reigns now, but He reigns in conflict with many enemies. All rival powers have yet to be subdued. But one day "all dominion, authority and power"—that is, those opposed to the Lord—will be brought to nothing. Included is death, personified as our enemy.

"The end" is synonymous with the accomplishment of Christ's final victories. His victories await His return to the earth in power. History will be climaxed when He comes to assert His full, direct authority on earth.

After His victory, Jesus will deliver the kingdom to His Father. He will not lose anything, but will resume His eternal relationship with His Father. He will have completed His redemptive assignment. There is no recorded revelation that He will revert to His pre-incarnate state, but He will forever live as a man with His Father.

Delivering His authority back to His Father will mean a change in administration. God's heyday will be ushered in. Christ's resurrection guarantees an ultimately perfected kingdom. It is the answer to the Lord's Prayer, "Your kingdom come, your will be done on earth as it is in heaven" (Matt. 6:10). Christ will fully and finally remove everything that stands between God and the sinful humanity.

B. Death Destroyed: vs. 26

The last enemy to be destroyed is death.

Jesus defeated death at His resurrection (2 Tim. 1:10), but death still works in the world. At Christ's return, death will be finally robbed of its power and all the captives of death will be set free (Rev. 20:14).

C. He Rules over All: vs. 27

For he "has put everything under his feet." Now when it says that "everything" has been put under him, it is clear that this does not include God himself, who put everything under Christ.

Paul quoted Psalm 8:6 to show that Christ's ultimate triumph was prophesied in the Old Testament. He made clear, however, that the Father was not under the Son's dominion. After the consummation of God's plan, the incarnate Son will resume His place in the Trinity, for the glory of the triune Godhead in all things.

There is no inequality or subordination as to essence in the Trinity. The Son is not competitive with the Father, but operates in cooperation with Him (John 6:38). There will be no lessening of the Son's distinction at that day, but the perfectly acknowledged rule of God so He will be "all in all."

The glory of God is the final end of Christ's work (Phil. 2:11). His co-equality with His Father will continue after He defeats all of God's enemies and turns His triumphant kingdom over to His Father.

III. OUR RESURRECTION BODIES: 1 CORINTHIANS 15:35-44

A. Illustrated by Nature: vss. 35-41

But someone may ask, "How are the dead raised? With what kind of body will they come?" How foolish! What you sow does not come to life unless it dies. When you sow, you do not plant the body that will be, but just a seed, perhaps of wheat or of something else. But God gives it a body as he has determined, and to each kind of seed he gives its own body. All flesh is not the same: Men have one kind of flesh, animals have another, birds another and fish another. There are also heavenly bodies and there are earthly bodies; but the splendor of the heavenly bodies is one kind, and the splendor of the earthly bodies is another. The sun has one kind of splendor, the moon another and the stars another; and star differs from star in splendor.

Corinth was full of scoffers who disbelieved the resurrection. Christians in other cultures were also puzzled about the nature of it. Paul quoted typical questions, then said they were foolish, because people should have learned something about the resurrection from observing how things work in nature. God teaches us eternal truth by what He does in the everyday world.

Paul pointed to the obvious fact that nothing grows unless the seed dies first. Jesus made the same point in John 12:24. This means that death is a necessary prelude to life. Unless our bodies die first, there will be no resurrection life.

Paul's next answer was that in the world of nature you do not plant the entire plant, but only the seed. What you sow is not what will be in the future. The seed does not look like the plant it will become. In considering our resurrection bodies, we must remember that they will be different from our present physical bodies.

Finally, Paul said, each seed brings forth its own kind of body. God has made a huge variety of plants. He makes new things according to His plan. So, if we can trust Him to do that in the plant world, we can expect that He will do the same for us.

Paul then illustrated our resurrection by looking at animal life. He noted the different kinds of bodies among animals, birds, and fish. From this fact we can believe that God can make a resurrection body that differs from the one we now have. "All flesh is not the same" (vs. 39), so we must not be surprised by the Christian doctrine that God will give the believers new bodies.

Next, Paul looked at the solar system. Variety and change are visible in the heavens. Sun, moon, and stars are not alike. They differ in "splendor." Therefore, it is not unreasonable to believe that God can give us resurrection bodies that will have a different kind of "splendor."

The two basic questions about the resurrection are how and what. "How" is answered by the power of God. The answer to "what" is the variety in God's creation. The key is difference—differences between seed and plant, between animals, bird, and fish, and between sun, moon, and stars. So it will be with the new bodies God will give us.

B. Contrasted to Our Physical Bodies: vss. 42-44

So will it be with the resurrection of the dead. The body that is sown is perishable, it is raised imperishable; it is sown in dishonor, it is raised in glory; it is sown in weakness, it is raised in power; it is sown a natural body, it is raised a spiritual body. If there is a natural body, there is also a spiritual body.

Paul applied his illustrations from nature by declaring four contrasts between our present bodies and our new ones: (1) perishable . . . imperishable; (2) dishonor . . . glory; (3) weakness . . . power; (4) natural . . . spiritual.

His first contrast is between perishable and imperishable. We readily acknowledge that our bodies are perishable, in spite of remarkable progress in medical discoveries that give us a longer life expectancy. We keep on aging and wearing out.

In contrast to that, our resurrection bodies will be imperishable. They will not be subject to disease and decay. They will be immune to all the things that now attack us. They will last forever without benefit of transplants. They will last forever without drugs and operations. "There will be no more death or mourning or crying or pain" (Rev. 21:4).

Paul's second contrast is between dishonor and glory. Our bodies are not dishonorable, but they can become instruments of dishonor by the way we use them. Our minds and wills control our bodies. Therefore, our bodies can be abused and used for sinful purposes.

Our present bodies do not show forth the glory that one day will be ours with our new bodies. These bodies are subject to humiliation and decay. One day they shall be free from both. That will be glory. Paul said the whole creation, including our bodies, groans as it waits for "the redemption of our bodies" (Rom. 8:23).

Paul's third contrast is between weakness and power. We are well aware of our finiteness. Despite amazing physical feats of prowess, there are limits to what our bodies can stand. We need rest, food, water, and air.

But our resurrection bodies will be marked by power. They will overcome all of the weaknesses of our present bodies. We will no longer be subject to the things that tire us out and wear us down.

Finally, Paul contrasted natural and spiritual bodies. This is perhaps his best summary of the differences, but it is the hardest to understand. How can you have a "spiritual" body when by definition "body" means something physical?

In terms of physical science, the two ideas are contradictory. But we have to see them in light of the radical differences Paul cited previously. He did not explain them in terms of modern science, because they are beyond such explanation. When we ask how such a resurrection body could be, we miss the point of Paul's illustrations about God's work in other things.

Somehow, by His power and wisdom, God will give us a different kind of body. Jesus had a resurrection body that was identifiable, but different. He looked like He did before His death, but His body had certain differences. It was a glorified body. That's as far as Paul went in explaining our resurrection bodies.

Paul gave us enough information to reassure us about our resurrection bodies. What more could we ask than a body that is no longer subject to the limitations of time, illness, and sin?

Discussion Questions

1. Why do some people not want to accept the New Testament facts about Christ's resurrection?
2. What difference does it make if you believe the resurrection or not?
3. How could you use Paul's answer to help someone with terminal cancer?
4. Why is it hard for some people to believe they will be given a new body?
5. Do you think Paul's explanation is adequate? Why?
6. What evidences of Christ's resurrection should we see in our lives today?

Contemporary Application

Somehow, Christ's resurrection power, and the assurance of resurrection bodies, gets lost when Easter turns into a kind of spring festival. We are thankful for every sign of new life in the spring. But we have to remember that these are just tokens of what lies in store for those who love and obey Jesus Christ.

Easter makes no sense unless we connect Christ's resurrection with His victory over sin and death. All of the signs of new life in nature will not do us any good unless we believe certain facts. We must accept Jesus Christ's death on the cross as the atonement for our sins. We must thank Him for dying in our place because of our sin.

God's power can easily be seen in nature, but it is seen supremely in the raising of His Son from the grave. The church at Easter celebrates this astounding fact. As Paul rightfully explained, if Jesus did not rise from the dead, we are hopelessly lost.

Easter means hope to those who understand and believe these things.

The Way of Love

DEVOTIONAL READING

1 John 4:7-21

DAILY BIBLE READINGS

Monday April 24
1 Corinthians 13:1-7 The Gift of Love

Tuesday April 25
1 Corinthians 13:8-13 Love Is the Greatest Gift

Wednesday April 26
1 John 2:7-17 Love: An Old New Commandment

Thursday April 27
1 John 3:11-17 Show Your Love for One Another

Friday April 28
1 John 3:18-24 Believe in Jesus, and Love One Another

Saturday April 29
1 John 4:7-12 Let Us Love as God Loves

Sunday April 30
1 John 4:13-21 We Abide in God If We Love

Scripture

Background Scripture: *1 Corinthians 12:31—13:13*
Scripture Lesson: *1 Corinthians 12:31—13:13*
Key Verse: *And now these three remain: faith, hope and love. But the greatest of these is love.* 1 Corinthians 13:13.
Scripture Lesson for Children: 1 Corinthians 13:4; Ruth 1:16-18; 2:2-3, 8-9, 11-12
Key Verse for Children: *Love is patient, love is kind.* 1 Corinthians 13:4.

Lesson Aim

To give priority to a Christian life of love.

Lesson Setting

Time: A.D. *55*
Place: *Written to Corinth from Ephesus*

Lesson Outline

The Way of Love
   I. Love's Values: 1 Corinthians 12:31—13:3
  II. Love's Strengths: 1 Corinthians 13:4-7
 III. Love's Triumphs: 1 Corinthians 13:8-13

Introduction for Adults

Topic: *What's Real Love?*

Real love is hard to come by because so many people give up trying to make it work. Even among church families we find disputes erupting, sometimes leading to separation and divorce, despite public vows to love until death separates us. We hear many reasons for these tragedies. A frequent reason is that one spouse wants to be free to find real love and happiness.

Another reason is that we have not fortified our minds and hearts by the biblical teaching about the supremacy of the way of love. Perhaps the last time we heard 1 Corinthians 13 was at a marriage ceremony. It sounded so lovely then.

But what about our commitment to make it work? This is where we need to shore up our values. If we seriously believe in Jesus Christ as Lord and Savior, then we must make every effort to make love work the way God intended.

Introduction for Youths

Topic: *What's Real Love?*

Young people in the market for a diamond engagement ring often are hoodwinked into buying something that looks like an expensive diamond but turns out to be something less. They are also cheated when it comes to finding real love. In fact, they see so many disasters arising from what supposedly were solid love relationships that they are skeptical of traditional marriage vows.

The Bible doesn't tell us how to spot a fake diamond, or a fake romance. But it does tell us how to live a genuine Christian life based on the values, strengths, and permanence of love. While television and the movies exploit lust, Christians are called to encourage one another with demonstrations of authentic love.

It may appear to teenagers that the kind of love taught in the Bible is irrelevant. Therefore, the task of Christian parents, teachers, and pastors is to make Christian love—with its purity, depth, and commitment—a reality by our example as well as by teaching.

Concepts for Children

Topic: *Showing Love for Others*

1. God sends us love in many ways, especially through family and friends.
2. Love is not just something we receive; it is something we give.
3. In 1 Corinthians 13, we find a very simple, practical description of love.
4. From the story of Ruth, we learn that God gives us many chances to be kind, courteous, patient, and helpful.
5. Sometimes we have to admit that it's hard to love people who cause us trouble.
6. When we are unloving, we can confess this to Jesus and ask Him to help us to be more loving.

The Lesson Commentary

I. Love's Values: 1 Corinthians 12:31—13:3

But eagerly desire the greater gifts. And now I will show you the most excellent way. If I speak in the tongues of men and of angels, but have not love, I am only a resounding gong or a clanging cymbal. If I have the gift of prophecy and can fathom all mysteries and all knowledge, and if I have a faith that can move mountains, but have not love, I am nothing. If I give all I possess to the poor and surrender my body to the flames, but have not love, I gain nothing.

In the church at Corinth there were apostles, prophets, teachers, workers of miracles, healers, helpers, administrators, and tongues speakers. Of course, others served in the church in different capacities as well, because Paul's list was not exhaustive. This is clear from 12:29-30.

Those who had the more public gifts would obviously be more visible, and perhaps envied as well. Paul reminded the church that God did not intend for every believer to have all the gifts. If they could not preach, teach, heal, or speak in tongues, they were not second-class Christians. He encouraged them to "eagerly desire the greater gifts" (vs. 31). But the "greater gifts" did not ensure the most effective ministry.

At that point, Paul turned to what he called "the most excellent way," the way of love. Paul's main point was that it is possible for Christians to have the "greater gifts" and still be useless for the cause of Christ. He mentioned some of these supposedly "greater" gifts: speaking in both human and angelic tongues; speaking with prophetic powers and insight into divine mysteries and knowledge; having faith strong enough to move mountains; sacrificial giving; even martyrdom.

However, Paul warned that the usefulness of these gifts would be diminished if the user did not exercise them in love. He ridiculed loveless tongues-speakers by saying they sounded like a noisy gong or cymbal. All kinds of spiritual activities, even martyrdom, can mask a lack of love. He made it very clear that despite what other accomplishments Christians might have, if they lacked love, their lives amounted to nothing.

Paul encouraged Christians to desire and use spiritual gifts, but he also warned of dangers. Even though we may think we are important, and even though we consider our works vital to the church, if we lack love everything is counted as nothing in God's sight. That's because our motives establish our value. If love drives my devotion to the truth, then my devotion counts with God.

The pervasive power of sin in our lives is so great that even the greatest of spiritual gifts can be corrupted. All of our gifts can be used selfishly, to boost our pride. Paul warned that our egos and pride are so strong that they can undo our good deeds.

Paul did not deride Christian service and the ministry of spiritual gifts, but he emphasized that they could easily be rendered worthless. He addressed the issue of motives and attitudes, not activity. The way of love makes the difference between spiritual gifts that are useful and those that are useless.

II. LOVE'S STRENGTHS: 1 CORINTHIANS 13:4-7

Love is patient, love is kind. It does not envy, it does not boast, it is not proud. It is not rude, it is not self-seeking, it is not easily angered, it keeps no record of wrongs. Love does not delight in evil but rejoices with the truth. It always protects, always trusts, always hopes, always perseveres.

After exposing the great danger of exercising spiritual gifts devoid of love, Paul went on to describe the amazing strengths of love. He listed fifteen strengths of love. If we measure up to his list, we can be sure that our spiritual gifts and activities will bring glory to God and build up the church. With these qualities of love, our service for God will be fruitful and the lives of other people will be enriched.

The first thing we notice here is that Paul's description of love is far removed from popular ideas about romantic, sentimental feelings of love. Christian love is always seen in how we treat others. It is love of deeds, not feelings.

Love produces patience and kindness that enable Christians to be long-suffering. Christians are kind beyond the point when patience would usually be exhausted. Why did Paul begin with patience? Probably because if we do not achieve patience we won't get very far with the other strengths of love.

Paul described love by including eight things love is not:

Love is not jealous, or envious. Envy makes it impossible to love. Some Christians at Corinth were jealous of others because they had different spiritual gifts. Love makes it possible, in Christ's body, for the "foot" to rejoice in the dexterity of the "hand," for the "ear" to rejoice in the brilliance of the "eye" (12:14-21).

Love is not boastful. Love doesn't even boast about itself. Love keeps Christians from seeking applause, approval, and esteem. Love keeps us from becoming ostentatious, and from talking too much about others.

Love is not proud. Pride is possibly a more severe form of boasting. It is empty conceit. Love makes us less conscious of ourselves.

Love is not rude. It is not discourteous or boorish. Love doesn't raise a blush. Love guards Christians from making fools of themselves.

Love is not self-seeking. Love does not insist on getting its own way. Love is unselfish. Love has a capacity for self-emptying.

Love is not easily angered. Love is not irritable. Love doesn't blow its top. Love isn't easily brought to the boiling point. Some Christians excuse their tempers by saying people provoke them. But when loves controls us, we will not be touchy and supersensitive.

Love keeps no record of wrongs. Love is not resentful. Love takes no account of personal hurts. Love sets Christians free from the bondage of grudges and revenge.

Love does not delight in evil. In the strength of love, Christians are never glad when someone falls into sin, even when it proves them "right."

After he defined love in terms of what love does not do, Paul gave the positive strengths of love:

Love rejoices with the truth. If we are interested in rejoicing with the truth, we will find it. Christians cannot be smug in the presence of unrighteousness, because the nature of Christ within them demands that they love truth and holiness. They are glad when fellow believers advance in holiness.

Love always protects. The Greek word used by Paul means to put a shield over someone, to keep them safe underneath. Loving Christians provide a canopy for others to keep them safe from evil. They are busy protecting those who may be unaware of sin, or untrained in spiritual living.

Love always trusts, or believes all things. Love credits others with good intentions. This does not mean that Christians believe everything that comes down the pike. They are not gullible. Scripture warns Christians against false teachers. However, motivated by love, Christians give others the benefit of the doubt in their personal relations. They are not automatically suspicious of the motives of others.

Love always hopes. If Christians do have some reason for suspecting another person, their love drives them to be optimistic rather than pessimistic. They hope for the best against all appearances. This is not unreasonable optimism, but rather a deep yearning for God's best for everyone.

Love perseveres, or endures all things. Christian love remains strong, regardless of difficulties. Love sustains Christians in their faith. To endure means to be active, positive, and strong in our attitudes. It is not groaning through our hardships.

III. Love's Triumphs: 1 Corinthians 13:8-13

Love never fails. But where there are prophecies, they will cease; where there are tongues, they will be stilled; where there is knowledge, it will pass away. For we know in part and we prophesy in part, but when perfection comes, the imperfect disappears. When I was a child, I talked like a child, I thought like a child, I reasoned like a child. When I became a man, I put childish ways behind me. Now we see but a poor reflection as in a mirror; then we shall see face to face. Now I know in part; then I shall know fully, even as I am fully known. And now these three remain: faith, hope and love. But the greatest of these is love.

Paul's final accolade to love is that it never fails. It outlasts everything, and it surpasses both faith and hope. This is Paul's summary of love's qualities. Love is eternal; it never collapses. Love never stops working. It never stops motivating Christians to care and to show concern for others.

Paul returned to his starting point, the earnest desire for higher gifts (12:31).

Of course, it was commendable to desire these gifts, but it was even more commendable to live under the everlasting power of love.

The so-called greater gifts—whether they be prophecy, tongues speaking, or knowledge (12:28—13:2)—will cease and pass away. In fact, Paul said, these gifts at best are "imperfect" (vs. 10). How so? Because compared to love they are finite, limited, and temporal. Prophecies will cease, tongues will be silenced, and knowledge will pass away. These gifts are useful now, but they will be replaced by love that endures forever.

Paul used two analogies to illustrate this point: (1) It was like passing from childhood to manhood, and (2) it was like looking at a poor reflection in a mirror. There are many childlike ways in all of us. Our perception of things, our evaluations of things, and our appreciation of things many times are imperfect. We can't dismiss spiritual gifts to build up the body. But just as the scaffolding is removed when the building is completed, so these gifts eventually will disappear.

Paul then looked down the long corridor of the future and revealed his own intense longing for a full knowledge of God. His knowledge was like looking at a poor reflection in a mirror. He had partial knowledge. But he anticipated the day when he would fully understand, because he would enjoy God's presence.

Paul's primary concern for the demonstration of Christian love followed his desire to show why God is chiefly interested in our attitudes. God is more concerned about the kind of people we are than about our various church activities. Spiritual gifts are vital to the life of the church, but they are imperfect, or partial, when compared to the full, final revelation of the knowledge of God.

Christians need the eternal perspective provided by love. They often struggle to find meaning in their lives. They may not be able to influence thousands. They may not be able to impress anyone with their achievements. But they know that when they invest their love in others, this will outlast everything else and have eternal significance.

Faith, hope, and love "remain" (vs. 13). Of course, these Christian virtues are important and essential. Why should we think that one is more important than the other? Paul did not say why he ranked love at the top, but he did. That must give us pause in making our own priorities.

Why is love "the greatest"? Perhaps because it is the reason and strength of both faith and hope. If we fail to love, our faith weakens and our hope fades. Faith and hope do not disappear with the spiritual gifts. They remain alone with love, but they are sustained by and overshadowed by eternal love.

When we look at Paul's positive and negative lists of what love does and does not do, we are reminded that the only person who has fully lived up to this remarkable standard is the Lord Jesus Christ. Paul's picture of love really is a portrait of Jesus. We read in the Gospels how He manifested love, even though

He often was provoked, tested, and finally denied, and then crucified. Yes, on some occasions Jesus showed righteous anger over the hypocrisy of the Pharisees, but He never retaliated against His accusers. His final act—death on the cross—was one of unselfish forgiveness and love.

Discussion Questions

1. Why is the "most excellent way" of love more valuable than the "greater" spiritual gifts?
2. Why does the absence of love cancel the effectiveness of these gifts?
3. What do you think about God's evaluation of gifted, but loveless Christians? Is it fair to say their gifts amount to nothing?
4. Is Paul's description of love realistic? Attainable?
5. How can Christians love people who irritate or injure them?
6. How would your church look if people practiced love according to God's standard?

Contemporary Application

We are astounded by the comprehensiveness and practicality of Paul's description of love. Nothing like it has ever been written. It sets Christian virtue far above any other standard to be found in the world.

At the same time, we have to confess how far short of this standard we fall. So far short, in fact, that we are tempted to dismiss it and give up. Too hard. Won't work in the real world. We are much better at making excuses than we are at asking God to do something special in our lives so we can be His loving people.

Perhaps the place to begin is with confession. As we read over this list, we must confess that we haven't done it. If we've been rude, we must confess. If we've been holding a grudge, we must confess it. Until we clear our hearts and lives of the sludge and silt of sin, we will not be refreshed by Christ's clear, living water of love.

Our churches invest greatly in programs, buildings, and staff. Perhaps we need to take an inventory of how much we invest in love. If our balance sheet is heavily weighted toward love, things will happen in our churches that we cannot possibly attribute to any program alone.

The Christian March of Triumph

Scripture

Background Scripture: *2 Corinthians 1-2*
Scripture Lesson: *2 Corinthians 2:4-17*
Key Verse: *But thanks be to God, who always leads us in triumphal procession in Christ and through us spreads everywhere the fragrance of the knowledge of him.*
2 Corinthians 2:14.
Key Verse for Children: *We work with you for your joy.*
2 Corinthians 1:24.

Lesson Aim

To forgive one another and celebrate Christ's triumph over sin and death.

Lesson Setting

Time: *A.D. 57-58*
Place: *Written to Corinth from Macedonia*

Lesson Outline

The Christian March of Triumph

  I. The Forgiveness of Christ: 2 Corinthians 2:4-11
     A. *Paul's Tears: vs. 4*
     B. *Sufficient Punishment: vss. 5-6*
     C. *Love Reaffirmed: vss. 7-8*
     D. *Forgiveness All Around: vss. 9-11*
  II. Paul's Unease: 2 Corinthians 2:12-13
III. The Aroma of Christ: 2 Corinthians 2:14-17
     A. *Triumph in Christ: vs. 14*
     B. *The "Life and Death" Fragrance: vss. 15-16a*
     C. *Speaking in Christ: vss. 16b-17*

Introduction for Adults

Topic: *From Sorrow to Joy*

A group of soldiers had just finished Army basic training and were eager to get some time off. They stood around in the railroad station, laughing and telling stories about what we were going to do on furlough. Their hopes were high. When the train pulled in, they rushed to the platform. Then they noticed a small cluster of people nearby. They were sober, not laughing. The reason soon became apparent: a casket was unloaded from the baggage car. The same train brought joy to one group but sorrow to another.

The apostle Paul said the "aroma of Christ" is like that. To those who receive the good news, it brings joy; to those who do not believe, it brings sorrow. This is a sobering fact that often we are reluctant to face.

We need only consider how this principle worked with Jesus Himself. His "aroma" attracted great crowds, because He offered forgiveness, peace, hope, and eternal life. At the same time, however, some of those who heard what He said called Him a maniac, a blasphemer, a tool of the devil.

Introduction for Youths

Topic: *Discipline from Love*

It's easy for young people to get discouraged by the struggles they see in the church. Sometimes they excuse themselves from worship, study, and service because of these imperfections. We have to remind ourselves that the apostle Paul could very easily have thrown in the towel and given up on the Corinthians with justifiable disgust.

However, he knew that God's people are believers in process. They have many rough edges. They cause problems. They offend each other. They fall into sin. He did not quit because he knew the value of discipline and love. He knew that sinners do repent; they are forgiven and restored; they are loved; they make fresh starts. This is good news, especially for teenagers.

They need discipline with strong doses of encouragement, love, and second chances. Where would any of us be without multiple opportunities?

Our great hope and confidence is that we are winners with Jesus. He calls us to join His victory parade. Perhaps we have stumbled, but He has not thrown us out of His triumphal procession.

Concepts for Children

Topic: *The Joy of Serving*

1. When we come to faith in Jesus, He gives us opportunities to serve others.
2. The apostle Paul served Jesus with a strong sense of being called by God.
3. On some occasions, difficulties arise that make it hard to serve.
4. Something as simple as "serving tables" counts for much in God's sight.
5. Our friends have many needs that we can meet in the name of Jesus.
6. We can learn how to serve Jesus by following the examples of others.

The Lesson Commentary

I. THE FORGIVENESS OF CHRIST: 2 CORINTHIANS 2:4-11

A. Paul's Tears: vs. 4

For I wrote you out of great distress and anguish of heart and with many tears, not to grieve you but to let you know the depth of my love for you.

The story of the apostle Paul's relations with the church at Corinth is not pleasant to reflect on. Paul had established the church and lived there 18 months (Acts 18:1-11), during which time he experienced many fears and anxieties. Because the city itself was such a godless place, and because Paul's authority in the church was questioned and usurped, he made little progress. Yet he persisted in ministering to the Corinthians, even though the process was painful.

The problems confronting Paul and the Christians at Corinth were attributed partly to the city's sordid moral character. Because of its unique location, with two seaports (consult Bible lands maps), Corinth was a thriving commercial center. Jews went there for trade, Romans for government business, and Greeks for selling local products. The city was jammed with sailors, business people, sales persons, and travelers from all over the Roman world.

Corinth was a boomtown, marked by luxury, display, sensuality, and sports. "To live as do the Corinthians" was a common epithet for the lowest kind of life. The temple of Aphrodite at Corinth represented pagan idolatry and gross immorality. More than 1,000 priestesses served as prostitutes.

In this atmosphere the Christians struggled to live like saints, and the apostle shed tears for them, even as he wrote his letters. In his second letter, as in his first, Paul reminded his readers that God had sent him to them with the good news about Jesus Christ. God had established Paul's spiritual credentials among the Corinthians. He had authenticated the apostle's message, and many people had turned from the vileness and ignorance of paganism to truth and holiness in Christ.

Paul had to write of his own authority from God because false teachers were seeking to subvert the truth of the Gospel and lead people astray. It was difficult for Paul to write this way, because he did not want to appear to be bragging. But his divine commission was important to the establishment of the truth.

Paul was fearless and forthright because of his dedication to Christian principles. He may have appeared tough to those whom he had disciplined. But he also had the great courage not to hide his tears (see also Acts 20:19, 31). Often it takes more courage to cry openly for people than it does to rebuke them.

Paul knew that part of being a pastor of God's flock meant assuring people of deep love, by shedding tears of affliction and anguish over the welfare of their souls. Paul loved and wept in spite of the existence of a faction in the church that opposed him.

B. Sufficient Punishment: vss. 5-6

If anyone has caused grief, he has not so much grieved me as he has grieved all of you, to some extent—not to put it too severely. The punishment inflicted on him by the majority is sufficient for him.

Paul then addressed the issue of what to do with the man who had been isolated from Christian fellowship because of his sin. (See Lesson 4, March 26, concerning 1 Corinthians 5:1-13, though not all scholars consider this the same situation.) This terrible situation had caused considerable grief. The church had carried out Paul's instruction to banish the offender, but that was enough. The church's integrity and purity had been established. The man's spiritual life had been redeemed.

The principle here seems clear. The Gospel sometimes demands actions that bring temporary pain and grief. The church cannot walk away from its responsibilities because the outcomes are likely to hurt. The larger issues of holiness and truth require corresponding actions. When the church is faithful to Christ, the outcomes are beneficial. The church is purified. The public learns that being a Christian requires living by God's laws. The offender is restored.

C. Love Reaffirmed: vss. 7-8

Now instead, you ought to forgive and comfort him, so that he will not be overwhelmed by excessive sorrow. I urge you, therefore, to reaffirm your love for him.

Discipline had brought the man to repentance. Therefore, he must be welcomed back to Christian fellowship in the church. If not, the man would be overwhelmed by the sorrow brought about by his sin and banishment.

We see here how God's principles of judgment and mercy work. *Redemption and restoration are the goals of discipline*, not permanent exclusion from the fellowship. "Throw your arms around him and welcome him back," Paul said, in effect.

The offender needed strong personal encouragement to resume his Christian walk. He could make a fresh start and grow to be a strong Christian witness. But he needed love to get back on track. How do you reaffirm love? In this case, it meant not just opening the church but their hearts and homes as well. He must be included in the church's social relationships as well as worship.

Just as Paul wept, showing his deep love, so the Corinthians would have to welcome this man back with tears of joy.

D. Forgiveness All Around: vss. 9-11

The reason I wrote you was to see if you would stand the test and be obedient in everything. If you forgive anyone, I also forgive him. And what I have forgiven—if there was anything to forgive—I have forgiven in the sight of Christ for your sake, in order that Satan might not outwit us. For we are not unaware of his schemes.

Of course, forgiveness was the key to the man's restoration to fellowship. Paul's letter of instructions about this case had been followed (vs. 9). He rejoiced that the church had exercised godly discipline. Now it was time to put the matter to rest.

Paul explained that he would forgive the man because the church had forgiven him (vs. 10). He trusted the spiritual discernment of his fellow believers at Corinth. Then he added that he was also extending the forgiveness of Christ. The translation is a bit awkward here. It could mean, "I mean that as the representative of Christ I have forgiven him for your sake," or, "I have forgiven him for your sake, in the presence of Christ."

Forgiveness, according to Jesus, always extends to both the human and divine levels. Because God has forgiven us in Christ, we are called to forgive one another. The grace of forgiveness transforms human relationships. Nothing worthwhile could result from this case, unless the man was forgiven both by Jesus and by his fellow believers.

Paul added another important reason why the man was to be forgiven, restored, comforted, and loved (vs. 11). He was at the mercy of Satan if he did not receive the tender mercies of the church. Paul knew that a major part of Satan's strategy is to consume discouraged, defeated, unloved Christians. Isolated from the church, any Christian is easy prey for the devil.

Satan must not gain the victory in this situation. The church that is aware of Satan's schemes will be successful in showing forgiveness, love, and acceptance to erring sisters and brothers who confess and repent of their sins.

II. PAUL'S UNEASE: 2 CORINTHIANS 2:12-13

Now when I went to Troas to preach the gospel of Christ and found that the Lord had opened a door for me, I still had no peace of mind, because I did not find my brother Titus there. So I said good-by to them and went on to Macedonia.

Paul wanted the Corinthians to understand his great unease because he lacked fresh information about their spiritual condition. He was intensely concerned, and therefore keenly disappointed when he could not connect with Titus at Troas (Acts 20:7-12).

Although not mentioned in Acts, Titus was one of Paul's most trusted companions. He acted as Paul's representative at Corinth during the year before Paul wrote 2 Corinthians, with the special task of organizing a collection. His much more delicate task was soothing over the tensions between Paul and the Corinthians. A comparison of 2 Corinthians 2 and 7 suggests that Titus carried a letter from Paul to the Corinthians, which was lost.

Titus eventually rejoined Paul in Macedonia (2 Cor. 7:5-6) with good news. As a result, Paul wrote 2 Corinthians, and Titus took the letter to Corinth (2 Cor. 8:17).

III. THE AROMA OF CHRIST: 2 CORINTHIANS 2:14-17

A. Triumph in Christ: vs. 14

But thanks be to God, who always leads us in triumphal procession in Christ and through us spreads everywhere the fragrance of the knowledge of him.

Out of his profound disappointment, Paul described how God had sustained him. This led him to write about the glory he had found in serving Christ. In the goodness of God, Paul had found encouragement in Macedonia when Titus reached him (7:6). Paul praised God. To tell how grateful he was to God, he used the picture of the triumphal procession of Roman generals.

However, his victory in Christ was much more significant than the great military conquests of the Romans. Nevertheless, Paul found an aspect of their conquests to illustrate what he had found in Jesus.

The "triumphal procession" was a technical term used to describe a victorious general's homecoming from the war, parading through the packed streets of Rome. Paul's victory march was "in Christ," and he rejoiced despite his setbacks and hardships.

Paul saw Christians as the victors. Joined to Christ by faith, they have defeated sin and death. They have triumphed because they are linked to Jesus.

B. The "Life and Death" Fragrance: vss. 15-16a

For we are to God the aroma of Christ among those who are being saved and those who are perishing. To the one we are the smell of death; to the other, the fragrance of life.

To the one we are the smell of death; to the other, the fragrance of life. Paul saw not only our victory in Christ, he saw something else to illustrate spiritual truth. He remembered the smell that accompanied the Romans' parades. He remembered the pungent smells of incense and perfume from the burning censers carried by captives. He remembered the aroma of the aromatic herbs strewn along the streets by the celebrating citizens.

The aromas were sweet to those praising the victors, but they were bitter to the doomed prisoners. This picture of the Romans' victory march shows the role of Christians in the world. Christians are led in Christ's triumphal parade. Therefore, they are responsible to spread the fragrance of Jesus everywhere.

How do Christians become "the aroma of Christ"? By staying close to Him in prayer, Bible study, worship, and obedience. Christians grow to become more and more like Jesus. God shapes them to be like His Son. As this happens, Christians become attractive to others. They are like the aroma of a bubbling stew in the kitchen. Their "smell" draws people to Christ.

Of course, not all people whom Christians influence receive the knowledge of Christ. Some do, and they are saved, but others do not, and they are lost. The same fragrance leads to different eternal destinies, depending on the person's receptivity to the Gospel. Christians cannot control the responses of others. Their duty is to carry the fragrance of Jesus everywhere.

C. Speaking in Christ: vss. 16b-17

And who is equal to such a task? Unlike so many, we do not peddle the word of God for profit. On the contrary, in Christ we speak before God with sincerity, like men sent from God.

Paul admitted that his picture of Christians spreading the aroma of Christ was hard to carry out. "Who is equal to such a task?" he asked. His answer was somewhat indirect, because he addressed it from his own experience. He posed two possible ways: either "peddle the word of God for profit" or speak "with sincerity, like men sent from God."

The first way, which he rejected, compares telling the good news to crass salesmanship. This way treats the Gospel as something to be "sold," like pots and pans. Such commercialization upset Paul, because it was phony, not sincere.

The second way requires honesty and sincerity, because "we speak before God." We speak about Jesus because we have been "sent from God." Telling other people about Christ's victory means being honest about ourselves and about the cost of believing in Jesus.

Christians do not "sell" Jesus because He is some kind of sedative, or tranquilizer to settle problems. He does not need to be peddled merely as a fire escape from hell. Jesus does offer peace, and He does promise eternal life in heaven. Sincere witnesses talk about His deity, His victory over sin and death, and the cost of discipleship. They testify to the abiding joys of marching in His victory parade.

Discussion Questions

1. How would you describe Paul's fears about the church at Corinth?
2. Why is it important to forgive and comfort those who have repented?
3. What makes it difficult to forgive?
4. How would you describe the "aroma of Christ"?
5. In what circles can Christians share "the fragrance of life"?
6. How can Christians sense that God is sending them to tell the good news with honesty and sincerity?

Contemporary Application

Can you imagine celebrating your team's victory if you're carrying a grudge against one of the players? Your enthusiasm will likely be tempered. Perhaps that's one reason the church has a hard time marching in Christ's victory parade. Too many people have yet to forgive someone who has offended them.

The apostle Paul knew that the church at Corinth would be stuck in reverse gear if people did not forgive, comfort, and love the one who had offended them. No parade for them.

The church must rid itself of hard feelings, and pull together as a united team. If we fail in this regard, the world at large will not "smell" the fragrance of Christ. Unbelievers are quick to "smell" bitterness and resentment. There can be no rejoicing in the streets unless we learn how to forgive, accept, and restore one another.

Trials and Triumphs of Christian Ministry

DEVOTIONAL READING

2 Corinthians 6:1-10

DAILY BIBLE READINGS

Monday May 8
2 Corinthians 4:1-7 God's Light Shines in Our Hearts

Tuesday May 9
2 Corinthians 4:8-15 God Raised Jesus and Will Raise Us

Wednesday May 10
2 Corinthians 4:16—5:10 We Walk and Live by Faith

Thursday May 11
2 Corinthians 5:11-21 Reconciled to be Reconcilers

Friday May 12
2 Corinthians 6:1-13 Open Wide Your Hearts

Saturday May 13
2 Corinthians 6:14—7:1 We Are Temples of the Living God

Sunday May 14
2 Corinthians 7:2-13 Paul's Joy at the Corinthians' Repentance

Scripture

Background Scripture: *2 Corinthians 4*
Scripture Lesson: *2 Corinthians 4:5-18*
Key Verse: *We are hard pressed on every side, but not crushed; perplexed, but not in despair; persecuted, but not abandoned; struck down, but not destroyed.*
2 Corinthians 4:8-9.
Key Verse for Children: *For we . . . preach . . . Jesus Christ as Lord.* 2 Corinthians 4:5.

Lesson Aim

To use God's power to overcome our afflictions.

Lesson Setting

Time: A.D. *57-58*
Place: *Written to Corinth from Macedonia*

Lesson Outline

Trials and Triumphs of Christian Ministry

  I. God's Power in the Gospel: 2 Corinthians 4:5-6
     A. Our Proclamation: vs. 5
     B. God's Glory in Christ: vs. 6
  II. God's Power in Weakness: 2 Corinthians 4:7-12
     A. Weak Human Vessels: vs. 7
     B. Severe Hindrances: vss. 8-9
     C. The Life of Christ: vss. 10-12
  III. God's Grace in Action: 2 Corinthians 4:13-15
     A. Resurrection with Christ: vss. 13-14
     B. Overflowing Praise: vs. 15
  IV. God's Eternal Perspective:
     2 Corinthians 4:16-18
     A. Renewal of the Inner Man: vs. 16
     B. Present Affliction and Eternal Glory: vs. 17
     C. Things Seen and Unseen: vs. 18

Introduction for Adults

Topic: *From Suffering to Triumph*

In his book, *Where Is God When It Hurts?* Philip Yancey has a chapter about Joni Eareckson Tada's journey from suffering to triumph. She told him, "God became incredibly close to me. . . . I had no other identity but God, and gradually He became enough."

Joni has written a number of books herself. Her speeches and her art have inspired thousands. But despite her witness, and that of the apostle Paul, we find it incredibly difficult to accept the fact that the road to triumph leads through suffering. This is the story of *Pilgrim's Progress*. It is the story of the life and suffering of the Lord Jesus Christ.

Jesus said, "Whoever serves me must follow me" (John 12:26). He described what it means to follow Him when He said, "Unless a kernel of wheat falls to the ground and dies, it remains only a single seed. But if it dies, it produces many seeds" (John 12:24).

Introduction for Youths

Topic: *Power from Weakness*

Power from weakness is an oxymoron in today's culture. Smart people tell us to use power to get ahead and make something of ourselves. The importance of power is the unwritten message that undergirds the media's assault on our minds. We are sold power cars, power computers, and power perfume.

However, the Gospel tells us, "In our own power, we're dead." So teenagers are forced to choose between society's power and Christ's power. Jesus was dismissed by the crowds because He refused to use His power to overthrow the Romans who had conquered, subjugated, and persecuted the Jews. They taunted Him to use His power to come down from the cross.

Instead, Jesus showed that real, eternal power comes only through His cross. To follow His way requires enormous courage and faith in today's culture. But the apostle Paul convincingly showed that by Christ's power he could not only endure hardships, but also live with hope and purpose. The Gospel's power really is better, and it lasts forever.

Concepts for Children

Topic: *The Joy of Telling Good News*

1. The good news about Jesus is much better than anything else.
2. The good news is not about ourselves, but about what Jesus has done and will do for us.
3. Because the light of Jesus shines in us, we can bring His light to others.
4. Because Jesus died for us, we can be set free from living selfishly.
5. Like Philip, we can use our Bibles to show others how to believe in Jesus.
6. Perhaps we think people are not interested in Jesus, but God creates spiritual hunger so they will look for saving faith.

The Lesson Commentary

I. GOD'S POWER IN THE GOSPEL: 2 CORINTHIANS 4:5-6

A. Our Proclamation: vs. 5

For we do not preach ourselves, but Jesus Christ as Lord, and ourselves as your servants for Jesus' sake.

In point of order written, some would say 2 Corinthians was the fourth of Paul's letters, preceded by 1 and 2 Thessalonians and 1 Corinthians. The theme is the apostle's personal vindication of his ministry at Corinth.

After his address and greeting, Paul praised God for his recent deliverance (1:3-11). He then defended his own conduct in general with regard to certain accusations and his relation to an offending brother (1:12—2:11). Next, he described his disappointment at Troas because Titus was not there. His disappointment led him to the glory of his own ministry (2:14—6:10).

Christ always led him in triumph. He was an able minister of the new covenant. In 4:1-6, we see the glory of the gospel of Christ; in 4:7, his thoughts turned to his own suffering for the cause of Christ. This theme, and his hope of eternal glory, carry through 5:10.

Paul strongly defended his commitment to the Gospel and to his life of service for the church. "We do not preach ourselves" refers to the fact that at Corinth certain people had set themselves in opposition to Paul's leadership and teaching. In effect, they were preaching themselves. Paul did not preach himself, he preached Christ as Lord. He was not the lord of the church, Jesus was. Because Jesus died and rose again, He was the authority in the church. Neither Paul nor his opponents were the focal point of preaching. Jesus must be exalted in the church, not the human leaders.

The apostle was not the dictator but the servant of the church. Although Paul exercised full apostolic authority, he did so as the servant of Christ. Paul was not looking for accolades, or for mindless obedience. He wanted both his message and his life to be a reflection of Jesus Christ. Our proclamation is Christ and we serve in His name.

B. God's Glory in Christ: 2 Corinthians 4:6

For God, who said, "Let light shine out of darkness," made his light shine in our hearts to give us the light of the knowledge of the glory of God in the face of Christ.

The church exists because it pleased God to call it into existence just like He called light to shine out of darkness at creation. The Church is His new creation in Jesus Christ. The Church is to manifest God's glory in Christ. The Church does not exist for its own exaltation or for the pride of its people and leaders.

Through the preaching of the Gospel, God made His light shine in our hearts. Without faith in Christ, we are lost in total darkness. Through the Gospel, we gain light into the knowledge of God's glory. There is no possible way to know

God apart from believing in His Son. God's glory is revealed "in the face of Christ."

God's power in the Gospel is so strong that it defeated sin and darkness. Jesus is the light of the world. "In him [Jesus] was life, and that life was the light of men" (John 1:4). Jesus said, "I am the light of the world. Whoever follows me will never walk in darkness, but will have the light of life" (John 8:12).

II. GOD'S POWER IN WEAKNESS: 2 CORINTHIANS 4:7-12

A. Weak Human Vessels: vs. 7

But we have this treasure in jars of clay to show that this all-surpassing power is from God and not from us.

Paul resisted the temptation to conform to Greek philosophy. He took the Gospel to Corinth in human weakness and found that God's power produced faith in the lives of many people. Because he overcame serious obstacles, he grew in his understanding of God's power.

His growth was costly. He suffered greatly. Paul recognized his weaknesses, but in spite of his afflictions, he demonstrated the life of Christ. Spiritual growth happened because God renewed Paul day by day.

God's power was seen in weak human vessels. Paul saw the Gospel as a treasure and himself as a container of no great value—like a paper bag. He made this comparison so that God would receive the credit, not himself. The "all-surpassing power" was the power unleashed in people's lives when they believed the Gospel.

B. Severe Hindrances: vss. 8-9

We are hard pressed on every side, but not crushed; perplexed, but not in despair; persecuted, but not abandoned; struck down, but not destroyed.

Severe hindrances confronted Paul in his Gospel ministry. (See Acts 13:44-52; 14:1-5, 19; 16:19-24; 21:27-32; 22:24; 27:13—28:10 for some of his experiences.) However, he did not succumb to the pressure. Although he was "hard pressed," "perplexed," "persecuted," and "struck down," he was not overcome by the opposition. Rather, he grew more fruitful in spite of it.

In one sense Paul thrived on his various afflictions. He described his resilient spirit in these words: "not crushed," "not in despair," "not abandoned," and "not destroyed." None of his hindrances throttled his growth, because his commitment to God's will enabled him to rise above them. Paul's staying power in the Lord was greater than the obstacles he met.

C. The Life of Christ: 2 Corinthians 4:10-12

We always carry around in our body the death of Jesus, so that the life of Jesus may also be revealed in our body. For we who are alive are always being given over to death for Jesus' sake, so that his life may be revealed in our mortal body. So then, death is at work in us, but life is at work in you.

In spite of his afflictions, Paul manifested the life of Christ. He understood what was happening. He saw the big picture. He interpreted the specific cases of suffering in the light of a larger principle. Therefore, he pressed on in spite of his circumstances.

Paul summarized his ministry as carrying out a death sentence for the sake of Jesus. God's purpose in his suffering was to reveal the life of Christ to a watching world. Christ's life is revealed "in our mortal body." This divine insight helps us to put suffering in the proper perspective.

Paradoxically, in God's economy, death brings life. In this case, God brought life to the Corinthians through what they saw of the apostle's suffering, and how he reacted to it. This is a principle of ministry for all of God's servants.

Christian growth costs self-denial, sacrifice, and suffering. The outcome is spiritual life and growth. In effect, we die so that others might live (see also John 12:24). This is both the ultimate cost and ultimate benefit of serving Christ.

III. God's Grace in Action: 2 Corinthians 4:13-15

A. Resurrection with Christ: vss. 13-14

It is written: "I believed; therefore I have spoken." With that same spirit of faith we also believe and therefore speak, because we know that the one who raised the Lord Jesus from the dead will also raise us with Jesus and present us with you in his presence.

Paul looked beyond his immediate problems at Corinth, and his own suffering, to the day when he and his fellow believers would be raised with Christ. Ultimately, this is where we must look, if we are to endure hardships in serving Christ. Christian hope is anchored in the certainty of Christ's resurrection. His resurrection gives meaning and purpose to life. His resurrection gives meaning to suffering.

Paul quoted Psalm 116:10 to defend his own faith and preaching. He lived and preached by faith. When we believe, we are called to speak. In that sense, Paul could not help himself. His faith compelled him to speak the Gospel at Corinth and elsewhere. His faith drove him to keep going, despite all the obstacles and suffering.

Because God raised Jesus from the dead, He will also raise all believers with Jesus. God's plan for Paul and the Corinthians was to unite them in the presence of Christ. This anticipated reunion kept Paul from swerving in his obedience.

B. Overflowing Praise: vs. 15

All this is for your benefit, so that the grace that is reaching more and more people may cause thanksgiving to overflow to the glory of God.

The thought of the church's eternal destiny with Christ moved Paul to overflow with praise to God's glory. Salvation's benefits are not simply for the good of believers; they are also intended to inspire praise to God.

"All this is for your benefit," Paul reminded his readers. But the purpose of God's blessings at Corinth was to extend God's grace to "more and more people." As the believers anticipated resurrection with Christ, they would be moved to promote His grace to others as well.

As God's grace reached more people through the preaching of the Gospel, it would stimulate overflowing thanksgiving to God. The purpose of Gospel ministry is to bring people to faith in Christ. As people believe, they praise and thank God for the blessings of their salvation—sins forgiven, righteousness with Christ, eternal life, and the presence of the Holy Spirit.

IV. God's Eternal Perspective: 2 Corinthians 4:16-18

A. Renewal of the Inner Man: vs. 16

Therefore we do not lose heart. Though outwardly we are wasting away, yet inwardly we are being renewed day by day.

The fact that Paul was not discouraged served as his conclusion to the matter of suffering. It also introduced the key to his perseverance. After telling what he endured—affliction, perplexity, persecution—Paul could have said he was discouraged. Discouragement often is the outcome of suffering. But Paul ended on a triumphant note: "We do not lose heart."

Why not? He anticipated our question. In 4:16—5:5 we find the reasons for his victory over discouragement. First, God renews the inner man every day. Paul's physical body was deteriorating ("outwardly"), but God was constantly renewing his inner nature ("inwardly"). Paul suffered from a constant problem—a "thorn in the flesh" (2 Cor. 12:7-8). He endured physical punishment, being stoned and beaten (2 Cor. 6:4-5). He suffered the normal toll of aging. He worked hard and carried out his own injunction to be a living sacrifice (Rom. 12:1).

Nevertheless, God renewed his inner nature. That inner renewal of heart, mind, and spirit came as he saw his sufferings in the light of future glory (vss. 17-18). Paul did not describe exactly how his spirit was renewed every day. From Philippians 4:13 we know that it was through the strength that Jesus gave him. When we are born again by faith in Christ, we become new creations (2 Cor. 5:17). We have new life and enablement.

Christians are renewed in Christ (Col. 3:10). We enjoy the fullness of the Godhead (2:9-10). We are blessed with every spiritual blessing in Christ (Eph. 1:3). He possessed the resurrection power of Christ (Eph. 1:19-20). Therefore, we can expect supernatural strength in the inner person—"the power that is at work within us" (Eph. 3:20).

B. Present Affliction and Eternal Glory: vs. 17

For our light and momentary troubles are achieving for us an eternal glory that far outweighs them all.

Next, Paul described one aspect of his daily inner renewal. It was related to the fact of eternity. He saw his present affliction as "light and momentary." An important reason for his not losing heart was that in the light of eternity, his suffering would not last very long. It was merely a second on God's timetable.

In light of eternity, present affliction was "light," that is, not as bad as it might seem to be. This may not seem to be true while we are enduring our trials, but we look at them from the perspective of eternity.

Paul also saw his present troubles as preparing him for eternal glory. To justify his hope, he made two paradoxical comparisons. His present troubles were "light," but his future glory "far outweighs them all." His eternal glory was of much greater value. His present afflictions were "momentary," but his future glory would be "eternal," it would last forever. His "troubles" would achieve "glory." In his mind, future glory was incomparable.

Based on these facts, Christians gain an understanding that gives meaning to their lives. Troubles are not meaningless. One day they will be worth far more than present sufferings.

C. Things Seen and Unseen: vs. 18

So we fix our eyes not on what is seen, but on what is unseen. For what is seen is temporary, but what is unseen is eternal.

How could Paul accept his troubles as "light and momentary"? By getting the proper perspective on what's really important in life. "What is seen" refers to all life's experiences, including hardships and suffering. Paul said, in effect, "Don't look at them. Don't let your mind dwell on them. They are not what is important."

Instead, he said, focus on "what is unseen." What did he mean? "Set your hearts on things above, where Christ is seated at the right hand of God. Set your minds on things above, not on earthly things" (Col. 3:1-2).

Reality lies not in what we see, because those things are temporary. They will not last; they will pass away. Reality lies in what we can't see with our physical eyes. Reality is what we see with our spiritual eyes. Those things are eternal; they last forever. If we choose to base our lives on what we can see physically, we are doomed. We will have nothing to show for it. But if we choose Jesus Christ and His eternal values—things we can't see physically—we will gain everlasting blessings and rewards.

Discussion Questions

1. How can we be sure our actions and words point only to Jesus Christ?
2. Why do you think God chose to reveal the Gospel in weak human vessels?
3. What evidence do you see of overflowing praise to God in your church and community?
4. What values do you see in Paul's hardships? In yours?

5. How can Christians be renewed inwardly day after day?

6. What is the key to staying focused on our eternal weight of glory?

Contemporary Application

We face the risk of skepticism when we read about the physical obstacles the apostle Paul faced and conquered in his ministry. We wonder how we would have responded to the same troubles he faced. Whether or not God calls us to face similar circumstances, the main fact is that Paul's answer is ours as well.

Paul succeeded because of his complete commitment to Jesus Christ. He loved Jesus so much, and he wanted to obey Him so completely, that he persevered and grew in spiritual wisdom and understanding. He finished the ministry race successfully.

There is no other way for Christians today. Despite many popular "secrets" on the market, we are challenged to find answers in our devotion to Jesus Christ. When we love and serve Him above everything else, He enables us to rise above our difficulties and setbacks.

The Collection for Jerusalem Christians

DEVOTIONAL READING

2 Corinthians 8:1-15

DAILY BIBLE READINGS

Monday May 15
*2 Corinthians 8:1-7
Exceeding Generosity*

Tuesday May 16
*2 Corinthians 8:8-15 Show
Your Love by Your Giving*

Wednesday May 17
*2 Corinthians 8:16-24 A
Generous Gift Glorifies God*

Thursday May 18
*2 Corinthians 9:1-9 God
Loves and Blesses Cheerful
Givers*

Friday May 19
*2 Corinthians 9:10-15
Generous Giving Brings Joy
to All*

Saturday May 20
*2 Corinthians 9:1-9 A
Collection for Jerusalem
Christians*

Sunday May 21
*Romans 15:22-29 Paul
Intends to Visit Roman
Christians*

Scripture

Background Scripture: *2 Corinthians 9*
Scripture Lesson: *2 Corinthians 9:1-13*
Key Verse: *Each man should give what he has decided
in his heart to give, not reluctantly or under compulsion,
for God loves a cheerful giver.* 2 Corinthians 9:7.

Lesson Aim

To experience the thrill and blessing of generous
giving.

Lesson Setting

Time: A.D. *57-58*
Place: *Written to Corinth from Macedonia*

Lesson Outline

The Collection for Jerusalem Christians

   I. Service to the Saints: 2 Corinthians 9:1-5
      A. Their Eagerness to Help: vss. 1-2
      B. Paul's Plan for Their Offering: vss. 3-5
  II. Sharing God's Abundance: 2 Corinthians 9:6-9
      A. Give Bountifully: vs. 6
      B. Give Willingly According to Plan: vs. 7
      C. Receive Enough to Share with Others: vss. 8-9
 III. Reaping God's Blessings: 2 Corinthians 9:10-13
      A. Harvest Righteousness: vs. 10
      B. Be Enriched through Generosity: vs. 11
      C. Overflow with Thanksgiving: vs. 12
      D. Acknowledge the Gospel: vs. 13

Introduction for Adults

Topic: *From Reluctance to Joyful Giving*

One day the famous Japanese church leader Toyohiko Kagawa was talking with the secretary of the Kobe YMCA. Debts had accumulated, and programs and services had been curtailed because of the lack of money. When he heard the gloomy report, Kagawa reached into his pocket and took out a letter. It included a check from one of his publishers.

Kagawa gave it to the secretary, who hesitated, but Kagawa urged him to accept it. When he got home, Kagawa received a letter from the man, who, knowing Kagawa's sparse living conditions, wrote, "You mustn't give money away like that."

"Why shouldn't I?" Kagawa wrote back. "When your friend is dying, there is only one thing to do. Give him your lifeblood."

Kagawa knew the joy of giving, which many Christians seem to miss today. They have not learned how to handle their money and other resources as a stewardship from God. They have missed the spiritual gift of giving.

Introduction for Youths

Topic: *Joy from Giving*

Teenagers know that decisions about money confront them day in and day out. Some decisions, large and small, have to be made about money almost every hour. They face some long-term decisions, such as buying a car and how much to save for their education. On the other hand, they have to decide how much to spend on their clothes, their dates, and their junk food.

On top of that, economic issues are extremely complicated. People lose their jobs, run up huge debts, and declare bankruptcy because they can't pay off their credit cards. Plastic has removed the sense of responsibility for many people.

But Christians have one irrevocable guideline that supersedes all of our personal desires and social and economic pressures. It is the earliest Christian creed, "Jesus is Lord" (1 Cor. 12:3). He is Lord of our recreation, our fun, our dates, our jobs, our money, and our savings accounts. The apostle Paul encouraged the Christians of his day to work out Christ's Lordship of their money.

Concepts for Children

Topic: *The Joy of Giving*

1. Hungry and homeless people are all around us, not just in distant countries.
2. Christians are asked by God to help all suffering people.
3. Children can put aside small sums regularly to give as their weekly offerings.
4. We can also help at special times by bringing bags of groceries to the church for needy people.
5. Even a little bit goes a long way when Jesus blesses our gifts.
6. God loves people who give cheerfully, not reluctantly.

The Lesson Commentary

I. SERVICE TO THE SAINTS: 2 CORINTHIANS 9:1-5

A. Their Eagerness to Help: vss. 1-2

There is no need for me to write to you about this service to the saints. For I know your eagerness to help, and I have been boasting about it to the Macedonians, telling them that since last year you in Achaia were ready to give; and your enthusiasm has stirred most of them to action.

Giving to meet the needs of fellow Christians was an outstanding characteristic of the first-century followers of Christ. There was no public welfare plan for the poor, the unemployed, and the disabled.

The apostle Paul taught sacrificial stewardship in the churches. Those in northern Greece (Macedonia) responded so generously for the poor in Jerusalem that he used them as an example to inspire similar patterns of giving among the Christians at Corinth in southern Greece. They actually begged him to be allowed to take part "in this service to the saints" (2 Cor. 8:4).

Second Corinthians 8 and 9 need to be studied together to grasp the full philosophy of Christian giving. Chapter 9 follows Paul's use of psychology with the Corinthians. He had been bragging to the Macedonians about the generosity of the Corinthians (vs. 2). He wrote to be sure that his boasting was not ill founded. Nevertheless, he wanted it to be clear that the gifts of the Corinthian believers really came spontaneously from their hearts, and not as a grudgingly given tax.

B. Paul's Plan for Their Offering: vss. 3-5

But I am sending the brothers in order that our boasting about you in this matter should not prove hollow, but that you may be ready, as I said you would be. For if any Macedonians come with me and find you unprepared, we—not to say anything about you—would be ashamed of having been so confident. So I thought it necessary to urge the brothers to visit you in advance and finish the arrangements for the generous gift you had promised. Then it will be ready as a generous gift, not as one grudgingly given.

Again, Paul reminded the Corinthians of the generosity of the Macedonians (2 Cor. 8:1-5). He wasn't losing faith in the Corinthians, but he did want to be sure that they were ready for the collection when "the brothers" arrived. Titus was among them (vs. 6). At the same time, of course, Paul did not want his confidence in them to be betrayed by any slackness on their part. Paul himself would come with the believers from Macedonia (9:4).

Apparently Paul decided that a two-stage effort was needed. The unnamed brothers would arrive in advance and make sure that the offering would be taken. The Corinthians could thus make sure that the funds would be ready to turn over to Paul when he arrived.

Paul did not emphasize how much was to be collected. He was much more concerned about the attitude of the givers than about the size of the collection. He wanted them to give generously, out of their own desire to help their fellow believers. He did not want them to give under apostolic pressure, or grudgingly, just to get him off their backs.

II. SHARING GOD'S ABUNDANCE: 2 CORINTHIANS 9:6-9

A. Give Bountifully: vs. 6

Remember this: Whoever sows sparingly will also reap sparingly, and whoever sows generously will also reap generously.

Paul used a principle of farming to illustrate the kind of giving that glorifies God. The farmer must sow his seed generously if he expects to harvest a bountiful crop. The spiritual principle of giving is the same.

Giving away one's money seems foolish unless Christian principles are effective. Human nature being what it is, people think that the more they keep for themselves, the more they will have in the end. However, by God's accounting, the stingy giver will receive a stingy harvest from the Lord. They may have more materially for awhile, but when they die it will be given to others. In the meantime, they will have missed out on the joy of the Lord while they were alive.

On the other hand, the faithful, trusting Christian steward will give bountifully, not worrying about the accumulation of wealth in this life. This person will be accumulating treasure in heaven, besides contributing to the relief of people in need.

B. Give Willingly According to Plan: vs. 7

Each man should give what he has decided in his heart to give, not reluctantly or under compulsion, for God loves a cheerful giver.

It is possible to give away one's money, but for the wrong reasons, or from the wrong motives. Some people give "reluctantly or under compulsion." They would rather not give, but perhaps they have been shamed into it, or coerced.

Paul wanted to avoid this false motive for giving. He did not lay guilt on people, or try to arouse their emotions with dramatic appeals. Paul also urged the believers to make up their own minds and plan carefully how much to give ("give what he has decided in his heart to give"). We should plan our giving and we should give cheerfully. "Cheerful" stands in sharp contrast to "reluctantly, or under compulsion." In some churches, stewardship has become a matter of onerous duty rather than glad joy. The word translated "cheerful" signifies readiness of mind and joyousness that prompt us to do anything.

C. Receive Enough to Share with Others: vss. 8-9

And God is able to make all grace abound to you, so that in all things at all times, having all that you need, you will abound in every good work. As it is written: "He has scattered abroad his gifts to the poor; his righteousness endures forever."

God loves happy givers and he provides for their needs. He gives them every blessing in abundance. Therefore, Christians can give generously and joyfully. They do not have to worry about how their own needs will be met; they do not have to begrudge the needy their due.

God's provision for Christian givers is two-fold: He sees to it that they have enough of everything; He sees that they have more than they need so their abundance can be used "in every good work," that is, given away. Quoting from Psalms (vs. 9), Paul showed that God meets the needs of the poor through His generosity to others, who are supposed to share their abundance.

The logic behind joyful Christian giving is simple: God provides in abundance for the Christians so they can in turn do the same for others. Christians know that God's material blessings are meant to be shared.

III. REAPING GOD'S BLESSINGS: 2 CORINTHIANS 9:10-13

A. Harvest Righteousness: vs. 10

Now he who supplies seed to the sower and bread for food will also supply and increase your store of seed and will enlarge the harvest of your righteousness.

In this section Paul continues to discuss God's generosity. He also connects people's response to the Gospel to how Christians give to meet the needs of others. To this point, he has tried to convince his readers that God will take care of them if they give generously. Now he wants to show how, apart from that, generous giving really is part of the Christian's obedience to Christ.

In terms of basic human needs, God is the faithful provider. He supplies the seed that ultimately produces bread on the table. For millions of people, this is what life is all about, growing enough food to eat. In America, most people depend on someone else to do this for them. They are not so keenly aware of the close relationship between seed and bread, or of God's hand in the whole process.

However, Paul thought more about another kind of harvest, a spiritual harvest of righteousness that comes to those who sow their money in the lives of other people through their generous gifts. The miracle of bread is duplicated by the miracle of a spiritual harvest.

This is how it works with money: God supplies it and then multiplies it when we give it away. Not in terms of actual cash, of course, but in terms of spiritual profit. Money given away according to God's will is increased in terms of righteousness. This is by far the best investment of our money.

B. Be Enriched through Generosity: vs. 11

You will be made rich in every way so that you can be generous on every occasion, and through us your generosity will result in thanksgiving to God.

The paradox of generous giving is that Christians who practice it will get richer and richer, not necessarily in their bank accounts, but "in every way," primarily morally, spiritually, and emotionally. As Paul noted before, Christians trust God to give them every blessing in abundance (vs. 8).

In some cases, Christians who have decided to give more and more have found that in unexpected ways their income has grown or their resources have stretched further, so they can keep on giving more. In other cases, Christians have decided ahead of time how much they should give for the coming year, perhaps beyond what their normal income would seem to permit. They make such a faith commitment, trusting God to bring in the needed funds.

God keeps His word to "make rich" those who give generously and sacrificially. Whether they see increased income or not, they are happier, stronger, less stressed, and more content than if they had been stingy, or reluctant givers.

C. Overflow with Thanksgiving: vs. 12

This service that you perform is not only supplying the needs of God's people but is also overflowing in many expressions of thanks to God.

In this verse, Paul cited two further results from Christian giving: the "needs of God's people" will be taken care of, and God Himself will be praised.

Paul did not dwell on the needs of the Christians in Jerusalem. This shows that if Christian giving springs from a generous heart, churches and organizations do not need to rely on public relations gimmicks. Paul simply wrote about the necessity of an offering for "the needs of God's people" (8:4; 9:1, 12).

Giving is a Christian service, a privilege, and a spiritual grace (8:7). The recipients of the offerings are blessed physically and spiritually. As their needs are met, their hearts overflow with praise and thanksgiving to God.

D. Acknowledge the Gospel: vs. 13

Because of the service by which you have proved yourselves, men will praise God for the obedience that accompanies your confession of the gospel of Christ, and for your generosity in sharing with them and with everyone else.

Generous contributions for physical needs and for supporting the ministries of churches, mission agencies, and others kinds of charitable services show that the donors are working out their obedience to the Lord Jesus Christ.

However, the apostle Paul made a connection between the Gospel and giving. The Gospel teaches that God grants forgiveness and pardon when we own up to our sins and receive Christ as our Savior. In that sense, no amount of money can entitle anyone to be saved. We cannot earn God's grace; He gives it freely to all who believe.

On the other hand, Christians who have been forgiven and redeemed by Christ sense that all of life, including their possessions, is really a sacrifice. Everything they have belongs to Jesus. Christ's love motivates them to be generous givers.

So, although giving does not earn salvation, it does demonstrate the integrity of our Christian profession. Christians who want to obey Christ will hear what He has to say about the snare of wealth and about the poverty-stricken widow who gave all that she had (Mark 12:42-44). Generous giving flows out of spiritual perception, the understanding that satisfaction in life does not come from material things but from being occupied with God's kingdom and His righteousness.

Paul closed this section with a reminder of how much God Himself gave (vss. 14-15). No one can out-give God. God gave what Paul called an "indescribable" (or "inexpressible," or "beyond words") gift, that is, His only, well-beloved Son, the Lord Jesus Christ.

Discussion Questions

1. Is stewardship a touchy subject in your church? Why?
2. Why do some Christians resent it when they are urged to give?
3. How would they respond to Paul's approach? Why?
4. Why do some organizations spend millions to raise money?
5. If you were to frame one main point from Paul's argument in verses 6-9, as far as your giving is concerned, what would it be?
6. Is there anything in vss. 10-15 that would motivate you to give more? Why?

Contemporary Application

Christians realize that their giving, whether to help feed and clothe people overseas or to help an unemployed neighbor with a huge medical bill, is one way they can help to correct the obvious inequities in this world. Therefore, in praying about how much to give, Christians look at both their own abundance and the serious plight of others. They respond generously because they know this is required of Christians who are affluent compared to most people in the world.

If we follow Paul's counsel, "taking the offering" during the worship service would not seem like an empty routine. Rightly understood, this part of the service gives Christians a chance to honor God, to demonstrate sacrifice, cheerfulness, and generosity, and to acknowledge that all they have is a gift from God. Their offerings render a service to others and inspire thanksgiving and praise to God from those who are blessed by the money.

Living in the Faith

DEVOTIONAL READING

Acts 4:32-37

DAILY BIBLE READINGS

Monday May 22
2 Corinthians 10:1-11
Paul Defends His Ministry

Tuesday May 23
*2 Corinthians 10:12-18 If
You Boast, Boast in the
Lord*

Wednesday May 24
*2 Corinthians 11:1-15
Paul and the False Apostles*

Thursday May 25
*2 Corinthians 11:16-29
Paul's Sufferings as an
Apostle*

Friday May 26
*2 Corinthians 12:1-10
Paul's Visions and Revelations*

Saturday May 27
*2 Corinthians 12:11-21
Paul's Concerns for the
Corinthian Christians*

Sunday May 28
*2 Corinthians 13:1-13 Live
in Faith: Christ Is in You*

Scripture

Background Scripture: *2 Corinthians 13:1-13*
Scripture Lesson: *2 Corinthians 13:1-13*
Key Verse: *Examine yourselves to see whether you are in
the faith; test yourselves. Do you not realize that Christ
Jesus is in you—unless, of course, you fail the test?*
2 Corinthians 13:5.
Scripture Lesson for Children: *2 Corinthians 13:11;
Acts 2:41-47*
Key Verse: *Be of one mind, live in peace.*
2 Corinthians 13:11.

Lesson Aim

To find security and peace by passing the test of
faith in Christ.

Lesson Setting

Time: *A.D. 57-58*
Place: *Written to Corinth from Macedonia*

Lesson Outline

Living in the Faith
  I. Paul's Strong Convictions: 2 Corinthians 13:1-4
    A. His Coming Visit: vs. 1
    B. His Proposed Actions: vss. 2-3
    C. Christ Was His Example: vs. 4
  II. Paul's Final Warnings: 2 Corinthians 13:5-10
    A. Take the Test: vss. 5-6
    B. Do What Is Right and True: vss. 7-8
    C. Respect My Motives: vss. 9-10
  III. Paul's Final Greeting: 2 Corinthians 13:11-13

Introduction for Adults

Topic: *From Confrontation to Growth*

A woman asked a pastor friend to visit her father in the hospital. He had suffered a heart attack after a flood had wiped out his business. She thought he would be open to spiritual counsel and turn to Christ in faith. Perhaps he would take the flood as God's warning for him to repent.

Sadly, however, he was angry with God for the flood. If it was God's final warning, he had paid no attention to it.

When Paul concluded his letter to the church at Corinth, he wanted to be sure that everyone was "in the faith." That's why he urged them to test themselves. Tests are not easy to take, especially tests about the reality and integrity of our faith in Christ.

But this is the most important test we can ever take. The outcome determines our eternal destiny. If Christ dwells in our hearts, we pass; if he doesn't, we fail. Paul's open approach is what we need to determine where we stand with Jesus.

Introduction for Youths

Topic: *Growth from Confrontation*

Family counselors tell us how important it is to confront one another when we feel something is wrong. It's disastrous to hide our true feelings for the sake of supposed harmony. Yet we find it is painfully difficult to confront our spouses and children. But from the apostle Paul's example, we learn that we must care enough to confront.

Confronting teenagers often leads to family explosions. Confronting fellow believers often produces hard feelings. This is one aspect of Christian living we would rather avoid at all costs. Therefore, we need to encourage one another to develop skills in confronting one another in love.

For example, confronting does not mean accusing someone of wrongdoing. It means raising honest concerns with a loving attitude and voice. Love causes us to ask questions with patience, not with anger. As with Paul, our desire must be to build one another's faith, not to tear it down. With prayer, and with tears, we can grow more Christlike through godly confrontations.

Concepts for Children

Topic: *The Joy of Peaceful Living*

1. We have to accept our failures as part of our growing in faith.
2. Living in peace means being honest with one another about our true feelings.
3. Faith is required to believe that God loves us and gives us peace, even in our difficulties.
4. The early Christians took care of one another.
5. We can look for opportunities to help one another in our families and churches.
6. As we worship together we grow in love and respect for one another.

The Lesson Commentary

I. PAUL'S STRONG CONVICTIONS: 2 CORINTHIANS 13:1-4

A. His Coming Visit: vs. 1

This will be my third visit to you. "Every matter must be established by the testimony of two or three witnesses."

Paul notified the church that he was coming again (2 Cor. 12:14). He explained that his motives had been misunderstood and misrepresented. He wasn't crafty and he wasn't trying to take advantage of them. His next major concern was that the sins in the church should be put away. That was the basis of his fears for the church (12:20-21).

Paul pictured himself in a law court, defending himself before the judges—the Christians at Corinth. Even so, he called them his "dear friends" (12:19). But his primary purpose was not to defend himself. Perhaps the Corinthians had received that impression from what they had read in this letter so far.

Therefore, following his court analogy, he said that he would act only on the testimony "of two or three witnesses." This was the rule given by Moses (Deut. 19:15). Both Jesus and Paul followed it. Paul wanted to assure the church that he was not going to act simply on the basis of hearsay evidence, or gossip.

B. His Proposed Actions: vss. 2-3

I already gave you a warning when I was with you the second time. I now repeat it while absent: On my return I will not spare those who sinned earlier or any of the others, since you are demanding proof that Christ is speaking through me. He is not weak in dealing with you, but is powerful among you.

Paul wrote again about what he proposed to do when he returned to Corinth. Perhaps his earlier warnings had been disregarded, or misunderstood. Most likely, his opponents in the church discounted him as a weakling, a man who talked big but failed to act. This warning was intended to dispel any such notions.

His warning was clear: he would not spare those living in sin or those who challenged his authority and leadership ("any of the others"). He knew their cleverness and their strong appeal. He knew how easy it was for them to discount his authority while he was away. Therefore, he strongly warned them not to mistake his intentions.

The issue seemed to be proof of his authority, which Paul claimed to be from Christ Himself. The false apostles had disputed his claim. In effect, they said, "If you really are from Christ, show us." That is what he intended to do.

The larger question at stake was the integrity of Jesus. Jesus is head of the church. His authority and power had to be maintained. Because of His power, the Gospel had come to Corinth and the church had been established. Christ's power was needed to maintain the purity and unity of the church. The church had to be pure in doctrine and in life. Christ does not approve of sinful behavior in His body. Sin must be judged, and Christ's rightful authority must be maintained. To do so, Paul would take the necessary steps to clear the church of sin, division, and rebellion.

C. Christ Was His Example: vs. 4

For to be sure, he was crucified in weakness, yet he lives by God's power. Likewise, we are weak in him, yet by God's power we will live with him to serve you.

Christ's life was a paradox. As God the Son, He had all power and authority from the beginning. Yet He allowed Himself to be put together "in weakness." The cross demonstrated His weakness for the sake of our sins. He willingly submitted to death on the cross in order to take the just judgment we deserved because of our sins. Our only hope of forgiveness and salvation lies in Christ's humiliation and weakness.

However, the cross was not the end of the story, because Jesus "lives by God's power." God raised His Son from the grave to triumph over sin and death. Jesus lives and therefore He rules in His church, which is His body. Jesus is alive in the church.

Paul said he followed Christ's example. He was weak and he suffered accordingly. Paul suffered not only physically, but also emotionally and spiritually in his care and concerns for the churches he had established. On the other hand, Paul lived by God's power, not to assume human power but for the sake of his spiritual authority in the church.

Paul's motives were the same as Christ's: to live to serve. Paul lived by Christ's resurrection power, so that he could serve believers for their spiritual growth and development. He wasn't interested in building institutions to glorify his name. He wanted only to see Christ formed in Christians. He wanted the church to be pure and strong, so that the Gospel could spread.

II. Paul's Final Warnings: 2 Corinthians 13:5-10

A. Take the Test: vss. 5-6

Examine yourselves to see whether you are in the faith; test yourselves. Do you not realize that Christ Jesus is in you—unless, of course, you fail the test? And I trust that you will discover that we have not failed the test.

As far as Paul was concerned, it was examination time in the church. How could he account for such incredible behavior? "Are you really Christians?" he asked, because, in effect, if they were, their conduct was inexplicable and totally inappropriate.

He had to begin at the beginning, so to speak, because it was possible that some among them had not truly been converted.

In any church there are those who go along for a variety of reasons, but who have not committed themselves to Jesus Christ as Lord and Savior. The root cause of immorality in the church at Corinth could very well have been some phonies in the ranks. Outwardly, they joined the church, but they had not truly received Christ.

"Test yourselves," Paul demanded. How does one do that? What questions are on this self-examination? How do you know if you have passed or not? Paul's test was very simple: Is Jesus Christ in you? If He is, then you pass; if not, you flunk.

He himself was supremely confident that he was "in Christ." What does that mean? It means you have confessed your sin, acknowledged your guilt before a holy God, and welcomed Jesus Christ to redeem you and save you from the just consequences of your sin. Jesus Himself gave the first clue to this faith relationship by explaining that those who loved and obeyed Him would have the privilege of hosting Him in their lives. He would actually live in them (John 14:23). He said this was like the unity of the vine and the branches. "Remain in me, and I will remain in you," He said (John 15:4).

That was the test Paul urged on the Corinthians. Had they really come to know and trust Jesus Christ? Was He really living in them?

B. Do What Is Right and True: vss. 7-8

Now we pray to God that you will not do anything wrong. Not that people will see that we have stood the test but that you will do what is right even though we may seem to have failed. For we cannot do anything against the truth, but only for the truth.

Paul tried to stem the influence of the minority who challenged his authority. He was concerned not only about the existence of moral misbehavior, but of the possibility that some false teachers could lead the entire church astray.

If they were in the faith, he could rightly pray that they would not do anything wrong, whether it was carrying on with their divisions, quarrels, gossip, and slander, or their gross immorality. He was not just looking out for his own reputation and self-justification. He even admitted that it was more important for them to follow in obedience to Christ than it was for him to claim victory. What people thought, and whatever they charged him with, did not really count with him.

The central issue was the truth of the Gospel—Christ's death and resurrection for our sins (1 Cor. 15:3-5). In dealing with conflict, he knew there was only one standard to apply: God's truth. He could not go against what God had revealed to him.

So, he appealed here not to the intellectual side of truth, but to the moral side. God's truth requires conduct consistent with His holiness. He knew some people could give intellectual assent to his doctrines, but still be unwilling to shape their lives to what Christ demanded of His followers.

C. Respect My Motives: vss. 9-10

We are glad whenever we are weak but you are strong; and our prayer is for your perfection. This is why I write these things when I am absent, that when I come I may not have to be harsh in my use of authority—the authority the Lord gave me for building you up, not for tearing you down.

It is generally assumed that conflict has to be destructive. However, conflict can bring about growth if it leads to positive steps for improvement. It is not enough to criticize others for their faults. They must be helped to do better.

Twice in his closing remarks Paul made his goal for the church clear: The believers were to be perfected (vss. 9, 11). Paul never yielded his desire for a perfect church, a pure church, a body of holy believers conformed to Christ. Despite the obvious problems at Corinth, he did not become cynical. Rather, he prayed, counseled, and admonished them so that they could always be pointed toward perfection.

Of course, his goal applied not just to individual spiritual maturity, but to the church as a whole. Individual holiness was required at Corinth, but so were unity and harmony. They had to learn to end their party splits and live peacefully with each other.

The word translated "perfection" refers to the proper working together of limbs and joints in the body, a resetting of what has been broken or dislocated, and a restoration to harmonious, efficient working. This is a graphic picture of what was wrong at Corinth, as well as of how the problem could be fixed.

"Whenever we are weak" (vs. 9) means "When we have no opportunity to show our power in punishment," or, "When there is no need to enforce my authority." "You are strong" (vs. 9) means strong in Christian character, and self-disciplined toward godliness.

Paul did not relish the idea of settling the issues by the "harsh" use of his God-given authority. He could have been severe, especially in light of the problems at Corinth, but he was restrained. To come in and knock people down right and left would be self-defeating. It would mean tearing them down, not building them up. This tactic would not help him reach his goal—the strengthening of the church.

If the people took to heart Paul's concerns, examined themselves, and repented, he would not have to exercise his authority. But there was an implied threat in his message (vs. 10). Obeying his written counsel would spare them stronger discipline in person.

Paul was not a tyrant, but an apostle. His authority came from God, not from his own ego. Conflicts are rarely settled when people think they are in win-lose contests. In Paul's mind, everybody should win.

III. Paul's Final Greeting: 2 Corinthians 13:11-13

Finally, brothers, good-by. Aim for perfection, listen to my appeal, be of one mind, live in peace. And the God of love and peace will be with you. Greet one another with a holy kiss. All the saints send their greetings.

Paul appeared confident of the outcome, that his warnings would lead to a change in their ways and make discipline unnecessary. Displays of force are impressive in the godless world at large, and sometimes people think force works in church as well. But rarely do power plays unite churches; most often they divide them and destroy the unity of Christ's body.

In his final greeting, Paul appealed for obedience to his exhortation and for unity among the believers at Corinth. If they listened to him, God's love and peace would dwell among them. Their lives together in the church would be what God intended.

Discussion Questions

1. Why was Paul so worked up about the problems at Corinth?
2. Why do today's churches seem to lack his enthusiasm for purity and unity?
3. What are the main problems in dealing with church conflicts?
4. How can Christians learn to be more confrontational with love?
5. Is it realistic to expect a perfect church? Why or why not?
6. We should "examine [ourselves] to see whether [we] are in the faith"?

Contemporary Application

Living in the faith requires both self-testing and the testing of others. Obviously, we are much more comfortable with self-tests. But as the apostle Paul realized, we also need to respect the tests of others. Many times they can help us to see where we stand before the Lord.

Only we ourselves can really know if we are "in the faith." Only we can tell that Jesus Christ is in us. On the other hand, sometimes we unknowingly stray into dangerous territory, and away from Christ. The devil tricks us into thinking we are safe when we really are in danger.

That's why accountability is such a valuable tool. We can find other Christians to whom we are accountable. We can join small groups of fellow believers to whom we are accountable. As we grow in love and trust for each other, we can admit our weaknesses, be vulnerable about our problems, and ask for prayer and wise counsel.

Being accountable on a regular basis helps us to avoid confrontations later on, when perhaps we are too proud to admit we have cooled in our love and obedience to Christ.

New Life in Christ

Unit I: Living in Christ

Unit II: Called to Be a New Humanity

Unit III: Christ above All

Living Is Christ

Scripture
Background Scripture: *Philippians 1:12-30*
Scripture Lesson: *Philippians 1:12-26*
Key Verse: *For to me, to live is Christ and to die is gain.* Philippians 1:21.
Key Verse for Children: *But these are written that you may believe that Jesus is the Christ, the Son of God.* John 20:31.

Lesson Aim
To find purpose, hope, and joy in living in Christ.

Lesson Setting
Time: A.D. *61 or 62*
Place: *Written to Philippi from Rome*

Lesson Outline
Living Is Christ
  I. The Advance of the Gospel: Philippians 1:12-14
      A. *Despite Chains: vss. 12-13*
      B. *Despite Fear: vs. 14*
  II. The Preaching of the Gospel: Philippians 1:15-18a
      A. *Out of Love: vss. 15-16*
      B. *Out of Selfishness: vs. 17*
      C. *Christ Is Preached: vs. 18a*
  III. Joy in the Gospel: Philippians 1:18b-26
      A. *Deliverance Expected: vss. 18b-19*
      B. *Exalting Christ: vs. 20*
      C. *Purpose in Christ: vs. 21*
      D. *Desire for Christ: vss. 22-24*
      E. *Joy in Christ: vss. 25-26*

Introduction for Adults

Topic: *Living Is Christ*

One day a Christian writer asked a college student what he was living for. The student said he wanted to graduate and get a good job. "Then what?" the writer asked. Well, he would like to get married and raise a family. "Then what?" He would like to have a successful career and make enough money to take care of his family and retire comfortably. "Then what?"

"What do you mean?" the college student asked, bewildered.

The Christian writer challenged him. "Is that all there is to life? And what about the life to come after you die? Then what?"

Like many people, the student had never thought about a higher purpose in life, or about his eternal destiny. Christians, too, must check their reasons for living. It is easy for Christians to follow the world's values and goals.

If we really believe that "living is Christ," we will devote ourselves to more than successful careers, money, and retirement. Jesus will determine our interests and how we spend our time, energy, and money.

Introduction for Youths

Topic: *Hope During Hardship*

During a high school wrestling match, Caleb "the underdog" appeared on the verge of losing. The state champion was about to pin him. But suddenly, in what seemed like a miracle, Caleb threw off his opponent and defeated him. Why? Because he never gave up hope in the midst of hardship.

Wrestling is a picture of the Christian life. The apostle Paul reminded his readers that they wrestled with powerful spiritual opponents. He himself demonstrated what it was like. Paul never quit, despite physical beatings, abuse, and imprisonment. Rather than succumb to defeat and despair, he came up rejoicing. He refused to be pinned.

What was his secret? Enduring confidence in the power and love of Jesus. He also counted on strong support from his fans. All of us need serious training to be strong in Christ. Just as wrestlers keep in top physical condition, so Christians need to work out every day in worship, prayer, Bible reading, and fellowship. We must encourage each other to be strong in Christ.

Concepts for Children

Topic: *Believing in Jesus*

1. Faith in Jesus is the only reliable cornerstone on which to build our lives.
2. Many times we have to choose between believing in Jesus and believing popular but false ideas.
3. The apostle Paul was imprisoned for his faith. Many Christians today are persecuted and imprisoned.

4. We can ask Jesus for courage to speak up for Him when people ask us what we believe.
5. The first church at Philippi grew because of Lydia's influence.
6. All of our friends represent people to whom we can introduce Jesus.

The Lesson Commentary

I. THE ADVANCE OF THE GOSPEL: PHILIPPIANS 1:12-14

A. Despite Chains: vss. 12-13

Now I want you to know, brothers, that what has happened to me has really served to advance the gospel. As a result, it has become clear throughout the whole palace guard and to everyone else that I am in chains for Christ.

The theme of this quarter's lessons is "New Life in Christ." The first unit, "Living in Christ" is taken from Philippians. The second, "Called to Be a New Humanity," is based on Ephesians. The third, "Christ above All," is taken from Colossians and Philemon.

Philippians was written about A.D. 62 when the apostle Paul was a prisoner at Rome. He emphasized rejoicing in Christ, regardless of circumstances. Paul's theme was "For to me, to live is Christ" (1:21).

The church at Philippi, a city of Macedonia [mass-uh-DOHN-yuh] (northern Greece), was founded by Paul on his second missionary journey about A.D. 52 (Acts 16:6-40). It was the first European city to receive the Gospel. Paul returned to Macedonia at the end of his third missionary journey, and went back three months later (Acts 20:1-3, 6).

This letter, which sounds the note of joy more than 18 times, was occasioned by a gift Paul had received from the Philippians (2:25; 4:10, 14). They had done this three times before, twice when Paul was at Thessalonica and once when he was at Corinth (4:15-16; 2 Cor. 11:9). Paul wrote to encourage their kindness and to promote a deeper sense of fellowship among them (Phil 2:1-3; 4:2).

After greeting the church, Paul told the Christians how thankful to God he was for them and their partnership in the Gospel (1:5). This was not an organizational partnership, but a partnership of the heart (1:7). He longed for them "with the affection of Christ Jesus" (1:8).

Paul's prayer (1:9-11) shows that he desired the highest spiritual goals for them. He prayed for their abounding love, for their discernment and purity, and for their fruitfulness in Christ. Then he wanted them to know that despite his imprisonment, the Gospel was advancing in Rome.

Of course, the Philippians worried that Paul's imprisonment meant the end of his preaching and possibly his execution as well. They knew his overwhelming commitment to spread the good news about Jesus Christ. How could he possibly survive in Rome? The empire as a whole was open to the Gospel, but Paul had been arrested in Jerusalem and had appealed his case to Rome.

Therefore, Paul quickly assured the church that his imprisonment had not stopped his preaching, but had furthered the Gospel. He was "in chains for Christ," but despite his chains the guards around him had been exposed to the Gospel. These guards were the imperial bodyguards, of whom the emperor was commander-in-chief. Paul's testimony also had reached beyond his guards to "everyone else," that is, to all the others in the emperor's entourage who had heard about this prisoner.

This news certainly reminded the Philippians of how Paul's imprisonment in their own city had led to the salvation of the jailer and his family. The church at Philippi had sprung from a prison cell (Acts 16:16-40) and from the conversion of Lydia (Acts 16:11-15).

B. Despite Fear: vs. 14

Because of my chains, most of the brothers in the Lord have been encouraged to speak the word of God more courageously and fearlessly.

Prison chains could not stop the Gospel, and neither could fear of possible arrest and execution. "The brothers in the Lord" were fellow believers in the church at Rome. Having learned of Paul's imprisonment, they were scared to speak out publicly, either on his behalf or for the Gospel.

But when they saw how Paul had witnessed to his guards, they decided to break out of their fear and defensiveness. Paul's example emboldened them to preach the Gospel "courageously and fearlessly." Not all of them did so, but most of them did. God used Paul not only to spread the Gospel himself, but also to inspire and motivate others to do so as well.

This story of triumph over imprisonment and fear has been repeated in the lives of Christians since Paul's time. The advance of the Gospel has always been opposed by civil and religious authorities. The church has moved ahead as bold, courageous, fearless believers have spoken for Christ, despite the potential dangers. Many have given up their lives for the sake of their testimony to Jesus.

II. THE PREACHING OF THE GOSPEL: PHILIPPIANS 1:15-18A

A. Out of Love: vss. 15-16

It is true that some preach Christ out of envy and rivalry, but others out of goodwill. The latter do so in love, knowing that I am put here for the defense of the gospel.

Strange as it seems, in the early church motives for proclaiming Christ varied from envy to love. Paul was wise enough to discern what was happening. He saw that some preached "out of goodwill . . . in love," because they appreciated that Paul was imprisoned at Rome for the "defense of the gospel."

Therefore, they linked arms with the apostle and strongly encouraged him. They preached freely in the city, while Paul's witness was limited to his guards and the emperor's household. It was possible for them to compare notes, pray together, and build the church's outreach.

B. Out of Selfishness: vs. 17

The former preach Christ out of selfish ambition, not sincerely, supposing that they can stir up trouble for me while I am in chains.

Those who preached Christ out of "envy and rivalry" apparently were jealous of Paul's leadership in the church. They preached "out of selfish ambition, not sincerely." Their motives were false (vs. 18). They resented his being looked up to as the chief spokesman for the Gospel. They wanted to gain superior positions and authority in the church at Paul's expense while he was locked up.

Nevertheless, it is hard to understand that they actually wanted to make matters worse for Paul in his chains. Perhaps they thought that the more they preached the new religion in pagan Rome, the tougher the guards would treat Paul. The guards could easily deny Paul the privileges of mobility in the city (Acts 28:17-31).

C. Christ Is Preached: vs. 18a

But what does it matter? The important thing is that in every way, whether from false motives or true, Christ is preached. And because of this I rejoice.

Somehow, Paul was not upset by those who opposed him. For him, the crucial matter was the preaching of the Gospel of Christ. He did not engage in an argument with those who preached to bring him harm. If they preached Christ, more people in Rome would hear the good news.

Paul rejoiced that Christ was preached. His supreme goal was that "in every way" the Gospel would advance throughout the Roman Empire. The fact that Rome was the citadel of pagan political and religious power did not deter him. When he learned how many Christians were making Christ known in the city, it brought joy to his heart. This joy was medicine for his soul, and kept him from feeling self-pity about his long-delayed appeal to the Roman authorities.

III. JOY IN THE GOSPEL: PHILIPPIANS 1:18B-26

A. Deliverance Expected: vss. 18b-19

Yes, and I will continue to rejoice, for I know that through your prayers and the help given by the Spirit of Jesus Christ, what has happened to me will turn out for my deliverance.

After telling the good news that his imprisonment had not held back the preaching of Christ, Paul went on to tell the Philippians about the condition of his soul. He knew that his readers were eager to know how he felt during the lonely hours when he was not engaged in Gospel witness. Was he really on top spiritually? How was he facing the prospect of a death sentence?

Paul boldly declared, "I will continue to rejoice." He could and would find his joy in Christ, despite his circumstances. This was not evidence of overconfidence on his part. He confessed that he needed the prayers of the church at Philippi, and he needed the help given by the Holy Spirit.

Paul knew that God works through other believers. Jesus helps us to find joy in our tough experiences through the prayers, support, and encouragement of fellow Christians. Motivated by the Holy Spirit's promptings, Christians become agents of healing. At the same time, the Holy Spirit Himself ministers to our emotional needs as well.

Paul anticipated deliverance from Rome. He never gave in to doubt and despair. With full confidence in God's wisdom and love, he looked forward to continued ministry of the Gospel. He knew that he was in Rome according to God's sovereignty. Therefore, he did not complain and second-guess the Lord.

"Deliverance," of course, was not limited to being set free physically. He also wanted to be delivered from shame and fear (vs. 20). Paul was delivered spiritually from fear and depression because he had learned to rejoice in Christ. His heart, soul, and spirit were not held captive by Rome. Because of his robust faith, Paul looked positively at his circumstances. The Holy Spirit nourished him day by day, and he was greatly encouraged by knowing that the church at Philippi stood with him.

B. Exalting Christ: vs. 20

I eagerly expect and hope that I will in no way be ashamed, but will have sufficient courage so that now as always Christ will be exalted in my body, whether by life or by death.

While Paul confidently anticipated his release, he acknowledged that it might be God's will for him to die in Rome. He did not dodge that possibility, but faced it realistically with "sufficient courage." For Paul, the prime issue was not whether he lived or died, but honoring Jesus Christ.

Many people look at death as the end of their existence. Indeed, life has little purpose if death is the end of it all. The Christian hope of eternal life after death gives meaning to the present. When we make Jesus Christ the central focus of our lives, then death ceases to be absurd.

How could Paul exalt Jesus "by death"? Because Jesus conquered death and lives at the Father's right hand. He also lives in every believer. By understanding these basic Christian truths we can share Paul's desire to exalt Christ "by life or by death."

At the same time, we appreciate Paul's need for courage to honor Christ in a hostile pagan environment. Thousands of Christians live under civil and religious powers that hate the Gospel. They face the prospect of life or death. Their desires and needs are the same as Paul's.

Exalting Christ includes regular worship, prayer, and witness. Beyond that, it means living in fellowship with Him and obeying His will. Paul gave us the pattern to follow. We exalt Christ by both the moral integrity of our lives and our public testimony at home and on the job.

C. Purpose in Christ: vs. 21

For to me, to live is Christ and to die is gain.

Paul gave an astonishing perspective on both life and death. He explained his philosophy of life in words that have become the foundation for faithful Christians ever since. His statement is the way to find meaning in life. Jesus is the reason for living; Jesus is the believer's whole life.

As we grow in our knowledge of Him, our personal goals and values change. We become more like Him. Many of our ways are distinctly different from the ways of the unbelieving world. We understand that only what we invest in our walk with Jesus brings lasting satisfaction, no matter what our circumstances.

Therefore, we take more time for reading His words and deeds. We allow the Gospel stories to saturate our hearts and minds. When we make decisions, they are shaped by His values and standards.

Paul considered death a plus because he would be transported into the presence of the living Christ. He had met the risen Christ at his conversion on the Damascus road. He was certain about his destiny. Christians gain the same confidence about death as Jesus looms larger in their daily desires.

D. Desire for Christ: vss. 22-24

If I am to go on living in the body, this will mean fruitful labor for me. Yet what shall I choose? I do not know! I am torn between the two: I desire to depart and be with Christ, which is better by far; but it is more necessary for you that I remain in the body.

However, Paul did not see death as an escape from the world's harsh realities. He was "torn," or hard pressed, when he considered what God's will might be for him. To "be with Christ" would be better. However, he also recognized that he was needed for future ministry. He was confident of more years of "fruitful labor" in the Gospel.

As much as he loved Christ, Paul also loved the Philippians. He had to trade what was a better prospect for himself (being with Christ) for the necessity of serving the church. After so many years of suffering and hardship, Paul probably felt it would be a great relief "to depart." But he stubbornly held to his commitment to be a servant of the church.

E. Joy in Christ: vss. 25-26

Convinced of this, I know that I will remain, and I will continue with all of you for your progress and joy in the faith, so that through my being with you again your joy in Christ Jesus will overflow on account of me.

"Fruitful labor" for Paul meant helping fellow believers to find "progress and joy in the faith." He saw the Christian faith as a growing, dynamic personal relationship with the Lord Jesus Christ. Christian faith is not static. It pulsates with the vibrancy of Christ's love and power.

Paul himself had found joy and he wanted to communicate joy. He wanted his disturbed readers to share his overflowing joy in believing in Christ. He anticipated seeing them again, when they could rejoice and praise God together.

Discussion Questions

1. How can Christians overcome their fears of public witness to Christ?
2. Why is it important for the church to stand against civil and religious opposition to the Gospel?
3. How can the preaching of Christ become the central focus and purpose of the church?
4. What was Paul's key to finding joy and confidence in his circumstances?
5. How can Christians develop the single-minded purpose: "To me, to live is Christ"?
6. How can Christians help one another in their "progress and joy in the faith?"

Contemporary Application

Paul's simple testimony sounds other-worldly to us. He can't be real, we think. How could he possibly rejoice while wearing chains and locked in a prison? How could he be so bold and so confident about his life's purpose and destiny? What a contrast to the aimlessness we see in people's lives all around us.

The church stands as a beacon of brightness to people lost in the fog of meaninglessness. How encouraging it is to hear the testimonies of people who say that Jesus Christ filled the emptiness in their lives.

We must never doubt the influence of a simple statement: "To me, to live is Christ." Perhaps we are ashamed or afraid to say this to people. We need courage to tell what Jesus means to us because people are spiritually hungry.

When Jesus means everything to us, others will be drawn to Him. Our joy will overflow in the lives of those who know so little joy.

Having the Mind of Christ

DEVOTIONAL READING

2 Peter 3:8-18

DAILY BIBLE READINGS

Monday June 5
Philippians 2:1-11 Imitate Christ's Humility in Your Lives

Tuesday June 6
Philippians 2:12-18 Rejoice in One Another's Faithfulness

Wednesday June 7
Philippians 2:19-24 Timothy, a Faithful Servant of Christ

Thursday June 8
Philippians 2:25-30 Welcome Epaphroditus in Christ

Friday June 9
1 Peter 3:8-12 Repay Evil with a Blessing

Saturday June 10
1 Peter 3:13-22 Suffering for Doing Right

Sunday June 11
2 Peter 1:1-11 You Are Participants in God's Blessings

Scripture

Background Scripture: *Philippians 2:1-18*
Scripture Lesson: *Philippians 2:1-13*
Key Verse: *Your attitude should be the same as that of Christ Jesus.* Philippians 2:5.
Key Verse for Children: *Let us do good to all people.* Galatians 6:10.

Lesson Aim

To confess our need of following Jesus in His humiliation.

Lesson Setting

Time: *A.D. 61 or 62*
Place: *Written to Philippi from Rome*

Lesson Outline

Having the Mind of Christ

I. The Call to Humility: Philippians 2:1-4
   A. *Unity: vss. 1-2*
   B. *Care: vss. 3-4*

II. The Example of Humility: Philippians 2:5-11
   A. *The Mind of Christ: vs. 5*
   B. *The Glory of Christ: vs. 6*
   C. *The Self-Emptying of Christ: vs. 7*
   D. *The Humiliation of Christ: vs. 8*
   E. *The Exaltation of Christ: vss. 9-11*

III. The Call to Obedience: Philippians 2:12-13
   A. *Our Work: vs. 12*
   B. *God's Work: vs. 13*

Introduction for Adults

Topic: *Genuine Humility*

Paul wanted the church at Philippi to change. He did not call for a conference on management. He called for a fresh look at the suffering Savior. Until the believers took Jesus seriously, they would not discover genuine humility.

A Christian pastor said, "A person who profoundly changed my life was not a preacher or the leader of a big organization. She was an office worker at the local bus company. She never married. She used her home and her slim resources to develop Christian maturity among college students. Many of them—including myself—went into the ministry at home and abroad."

Few of us recognize the power of humility. But when the books are revealed, we may be surprised to learn that the major influences in God's kingdom came from humble, unselfish, loving servants. Our own lives and our churches are immeasurably enriched when we follow the mind of Christ.

Introduction for Youths

Topic: *Setting Aside Privileges*

Jim, a Christian who started out his career as a sports reporter, thoroughly enjoyed the privileges that came with the job—passes to sports events, access to players, and stuff like that. Later on, he had to make a big career decision. Should he stay in the newspaper business, or should he enter Christian service? If he chose the latter, he knew he was saying good-bye to his last free pass.

Nevertheless, Jim set aside those privileges and says, "I have never regretted the decision. God more than made up for any passes I relinquished. He gave me the most satisfying work I could do in editing, writing, teaching, and preaching."

Sometimes it's hard to choose what we know to be God's will. Sometimes we're afraid God will cheat us out of something good. Do you ever think about what Jesus thought when God asked Him to set aside His privileges in heaven, to come to earth and take on human limitations, and to die a criminal's death for our sins?

Christ's humiliation and exaltation prove that God will never let us down. We can trust Him completely to do the very best for us.

Concepts for Children

Topic: *Being Like Jesus*

1. God wants us to live unselfishly with one another.
2. Jesus calls us to look for ways to help others.
3. Sometimes it is hard to give up our own ambitions for the sake of others.
4. Early Christians were able to help people who suffered from various ills.
5. Jesus came from heaven and suffered so that we might have eternal life.
6. One day Jesus will come back and the whole world will submit to Him.

The Lesson Commentary

I. THE CALL TO HUMILITY: PHILIPPIANS 2:1-4

A. Unity: vss. 1-2

If you have any encouragement from being united with Christ, if any comfort from his love, if any fellowship with the Spirit, if any tenderness and compassion, then make my joy complete by being like-minded, having the same love, being one in spirit and purpose.

Paul began his letter to the church at Philippi with thankfulness for the church's "partnership in the Gospel" (1:5). He wanted the Christians to know that they were solidly linked both in his imprisonment in Rome and in their witness in Philippi. He urged them to strive side by side for the Gospel with one spirit and one mind (1:27). They were in a hard battle for the Lord, and an important key to victory was their unity.

How can a diverse group of people discover unity? By understanding and practicing Christian humility. He asked the Philippians to complete his joy by standing together in humility and love.

Paul set forth an astonishingly high standard: "Like-minded . . . the same love . . . one in spirit and purpose." J. B. Phillips paraphrased it this way: "Live together in harmony, live together in love, as though you had only one mind and one spirit between you." Christians are to think and feel alike in terms of their love for one another and their common goals.

Christian unity and love relate to the importance of striving together for the truth of the Gospel and for our own spiritual growth. It does not mean that all believers see eye-to-eye on everything in private and public life. For example, we don't have to like the same kind of music, or vote for the same party's candidates.

Having considered Paul's high standard of unity, we have to look at the basis of his appeal. He based it on four facts of Christian experience: (1) encouragement from Christ; (2) comfort from Christ's love; (3) fellowship with the Holy Spirit; and (4) personal affection and sympathy.

Paul concluded that when Jesus Christ has transformed our lives, we would find in Him all the incentive we need to live in love and unity. Because the Holy Spirit lives in all believers, we belong to each other in a special partnership. Because of our common fellowship in the Spirit, we can be one in spirit and purpose.

B. Care: vss. 3-4

Do nothing out of selfish ambition or vain conceit, but in humility consider others better than yourselves. Each of you should look not only to your own interests, but also to the interests of others.

These two verses flesh out the practical implications of Paul's appeal. He called for the church to rid itself of two major hindrances to Christian love and unity— selfishness and conceit. Selfish strife and petty ambition must be yielded to Christ's lordship in the church.

Humility is the cornerstone of unity and love in the church. Humility is hard to define, but it is generally understood as the opposite of pride. Paul gave two ways to practice humility: (1) consider others better than ourselves; and (2) look out for the interests of others, not just our own.

We have to recognize the strengths and gifts of our fellow believers, while admitting our own deficiencies. No believer is inherently better than another, yet sometimes we fall into that kind of thinking. That is not the way to love and unity.

Instead of putting our own ideas first, and insisting on them, humble Christians are sensitive to what others think. When we practice humility, and when we honor and love one another, the seemingly impossible happens. The church is unified, marked by love, and strengthened in its witness to the unbelieving world.

II. THE EXAMPLE OF HUMILITY: PHILIPPIANS 2:5-11

A. The Mind of Christ: vs. 5

Your attitude should be the same as that of Christ Jesus.

The Greek word translated "humility" popularly conveyed the idea of a base, servile spirit. Today, people often think of humble people as doormats.

However, Paul's apostolic teaching reveals an entirely different perspective. In Christian understanding, humility becomes a strength and a virtue, not a weakness and a liability. This radical change came about because of the example of Christ's humility. Rightly understood, humility is good for us, it exalts Christ, and it promotes love and unity in the church.

In Philippians 2:1-11, we have to remember that Paul used the example of Christ's humility to teach how believers should relate to one another in the church (vss. 1-4). How do we attain his high ambition for the church? "Your attitude should be the same as that of Christ Jesus."

This means we practice looking at our lives and circumstances—and the lives of our fellow believers—from the perspective of Jesus. We do this because we are one in Christ. Jesus is not a philosophical example; He is a living person whose Holy Spirit lives in us and empowers us to live according to this high standard.

Therefore, it is possible for Christians to foster the same disposition that Jesus had. We look to Him for our inspiration and example. Humility comes from allowing the fullness of Christ to be expressed in our lives.

B. The Glory of Christ: vs. 6

Who, being in very nature God, did not consider equality with God something to be grasped.

We have to consider Christ's humility from the perspective of His preincarnate glory with the Father (John 1:1-2; 17:5, 24). Paul declared that Jesus possessed the "very nature of God" and was therefore equal with God. These facts help us to understand the dramatic contrast between Christ's eternal deity and what He became and did for us.

Jesus first demonstrated humility by voluntarily relinquishing the full pre-rogatives of deity when He came to earth. Though Jesus did not surrender His deity, He did forego the rights of that heavenly environment. Jesus knew hunger, thirst, pain, and temptation. When His executioners dragged Him to the cross, Jesus could have called down a legion of angels, but He didn't.

So, we are called to follow the same principle in our behavior. Christians lay aside their personal rights for the sake of ministering to others.

C. The Self-Emptying of Christ: vs. 7

But made himself nothing, taking the very nature of a servant, being made in human likeness.

"But" introduces Paul's contrast between the glory of Christ and His self-emptying. This is our peek into the great mystery of the Godhead and of our salvation. We have no details about what went on in the triune Godhead—Father, Son, and Holy Spirit. We know little about Christ's decision to leave heaven, other than that the Father sent Him on His mission and He obeyed (John 20:21).

Paul described three steps in Christ's mission. He "made himself nothing"; He took "the very nature of a servant"; and He was "made in human likeness." He "made himself nothing" in the sense that He laid aside His heavenly glory when He came to earth. It does not mean He was worthless. In His humanity, Jesus lived as a servant. That was how He characterized His mission (Mark 10:45).

From birth to death, Jesus lived in humility. He was born in a stable. His parents were refugees in Egypt. He grew up in obedience to His parents. He worked at a humble trade, as a carpenter. He cried with those who grieved. He washed the feet of His disciples. Paul summarized Christ's self-emptying this way: "Though he was rich, yet for your sakes he became poor, so that you through his poverty might become rich" (2 Cor. 8:9).

"Have the same attitude," said Paul. This requires prayerful meditation on Jesus' humility and disciplined study of His words and deeds. We confess we cannot do it on our own; we need the Holy Spirit's empowerment.

D. The Humiliation of Christ: vs. 8

And being found in appearance as a man, he humbled himself and became obedient to death—even death on a cross!

The supreme demonstration of Christ's humility was His willingness to go to the cross. His leaving heaven and "being made in human likeness" was the first step in His humiliation. It culminated at Calvary. When we look at Jesus on the cross, we understand what it means to "look not only to your own interests, but also to the interests of others" (vs. 4).

Jesus lived completely obedient to His Father, to the extent that He died like a common criminal for our sins. The enormous pain of His humiliation was described by the prophets, the psalmists, and the writers of the four Gospels.

317

In this letter to the Philippians, Paul did not dwell on the details of Christ's unjust trials, the way He was mocked, beaten, and nailed to the cross. Rather, he emphasized the stigma of being executed on the cross.

To the Jews, crucifixion was the epitome of shame, because it showed that the victim was beyond God's covenant (Deut. 21:23; Gal. 3:13). To the Romans, crucifixion was repulsive. The Roman historian Cicero wrote: "Far be the very name of the cross, not only from the body, but even from the thought, the eyes, the ears of Roman citizens."

Christians know little, if anything, about this kind of humiliation. That's why Paul tells us to look squarely at the cross if we are to grasp what it means to serve in the church with love, humility, and unity.

E. The Exaltation of Christ: vss. 9-11

Therefore God exalted him to the highest place and gave him the name that is above every name, that at the name of Jesus every knee should bow, in heaven and on earth and under the earth, and every tongue confess that Jesus Christ is Lord, to the glory of God the Father.

The cross was not the end of the story. Christ's humiliation led to His exaltation. Jesus taught and lived by this principle: no suffering, no glory. It was taught by the prophet Isaiah: "He was despised and rejected by men . . . he was pierced for our transgressions, he was crushed for our iniquities . . . My servant . . . will be raised and lifted up and highly exalted" (53:3-5; 52:13).

The scorned and rejected Jesus is now exalted "above every name." One day the world will confess Him as Lord. Because Jesus endured the worst that unbelievers could hurl at Him, God has established Him as the supreme ruler of the universe.

The Lord Jesus Christ owns the name above all names. He has the highest honor and authority. The name given Him is Lord (Acts 9:5; 2:36). His name clearly identifies who Jesus is, and the kind of person He is.

The name "Lord" is rooted in the Old Testament. It is the name of God Himself. Only that name is above every name. It is the name by which Jesus Christ is to be publicly acclaimed and worshiped.

The exaltation of Jesus means He is to be the object of universal homage and praise. "Every knee should bow . . . every tongue confess." Kneeling is a sign of homage as people openly proclaim the lordship of Jesus Christ.

III. The Call to Obedience: Philippians 2:12-13

A. Our Work: vs. 12

Therefore, my dear friends, as you have always obeyed—not only in my presence, but now much more in my absence—continue to work out your salvation with fear and trembling.

"Therefore," in light of what Jesus has done and will do, Christians are called to live out their salvation with a healthy respect for His suffering and glory. Paul urged the Philippians to keep on doing this, as they had done.

Eternal salvation comes through faith in Christ alone. Nothing we can do will earn salvation. Confessing faith in Christ is the entrance into eternal life. Then we are called to follow the principles of Jesus. We are to work out in the church what we know to be true of Him. "Fear and trembling" do not stand for insecurity, but for earnestness, hard work, and seriousness in being the kind of people Christ wants us to be.

B. God's Work: vs. 13

For it is God who works in you to will and to act according to his good purpose.

Our great comfort in the Christian life is that God continually works His good and perfect will in us. We always live in the tension between working for God and His kingdom as faithfully and diligently as we can, and allowing God to inspire and train us to do what He desires.

We are not in the battle alone. Paul's assurance that "God works in you" builds our confidence and gives us hope that we can fulfill His purposes for us and for His church. Paul set a high standard for Christian humility, love, and unity. He knew that God works in His people to reach that standard.

Discussion Questions

1. How would you define Paul's standards for the church?
2. What does unity in your church look like?
3. How do we develop humility and dispose of selfish ambitions?
4. What effects does Christ's humiliation have on the Christian's outlook on life? On the life of the church?
5. Why is it hard to live by the principle that exaltation follows humiliation?
6. How might your church's business meetings be different if Philippians 2:1-11 was read thoughtfully before the meeting started?

Contemporary Application

Have you ever seen an advertisement for a seminar on humility? There are lots of ads about how to be successful, how to get ahead, and how to be number one. But how to be humble? Forget it.

When Christians take seriously the high standards of the Gospel, they run smack into the world's way of thinking. That's why one of our most powerful influences on society is our model of humility. People cannot deny that Jesus makes a difference when they see Christians following the humility of Christ.

Our churches would also find larger responses if they were known as communities where people put the interests of others ahead of their own. Too often, it seems, the public sees more fighting than humility among God's people. Having the mind of Christ shapes the church and shakes the world.

Pressing On in Christ

Scripture

Background Scripture: *Philippians 3*
Scripture Lesson: *Philippians 3:7-21*
Key Verse: *I press on toward the goal to win the prize for which God has called me heavenward in Christ Jesus.* Philippians 3:14.
Key Verse for Children: *"Believe in the Lord Jesus, and you will be saved—you and your household."* Acts 16:31.

Lesson Aim

To make knowing and serving Christ our chief aim in life.

Lesson Setting

Time: A.D. *61 or 62*
Place: *Written to Philippi from Rome*

Lesson Outline

Pressing On in Christ

I. Paul's Radical Reevaluation: Philippians 3:7-11
   A. *Counting Gains as Losses: vs. 7*
   B. *The Supreme Value of Knowing Christ: vss. 8-9*
   C. *The Power of Knowing Christ: vss. 10-11*

II. Paul's Race for the Prize: Philippians 3:12-16
   A. *His New Relation to Jesus: vs. 12*
   B. *His Single Objective: vss. 13-14*
   C. *His Call to Press On: vss. 15-16*

III. Paul's Vision of the Future: Philippians 3:17-21
   A. *Follow His Pattern: vs. 17*
   B. *Beware of Christ's Enemies: vss. 18-19*
   C. *Await the Savior: vs. 20*
   D. *Christ Will Transform Us: vs. 21*

Introduction for Adults

Topic: *Striving to be Christlike*

Sadly, when people talk about "church," they often focus on programs, staff, buildings, and denominational differences. There's more than enough criticism to go around, which means outsiders frequently are turned off by what they see and hear.

However, the essence of Christianity is none of these. Those things often get in the way of real Christian faith, which means trusting in Jesus Christ and obeying His will. The apostle Paul had to get rid of a lot of religious baggage that kept him from knowing and serving Christ. We have to do the same.

Striving to be Christlike is more important than anything else. If we find anything in religion that keeps us from knowing Him, and living like Him, we have to discard it. This may mean radical changes for some people who have been in church for years. If some kinds of church experiences keep us from Christ, we can make fresh starts. There is no use wasting time arguing about things that may seem important, but are really dangerous if our Christian growth is stunted.

Introduction for Youths

Topic: *Press Ahead!*

One of the favorite ways to prove a diet works is to show before and after pictures. You know, the photo on the left shows an obese man weighing 300 pounds, but the photo on the right shows the same man, trim and fit, weighing 175 pounds. This could be you, if you stick to our diet, the ad says.

The apostle Paul's story is something like that. He told us what he was like before he met Christ, and then he told us the remarkable changes that occurred after his conversion. You can pick out the dramatic changes in Philippians 3.

Of course, the key to weight loss is sticking to the diet, not just for a few weeks but forever. The same was true for Paul. He kept on pressing ahead toward his goal of spiritual maturity and Christlikeness. He never said he had arrived at the place where he could relax. Many people start the Christian walk, but fail to keep at it. They do not pursue the goal as doggedly as Paul did. His example should motivate us to keep shedding the weight of sin and keeping trim to win our faith race with Jesus.

Concepts for Children

Topic: *Telling the Good News*

1. Like the apostle Paul, we can single-mindedly pursue our walk with Jesus.
2. Sometimes we think other things are more valuable than trusting in Jesus.
3. When we follow Jesus, we have opportunities to speak to others about Him.
4. The apostles were persecuted for telling the good news.
5. God saved many people through the faithful witness of Paul and Silas.
6. Paul's counsel to the jailer to believe on Jesus is the heart of the good news.

The Lesson Commentary

I. PAUL'S RADICAL REEVALUATION: PHILIPPIANS 3:7-11

A. Counting Gains as Losses: vs. 7

Whatever was to my profit I now consider loss for the sake of Christ.

Before he talked about pursuing his spiritual goal as a Christian, the apostle Paul looked back to his life as a zealous Jew (Phil. 3:4-6). In many ways, he was an outstanding person. His achievements were so remarkable that he ranked at the top among his peers. Not only had he been born and raised a Jew, he excelled as "a Hebrew of the Hebrews." He followed the law strictly as a Pharisee, to such an extent that he considered himself "faultless." In addition, he tried to keep the Jewish faith "pure" by persecuting the Christ-followers with a vengeance.

However, when he looked at his spiritual balance sheet he made an amazing discovery. All of his assets turned out to be liabilities. He had to transfer his assets to the loss column in the ledger book, because these things had kept him from knowing Christ.

"Profits" became "losses" for the sake of Christ. Paul's spiritual bookkeeping is a powerful lesson to those of us who trust in our religious upbringing, zeal, and achievements for salvation. These things keep people from Christ and salvation.

B. The Supreme Value of Knowing Christ: vss. 8-9

What is more, I consider everything a loss compared to the surpassing greatness of knowing Christ Jesus my Lord, for whose sake I have lost all things. I consider them rubbish, that I may gain Christ and be found in him, not having a righteousness of my own that comes from the law, but that which is through faith in Christ—the righteousness that comes from God and is by faith.

Paul drove to the heart of the issue he had to face, and so must we. He put all of his assets on the scales and found they came up short. Everything he considered valuable he now considered worthless. Why? Because knowing Christ far outweighed them all.

There really was no comparison, because knowing Christ is incomparable. Paul called it "surpassing greatness." Three times Paul spoke of his basic spiritual transaction: "I now consider loss" (vs. 7); "I consider everything a loss" (vs. 8); "I consider them rubbish" (vs. 8). Only when we see ourselves as spiritually bankrupt and helpless will we flee to Christ for salvation. Because knowing Him is life's supreme value, everything else must go—even things that appear to be religiously motivated.

This was not theory with Paul. He actually had "lost all things." Everything he had trusted in was gone. From being the zealous leader of the Jews in Jerusalem, he had now become a hunted criminal and even a prisoner. But never mind, said Paul, because what he lost was only rubbish anyway. ("Rubbish" is a nice word for the Greek, which means garbage or dung.)

But Paul's losses were nothing compared to what he had gained. He had gained Christ, and he had received righteousness as a gift by faith. His supposed spiritual assets had been accumulated by legalistic zeal—his own works. But they not only counted for nothing, they barred him from knowing Christ. To gain Christ and be counted righteous in Him, Paul had to trust Him by faith.

Each person, then, must decide if the value of gaining Christ is worth considering all of one's religious works as so much garbage. Paul's radical reevaluation of his life led him to the conclusion that knowing Christ and gaining righteousness as a gift by faith were worth more than anything else.

C. The Power of Knowing Christ: vss. 10-11

I want to know Christ and the power of his resurrection and the fellowship of sharing in his sufferings, becoming like him in his death, and so, somehow, to attain to the resurrection from the dead.

For Paul, knowing Christ opened the door to limitless spiritual possibilities. His supreme goal of knowing Christ led him to desire the power of Christ's resurrection. Such power is available because Jesus is alive and lives in those who have committed themselves to Him. This spiritual power inspires godly living, worship, praise, and service for others.

The power of Christ's resurrection was rooted in His self-denial that led to the Cross. Jesus had said that His followers would have to take up their own crosses. Paul realized there was spiritual power in sharing Christ's sufferings. Paul willingly faced incredible hardships for the sake of obeying Christ. Everything he did was out of obedience to Christ, becoming "like him," because Paul's ultimate goal was eternal life with God ("to attain . . . resurrection from the dead").

II. PAUL'S RACE FOR THE PRIZE: PHILIPPIANS 3:12-16

A. His New Relation to Jesus: vs. 12

Not that I have already obtained all this, or have already been made perfect, but I press on to take hold of that for which Christ Jesus took hold of me.

Paul realized, of course, that he was still a believer "in process," as we all are. He had gained Christ and he had received God's righteousness as a gift. Nevertheless, he looked ahead to reach the goal for which Jesus had saved him. Paul's concept of the Christian life was that of a mountain climber continually working his way to the summit. He was not content to stop at a lower level.

That's why he pressed ahead. He wanted to grasp that for which Christ had gripped him. He saw salvation not as an entry pass into a life of ease, but as the beginning of a lifelong pursuit to achieve God's will.

Such a view transforms a dull, static concept of Christian living. We constantly ask ourselves if we are being what Jesus wants us to be, and doing what He wants us to do. Why does Jesus save us and make us righteous? Not for our self-fulfillment, but for the fulfillment of *His* purposes. Jesus takes hold of every believer for a specific lifelong purpose. Finding and doing that purpose brings ultimate satisfaction.

B. His Single Objective: vss. 13-14

Brothers, I do not consider myself yet to have taken hold of it. But one thing I do: Forgetting what is behind and straining toward what is ahead, I press on toward the goal to win the prize for which God has called me heavenward in Christ Jesus.

Nothing could be clearer or more forceful than this statement of Paul's purpose in life. He was certain that Jesus had called and saved him. He wanted his life to fit squarely with what Jesus had in mind. Although he confessed that he had not yet fully achieved Christ's purpose, he was totally dedicated to reaching it.

He never looked back. Instead, he kept pushing ahead with all his strength. He reminds us of a distance runner. The first rule is never look back to see where your opponents are. Paul's graphic picture tells us that the Christian life must be marked not only by intense effort, but also by clear purpose.

Having a clear purpose, or vision, kept Paul from going into blind alleys. His goal was simple: Win the prize for which God had called him. Everything else was secondary. The prize was in heaven with Jesus, so Paul kept his eyes on Jesus. Because of Jesus he had counted his religious zeal and works as garbage. Because of Jesus he had gained righteousness. Because of Jesus he was willing to suffer. Because of Jesus he was confident of his own resurrection. Because of Jesus he relentlessly pursued his vocation of spreading the good news.

C. His Call to Press On: vss. 15-16

All of us who are mature should take such a view of things. And if on some point you think differently, that too God will make clear to you. Only let us live up to what we have already attained.

Paul had plumbed new depths of spiritual maturity and insight, perhaps too deep for some to follow. Could everyone be as intense as he was in his pursuit of Christ and His will? Possibly not. But those who had reached some degree of spiritual maturity could accept Paul's testimony.

Paul was confident that in time God would graciously help others reach his own understanding of what it meant to know and serve Christ. In the meantime, all believers could press on in the light of what they already knew.

His main point is that we must not quit, we must not give up our pursuit of the highest goals in Christ. The race goes on, one step at a time. As we live in obedient faith, Jesus makes clear to us the full scope of why He has called us to himself.

III. PAUL'S VISION OF THE FUTURE: PHILIPPIANS 3:17-21

A. Follow His Pattern: vs. 17

Join with others in following my example, brothers, and take note of those who live according to the pattern we gave you.

Paul's vision of the future began with serious concerns about the present. But he looked beyond those concerns to the ultimate transforming power of Christ. He was not reticent about holding himself up as an example to follow. He encouraged his readers to follow the pattern he had set.

Paul's pattern, as we have seen, was to put Christ first in everything. All remnants of "good works theology" had to be discarded. The church was to follow him in single-minded devotion to Christ.

B. Beware of Christ's Enemies: vss. 18-19

For, as I have often told you before and now say again even with tears, many live as enemies of the cross of Christ. Their destiny is destruction, their god is their stomach, and their glory is in their shame. Their mind is on earthly things.

Paul appealed for the strength that comes from unity in the church. The believers were to stand together in following his example, so that they could withstand the enemies of Christ. Paul narrowed his audience to two groups: (1) those who followed his teachings; (2) those who lived as enemies of Christ.

Perhaps the church was in danger of being infiltrated by those described in vs. 19. Their condition was so serious that Paul had often warned against them, and did so again with tears. The danger was that they would lead people away from Christ and away from salvation by faith alone.

These people were earthly minded and seemed to glory in the extravagance of their sensual appetites. Rather than seeking Christ, they sought their own physical desires.

C. Await the Savior: vs. 20

But our citizenship is in heaven. And we eagerly await a Savior from there, the Lord Jesus Christ . . .

The destiny of the earthly-minded is destruction (vs. 19); the destiny of the heavenly-minded is heaven and the coming of Jesus Christ. Because Christians are citizens of heaven, Paul argued that they should not live like those who fight against Christ by their immoral living.

Our citizenship in heaven and our hope of Christ's return give meaning and purpose to Christian experience. Our focus is on Him because we belong to Him and His kingdom. Christians obey Christ and live godly lives as they anticipate His return. Being a citizen of heaven makes a difference here and now.

D. Christ Will Transform Us: vs. 21

. . . who, by the power that enables him to bring everything under his control, will transform our lowly bodies so that they will be like his glorious body.

Paul's testimony climaxed with a wonderful vision of what Jesus will do for us. Because Jesus is Lord He controls all things. We know that He will bring righteousness and peace. We pray for His return so that the world will be restored to His rule. The reason we look for Him with eager anticipation is that He will assume His rightful place as King of kings and Lord of lords.

Here, Paul says that Christ's power will even transform "our lowly bodies" to be like His own. Lowly bodies will become glorious bodies. This article of faith sustains our hope, and keeps us pursuing the knowledge of Christ and His will. Salvation by faith is His gift, and so is the changing of our bodies.

Paul's radical reevaluation cost him everything. In return, he gained Christ and the assurance of one day being made like Him.

Discussion Questions

1. What pros and cons did Paul weigh in his radical reevaluation of himself?
2. Why is it so hard to consider our religious deeds as so much garbage?
3. What do people you know find it hardest to throw on the "loss column" in order to gain Christ?
4. How can Christians help one another to pursue a single-minded goal of reaching the prize of God's calling?
5. What makes the difference between Christians like Paul and many others who seem to lack his zeal for Christ?
6. How should citizens of heaven live in today's world?

Contemporary Application

Some churches that have a "new building" plan or some other program of giving will put a huge thermometer painted on a sign in the foyer. At the top is the financial goal, perhaps $500,000 or even one million. Each week the red line goes a little higher. Every Sunday people are reminded of how far they have to go to reach the top.

What if we had the same kind of device to measure our devotion to Christ, and our zeal to know Him and do His will? Perhaps the red line would vary from week to week. But we would hope that gradually the line would move upward as people pressed on in spiritual growth and development.

However, to be honest, in some cases it's easier to get excited about reaching a financial goal than a spiritual goal. Why are we so reluctant to take our spiritual temperature? Surely we can confess that all of our other goals should be secondary to this one. We confess that our relationship with Christ should be our first concern. Too easily we have allowed our minds to focus on earthly things. Too easily we have let the supreme value of Christ slip away from us. Anything less, no matter how much we strive for it, is rubbish.

Rejoicing in Christ

DEVOTIONAL READING

1 Thessalonians 1:2-10

DAILY BIBLE READINGS

Monday June 19
Philippians 4:2-7 Rejoice, and Be Gentle with One Another

Tuesday June 20
Philippians 4:8-14 Keep On Keeping On in Christ

Wednesday June 21
Philippians 4:15-23 Paul's Thanks for the Philippian Church

Thursday June 22
Acts 2:43-47 Life among the Early Believers

Friday June 23
1 Thessalonians 1:1-10 Paul's Thanks for the Thessalonian Church

Saturday June 24
1 Thessalonians 4:1-12 Lives Pleasing to God

Sunday June 25
3 John 1-8 Faithfulness Brings Great Joy

Scripture

Background Scripture: *Philippians 4:4-20*
Scripture Lesson: *Philippians 4:4-18*
Key Verse: *Rejoice in the Lord always. I will say it again: Rejoice!* Philippians 4:4.

Lesson Aim

To discover genuine joy and peace in Christ.

Lesson Setting

Time: A.D. *61 or 62*
Place: *Written to Philippi from Rome*

Lesson Outline

Rejoicing in Christ

I. The Peace of God: Philippians 4:4-9
   A. *Our Joy: vs. 4*
   B. *Our Gentleness: vs. 5*
   C. *Our Prayer: vs. 6*
   D. *Our Guard: vs. 7*
   E. *Our Thoughts: vs. 8*
   F. *Our Practice and Our Peace: vs. 9*

II. The Strength of God: Philippians 4:10-13
   A. *The Concern of Others: vs. 10*
   B. *The Secret of Contentment: vss. 11-12*
   C. *The Source of Strength: vs. 13*

III. The Fellowship of Believers: Philippians 4:14-18
   A. *Faithful Support: vss. 14-16*
   B. *Fragrant Offerings: vss. 17-18*

Introduction for Adults

Topic: *Deep Joy*

How do you define deep joy? How is it different from the happiness we feel at a family party, or the excitement at a football game? Does the Gospel really open a new dimension of experience that surpasses everything else?

Sometimes the Gospel is rejected as a crutch for weak people. Some people think that if you're strong, you don't need Christ. But as we read the apostle Paul's testimony, it does not appear that his faith in Christ was a crutch. Paul was not a weak person. He exuded remarkable strength under stress.

The Gospel offers answers to our deepest longings for joy, security, and freedom from worry. The Gospel is not a psychological formula; the Gospel is a person—Jesus Christ. This makes Christianity distinctive. Christians live in Christ and He lives in them.

Only Jesus brings deep, satisfying joy that's not dependent on circumstances. Only Jesus gives joy that sustains us in our darkest hours. It is our privilege to know Him better each day. The better we know Him, the deeper our joy.

Introduction for Youths

Topic: *Rejoicing in Christ*

One of America's great distance runners was Gil Dodds. He was a Christian and when he signed his autograph he added "Phil. 4:13." People thought he had run the mile in Philadelphia in four minutes and thirteen seconds, hardly a great accomplishment. They did not know "Phil. 4:13" was a reference to Paul's claim that he could do everything through Christ. Gil Dodds tried to give credit to Jesus for his athletic achievements.

However we do it, we must show people that Jesus makes a difference. Our attitudes and our conduct must be shaped by Jesus. Many times, the supreme test comes in how we handle problems and difficulties. Does Jesus give us peace and joy when we're disappointed and hurt? When a tragedy occurs?

Unbelievers are quick to size up Christians when they are under the gun. That's why it's so important to rejoice in Christ, and to point people to Him for whatever He has enabled us to do. Admittedly, this is a tough assignment. That's why Paul urged us to pray at all times, and to ask Jesus for His joy.

Concepts for Children

Topic: *Rejoicing Together*

1. Jesus wants us to rejoice in His goodness.
2. When things go wrong, it's hard to rejoice, so we are called to prayer.
3. Anxiety, fear, and worry attack our minds, so we need to pray for God's peace to guard our hearts and minds.
4. Living with God's peace helps us to encourage others.
5. Joy grows from our faith in the Lord Jesus Christ.
6. Often we have to choose between what the unbelieving world offers as joy, and what Jesus offers as joy.

The Lesson Commentary

I. THE PEACE OF GOD: PHILIPPIANS 4:4-9

A. Our Joy: vs. 4

Rejoice in the Lord always. I will say it again: Rejoice!

Paul's letter to the church at Philippi has rightly been called the epistle of joy. He rejoiced in the outcome of his imprisonment (chap. 1). He rejoiced in the example of Christ (chap. 2). He rejoiced in the gift of righteousness by faith in Christ (chap. 3). He rejoiced in God's peace and in the provision for his needs by his friends in the church (chap. 4).

Therefore, when he told the church to rejoice always, he was not speaking theoretically. He knew what it meant to rejoice in the Lord. He so strongly desired the church to share his joy that he gave the command twice.

This was not pop psychology intended to paper over Paul's troubles in Rome. Paul touched the uniqueness of Christian faith when he told the believers to rejoice. Christian joy is "in the Lord." This means it is not in circumstances, or good luck. Christians rejoice in Christ because of what He has done for them, and because He keeps His promise to give His children joy and peace (John 14:27; 15:11).

Therefore, Christian rejoicing is not like the world's joy. Christians rejoice "always," regardless of the difficulties and hardships. This does not mean Christians are perpetual happiness freaks. They cry and they hurt; they don't smile and laugh all the time. But when they suffer loss and pain, they commit their way to Jesus. They ask Him for the joy that comes only from their faith and hope in Him. They know that He will never abandon them. That is the mark of a mature Christian.

B. Our Gentleness: vs. 5

Let your gentleness be evident to all. The Lord is near.

The Christian life is not only characterized by joy but also by gentleness. The word used by Paul means "yieldingness." Or, we might say "reasonableness." In other words, Christians don't ride roughshod over others, insisting on their own way, but yield when necessary for the good of the fellowship. This virtue was expressed previously by Paul: "Each of you should look not only to your own interests, but also to the interests of others" (2:4).

Paul reminded his readers of the continual presence of Christ. When interacting with fellow believers, keep in mind that Jesus is looking over your shoulder. We cannot escape His presence. Therefore, our behavior is shaped by the indwelling Christ.

C. Our Prayer: vs. 6

Do not be anxious about anything, but in everything, by prayer and petition, with thanksgiving, present your requests to God.

Anxiety is a killer. Anxiety kills joy and peace. But prayer is God's solution for anxiety. "Do not be anxious about anything" reminds us of our Lord's command not to worry about anything (Matt. 6:25-34). We need to meditate on His words regularly.

The Philippian believers had many reasons to be anxious, not only for Paul's welfare, but also for their church in a hostile environment. They also faced the worries and fears common to all people, such as employment, housing, income, children, and health.

Perhaps they felt that as Christians they would not suffer the usual stresses and strains of life. However, Christians are not immune to the world's problems, and we suffer accordingly. But Christians can be delivered from anxiety about our daily concerns. Prayer is the key.

Let God know how you feel, Paul said in effect. Tell Him everything. Bring your requests to Him, whatever they may be, silly as they may seem. God cares about the details of everyday life. There's nothing too insignificant to talk to God about.

Paul encouraged thanksgiving as well as specific requests. When we focus on what God has done for us, and develop a spirit of praise and thanksgiving, somehow our cares seem to fade away. The circumstances don't change, but our outlook does. Suddenly, fear is replaced by joy, and we can sing to the Lord.

Reminding ourselves of Christ's promises, and reading the psalms and the stories of the Old Testament, also helps to shape our prayers. The Word of God brings change to our minds and hearts and delivers us from anxiety.

D. Our Guard: vs. 7

And the peace of God, which transcends all understanding, will guard your hearts and your minds in Christ Jesus.

Our minds and our hearts need heavenly guards, or protectors, because the enemy of our souls seeks to drag us down into anxiety, despair, depression, and anger with God. He stirs up a cauldron of bitterness. Paul promised that when we commit everything to God in prayer, He would send His peace to be our guard.

This is one of the cornerstone promises of the Bible, which Christians turn to again and again. They find peace in the midst of turmoil, illness, death, disappointment, and grief. Paul said God's peace "transcends understanding." There is no human way to explain what God does for us.

Of course, we can testify to the many times God has intervened and provided His peace to protect us, but we can't actually explain how it works. Every time God shows His faithfulness, we can encourage others to turn over their anxieties and worries to Him as well.

The only safeguard of our hearts and minds is God's peace in Christ Jesus.

His peace is not like a temporary, artificial panacea. Christians don't try to find peace by following the world's plunge into alcohol and drugs, for example. Rather, they anchor their hearts and minds in Christ.

We also need to recognize our weaknesses and ask for God's protection. Our hearts may need strong emotional undergirding; our minds may need to recall the basic facts of our faith. When Christians fall into despair, it's often because they fail to remember that the facts about God and about Christ haven't changed, even though their feelings may be low. Circumstances and feelings do not change God's wisdom, love and power. They do not change Christ's promises to be with us and take care of us.

Peace follows prayer, so we must continually exercise the discipline of prayer, alone and with other believers. This is our protection.

E. Our Thoughts: vs. 8

Finally, brothers, whatever is true, whatever is noble, whatever is right, whatever is pure, whatever is lovely, whatever is admirable—if anything is excellent or praiseworthy—think about such things.

Prayer must be followed by the disciplined use of our minds. When our minds get off the track, we can lose the sense of God's peace and protection. He is always there, but if we allow ourselves to think about ungodly things, our joy and peace will be destroyed.

Paul set a high standard to shape what we think about. Of course, what we think about is shaped by what we read, talk about, and watch on television and the movies. We are asking for trouble and spiritual disaster if we fail to apply these tests to everything that enters our minds, whatever the gateway.

Truth is the first test, followed by what is "noble," or worthy of respect. Then whatever is right, as opposed to what is wrong; whatever is pure, as opposed to immoral, rotten, indecent; whatever is lovely, as opposed to unseemly and inappropriate; whatever is admirable, excellent, or praiseworthy, as opposed to what is unworthy, inferior, or self-centered.

When we look at the menu offered by the world, we have no trouble understanding what Paul had in mind. Most of the time the world is occupied with things that fall far short of Paul's standards.

F. Our Practice and Our Peace: vs. 9

Whatever you have learned or received or heard from me, or seen in me—put it into practice. And the God of peace will be with you.

Paul closed his appeal by asking the Philippians to consider his own teaching and practice. What a remarkable statement this was, yet Paul was confident that both his teaching and his life would hold up. The new believers could confidently follow the apostle's example. Both his words and his life rang true.

Paul returned to the promise of God's peace. He knew that the Philippians were engaged in serious spiritual battles. They needed his reassurance that as they practiced prayer, and focused their minds on holy, godly thoughts, they would enjoy God's amazing peace. This peace did not mean the absence of conflict, but peace that would keep them steady and protect them from fear and despair.

II. THE STRENGTH OF GOD: PHILIPPIANS 4:10-13

A. The Concern of Others: vs. 10

I rejoice greatly in the Lord that at last you have renewed your concern for me. Indeed, you have been concerned, but you had no opportunity to show it.

Paul not only preached joy, he practiced it. Despite his dire circumstances under house arrest in Rome (Acts 28:16, 20), he rejoiced greatly in the Lord. One of the reasons for his joy was the concern expressed by the church at Philippi.

Paul was thankful for their renewed concern, but was careful not to blame them for apparently not sending more timely relief. Because of difficulties, the believers had not been able to get their aid through to Paul until the arrival of Epaphroditus [ee-paff-roh-DIE-tus] (2:25; 4:18).

B. The Secret of Contentment: vss. 11-12

I am not saying this because I am in need, for I have learned to be content whatever the circumstances. I know what it is to be in need, and I know what it is to have plenty. I have learned the secret of being content in any and every situation, whether well fed or hungry, whether living in plenty or in want.

During the time when the gifts of the Philippians had been delayed, Paul had learned a profound spiritual lesson—how to be content whatever the circumstances. Of course, his testimony is a graphic picture of what it means to be protected by God's peace. Because he was at peace, Paul was content.

For him, contentment did not depend on his being free and well-fed. That is the way we naturally look at life. But Paul turned things upside down. He said he was content, even though he was in prison, in need, and hungry. This conclusion did not come easily; it was something he had to learn.

On the other hand, he knew what it was to be content when he had everything he needed. This is also a hard lesson to learn, because many times the more we prosper the more we want to acquire things we don't have. "Living in plenty" does not guarantee contentment.

C. The Source of Strength: vs. 13

I can do everything through him who gives me strength.

What was the secret of Paul's contentment, in need and in plenty? Jesus Christ. How could he find peace in prison? Jesus was with him. How could he endure being cut off from friends and their help? By trusting in Jesus.

He did "everything," that is, he endured all circumstances good and bad, in the strength of Christ. The indwelling Savior provided strength, hope, and courage as the apostle needed it. That is how he could write about rejoicing and about the peace of God.

Paul gave no complicated explanation of the secret of his spiritual triumph. He wanted believers simply to find all their needs met in Christ. Faith, hope, and trust are anchored in Him. Each day brings opportunities to find Christ's strength, no matter how heavy the load. This is what He promised (Matt. 11:28-30).

III. THE FELLOWSHIP OF BELIEVERS: PHILIPPIANS 4:14-18

A. Faithful Support: vss. 14-16

Yet it was good of you to share in my troubles. Moreover, as you Philippians know, in the early days of your acquaintance with the gospel, when I set out from Macedonia, not one church shared with me in the matter of giving and receiving, except you only; for even when I was in Thessalonica, you sent me aid again and again when I was in need.

Paul knew that Jesus was with him. He also knew that Jesus was with the believers at Philippi, who were the means of sending him help. He did all things in Christ's strength, but Christ's strength came to him through the faithful support of the church.

This is a wonderful picture of how Jesus works in the church. He uses fellow believers to strengthen other believers when they are in difficulties. Our responsibility is to allow Jesus to use us to share the troubles of others and bring them peace, hope, and encouragement.

Faithful support was not a one-time thing. Paul recalled how the Philippians had ministered to him again and again. In fact, they were the only church that had helped him on his missionary journeys. It's interesting that they did this as a young church. The believers knew that partnership was essential, so they helped Paul again and again.

B. Fragrant Offerings: vss. 17-18

Not that I am looking for a gift, but I am looking for what may be credited to your account. I have received full payment and even more; I am amply supplied, now that I have received from Epaphroditus the gifts you sent. They are a fragrant offering, an acceptable sacrifice, pleasing to God.

Paul lifted material aid from the purely physical to the highest spiritual plane. He wasn't looking for more money or goods from Philippi. He wanted the believers to know how special their gifts were.

Their gifts not only amply supplied his needs, they would be credited to the Philippians as "a fragrant offering, an acceptable sacrifice, pleasing to God." In this brief statement we find the key to spiritually motivated giving for God's work. Christians give to meet human needs, but their gifts go far beyond that. The act of giving ascends to heaven and is accepted by God as an offering to Him.

When the offering plate is passed, we need to ask if our gifts are an acceptable sacrifice to Almighty God. Sacrifice is the key. Do our gifts bring pleasure to God as a sweet-smelling offering? Not if we give grudgingly, or out of our excess.

Paul added the wonderful promise that if we give sacrificially, beyond what we think we can afford, God will take care of us out of His glorious riches in Christ (vs. 19). This promise greatly encouraged the Philippians in their giving and showed how the fellowship of Christians extends to sacrificial giving for one another.

Discussion Questions

1. Why is it sometimes hard to rejoice?
2. Do you think Paul had unrealistic expectations for Christian joy?
3. It seems simple to say that prayer is the key, but why do we find consistent prayer difficult to practice?
4. What guidelines can we give to help us discipline what we think about?
5. Why is discontentment such a peril to Christian joy?
6. How could Paul's letter change your attitude toward giving?

Contemporary Application

The high calling of God includes peace in the midst of conflict. Personal peace and joy are the priceless privileges of Christians. In light of this, we have to ask why so many are troubled, confused, and worried. Anxiety takes a heavy toll.

Perhaps one reason is that we have missed the simplicity of living by faith in Jesus Christ. We look for many avenues of relief, without calling on Jesus to do what He has promised. We neglect the practice of prayer. We allow our minds to be filled with unworthy ideas. The world forces us into its way of thinking. We have not learned to be content in Christ. We have not learned how to be sacrificially helpful to those in need.

While we prosper outwardly with unparalleled abundance, our souls are lean. That's why we need God's reminder to allow His peace and joy to control our lives. It's a matter of faith to believe that Jesus wants to give us His strength for whatever life may bring. The secret of joy and peace is Jesus.

Called to Spiritual Blessings in Christ

Scripture

Background Scripture: *Ephesians 1*
Scripture Lesson: *Ephesians 1:1-14*
Key Verse: *Praise be to the God and Father of our Lord Jesus Christ, who has blessed us in the heavenly realms with every spiritual blessing in Christ.* Ephesians 1:3.
Key Verse for Children: *He [God] predestined us to be adopted as his sons through Jesus Christ.* Ephesians 1:5.

Lesson Aim

To live by the great facts of God's blessings in Christ.

Lesson Setting

Time: *Between A.D. 60 and 62*
Place: *Written to Ephesus from Rome*

Lesson Outline

Called to Spiritual Blessings in Christ
  I. Paul's Greeting: Ephesians 1:1-2
      A. An Apostle of Christ: vs. 1
      B. Grace and Peace: vs. 2
  II. What God Has Done: Ephesians 1:3-10
      A. Blessed Us in Christ: vs. 3
      B. Chose Us to be Holy and Blameless: vs. 4
      C. Adopted Us as Sons: vs. 5
      D. Gave Us Grace: vs. 6
      E. Gave Us Redemption and Forgiveness: vss. 7-8
      F. Planned to Bring All Things under Christ: vss. 9-10
  III. Our Destiny in Christ: Ephesians 1:11-14
      A. To Live for His Glory: vss. 11-12
      B. To Receive Our Inheritance: vss. 13-14

Introduction for Adults

Topic: *Claim Your Spiritual Blessings*

Millions of dollars are given away every year to winners of state lotteries. To claim your prize, you have to produce a ticket showing the winning numbers. On some occasions officials wait for days for someone to show up with a rightful claim to the money. Many weeks no one claims the prize, because no one matches the numbers, and the jackpot is rolled over.

From the madness surrounding multimillion-dollar prizes, one would think the lottery is the biggest thing you could ever win in your life. Meanwhile, what is really the biggest jackpot of all often goes unclaimed. It is a prize that brings lasting satisfaction and eternal life—nothing a lottery prize can ever do for you.

People fail to realize what God has done for them in Christ, so they do not claim the wealth that comes from faith in Him. The multitude of God's blessings in Christ are waiting to be claimed, and you do not need to buy a lottery ticket to win. God has blessed believers in Christ with every spiritual blessing. The question is, what do we value?

Introduction for Youths

Topic: *That's the Spirit!*

This is the time of year when young people set their sights on the future. Many start new jobs or new educational programs. Their goal is to claim the best opportunities that life offers them.

One young man who graduated from college had his heart set on playing professional baseball, but when none of the Major League teams drafted him, his dream was smashed. What should he do? Because he was committed to Christ, he sought God's will. He entered graduate school in theology and began an internship working with his church's youth. Two years later he was on his way to a foreign country to coach baseball and to introduce kids to Christ.

Most important was his basic decision to follow God's will. At this season of life we must make clear that all of our choices for the future must be committed to God's good and perfect will. Because He has chosen us to be His sons and daughters, we can accept and do His will with supreme confidence.

Concepts for Children

Topic: *We Are God's Children*

1. The greatest thing in life is to belong to God's family by faith in Jesus.
2. Living in His family means enjoying forgiveness of our sins and eternal life.
3. Knowing God loves and accepts us means we can accept ourselves as valuable in His sight.
4. Sisters and brothers take care of one another in God's family, too.
5. God's loving pleasure enables us to live for His glory.
6. We know that God works to bring all things under the lordship of Christ.

The Lesson Commentary

I. PAUL'S GREETING: EPHESIANS 1:1-2

A. An Apostle of Christ: vs. 1

Paul, an apostle of Christ Jesus by the will of God, to the saints in Ephesus, the faithful in Christ Jesus.

Paul wrote this letter about A.D. 62 while he was under house arrest in Rome. Although the letter takes its name from the church at Ephesus, where Paul had a significant ministry, it seems that it was intended as a circular letter for a number of other churches in the area as well. Ephesus was one of the three great cities of the eastern Mediterranean, along with Alexandria, Egypt, and Antioch, Syria.

At the close of his second missionary journey, Paul spent a weekend at Ephesus, bringing Priscilla and Aquila with him. Leaving them there, he promised he would return (Acts 18:18-21). On his third missionary journey he stayed at Ephesus three years (Acts 19; 20:31). On his last voyage to Jerusalem he touched at Miletus, thirty miles south of Ephesus, where he gave his last instructions to the Ephesian elders (Acts 20:17-38).

In his greeting, Paul first identified himself as an apostle of Christ Jesus. He was not a self-appointed apostle, but became one by God's will. "Apostle" derives from the Greek verb, *apostello*, which means "to send." More precisely, *apostello* came to mean "to send with a particular purpose." Therefore, the force of "apostle" is "one commissioned," that is, by Jesus Christ. This was the essence of Paul's testimony in Acts 26:17-18. His encounter with Jesus and his obedience to God's will were the cornerstones of his life, and the basis of his authority in the churches he established.

Paul greeted his readers as "saints" and "the faithful." In his letters, Paul used "saints" as an all-inclusive term for believers. The Greek word, *hagios*, has the fundamental meaning of distinctiveness in the world, or of consecration to God. It speaks of holiness of life, of Christlike character. The New Testament everywhere emphasizes the ethical character of holiness. All Christians are made holy by Christ's death.

B. Grace and Peace: vs. 2

Grace and peace to you from God our Father and the Lord Jesus Christ.

Paul's greeting was also a blessing. He brought grace and peace from God the Father and the Lord Jesus Christ. The believers at Ephesus had received grace and peace when they received the Gospel.

Paul's greeting reminded them that grace and peace are not static theological concepts, but the driving force of everyday life. Each day God's children are to enjoy living with the manifold blessings of His grace and peace. God's grace gives them forgiveness; His peace enables them to live with security and confidence.

II. What God Has Done: Ephesians 1:3-10

A. Blessed Us in Christ: vs. 3

Praise be to the God and Father of our Lord Jesus Christ, who has blessed us in the heavenly realms with every spiritual blessing in Christ.

Paul immediately launched into a magnificent description of what God has done for believers in Christ. There is nothing quite like this profile in all of Scripture. It surveys all that accrues to people the moment they commit themselves to Christ, not just for "super" Christians, but of every one of God's children.

Paul began with a general call to thanksgiving and praise to God for all He has done. Praise is God's antidote to fear and doubt. These facts are true, whether we feel good or not.

Paul cited the source of our blessings ("in the heavenly realms") and the scope of our blessings ("every spiritual blessing in Christ"). God's salvation plan issued from heaven. He sent His Son Jesus from heaven to be our Savior and Lord. Jesus rose from the dead and returned to heaven, where He carries on His work for us. Heaven is the object of our desires and our eternal home. "Set your hearts on things above, where Christ is seated at the right hand of God. Set your minds on things above, not on earthly things," Paul said (Col. 3:1-2).

In Christ we have received all we shall ever need for our spiritual growth and welfare. We cannot own more than we already possess. Everything in Christ is ours. This is the cornerstone of our Christian faith and experience. Yet, paradoxically, we are told to grow in the grace and knowledge of Christ (2 Pet. 3:18), which means we have to be diligent in using our unlimited blessings in Christ. Weak Christians are poverty-stricken, not because they have not been supremely blessed in Christ, but because they do not walk in obedience and love with Him. They possess ultimate spiritual riches, but do not use them.

B. Chose Us to Be Holy and Blameless: vs. 4

For he chose us in him before the creation of the world to be holy and blameless in his sight.

Paul followed his call to praise by spelling out what he meant by "every spiritual blessing in Christ." He began by reaching back "before the creation of the world" to find God's choice of His children to be holy and blameless.

God made His choice of us *in Christ*. We cannot be holy and blameless on our own. Our holiness rests entirely on Jesus. God made Him to be our righteousness (1 Cor. 1:30; 2 Cor. 5:21). Therefore, that's our standing in Christ.

Are we blessed by being made holy and blameless? This is the basis of our security before God's judgment. God sees believers not in our sins but clothed in Christ's perfection (Heb. 10:10). Therefore, we have eternal fellowship with the Father because of what He has done for us in Christ. We can do nothing of our own efforts to add to this blessing. Since we know why God chose us, we live according to His holy standards.

C. Adopted Us as Sons: vs. 5

In love he predestined us to be adopted as his sons through Jesus Christ, in accordance with his pleasure and will.

The next great blessing we have in Christ is God's adoption of us as His children. He did this according to His "pleasure and will" fixed in eternity past ("predestined us"). God's choice to adopt us was rooted in His good and perfect will. He does all things for His pleasure. We are not His children because we deserve the honor.

His adoption plan became effective with the Gospel of Christ. When God the Father sent His Son to die for our sins, He made it possible to receive us into His family. Otherwise, there would be no hope for us. Sin separates us eternally from God. Our willful disobedience alienates us from Him. But when we receive Christ, He gives us the authority to become His sons and daughters (John 1:12). This is the heart of the Gospel. This is what the new birth is all about.

D. Gave Us Grace: vs. 6

To the praise of his glorious grace, which he has freely given us in the One he loves.

God's adoption of us is intended to inspire our praise of "his glorious grace." God's grace simply means that He gives us what we do not deserve and can never earn. We can never be good enough to earn God's favor. Instead, we glorify and magnify the wonders of His grace, never ceasing to give Him praise, honor, and glory.

We experience God's grace in many ways, but supremely in Jesus Christ. God's grace in Christ is free. A member of a New York street gang once remarked that the greatest thing about the Gospel is that salvation is free, you don't have to pay anything for it.

E. Gave Us Redemption and Forgiveness: vss. 7-8

In him we have redemption through his blood, the forgiveness of sins, in accordance with the riches of God's grace that he lavished on us with all wisdom and understanding.

God's choice to bless us is not religious speculation. It is rooted in history. Our security rests in what Jesus Christ did for us when He was on earth. So Paul pointed to Christ's death on the cross ("his blood") as the effective means by which God carried out the pleasure of His will. All of our blessings in Christ depend on Christ's willingness to suffer death for us.

Our blessings include redemption and forgiveness. Redemption means that God purchased us for Himself, and Christ's death was His payment. Otherwise, we are doomed to live in Satan's control and in his kingdom of darkness. Christ's blood satisfied the demands of God's righteousness. "The wages of sin is death" (Rom. 6:23) and that's the price Jesus paid on our behalf. Because of Christ's death, a holy and righteous God can forgive us for our sins and offenses against Him.

Paul attributed the blessings of redemption and forgiveness to the richness of God's grace lavished upon us. However, unless we tap the wealth of His grace in Christ, we cannot be redeemed and forgiven. Faith in Jesus locks us into God's unbounded wealth, wisdom, and understanding.

F. Planned to Bring All Things under Christ: vss. 9-10

And he made known to us the mystery of his will according to his good pleasure, which he purposed in Christ, to be put into effect when the times will have reached their fulfillment—to bring all things in heaven and on earth together under one head, even Christ.

Paul looked from the past to the consummation of all things in eternity future. He noted that the revelation of the future was God's mystery until the Gospel came in Christ. Again, the future rests in God's "good pleasure," which is anchored in Christ.

We cannot contemplate the future without Jesus at the center. He is the focal point of all history. Everything will be brought under His headship.

Paul did not speculate when Christ will return to rule everything in heaven and on earth. He was content to trust God to know when the time is ripe. We don't know when this will happen, but our confidence is in God's will and power. Therefore, we rejoice in the blessing of knowing what the future holds for us and the world.

III. OUR DESTINY IN CHRIST: EPHESIANS 1:11-14

A. To Live for His Glory: vss. 11-12

In him we were also chosen, having been predestined according to the plan of him who works out everything in conformity with the purpose of his will, in order that we, who were the first to hope in Christ, might be for the praise of his glory.

To be sure that his readers did not miss his main point, Paul summarized their duty in light of the facts about their blessings in Christ. It comes at the end of vs. 12: that we "might be for the praise of his (God's) glory."

He rehearsed the wonders of God's eternal plan. He reaffirmed the sovereignty of God's purposes. God did all of this so that those who "hope in Christ" will live to bring praise to God's glory. In the light of all that God has done for us in Christ, we must somehow cause His glory to be praised.

Christians do this as they worship together, in their hymns and prayers, and in their testimonies to God's saving grace. They live for His glory by the way they conform to His moral and ethical demands. They praise His glory by honoring Jesus in all they do. They praise Him by loving Him above everything else.

B. To Receive Our Inheritance: vss. 13-14

And you also were included in Christ when you heard the word of truth, the gospel of your salvation. Having believed, you were marked in him with a seal, the promised Holy Spirit, who is a deposit guaranteeing our inheritance until the redemption of those who are God's possession—to the praise of his glory.

For the first time Paul described how the Ephesians had responded. What was their part in God's wise and loving plan? They heard the Gospel ("the word of truth") and they believed it. This act of mind and will ushered them into all of the blessings just described.

Faith also affords us the "seal" of the Holy Spirit. He comes to live in Christians. Part of His work is to assure us of our eternal inheritance in Christ. Of course, the Holy Spirit guides, corrects, and comforts us, but He also serves as a deposit, or down payment, of our inheritance.

What lies ahead? The redemption of all those who belong to God in Christ. This will be the fruition of God's eternal plan from eternity past. Paul described this more fully in Romans 8:22-23.

Discussion Questions

1. In what ways do Christians experience God's grace and peace?
2. How does God's choice of us to be holy and blameless affect how we live?
3. Why is it so difficult to accept grace?
4. How do we invite others to respond to God's invitation to become His sons?
5. What does it mean to live to the praise of God's glory?
6. What difference does it make that our future inheritance is guaranteed?

Contemporary Application

How quickly our culture saturates our minds with "truths" that affect our wills and emotions. Every day we are bombarded with messages about how to stay well, how to get rich, how to succeed, how to be popular, and so forth. When things don't work out the way these messages suggest, we wonder what's wrong with us.

As Christians, we can't escape these messages about the world's values, so we have to fortify our minds with the facts God has revealed to us. God's truths are not broadcast the same way the world's ads are, so we have to work hard to set aside time to think God's thoughts.

Every day we can pick up our Bibles and build our faith. We can read texts like Ephesians 1 and rejoice in the goodness of the Lord. We can realize that the really important things in life are God's choice of us to be His children, His incomparable blessings in Christ, His redemption and forgiveness, and His guarantee of an eternal inheritance. When we think about these things, somehow what the world tells us fades into insignificance. Our lives achieve purpose, order, and composure. We find grace and peace.

Called to Oneness in Christ

DEVOTIONAL READING

John 17:1-11, 20-23

DAILY BIBLE READINGS

Monday July 3
Ephesians 2:1-10 Saved and Made Alive by Grace

Tuesday July 4
Ephesians 2:11-16 One Body in Jesus Christ

Wednesday July 5
Ephesians 2:17-22 God Dwells in You

Thursday July 6
John 17:1-6 Jesus Commits Disciples to God's Care

Friday July 7
John 17:7-13 Jesus Prays for the Disciples' Protection

Saturday July 8
John 17:14-21 Jesus Prays for the Disciples' Unity

Sunday July 9
John 17:22-26 May God's Love Be in Christ's Disciples

Scripture

Background Scripture: *Ephesians 2*
Scripture Lesson: *Ephesians 2:8-22*
Key Verse: *Consequently, you are no longer foreigners and aliens, but fellow citizens with God's people and members of God's household.* Ephesians 2:19.
Key Verse for Children: *Consequently, you are . . . members of God's household.* Ephesians 2:19.

Lesson Aim

To bring to peace all the differences with our fellow Christians.

Lesson Setting

Time: *Between A.D. 60 and 62*
Place: *Written to Ephesus from Rome*

Lesson Outline

Called to Oneness in Christ
   I. God's Workmanship: Ephesians 2:8-10
      A. He Saved Us: vss. 8-9
      B. He Created Us to Do Good Works: vs. 10
  II. From Exclusion to Inclusion: Ephesians 2:11-13
      A. Separate from Christ: vss. 11-12
      B. Joined to Christ: vs. 13
 III. The Accomplishments of Jesus: Ephesians 2:14-18
      A. He Made the Two One: vss. 14-15a
      B. He Created One New Man: vs. 15b
      C. He Put Hostility to Death: vs. 16
      D. He Preached Peace: vs. 17
      E. He Gave Access to the Father: vs. 18
 IV. The Blessings of God's Family: Ephesians 2:19-22
      A. Common Citizenship: vs. 19
      B. Common Foundation: vs. 20
      C. Common Builder: vs. 21
      D. Common Purpose: vs. 22

Introduction for Adults

Topic: *Claim Your New Status*

Human differences are a fact of life, and we spend most of our lives trying to accommodate them. Of course, some people never do. In extreme cases, people fight and die to keep their distinctives alive. Even when our differences do not lead to bloodshed, they cause unhappiness and despair.

Looking at how hard it is to resolve problems brought on by racial, religious, national, and economic differences, we are tempted to say there is no hope. But the Gospel of Jesus Christ offers us the only hope we have to bring people together, despite their differences.

Our mission as Christians is to help people really understand who Jesus is and what He can do. Of course, we have to claim our new status as part of God's family. We have to demonstrate in Christ's body how we can overcome our differences. We must never give up on God's plan to bring people together in peace and harmony under Christ's lordship.

Introduction for Youths

Topic: *All For One!*

"All for one and one for all" is a great rallying cry for French musketeers, political movements, and football teams. It sounds so wonderful. It assumes that each individual will willingly lay aside his or her own preferences for the sake of a common goal.

But when we allow the Lord Jesus Christ to break down barriers, we do much more than paper over our differences. We have to confess and acknowledge that barriers and hostility do exist. We have to admit that unless we allow Jesus to change us from within, we won't be able to achieve oneness in human relationships.

Because Jesus gives us new hearts and new motivations, we can seek His help and power to get along with everyone, regardless of our differences. We accept people as they are, and see them as objects of God's love in the Gospel. We refuse to see ourselves as superior in any way. Rather, we show humility and love, demonstrating Christlikeness to people who are very different from ourselves.

Concepts for Children

Topic: *Members of God's Family*

1. Because we believe in Jesus, we can enjoy fellowship with others in His family.
2. The church is made up of people with many social differences.
3. The church is the only body where membership does not depend on exclusive human qualifications.
4. The Lord Jesus breaks down barriers that divide people.
5. Jesus asks us to do His work of loving and accepting all people.
6. Belonging to God's family brings special responsibilities to care for and build up each other.

The Lesson Commentary

I. GOD'S WORKMANSHIP: EPHESIANS 2:8-10

A. He Saved Us: vss. 8-9

For it is by grace you have been saved, through faith—and this not from yourselves, it is the gift of God—not by works, so that no one can boast.

Paul prayed that believers would understand "the riches of (their) glorious inheritance" in Christ (1:18). We have already glimpsed what those riches include (1:1-14). In chapter two of Ephesians, Paul cited two outcomes of our inheritance: (1) new life in Christ (2:1-10), and (2) new unity in Christ (2:11-22).

The foundation of Christian unity is God's gift of salvation by faith alone. Every believer comes to God by the same route—faith plus nothing. "Not by works" means that no one can ever be "good enough" to merit salvation. No amount of charitable works and good deeds will qualify anyone for heaven. It doesn't matter if our good deeds outweigh the bad stuff 99 percent to 1! We are still entirely dependent on God's grace. We do not earn salvation; it is a gift from God, to be received with gratitude.

B. He Created Us to Do Good Works: vs. 10

For we are God's workmanship, created in Christ Jesus to do good works, which God prepared in advance for us to do.

Christian doctrine is very clear: We are not saved by good works, but good works are expected to follow our conversion.

God's grace comes to the forefront because our good works really are His good works. In fact, God has prepared His "good works" agenda for us. This fact offers tremendous release from trying hard to please God. Instead, we ask Him to show us what His agenda is. Then we seek to do what He wants us to do.

Paul's picture of God's new community rests on a solid theological foundation: salvation by faith alone and good works by faith alone. Without this foundation, there is no hope of achieving the unity He described for the church.

II. FROM EXCLUSION TO INCLUSION: EPHESIANS 2:11-13

A. Separate from Christ: vss. 11-12

Therefore, remember that formerly you who are Gentiles by birth and called "uncircumcised" by those who call themselves "the circumcision" (that done in the body by the hands of men)—remember that at that time you were separate from Christ, excluded from citizenship in Israel and foreigners to the covenants of the promise, without hope and without God in the world.

Prior to coming to faith in Christ, Gentiles were not only cut off from Christ, but they were also beyond the promises God had given to Israel. The differences between Gentiles and Jews were both physical (Gentiles were not circumcised like the Jews were) and spiritual. The Jews had been the recipients of God's choice beginning with Abraham. "The covenants of promise" were given to the Jews, not to the Gentiles. These promises included both national and spiritual blessings, the greatest of which was the hope of Messiah's coming.

B. Joined to Christ: vs. 13

But now in Christ Jesus you who once were far away have been brought near through the blood of Christ.

Now, however, the Gentiles have been brought into God's family and inherited His promises. They came the same way Jewish believers had come—by faith in Christ as a gift from God. The key is being "in Christ."

The Gentiles who were once excluded are now included, thanks to the blood of Christ. "Far away" refers to how lost we are apart from Christ, while "brought near" refers to our salvation. No longer without hope and without God, we are joined to Christ because of His suffering and death for us on the cross.

Of course, the "you" in this verse refers to Gentile believers. We have to appreciate what an astonishing fact this was for the Jewish believers in the church to accept and assimilate. The early church leaders argued over this point. Peter received a vision from the Lord to convince him to preach to the Gentiles (Acts 10). He had to defend his actions before the church in Jerusalem (chap. 11). The Jerusalem Council debated the issue (chap. 15). However, their decision to welcome Gentile believers into the church without requiring adherence to the laws of Moses did not sit well with everyone in the church.

III. THE ACCOMPLISHMENTS OF JESUS: EPHESIANS 2:14-18

A. He Made the Two One: vss. 14-15a

For he himself is our peace, who has made the two one and has destroyed the barrier, the dividing wall of hostility, by abolishing in his flesh the law with its commandments and regulations.

Paul's effort to bring Gentile and Jewish believers together in the church rested on what Jesus Christ has done for both groups. Through His reconciling death on the cross He "made the two one." This monumental accomplishment shattered long-standing barriers and hostility between them.

The barriers and the hostilities were rooted in thousands of years of traditions. Of course, God had told His people Israel to stay away from the gods and immoral practices of the surrounding Gentiles. He prohibited intermarriage. At the same time, however, God instructed the Jews to be hospitable to Gentile aliens, and the prophets foresaw the time when God's kingdom would include Gentiles.

However, by the time of Jesus and Paul, the concept of Jewish separation had become so warped that it amounted to racial and religious prejudice. For example, Jews would not enter Gentile homes. They erected an impregnable social wall around themselves. Instead of bringing spiritual light to the Gentiles, the Jews had consigned them to outer darkness.

For the Jews, of course, the law was the dividing wall between them and the

Gentiles. Jesus broke down the law by abolishing it "in his flesh." The law was a wall because it embodied God's judgment of human sin. But when He died on the cross, Jesus fulfilled the requirements of the law—a blood sacrifice for sin—and thus abolished the law's power to condemn us. He did not set aside God's eternal moral principles. He brought God's way for us to be righteous before God.

B. He Created One New Man: vs. 15b

His purpose was to create in himself one new man out of the two, thus making peace.

Peace between Jews and Gentiles could only be achieved by the work of Jesus. He did it by creating a new humanity in Himself. This spiritual creation is His body, the Church. God, in effect, created a new race of people when Jesus came. Part of the Gospel's power includes taking radically different people and making them one. Keep in mind that God's "one new man" is not a human creation. This is a divine creation attainable only in the Lord Jesus Christ.

C. He Put Hostility to Death: vs. 16

And in this one body to reconcile both of them to God through the cross, by which he put to death their hostility.

No one living in the days of Jesus and Paul would ever have imagined that the hostility between Jews and Gentiles could be wiped out. In our time, it would be the same as saying that the enmity between Jews and Arabs will disappear. But the cross of Christ marked an end to any reason for hostility, and made reconciliation between the enemies possible.

This reconciliation takes place in Christ's "one body," the church. Those who have been redeemed and forgiven "in Christ" must love and forgive one another "in Christ." In Christ, we are God's new creation; the old assumptions and attitudes have passed away (2 Cor. 5:17).

D. He Preached Peace: vs. 17

He came and preached peace to you who were far away and peace to those who were near.

When Jesus was born, the angels announced peace. Jesus preached peace in the sense that He offered Himself as the only way to have peace with God, and the only valid way to live at peace with one another. When we receive the Gospel, sin—the barrier to peace—is forgiven. We are made righteous in Christ. Therefore, in His righteousness we can have peace with people of different backgrounds.

Jesus preached to those "far away," that is, to Gentiles, and to those "who were near," that is, the Jews. They were "near" in the sense that they had the advantages of the Messianic promises of the prophets (Rom. 1:2).

E. He Gave Access to the Father: vs. 18

For through him we both have access to the Father by one Spirit.

By His death on the cross and by His resurrection and ascension into heaven,

Jesus opened the way to God. This is the heart of the Gospel. Sin barred the door to God for Jews and Gentiles alike (Rom. 2). Jesus is called a new and living way to God (Heb. 10:20). He Himself said He was the only way to God (John 14:6).

Note Paul's emphasis on oneness in Christ's body: "we both (that is, Jews and Gentiles) have access to the Father." The same Holy Spirit indwells believers from all backgrounds. Since we have the same Spirit, we are one.

IV. THE BLESSINGS OF GOD'S FAMILY: EPHESIANS 2:19-22

A. Common Citizenship: vs. 19

Consequently, you are no longer foreigners and aliens, but fellow citizens with God's people and members of God's household.

After listing all that Jesus did to bring about oneness, Paul presented four blessings that result from our unity in Christ's new humanity. The first is common citizenship. Outside of Christ, we are like aliens in a foreign land. In Christ, we are fellow-citizens with all God's people and members of His family. Therefore, when we have to pass God's immigration inspection, we gain entrance to His kingdom because of what Jesus has done for us.

B. Common Foundation: vs. 20

Built on the foundation of the apostles and prophets, with Christ Jesus himself as the chief cornerstone.

Paul changed the metaphor from family to building, from household to house. Christ's church stands on the secure foundation of what the prophets and the apostles revealed as God's word. The church did not originate with any human ideas. Its doctrines were revealed by God. Therefore, we have complete confidence in our foundation.

We also are secure because Jesus Himself is our chief cornerstone. He is our only hope of salvation. He alone offers pardon, forgiveness, righteousness, and eternal life. He is the one of whom the prophets spoke. He fulfilled the Old Testament promises. He is the one through whom we come to know God.

C. Common Builder: vs. 21

In him the whole building is joined together and rises to become a holy temple in the Lord.

All of us in the church are blessed by the work of our common builder, the Lord Jesus. The church is built on Him and lives in Him. The people of the church are a holy temple to the Lord. They are not separate pieces of wood and plaster. Jesus is the head of the church. In Christ "all things hold together" (Col. 1:17). Therefore, all of our worship and service center in Him.

D. Common Purpose: vs. 22

And in him you too are being built together to become a dwelling in which God lives by his Spirit.

This magnificent vision shows God's purpose for the church. The great expectation is that all believers, regardless of race, nationality, and social background, will be "built together" to become God's dwelling. Difficult as it sometimes appears to be, God lives in the unity of His people in the church. This is why our oneness is not optional. It must come first, because that is God's desire for us.

It will help us if we look at the "before" and "after" of Paul's discussion. He began with our being dead in sin and cut off from God. He moved to the wonder of salvation by faith alone, and the call to do good works as a result. He described the terrible hostility between Jews and Gentiles. Then step-by-step he showed all that Jesus has done to reconcile us and to create a new humanity out of these former enemies. He concluded by bringing all of us together in God's family and in His holy temple. The Gospel shows that all people can be built together into God's dwelling place.

Discussion Questions

1. What causes separation between God and us? Between others and ourselves?
2. How do religious traditions separate people?
3. How can we help people to understand the difference between tradition and a personal knowledge of God through faith in Christ?
4. What kinds of differences need to be reconciled in your church? How?
5. What must both parties do to bring peace? How can we be peacemakers?
6. How can Christians show practically that they have been created "one new man" in Christ?

Contemporary Application

Jesus takes total strangers and makes them into a family. Our church life is intended to reflect this fact. Jesus has done everything to make good family relations possible in the church.

However, we have to confess that sometimes we fall short of achieving His will. To our shame, we have to admit that our divisions stand out more than our oneness. In the church we sometimes treat fellow believers as though they are our enemies. How tragic when we attack one another and spread gossip and build party spirits.

Therefore, we all need to receive a fresh vision of God's ideal. In Christ, He has brought us together and broken down the barriers between us. His church is supposed to work like a unified body, not like a splintered group of individuals.

How can we achieve God's purpose? By listening to the Lord Jesus instead of giving in to our selfish desires. Cleansed and forgiven by Jesus, we are free from sin's power in this regard.

Called to Use Your Spiritual Gifts

DEVOTIONAL READING

Ephesians 3:14-21

DAILY BIBLE READINGS

Monday July 10
Ephesians 3:1-6 Gentiles Are Fellow Heirs in Christ

Tuesday July 11
Ephesians 3:7-13 Gentiles Receive the Gospel's Riches

Wednesday July 12
Ephesians 3:14-21 Paul Prays for the Ephesian Christians

Thursday July 13
Ephesians 4:1-10 Unity in the Body of Christ

Friday July 14
Ephesians 4:11-16 Grow to Maturity in Christ Jesus

Saturday July 15
Ephesians 4:17-24 Live in Righteousness and Holiness

Sunday July 16
Ephesians 4:25-32 Live a New Life in Christ

Scripture

Background Scripture: *Ephesians 4:1-16*
Scripture Lesson: *Ephesians 4:1-16*
Key Verse: *But to each one of us grace has been given as Christ apportioned it.* Ephesians 4:7.
Key Verse for Children: *In all things grow up into him . . . that is, Christ.* Ephesians 4:15.

Lesson Aim

To build the body of Christ by using our spiritual gifts.

Lesson Setting

Time: *Between A.D. 60 and 62*
Place: *Written to Ephesus from Rome*

Lesson Outline

Called to Use Your Spiritual Gifts

   I. Unity in the Church: Ephesians 4:1-6
     A. The Command: vss. 1-3
     B. The Foundation: vss. 4-6
  II. Gifts to the Church: Ephesians 4:7-13
     A. The Work of Christ: vss. 7-10
     B. Gifted Leaders: vs. 11
     C. Their Function: vss. 12-13
 III. Growth in the Church: Ephesians 4:14-16
     A. Hindrances to Growth: vs. 14
     B. Goal of Growth: vss. 15-16

Introduction for Adults

Topic: *Claim Your Ministry*

If you served in the Army, you know that the Army has a designated code for every soldier. It's called your MOS (Military Occupation Specialty). Your MOS number determines what you do in the Army. In other words, every single soldier is assumed to play an essential role in the Army's overall plan.

The church works something like that too. In one sense, the Lord Jesus Christ has assigned an essential role to every believer. The effectiveness of the church depends to a large degree on how each member carries out that role.

Of course, there is a major difference between the Army and the church. The latter is a voluntary fellowship of people who have confessed their faith in Christ. No one can say to you when you join the church, "Here is your job. Now do it, or else!" Instead, the voluntary fellowship depends on each member's willingness to find and use her or his spiritual gifts to build the spiritual vitality of the church.

Introduction for Youths

Topic: *Use Your Gifts!*

When we raise our children, we have certain hopes for them: good health, sound minds, happiness, faith in Christ, and eventually responsible maturity and independence. We also pray that they will find and use their spiritual gifts.

Some health clubs are filled with expensive equipment designed to build the muscles and stamina of high school athletes. One admires these young people's dedication and hard work to achieve excellence in athletics. Some of them, it seems, will endure anything to gain an edge on their fellow athletes.

In the same way, we can help teenagers in our churches to develop and use their spiritual gifts. This does not mean we try to push them into a certain career path or religious vocation. Rather, it means we try to help them focus on what the really important goals in life are. In the long term, we want them to become more and more like Jesus, whatever they do. We want them to use their education and their vocational and professional skills for the growth and advancement of God's kingdom. Along the way, we shall have to give them increasing responsibilities in the church.

Concepts for Children

Topic: *Grow Up in Christ*

1. God wants us to grow spiritually as we grow physically.
2. Part of growing up spiritually is learning to serve Jesus in the church.
3. As we pray and talk with friends, we can learn what God wants us to do.
4. We can also work outside the church to reach those who do not know Jesus.
5. Since Jesus is the head of the church, He assigns us to various responsibilities.
6. Our spiritual gifts include not only teaching and preaching, but also praying with and encouraging one another to be faithful to Jesus.

The Lesson Commentary

I. UNITY IN THE CHURCH: EPHESIANS 4:1-6

A. The Command: vss. 1-3

As a prisoner for the Lord, then, I urge you to live a life worthy of the calling you have received. Be completely humble and gentle; be patient, bearing with one another in love. Make every effort to keep the unity of the Spirit through the bond of peace.

In the first three chapters of Ephesians the apostle Paul described the many values inherent in becoming a Christian. In the last three chapters he took a more practical turn. He related Christian doctrine to a number of pressing matters of ethics and morality.

In the first part of chapter four he called for unity of Christian life and experience. Then he showed how unity is manifested in the exercise of our spiritual gifts for the mutual upbuilding of the church. Paul saw a lack of maturity among the Ephesians. He wanted them to see how they could stand together in the faith and grow together in the use of their spiritual gifts and ministries.

Interestingly, Paul based his call for Christian unity on his status as a prisoner for Christ. Their calling to faith in Christ was a gift from God that conferred certain responsibilities on them (2:8-10). The whole tone of their lives was to demonstrate Christ's call and His ownership of their lives. He urged them to live up to their high calling in Christ. When other people saw them, they were to see unmistakable signs of Jesus. (If someone accused you of being a Christian, would there be enough evidence to "convict" you?)

In this text Paul named certain characteristics of our Christian calling. This is not a complete list of Christian virtues, but these are fundamental to our calling: humility, gentleness, patience, and forbearance. In his letters, Paul returned to these themes again and again (4:25-32; Phil. 2:1-4; Col. 3:12-14). Paul then added that part of our calling is to live in unity and peace with one another in the church. (Of course, if we are humble, gentle, patient, and forbearing, unity and peace will be easier to achieve. People will not fight for their own rights, criticize others, and lose their tempers.)

Achieving unity and peace requires hard work. However, our task is not to put on an outward appearance of unity, but to "keep" the unity we already have in the Holy Spirit. Our task is to so live at peace with one another that we will not destroy our spiritual unity. We are one in Christ, so we must live together in light of that fact.

B. The Foundation: vss. 4-6

There is one body and one Spirit—just as you were called to one hope when you were called—one Lord, one faith, one baptism; one God and Father of all, who is over all and through all and in all.

If we were to make a sign indicating the major characteristic of the Church, it might simply say "ONE." Seven times Paul used the word "one" to describe who we are as Christians. But do Christian people appear to be one? The fact that we sometimes fail does not alter the truth of God's Word.

One body (Christ's Church), one Holy Spirit, one hope of eternal salvation, one Lord (Jesus Christ), one common faith, one baptism into Christ's body, and one God and Father. These are the great foundation stones of our unity. These are the reasons why we are called to keep the unity of the Spirit. Without these truths there is no way to live in unity.

These truths supersede our denominational distinctives and our historic church traditions. While we are free to choose the local church that we want to join, we are not free to emphasize its distinctives over what God has revealed here. When that happens, we fracture Christ's body. We have to confess that we are Christians first, and Presbyterians or Baptists or whatever second.

To look at it another way, there are not many bodies of Christ, not many Holy Spirits, many Christs, many faiths, many baptisms, and many gods. Because unbelievers sometimes get that impression from us, we have to redouble our efforts to show that we really are one in Christ, despite our different church labels.

II. GIFTS TO THE CHURCH: EPHESIANS 4:7-13

A. The Work of Christ: vss. 7-10

But to each one of us grace has been given as Christ apportioned it. This is why it says: "When he ascended on high, he led captives in his train and gave gifts to men." (What does "he ascended" mean except that he also descended to the lower, earthly regions? He who descended is the very one who ascended higher than all the heavens, in order to fill the whole universe.)

Paul emphasized what Christians have in common. Then he added an important fact in verse 7: Christ's gifts to Christians are personal and individual. He has assigned grace-gifts to every believer. Many Christians, of course, have received similar gifts. Our task is to use our spiritual gifts in unique ways according to our personalities, skills, qualifications, education, and experience.

Paul then quoted Psalm 68:18 and applied it as a prophecy of what Jesus has done for His church. His main point was to show that in giving gifts to His people Jesus was doing something consistent with Scripture. This was an important point for the apostles to establish with Jewish believers.

At this point Paul went beyond the subject of spiritual gifts and explained his quotation from Psalm 68. The picture is of a triumphant warrior lifted to his throne as he returns from battle with his prisoners. He has received gifts from the people he conquered and he is passing out gifts to his loyal followers. Paul applied this to the ascension of Jesus to heaven after His descent to the "lower" regions (which some take to mean Hades, though the NIV apparently takes it to mean the earth). He previously described Christ's exaltation over all things in 1:20-23.

Paul wanted to establish that the work of Christ in apportioning gifts to the Church was no insignificant thing, and was part of His larger cosmic ministry of defeating sin, death, and Satan. Christ alone is worthy of establishing the purpose of believers to do His work in the Church. When we serve His Church, we are not carrying out a human assignment.

B. Gifted Leaders: vs. 11

It was he who gave some to be apostles, some to be prophets, some to be evangelists, and some to be pastors and teachers.

Paul then listed some of the gifted people Jesus gave to the Church. Keep in mind that verse 7 says "each one of us" has received a grace-gift. Paul picked out four leadership roles in the Church to illustrate his point. If we do not fall into one of these roles, that doesn't mean Jesus has not gifted us. In his letters to Corinth and Rome Paul listed other spiritual gifts (1 Cor. 12; Rom. 12).

Jesus had said that He would build His church and this is how He does it. This is an important truth, lest anyone think the church functions merely as a business organization. Church ministry is not a human work alone. Humans do the work, of course, but Jesus gives them the necessary wisdom, skills, and spiritual insights for their service.

Apostles, of course, were those first chosen by Jesus to be with Him and to do ministry under His direction. Later on, some others—including Paul—were also called apostles. This special group was unique in Christ's plan for His church. Essentially, they proclaimed foundational truth. Paul was instrumental in spreading the Gospel throughout the Mediterranean basin, while other apostles took the good news eastward into Asia and southwestward into Africa.

Prophets occupied a place of importance second to the apostles. They preached and taught the doctrines of the faith, because in the early years there were no written documents other than the Old Testament. The prophets also spread the Gospel, especially among the Gentiles. For example, Judas and Silas exhorted and confirmed the Gentile believers in Antioch (Acts 15:32).

Evangelists spread the good news as well. Their role is not spelled out, but we can see in Paul's mind that they stood between apostles and prophets on the one hand, and pastors and teachers on the other. But as their title implies, they preached and won people to faith in Christ. They prepared the way for pastors and teachers.

"Pastors" and "teachers" reflect two sides of one ministry, not two. We might call them pastor-teachers. They were involved with local congregations as their shepherds and instructors. This does not mean they never evangelized. They were witnesses to Christ and the Gospel, empowered by the Holy Spirit (Acts 1:8).

C. Their Function: vss. 12-13

To prepare God's people for works of service, so that the body of Christ may be built up until we all reach unity in the faith and in the knowledge of the Son of God and become mature, attaining to the whole measure of the fullness of Christ.

Whatever our specific role or gift, we must keep God's larger goals in sight. First, we are to prepare others so that the church will grow and develop. Second, our long-range goal is bringing people to full spiritual maturity in Christ. Leaders don't do all the work themselves; their main job is to train *all* of God's people for service in the church. Knowing God's blueprint for how the church should work is vitally important. Every believer's gifts are critical for building up Christ's body. We cannot leave this to the professional church staff. Every church needs to be sure that ongoing training and development of all spiritually gifted people is carried out.

What will such a church look like? Paul listed the important characteristics: unity and maturity. Unity is found in our common faith and in the knowledge of our common Savior. Paul's description of maturity explodes our usual attitude toward ministry in the church. We are not playing church. We are moving toward "the fullness of Christ." That's why using our spiritual gifts is so important. If we don't use them, we lose and the whole church suffers. We fail to reach all that Jesus wants to do for us.

III. GROWTH IN THE CHURCH: EPHESIANS 4:14-16

A. Hindrances to Growth: vs. 14

Then we will no longer be infants, tossed back and forth by the waves, and blown here and there by every wind of teaching and by the cunning and craftiness of men in their deceitful scheming.

Sadly, if we don't use our spiritual gifts to build up the body of Christ, some believers won't "grow up." Instead of becoming mature, they will still be spiritual babies. They will be insecure because they are not grounded in Christian truth. Paul compared them to corks bouncing around on the waves.

Immature Christians can be misled with false teaching by enemies of the church. These false teachers are cunning, crafty, and deceitful. This is why we need to use all of our spiritual gifts in the church, to keep ourselves and others from being led astray.

B. Goal of Growth: vss. 15-16

Instead, speaking the truth in love, we will in all things grow up into him who is the Head, that is, Christ. From him the whole body, joined and held together by every supporting ligament, grows and builds itself up in love, as each part does its work.

The answer to false teaching is the truth of the Gospel and the apostles' doctrine. God's Word is our strong defense. But we are not rough with infants; we handle them carefully so they will grow. Using our spiritual gifts means teaching with love, patience, and understanding. Our purpose is growth, not destruction.

Our goal is to promote growth "in all things," to become like the Lord Jesus, our Head, who builds us together. As we consider the importance of using our gifts, we can see why everyone's gift is essential to the welfare of the church. Of course, Christ is the source of our gifts and supplies all we need to serve the church.

Paul used the human body as an illustration. Every gifted church member is like a ligament in the body. The body grows because all parts work together. The same is true of the church. The church is weakened when members fail to serve one another. But when love motivates and permeates our service, everything fits and everyone grows. Our Lord is honored and praised.

Discussion Questions

1. Why is it sometimes hard to keep the unity of the Spirit?
2. Why do we tend to make more of our differences than of what we share in common?
3. How does the fact of our giftedness help us to understand our roles in the church?
4. How can we use our gifts to build up the body?
5. How can we better understand our pastor's role according to Paul's teaching?
6. How does knowing Christ's goal for the church help us to do our part?

Contemporary Application

In our culture, which maximizes individuality and personal fulfillment, the concept of having things in common or working for the larger good is hard to achieve. However, Jesus, the Church's Head, endows individual believers with spiritual gifts, not for their own sakes, but for the sake of His body.

That's why Paul's picture of how we work together to build up the Church is so instructive. Paul's Church body is alive. He sees all believers doing their "works of service." The body's functions are enhanced because all the "supporting ligaments" work together.

Everywhere there is steady growth from infancy to adulthood and maturity in Christ. The body beats with the heartbeat of mutual love and unity. The entire organism throbs with the vital warmth of God's love in Christ.

The secret to making this picture a reality is the Head, the Lord Jesus Christ. Each member "ligament" grows into Him with ever-deepening fellowship, worship, and obedience. From Him each member draws on His fullness for all their needs as they use their spiritual gifts.

Called to Responsible Living

DEVOTIONAL READING

Ephesians 5:6-20

DAILY BIBLE READINGS

Monday July 17
*Ephesians 5:1-5 Turn Your
Backs on Pagan Ways*

Tuesday July 18
*Ephesians 5:6-14 Live as
Children of the Light*

Wednesday July 19
*Ephesians 5:15-20 Serve
and Worship with Thanks*

Thursday July 20
*Ephesians 5:21-27 Words
for Christians in Families*

Friday July 21
*Ephesians 5:28-33 Love as
Christ Loved the Church*

Saturday July 22
*Ephesians 6:1-9 Treat
Everyone with Love and
Respect*

Sunday July 23
*Luke 6:43-49 Hear God's
Word and Obey*

Scripture

Background Scripture: *Ephesians 5—6:4*
Scripture Lesson: *Ephesians 5:1-5, 21-29; 6:1-4*
Key Verse: *Submit to one another out of reverence for
Christ.* Ephesians 5:21.
Key Verse for Children: *Let us love one another, for
love comes from God.* 1 John 4:7.

Lesson Aim

To develop new patterns of obedience to biblical
norms.

Lesson Setting

Time: *Between A.D. 60 and 62*
Place: *Written to Ephesus from Rome*

Lesson Outline

Called to Responsible Living
   I. Christian Conduct: Ephesians 5:1-5
      A. Live a Life of Love: vss. 1-2
      B. Avoid Sexual Immorality: vs. 3
      C. Avoid Obscene Language: vs. 4
      D. Keep Your Inheritance: vs. 5
  II. Christian Marriage: Ephesians 5:21-29
      A. Mutual Submission: vs. 21
      B. Wives: Submit: vss. 22-24
      C. Husbands: Love: vss. 25-29
 III. Christian Family: Ephesians 6:1-4
      A. Children: Obey: vss. 1-3
      B. Fathers: Instruct: vs. 4

Introduction for Adults

Topic: *Claim Your Responsibilities*

When it comes to claiming our responsibilities as Christians, not understanding what they are isn't the problem. God's commands are simple and clear. Our difficulties arise when, knowing what we are supposed to do, we lack the courage, faith, and will to act.

We have not understood the nature of spiritual warfare and how important basic training is. We have not invested time and energy in growing our faith, in studying God's Word, in praying, and in being filled with the Holy Spirit.

We can read God's guidelines for happy marriages and family life, but for these guidelines to help us we must have a vital faith. We can't obey our responsibilities if we have a weak faith. Jesus Christ must be Lord of everything in our lives. Our supreme desire must be to please Him.

Introduction for Youths

Topic: *A Place for Me!*

Sociologists tell us we have yet to see the fruit of family breakdown in the United States. But anyone in touch with teenagers knows very well how bitter that fruit is in their lives. What we used to consider the traditional family barely survives. Many teenagers live with single parents, or as part of "blended" families. They are trying to make some sense out of separation and divorce.

Therefore, the apostle Paul's picture of marriage and family life reads like a fairy tale, an impossible dream. We need to take a lot of time, in groups and one-on-one, to try to rebuild these shattered lives and dreams. Above all, we need to offer hope in Jesus Christ.

We do not abandon God's Word because so many have violated His design. Rather, we continue to love, serve, teach, and train—not by words only, but by the integrity of our own commitment to Christ and His will.

Concepts for Children

Topic: *Love One Another*

1. We are called to love one another as God loved us in Christ.
2. As Christians, we obey God's rules about our sexual conduct.
3. When others around us tell dirty stories, we can turn away and not listen.
4. In Christian families, we submit to one another because we love Jesus and because this is the way to happiness.
5. Jesus is the example all parents should follow in their relationship with their children.
6. God calls us to obey our parents as part of our obedience to Him.

The Lesson Commentary

I. CHRISTIAN CONDUCT: EPHESIANS 5:1-5

A. Live a Life of Love: vss. 1-2

Be imitators of God, therefore, as dearly loved children and live a life of love, just as Christ loved us and gave himself up for us as a fragrant offering and sacrifice to God.

In Ephesians 4, after calling for love and unity in the church, and the use of our spiritual gifts to build Christian maturity, Paul began a long section on responsible Christian living (4:17). Basically, he told the Ephesian Christians to stop living like the pagans around them. In Christ, they were called to a higher standard of conduct. "Put off your old self and put on your new self," he urged (vss. 22-24).

Then Paul listed the kinds of behavior that are inconsistent with a Christian profession of faith (vss. 25-31). He returned to his list in 5:3-14, but before doing so he wrote a powerful motivation to holiness: God's love in Jesus Christ.

Responsible Christian living is not a matter of following rules, but of becoming more like Christ. "Imitate God" is a lofty command, but Paul based it on the fact that we are God's "dearly loved children." We belong to His family and therefore our lives should reflect our divine heritage.

Paul cited the Lord Jesus as our example. The extent of His love was the cross. The key phrase here is that Jesus "gave himself up for us." He sacrificed Himself to God on our behalf and atoned for our sins, making salvation possible.

His "fragrant offering" satisfied God's righteous demands of the perfect sacrifice for sins. Further, when we receive Christ we not only are born again into God's family, we also receive the power to live a life of love. Apart from Jesus we are powerless, held in sin's grip, but with Christ we are freed to love Him and one another.

B. Avoid Sexual Immorality: vs. 3

But among you there must not be even a hint of sexual immorality, or of any kind of impurity, or of greed, because these are improper for God's holy people.

Responsible Christian living means staying away from sexual immorality. "God's holy people" refrain from the customs of unbelievers, who think nothing of violating God's commands regarding fornication and adultery. God expects His people to avoid "even a hint of sexual immorality, or of any kind of impurity." This means we do not "play with fire," we do not flirt, we do not read or watch harmful, immoral stories, we refrain from premarital sex, and we are faithful to our spouses.

Paul included greed in the list here and in vs. 5. Greed is usually associated with coveting money, possessions, and position. But there is also sexual greed. Of course, greed of any kind is ruled out of bounds for God's "holy people." Responsible living is holy living, because it conforms to God's character.

C. Avoid Obscene Language: vs. 4

Nor should there be obscenity, foolish talk or coarse joking, which are out of place, but rather thanksgiving.

Coarse, flippant talk is inappropriate for Christians. Jesus said, "For out of the overflow of the heart the mouth speaks" (Matt. 12:34). What does our way of speaking say about what is in our hearts? Paul said we are to avoid obscene language of any kind. When bad language becomes a habit, we need to pray and ask God to deliver us. Paul said we should focus on praising God, rather than on sexual humor.

D. Keep Your Inheritance: vs. 5

For of this you can be sure: No immoral, impure or greedy person—such a man is an idolater—has any inheritance in the kingdom of Christ and of God.

Paul warned that those who practice sexual immorality and greed will not gain God's kingdom. He observed that when we yield to immoral, impure, and greedy desires, in effect we become idolaters. We put those things in the place God should have in our lives. It's not off-base to say our culture idolizes sex.

Paul's warning does not mean that such people cannot be redeemed after repenting and receiving Christ. Rather, he used this as a test of lifestyle. People whose lives are characterized by these things will not be saved. If we claim to be Christians, our lives should be marked by conformity to God's will and the standards of Christ's kingdom.

II. CHRISTIAN MARRIAGE: EPHESIANS 5:21-29

A. Mutual Submission: vs. 21

Submit to one another out of reverence for Christ.

Paul compared the difference between godly and ungodly living to the difference between light and darkness (vss. 8-14). He said the best way to live responsibly is to be filled with the Holy Spirit (vs. 18). One of the evidences of the Spirit-filled life is mutual submission. It is important to consider this important responsibility in light of the following rules about holiness in our marriages.

We don't like submission because it seems to inhibit our freedom. When we apply this word from the Lord, we run smack into popular ideas which tell us to please ourselves first, and not allow ourselves to be restrained by others. Because mutual submission is a distinctively Christian concept, we should not be surprised when it is met with hostility and ridicule. We live in a world of self-indulgence, not sacrifice for the sake of others.

First, we have to understand what Paul meant by "submission." The word has nothing to do with subjugation, inferiority, or servitude. Rather, it means we willingly serve the needs of others. It means loving and blessing others. Our constant concern must be the welfare and feelings of others, not our own self-fulfillment.

In the context of the church, we look for ways to help others to grow spiritually. We also put their physical and social needs ahead of our own priorities. In the family context, mutual submission means that wives, husbands, and children submit to the loving requirements of each other, depending on their circumstances and needs. It has to be worked out in terms of personal priorities. Family members voluntarily relinquish something they want, or their time, for the sake of another family member.

Christians do this because they reverence, or honor, Christ and want to please Him. They want to follow His example. Our mutual submission is based on Christ's submission to the cross for us. He came not to be served, but to serve (Mark 10:45). We must catch this spirit if mutual submission is to work.

Understanding mutual submission helps us to avoid some of the nasty arguments that often arise over our rights when it comes to husband-wife and parent-child relationships. Family fights, separation, and divorce could in large measure be avoided if we practiced mutual submission.

B. Wives: Submit: vss. 22-24

Wives, submit to your husbands as to the Lord. For the husband is the head of the wife as Christ is the head of the church, his body, of which he is the Savior. Now as the church submits to Christ, so also wives should submit to their husbands in everything.

Women rightly resent being cast into an inferior role in marriage. This is not God's plan. In His plan, the marriage union produces oneness and partnership, not competition and dictatorship. Not only in marriage but also in Christ there is oneness and equality (Gal. 3:28).

Nonetheless, Paul's dictum, "Wives, submit to your husbands," is often ridiculed as suppressing women's rights. However, God's plan for the family does not violate godly aspirations of women. Christian wives need not apologize for this principle, because it does not mean they are in any way inferior to their husbands.

God has designed a certain family order so that two different persons can live together amicably as one. In this setup, wives are to submit to their husbands. The basic Greek word means "to place or rank under." There is nothing inherently servile or second-class in this setup. It does not deny wives' unique qualities, personalities, gifts, or desires.

Of course, their highest submission is "to the Lord" (vs. 22). As wives follow God's plan in marriage, they bring honor and pleasure to Christ. When others see her willing submission, they are drawn to Christ as a result. There is a unique divine relationship at work in the Christian family.

Paul went on to explain the profound theological reasons for wives submitting to their husbands (vss. 23-24). The key word is "head." In Christian marriage, the husband holds a similar relation as head of the family as Christ holds to the church. (Some scholars understand the meaning of "head" to be "source," citing Gen. 2:21-23 as background.)

Therefore, many Bible students believe that in the Christian family, authority and government rest with the husband. The family finds its unity, center, and direction in him. From him the wife receives the help, love, and encouragement she needs.

Christian wives are to submit "in everything," just as the church submits to Christ. Does "everything" mean how wives spend their money, how to vote, and the color of the drapes? No. Husbands are not to insist on having their own way. That is not mutual submission. "Everything" includes the husband's responsibilities for leadership and order in the family and participating in a way that works with him, not against him.

Godly submission of Christian wives to their husbands is not given grudgingly, but out of deep affection and love. In God's design, the husband's headship and the wife's submission are not in painful tension. Rather, they blend in affectionate adjustment for unity, harmony, and happiness. (Many other Bible students hold a more equalitarian view than this traditional one.)

C. Husbands: Love: vss. 25-29

Husbands, love your wives, just as Christ loved the church and gave himself up for her to make her holy, cleansing her by the washing with water through the word, and to present her to himself as a radiant church, without stain or wrinkle or any other blemish, but holy and blameless. In this same way, husbands ought to love their wives as their own bodies. He who loves his wife loves himself. After all, no one ever hated his own body, but he feeds and cares for it, just as Christ does the church.

Many women have suffered because their husbands have taken advantage of their wives' submission. This is terribly wrong! God's plan does not permit tyranny. The headship spoken of in Scripture is characterized by sacrificial love, patience, and kindness, not selfish power.

Husbands have awesome duties to God and their wives and children. As head of their families, they must provide physical and spiritual nurture. They must establish the overall spiritual tone of the family and provide for the needs of their wives and children.

Paul said Christian husbands are to love their wives "as Christ loved the church." This command removes the unrighteous exercise of headship. The husbands' love is to be measured by Christ's sacrificial self-giving, even unto death. Husbands are to love their wives with devotion, affection, and tenderness. Their love is to be unselfish, because they are anxious above all and by any sacrifice to secure the welfare and happiness of their wives. If husbands love their wives as Christ loved the church, Christian women will have no difficulties finding joyful satisfaction in their role in marriage.

In verses 26 and 27 we find Paul's magnificent description of what Jesus does for His church. "In this same way," Christian husbands should love their wives. Paul did not say, "Love your wife the way you love your own body." He said,

"Love your wife the way Christ loves His body, the Church." The difference is this: Husbands are to imitate Christ's self-giving love, not their own selfish love.

"He who loves his wife loves himself" (vs. 28), is based on the oneness of husbands and wives. Because of their oneness in marriage, when husbands love their wives they are in effect loving themselves.

Paul looked at how Christ cares for the Church (vss. 26-27) and chose two words to summarize it: "feeds and cares for it" (vs. 29). Husbands, of course, take care of their own bodies, but Paul used this truism to point to a much loftier truth to guide husbands in the care of their wives. "Feed" is a somewhat prosaic translation of a word that means to be careful for another's well-being and comfort. Husbands are responsible for much more than a house, food, and clothing, because the example Jesus gave went far beyond those material things. Husbands must provide love, loyalty, honor, support, and respect, and do all they can to foster the spiritual and intellectual growth of their wives.

God's design for marriage is based on the oneness of husbands and wives (vs. 31). Paul quoted Genesis 2:24, where oneness rests on the woman's being taken out of man. Here, Paul argued for oneness based on common membership in Christ's body (vs. 30), and on the far higher sanction of the oneness of Christ and the Church (vs. 32).

III. CHRISTIAN FAMILY: EPHESIANS 6:1-4

A. Children: Obey: vss. 1-3

Children, obey your parents in the Lord, for this is right. "Honor your father and mother"—which is the first commandment with a promise—"that it may go well with you and that you may enjoy long life on the earth."

Living responsibly as Christian children means obeying parents. Paul's command was simple and direct. Obedience is "in the Lord," that is, it is part of the children's acknowledgement of Christ's lordship in their lives. Such obedience is also "right," which means it accords with natural moral law. It is best for both children and parents and assures well-ordered family life rather than conflict and disruption.

Children's obedience to their parents is also anchored in the law of God, specifically the fifth of the Ten Commandments. Paul quoted this command and commented that it included the promise of God's blessing on the family.

B. Fathers: Instruct: vs. 4

Fathers, do not exasperate your children; instead, bring them up in the training and instruction of the Lord.

Paul's word to fathers included both a prohibition ("Do not exasperate your children") and a positive rule ("Bring them up in the training and instruction of the Lord"). All too often overstressed parents can be overbearing, harsh, and inconsistent. The needs and immaturity of children can feel insignificant alongside the demanding pressures of jobs and making the money stretch, and it's easy to brush their needs aside.

But responsible parents are called to teach as well as discipline. Good teaching involves not only content but delivery. If we are often frustrated and angry with our children, they will remember our anger, not our instruction. Positive discipline and training must take place within a climate of acceptance, love, and security. This training and instruction should be based on God's Word, not the latest social theories. Christian parents must know God's Word, obey it ourselves, and teach it to our children in a responsible, loving way.

Discussion Questions

1. How does God's love in Christ motivate and guide us in responsible living?
2. What can we do to protect ourselves from the onslaught of sexual immorality?
3. How would you define and describe mutual submission?
4. What are the benefits of (1) wives submitting to their husbands, and (2) husbands loving their wives?
5. What are the practical outcomes when husbands love and care for their wives according to the example of Christ and the Church?
6. How can parents and their children find common ground and satisfaction working together under Christ's lordship?

Contemporary Application

Responsible Christian living, according to God's Word, starts in the Christian family. In the church family, we are called to love and purity. In our physical families, we are called to mutual submission, respect, love, and obedience. The apostle Paul's teaching will not win secular approval in a society based on "personal rights," which means Christians have to stand out not only by what they say but also by how they live. The best defense of these principles is a godly example.

Therefore, when we see Christian families crumble, it is a wake-up call to the Church. When we see conflicts, it's a call to prayer and wise intervention. It will take great courage for the Church to stand publicly for God's design for marriage and family life. But our culture desperately needs Christians who will not yield to popular culture.

Family stability is at stake, but so is the honor of Christ and the integrity of God's Word. If we fail here, we confess to unbelievers that the Jesus way of love doesn't work. If we can trust Him for our eternal salvation, we can trust Him to take care of our marriages and children.

Called to Stand Firm

Scripture
Background Scripture: *Ephesians 6:10-24*
Scripture Lesson: *Ephesians 6:10-24*
Key Verse: *Be strong in the Lord and in his mighty power.* Ephesians 6:10.

Lesson Aim
To find strength from God to overcome all obstacles to faith and obedience.

Lesson Setting
Time: *Between A.D. 60 and 62*
Place: *Written to Ephesus from Rome*

Lesson Outline
Called to Stand Firm
   I. Strength in God: Ephesians 6:10-13
      A. Be Strong: vs. 10
      B. Defeat Satan: vss. 11-12
      C. Stand Your Ground: vs. 13
  II. Strength in God's Armor: Ephesians 6:14-17
      A. Truth and Righteousness: vs. 14
      B. The Gospel of Peace: vs. 15
      C. Faith: vs. 16
      D. Salvation and the Word of God: vs. 17
 III. Strength in Prayer: Ephesians 6:18-20
      A. At All Times: vs. 18
      B. For Christ's Ambassadors: vss. 19-20
 IV. Strength in Friendships: Ephesians 6:21-24
      A. Mutual Encouragement: vss. 21-22
      B. Benediction to the Brothers: vss. 23-24

Introduction for Adults

Topic: *Claim Your Power Base*

Christians are in a battle with the forces of evil. That fact may inspire different visions of various battles, because we do not lack righteous causes for which to fight. It's interesting, however, that when Paul told the Christians to stand firm, he did not mention any specific battles.

He pictured Christians holding their ground against the devil's schemes, the spiritual forces of evil, and the devil's flaming arrows. Therefore, we need to be spiritually alert and sensitive, so that we do not fight the wrong battles. We need spiritual wisdom and discernment, so we do not deplete our forces on inappropriate causes. For example, political battles often engage Christians against each other.

Perhaps if more Christians wore and used God's full armor, we would see more strong resistance to evil in our society. The greatest dangers we face are not recognizing the real enemy and fighting with the wrong weapons.

Introduction for Youths

Topic: *Stand Firm!*

Remember playing king of the mountain at recess or with friends in your neighborhood? If there ever was a time to stand firm, that was it. Later on, the football scrimmage line represented the place to stand firm if you were playing defense.

The most important place to stand firm is in our faith and morality. We see teenagers dropping like flies all around us, because they cannot stand firm against the inroads of drugs, illicit sex, alcohol, and cigarettes. Of course, part of the reason they fall is because they lack teaching and encouragement in the Christian faith.

Our great responsibility is to pick each other up when we see the possibility of slipping away. Christian teens are the real hope of our churches and schools. But we need to take the time, and pray for patience, and wisdom to show them how to use God's full armor of spiritual protection.

Concepts for Children

Topic: *Be Strong!*

1. Jesus gives us strength and courage to be spiritually strong.
2. God's armor includes everything we need to be strong.
3. Like soldiers taking basic training, we need to learn how to use God's spiritual weapons.
4. Knowing and believing the Gospel of Jesus is the foundation for becoming strong.
5. We need to exercise our faith muscles by trusting God in tough situations.
6. We all need the prayers and encouragement of each other to stand faithful to Christ.

The Lesson Commentary

I. STRENGTH IN GOD: EPHESIANS 6:10-13

A. Be Strong: vs. 10

Finally, be strong in the Lord and in his mighty power.

Writing to the church at Ephesus, Paul first blessed them with the magnitude of their spiritual wealth in Christ. Next, he begged them to live in a way that corresponded to their superlative position in Christ (4:1). They were to get rid of their old sinful ways and put on the nature of God Himself as they lived "in true righteousness and holiness" (4:24). Paul mentioned a host of bad habits that had to go. They were to be replaced by the dynamic power of the Holy Spirit (5:18). With such spiritual resources, the Ephesians could radically change their family and social relationships (5:21—6:9).

But it would not be easy. The powers of wickedness were arrayed against their desires to obey Christ. They knew what was right to do, but they needed strength beyond themselves to actually do it. They needed God's armor and His strength.

The apostle's command was very simple: "Be strong." He assumed the role of the squad leader of a platoon of infantrymen about to go into battle. "Take courage. Do not retreat," he said. The clear implication is that the Christian life is a daily battle.

It is also clear, in this section at least, that Paul saw the battle as defensive. He saw Christians under attack from the enemy, at risk from powerful forces. He did not want them to yield one inch of territory to their foes.

To hold their ground, Christians must look to God and His power, not to their own defenses. The courage comes from God. The power comes from God. This includes spiritual and moral power, power that strengthens our minds, hearts, and wills to be faithful to Christ, no matter what.

B. Defeat Satan: vss. 11-12

Put on the full armor of God so that you can take your stand against the devil's schemes. For our struggle is not against flesh and blood, but against the rulers, against the authorities, against the powers of this dark world and against the spiritual forces of evil in the heavenly realms.

After issuing his opening battle cry, Paul told the Christian soldiers how to be strong in the Lord and how to recognize their enemy. "Put on the full armor of God," he twice urged them (vss. 11, 13). We can be strong because God provides spiritual protection against Satan's schemes.

Success in battle depends on knowing who and how to fight. Sadly, too often we blame the government, our families, our employers, or some ungodly neighbors. We even blame fellow Christians for our woes. Paul said that we have to look beyond our human aggravations, worries, and fears to our real enemy.

Spiritual forces of evil are behind the attacks on God and His people. Paul called them rulers, authorities, and powers. With such awesome foes in view, is it any wonder that Paul appealed to the church to fight in God's strength, armor, and power? How foolish to attempt to resist this array of dark forces in our own strength.

C. Stand Your Ground: vs. 13

Therefore put on the full armor of God, so that when the day of evil comes, you may be able to stand your ground, and after you have done everything, to stand.

Paul's primary concern was that Christians should stand their ground against the enemy's attacks. There is no doubt in his mind that the day of attack will come.

"The day of evil" takes different forms for different believers. We cannot predict what tactics the enemy will use in every case. Nor can we assume that all of our troubles have satanic origins. Some of them are caused by outright sin, disobedience, ignorance, and spiritual laziness. Sometimes it's hard to tell when we are being attacked by Satan and when we are suffering the just consequences of our behavior. Other times God is testing us.

"The devil made me do it" is a lame excuse. At the same time, we know he attacks us to move us out of our strong position in Christ. "To stand" means to stand in our faith and confidence in the Lord Jesus Christ. Satan wants us to doubt and deny Christ. He wants us to abandon our hope and faith. Whatever happens, our duty is not to ask why, but to anchor ourselves in Christ's love, wisdom, and power.

II. STRENGTH IN GOD'S ARMOR: EPHESIANS 6:14-17

A. Truth and Righteousness: vs. 14

Stand firm then, with the belt of truth buckled around your waist, with the breastplate of righteousness in place.

Paul's battlefield imagery gives us a clear picture of the basic equipment of the Roman infantryman in Caesar's legions. They were almost completely protected from head to foot. So are God's people in His armor.

Paul considered the first two pieces of basic equipment—the belt and the breastplate. To them he assigned spiritual realities—truth and righteousness. Paul meant the truth of the Gospel and the righteousness that comes by faith in Christ. Christians are protected by "buckling" the truth around us (like a belt), which is the good news of Christ's death and resurrection for our sins.

The truth about God's holiness, righteousness, and love also includes the facts about our sin and the necessity of repentance and faith. The Gospel message tells us that Jesus died on our behalf to meet the just demands of a holy God. Once we have "buckled on" the truth of the Gospel, we are also clothed in God's righteousness (the breastplate).

Wearing these truths protects us from Satan's attacks, which seek to get us to distrust God and His gift of salvation by faith alone, based on Christ's atoning death. Satan will do anything to move us away from the confidence of our forgiveness, eternal life, and righteousness through Christ alone.

B. The Gospel of Peace: vs. 15

And with your feet fitted with the readiness that comes from the gospel of peace.

Shoes were a critical part of the soldier's equipment, because armies advance on their feet. In Paul's metaphor of the Christian soldier, he compared shoes to "the Gospel of peace." Peace in the midst of a picture of battle? But the Gospel gives us peace in the midst of conflicts, because God's love is a reconciling love—reconciling sinners with Himself and reconciling our broken relationships with each other. Jesus Christ is our peace in the midst of conflicts and difficulties.

Three times Paul told the church to stand firm. We stand on our feet with shoes of peace that not only protect us, but give us firmness and stability in our faith.

C. Faith: vs. 16

In addition to all this, take up the shield of faith, with which you can extinguish all the flaming arrows of the evil one.

In ancient times, attacking armies assaulted fortresses with flaming arrows before they advanced directly to the walls. "Flaming arrows" are the equivalent of direct attacks. Christians are subject not just to subtle attacks from the evil one, but straightforward attacks as well. For that reason God gives us the shield of faith. The devil's arrows are aimed at our faith. He will do anything to subvert our faith, so we will turn against God and refuse to follow Christ.

To deflect these attacks, we must be skilled handlers of God's shield. We must know how to defend ourselves with faith. Is faith adequate protection? We often think there must be some stronger defense than our faith, which often wavers. But throughout Scripture we find that faith is the only answer for God's people. We are actually helpless to fight these spiritual battles in our own strength. We must have faith in God's power to defeat Satan. We are called to trust God implicitly, even when it seems the battle is going against us.

D. Salvation and the Word of God: vs. 17

Take the helmet of salvation and the sword of the Spirit, which is the word of God.

Helmets protected soldiers from flying missiles, spears, and swords. Paul said God's salvation is our helmet of protection from our enemies. Salvation encompasses all that God has done for us in Christ. As the "helmet" in our armor, it covers us "from the head down" in the blood of Christ. The enemy's attacks bounce off our heads when we wear God's helmet of salvation.

The sword, on the other hand, is an offensive weapon. Imagine a soldier fighting with his helmet, belt, breastplate, shield, and shoes, but no sword.

Even his defense would be incomplete. Sometimes the best defense is a good offense. He would need to use his sword to keep his enemies at bay.

Our sword is the Bible, the Word of God. Without it we are helpless. Christians need to be skilled fighters with Scripture. We must be trained in how to use the Bible to build our faith and knowledge. We need to know the Bible to answer the attacks of critics. We need the comfort and courage of the Bible in difficult times.

Best of all, the Bible is the Holy Spirit's weapon of choice. When we use the Bible, we bring the Holy Spirit into warfare with our enemies. He inspired the Bible and He uses it to help us and to drive away our enemies.

III. STRENGTH IN PRAYER: EPHESIANS 6:18-20

A. At All Times: vs. 18

And pray in the Spirit on all occasions with all kinds of prayers and requests. With this in mind, be alert and always keep on praying for all the saints.

Christians can stand firm because we find our strength in God through prayer. Battles are lost and Christians retreat when we do not pray. We quit the faith race, drop out of worship and service, and lose our love for Christ when we fail to pray.

Knowing this, Paul instructed the Ephesians to pray: (1) in the Spirit; (2) on all occasions; (3) with all kinds of prayers and requests; (4) and with alertness and persistence. What a difference this makes in battle! The fully equipped soldier of Christ advances with prayer. By following Paul's counsel the church advanced into hostile territory. God's people will be strong in the Lord when we pray.

B. For Christ's Ambassadors: vss. 19-20

Pray also for me, that whenever I open my mouth, words may be given me so that I will fearlessly make known the mystery of the gospel, for which I am an ambassador in chains. Pray that I may declare it fearlessly, as I should.

Paul's appeal to stand firm took a decidedly personal turn. To be strong in the Lord we need to pray for each other. He called himself "an ambassador in chains," which is dramatic evidence that he never gave up witnessing for Christ. But in prison he might easily feel defeated and discouraged.

Therefore, he asked for prayer. He appealed for boldness and courage in his witness in Rome. Courage to speak out. Wisdom to know what to say. Twice he asked that he might speak "fearlessly." Fear is a greatest hindrance to our witness. We need to follow this model prayer for one another.

IV. STRENGTH IN FRIENDSHIPS: EPHESIANS 6:21-24

A. Mutual Encouragement: vss. 21-22

Tychicus, the dear brother and faithful servant in the Lord, will tell you everything, so that you also may know how I am and what I am doing. I am sending him to you for this very purpose, that you may know how we are, and that he may encourage you.

369

To be strong in the Lord we must encourage one another in our faith and obedience. That's what Paul did as he recalled his friend Tychicus [TICK-ih-kuss] and all the "brothers" in Christ. Paul's heart was so big that he never lost sight of the personal element in ministry.

Our friends are "dear brothers" and "faithful servants." Our friends tell us what God is doing in their lives, and they help us to see what He is doing in our lives.

B. Benediction to the Brothers: vss. 23-24

Peace to the brothers, and love with faith from God the Father and the Lord Jesus Christ. Grace to all who love our Lord Jesus Christ with an undying love.

To encourage means to put heart in people. It means to extend peace, love, and faith to one another in Christ. He is the focus of our friendship. Paul pronounced God's grace on those who love Christ. We can also bring that blessing into the lives of our friends. What a beautiful picture of Christian fellowship, which is so vital to our standing firm for God.

Discussion Questions

1. Why do you think Paul wrote about our Christian life as a battle with Satan?
2. In what areas of our lives do we need God's strength?
3. In how many different ways does the enemy attack us?
4. How can we be better trained in using the Spirit's sword?
5. What exercises can we practice to become skillful users of the shield of faith?
6. What are some common excuses for our not being disciplined in prayer, and how can we overcome them?

Contemporary Application

Perhaps Paul's metaphor would be more contemporary if he described a football player's equipment. Most of us have never seen a Roman soldier, so we have to trust the sketches in our history books. However, the main point is the same: we need serious protection if we are going to stand firm for the Lord.

The newspaper once carried a story about a platoon of soldiers that threw away their gas masks. They were too awkward to carry, and besides, they figured they wouldn't need them anyway. As you can guess, they made a fatal mistake.

Perhaps some Christians are like that. Talking about using God's armor doesn't appeal to them because they don't see any need for it. They have no idea they are engaged in spiritual warfare with Satan. They coast through life not on a wartime footing, but in a vacation mode. Therefore, we lose many soldiers and others drop out. They are easy prey for the enemy.

We must know the enemy's schemes and flaming arrows. We must know, trust, and use God's armor. We have no excuses for our failures, because He has given us all we need to triumph.

The Supremacy of Christ

DEVOTIONAL READING

John 1:1-5, 9-18

DAILY BIBLE READINGS

Monday July 31
Colossians 1:1-8 Paul Gives Thanks for the Colossians

Tuesday August 1
Colossians 1:9-14 Paul Prays for the Colossian Christians

Wednesday August 2
Colossians 1:15-20 The Fullness of God Dwelled in Christ

Thursday August 3
Colossians 1:21-29 God's Mystery Revealed to the Saints

Friday August 4
John 1:1-9 Jesus Christ: God's Word and Light

Saturday August 5
John 1:10-18 God's Word Lived among Us

Sunday August 6
Hebrews 1:1-14 Christ Is Superior Even to Angels

Scripture

Background Scripture: *Colossians 1*
Scripture Lesson: *Colossians 1:15-28*
Key Verse: *For God was pleased to have all his fullness dwell in him, and through him to reconcile to himself all things, whether things on earth or things in heaven, by making peace through his blood, shed on the cross.* Colossians 1:19-20.
Key Verse for Children: *"The God who made the world . . . is the Lord of heaven and earth and does not live in temples built by hands."* Acts 17:24.

Lesson Aim

To worship and serve Jesus Christ because of who He is.

Lesson Setting

Time: *A.D. 60-62*
Place: *Written to Colosse from Rome*

Lesson Outline

The Supremacy of Christ

   I. Over the World and the Church: Colossians 1:15-19
      A. His Deity: vs. 15
      B. His Creatorship: vss. 16-17
      C. His Headship: vs. 18a
      D. His New Beginning: 18b
      E. His Person: 19
  II. In Reconciliation: Colossians 1:20-23
      A. Through the Cross: vs. 20
      B. Why It Is Needed: vs. 21
      C. Its Means and Purpose: vs. 22
      D. Our Responsibility: vs. 23
 III. In Paul's Ministry: Colossians 1:24-28
      A. His Rejoicing: vs. 24
      B. His Calling: vs. 25
      C. His Message: vss. 26-27
      D. His Purpose: vs. 28

Introduction for Adults

Topic: *The Source of Life*

    Tony faithfully talked about Jesus with a friend who wanted to discuss religion in general. Tony gently refused and left his friend with one question, "Do you have life?" The issue is life, not religion, he explained. One day several months later the friend came to Tony and said, "I've got life!" He had trusted in Jesus for eternal life.

    The supremacy of Christ in our lives begins when we invite Him to become our Lord and Savior. He said that He came to give us life to the full (John 10:10). No one else can give us life. We need life because we are dead in sin. There is no true life available to us, other than in Christ.

    So we have to make choices. Even Peter, the Lord's disciple, had to decide. When Jesus confronted him, Peter answered, "Lord, to whom shall we go? You have the words of eternal life" (John 6:68). Jesus said, "I am the way and the truth and the life" (John 14:6). Receive Jesus by faith and live.

Introduction for Youths

Topic: *The Image of God*

    One day Philip the disciple demanded of Jesus, "Lord, show us the Father and that will be enough for us" (John 14:8). Many young people are asking the same thing. They want to see authentic Christianity lived by those who profess to be Christians. They are not directly demanding to see God, but they rightly expect to see Him in the lives of those who say they are believers.

    Jesus was the only one who perfectly bore God's image. But the apostle Paul said that in Christ we, too, can be regarded as holy and perfect. As others see Christ in us they get a taste of what it means to see God's image.

    Jesus said that He would reveal Himself to others by living in us. He promised to show Himself when we love and obey Him. Therefore, Christians stand in the gap between God and the unbelieving world.

Concepts for Children

Topic: *Jesus Is over All*

1. Many people today worship false gods.
2. The one true God has revealed Himself in nature, in the Bible, and in His Son, the Lord Jesus Christ.
3. As Christians, we live under Christ's authority.
4. Our faith is often tested by those who ridicule us and say they do not believe in God.
5. We are called to be faithful to the Gospel as Paul was to the men of Athens.
6. By prayer and study we can be better witnesses to the supremacy of Christ.

The Lesson Commentary

I. OVER THE WORLD AND THE CHURCH: COLOSSIANS 1:15-19

A. His Deity: vs. 15

He is the image of the invisible God, the firstborn over all creation.

Colossians was written by Paul under house arrest in Rome. Colosse [kuh-LAH-see] was a small town in Phrygia near Laodicea. From what we know, Paul never visited Colosse. The Gospel came there through some of Paul's converts, men such as Epaphras [EPP-uh-frus] (1:7) and Philemon, at whose house the church met (Philem. 2). The church at Colosse was an outgrowth of the far-reaching ministry of Paul at Ephesus (Acts 19:10).

Paul began this letter with thanksgiving for what God had done in raising up the church at Colosse (Col. 1:3-8). He reminded the believers of their priceless spiritual heritage. Then he penned a magnificent prayer for them (vss. 9-14). He concluded his prayer with thanksgiving for God's deliverance from the power of darkness, and for redemption and forgiveness in Christ. This magnificent reality led him to comment on the supremacy of Christ over the world and the church.

Paul's teaching about Christ's supremacy was needed at Colosse because the church was infiltrated by false teachers. They had introduced inferior created beings, angelic mediators, in place of Christ (2:8, 18). The believers had to be reminded that Jesus is the full and final revelation of God, and all human ideas must be brought in subjection to Him. The only adequate response to false teaching is a correct understanding of and commitment to Jesus Christ as Lord. (See also Ephesians 1:20-23 and Philippians 2:6-11).

Paul declared that Jesus is the "image" of God. "Image" means the exact likeness or representation of God, who is invisible. God's nature is essentially spiritual (John 4:24; Rom. 1:20). However, when Jesus came to earth, He expressed God's nature in physical form and made God visible. That's why Jesus said, "Anyone who has seen me has seen the Father" (John 14:9). "No one has ever seen God; but God's only Son, he who is nearest to the Father's heart, he has made him known" (John 1:18, NEB). Apart from the image of God in Christ, there is no visible physical likeness of God.

Paul's description of Christ as "the firstborn over all creation" might suggest that Jesus was simply the first of all created beings. But it means that Jesus existed prior to all creation, another evidence of His deity and supremacy. He was the antecedent of every creature and all creation.

Jesus was not a created being, but the agent of creation. This places Him above creation. "Firstborn" means supreme, not born first. Jesus existed eternally with His Father before the world was made (John 1:1-2; 17:5).

B. His Creatorship: vss. 16-17

For by him all things were created: things in heaven and on earth, visible and invisible, whether thrones or powers or rulers or authorities; all things were created by him and for him. He is before all things, and in him all things hold together.

Paul expanded Christ's supremacy to creation with three facts: (1) Jesus was the unique instrument of creation; (2) the created world exists for His glory; (3) He holds the physical world together. To be certain nothing was beyond the scope of Christ's creatorship, Paul used the term "all things" four times.

His "all things" included everything in heaven as well as on earth—every rank of earthly and supernatural powers. Christians at Colosse were speculating about the beings who inhabited the unseen world. Paul spoke of them as real entities, but definitely under Christ's authority.

Paul declared not only that Jesus made all things, but also that everything exists for His pleasure and glory. Jesus is "before all things" in terms of rank and authority. Paul added the astonishing fact that everything "holds together" in Christ, suggesting that the created world would disintegrate, were it not for Christ's power.

C. His Headship: vs. 18a

And he is the head of the body, the church.

Next, Paul extended Christ's supremacy to the Church. Jesus is supreme in the Church because it is His body and He gave His life for it. No human authority can usurp Christ's supremacy in the Church.

Paul's doctrine of the Church as the body of Christ is also important because it shows how believers relate to each other under Christ's headship. He is united with every believer in His body. He has full control of the members. They are subject to Him and relate to one another as fellow members.

D. His New Beginning: vs. 18b

He is the beginning and the firstborn from among the dead, so that in everything he might have the supremacy.

Supreme in creation (vs. 15), Jesus is likewise supreme in God's family. As our crucified and risen Savior, He stands as "the firstborn from among the dead." By calling Jesus the "beginning," Paul emphasized the fact of His precedence in establishing a new creation (2 Cor. 5:17), a spiritual creation in contrast to the physical creation.

All believers anticipate rising from the dead because of Christ's resurrection. Beyond that, Paul spoke of Christ's resurrection and His victory over death to prove that He is preeminent. That is Paul's major theme. He showed that both in creation and in the Church Jesus is supreme.

E. His Person: vs. 19

For God was pleased to have all his fullness dwell in him.

Christ's claim to supremacy is based not only on His creative and redemptive work, but also on His own person. The fullness of God dwells in Him. There is no clearer statement about the person of Christ than this one. God's "fullness" means the completeness of His divine attributes. Jesus is nothing less than God.

When we confess the truth of Paul's statement about Jesus, at the same time we also deny competing claims of other religions. A yes to the supremacy of Jesus is a no to everyone and everything else for spiritual supremacy.

II. In Reconciliation: Colossians 1:20-23

A. Through the Cross: vs. 20

And through him to reconcile to himself all things, whether things on earth or things in heaven, by making peace through his blood, shed on the cross.

The supremacy of Jesus is not just a religious claim. It is based on what He accomplished on the cross. Jesus did not bring a new philosophy or religious theory; He *did* something about our profound spiritual needs.

Paul used the word "reconcile" to describe what Jesus did for us. Jesus was at the center of God's salvation plan. "Through him" salvation was made possible. There is no other way to be reconciled to God. "To reconcile" means to bring enemies together, in this case, God and us because of our sins. Jesus "made peace" between God and us because God accepted His sacrificial, atoning blood on our behalf.

Christ's supremacy in reconciliation includes "all things." We cannot be dogmatic about what "things in heaven" need to be reconciled to God. Paul did not tell us. It seems best to take this to mean the restoration of all things to a state of harmony with God. Whatever discord and rebellion came into the world because of sin, in some way also it affected the realm of angels.

B. Why It Is Needed: vs. 21

Once you were alienated from God and were enemies in your minds because of your evil behavior.

Paul revealed two facts about why we must be reconciled to God: (1) we were His enemies in heart and mind, and (2) our deeds were evil. This is our basic spiritual condition. This is why we need salvation.

Our root problem lies in our alienation from and hostility to God. We are born rebels. Our sinful deeds and thoughts arise from our refusal to accept God's will and authority.

C. Its Means and Purpose: vs. 22

But now he has reconciled you by Christ's physical body through death to present you holy in his sight, without blemish and free from accusation.

The means of our reconciliation to God is Christ's death. The purpose of it is to present us "holy . . . without blemish and free from accusation." Or, as the Revised Standard Version has it, "holy and blameless and irreproachable before him." Not only does the supremacy of Jesus guarantee our peace with God, it also brings us the virtues and blessings of holiness and freedom from God's condemnation.

Paul clearly stated that salvation by faith includes much more than pardon for our sins. Jesus makes us so holy that we are actually good enough to stand before God. Our holiness is also guaranteed because Jesus is supreme.

D. Our Responsibility: vs. 23

If you continue in your faith, established and firm, not moved from the hope held out in the gospel. This is the gospel that you heard and that has been proclaimed to every creature under heaven, and of which I, Paul, have become a servant.

Paul knew that some people in the church at Colosse had to choose between Jesus and the ideas of the false teachers. They were at the crossroads. So he exhorted them to "continue in your faith." They had to remain strong in their commitment to Jesus as proclaimed by Paul in the Gospel. He appealed on the basis of all they had gained in Jesus not to move away from Him. They had to develop a strong, firm faith so they would not be dislodged from their hope in Christ.

Paul offered himself as the example to follow. He had brought the Gospel because he was a servant of the Gospel. In effect, then, the people had to stick with Paul's testimony and his doctrines about the supremacy of Christ. If they departed, they would lose their "hope" and everything guaranteed by Christ's supremacy.

III. IN PAUL'S MINISTRY: COLOSSIANS 1:24-28

A. His Rejoicing: vs. 24

Now I rejoice in what was suffered for you, and I fill up in my flesh what is still lacking in regard to Christ's afflictions, for the sake of his body, which is the church.

Jesus was also supreme in Paul's ministry. This paragraph may seem like a digression from his main point, but it isn't because it shows how Paul saw his ministry in light of what he had just written.

Paul saw himself as an extension of Christ's sufferings for the church. He could not add to the saving and reconciling merits of Christ's sufferings, but if his sufferings as a prisoner for Christ furthered the cause of the Gospel, he rejoiced.

B. His Calling: vs. 25

I have become its servant by the commission God gave me to present to you the word of God in its fullness.

Paul's calling was to spread God's word "in its fullness." He was not on a self-appointed human mission, but on God's. God gave him his assignment not for his own glory, but for the good of the churches. Paul's statement reveals how important it was to assert his God-given credentials to the Colossians. Paul faithfully taught God's Word in spite of great hardships and suffering, because Jesus was supreme in his life.

C. His Message: vss. 26-27

The mystery that has been kept hidden for ages and generations, but is now disclosed to the saints. To them God has chosen to make known among the Gentiles the glorious riches of this mystery, which is Christ in you, the hope of glory.

"The word of God in its fullness" meant the revelation of "the mystery" (something previously hidden from us), which is "Christ in you." Christ's supremacy in this regard has been disclosed to "the saints," all the believers in Christ who make up His Church.

Paul compared the indwelling presence of Christ to "glorious riches." In his ministry he had been given the inestimable privilege of announcing what had been hidden for ages past. Most believers at Colosse were Gentiles, so they would appreciate Paul's declaration that God had been pleased to reveal Christ to them.

D. His Purpose: vs. 28

We proclaim him, admonishing and teaching everyone with all wisdom, so that we may present everyone perfect in Christ.

No wonder Paul was excited about preaching Christ! He gave all his heart, wisdom, and energy to bringing people to perfection in Christ. He did not stop when a few people professed faith in Christ. He wanted them to grow into Christ's perfection. Jesus is supreme in our salvation and our ongoing spiritual growth.

Discussion Questions

1. How is Christ's supremacy being challenged in our lives?
2. How is His supremacy being challenged in our churches?
3. In what areas of our lives is it hard to live under Christ's preeminence?
4. What does it mean to "continue in your faith"?
5. How can we show that "Christ in you" is the preeminent goal in our lives?
6. What does perfection in Christ look like in our daily lives?

Contemporary Application

New theories about religious knowledge and spiritual attainments hit us every year. They are promulgated widely in the media as evidence of progress in human development. The implication is that traditional Christian ideas are outmoded.

Our task is to show that the power and love of Jesus Christ have not been diminished by time. We have to reassert His claims to supremacy—His supremacy in creation, redemption, and in the lives of all believers, the Church.

Jesus Christ alone is fully sufficient for our time and for all our needs. If the world is to see the difference He makes, Christians must "continue" in their faith, "established and firm." This is no time to make lame excuses for what we believe.

People in general are looking for forgiveness and hope. What a privilege we have to tell them it is possible, in Christ, to stand accepted before God.

A Complete Life in Christ

DEVOTIONAL READING

Romans 8:31-39

Scripture

Background Scripture: *Colossians 2:6-19*
Scripture Lesson: *Colossians 2:6-19*
Key Verse: *So then, just as you received Christ Jesus as Lord, continue to live in him, rooted and built up in him, strengthened in the faith as you were taught, and overflowing with thankfulness.* Colossians 2:6-7.
Key Verse: *God did not give us a spirit of timidity, but a spirit of power, of love and of self-discipline.* 2 Timothy 1:7.

Lesson Aim

To experience what it means to be complete in Christ.

Lesson Setting

Time: *A.D. 60-62*
Place: *Written to Colosse from Rome*

Lesson Outline

A Complete Life in Christ
  I Living in Christ: Colossians 2:6-7
    A. By a Personal Relationship: vs. 6
    B. By Developing Spiritual Roots: vs. 7
  II. Fullness of Life in Christ: Colossians 2:8-12
    A. Wrong Philosophy: vs. 8
    B. True Theology: vs. 9
    C. The Gift of Fullness: vs. 10
    D. The Exercise of Fullness: vss. 11-12
  III. Victory in Christ: Colossians 2:13-15
    A. Over Spiritual Death: vs. 13
    B. Over the Law: vs. 14
    C. Over Evil Powers: vs. 15
  IV. Holding Fast to Christ: Colossians 2:16-19
    A. Forget the Rules: vs. 16
    B. Reality in Christ: vs. 17
    C. False Worship: vs. 18
    D. Growth in Christ: vs. 19

Introduction for Adults

Topic: *The Fullness of Life*

A young father of two children lost his wife when their second child was born. One night as he was praying for strength, God directed him to Colossians 2:10. God spoke to him and reminded him that he was complete in Christ, despite the death of his wife.

The Holy Spirit touched him. He confessed that he did not need anything more than he had in Jesus—not even a wife and mother for his children. God comforted him with the fullness of life he already had in Christ. His heart and mind came to rest and peace.

Too often, it seems, we come to God with complaining spirits. We wish we had something more. Then we would be satisfied. But no matter how much we have, we can find true satisfaction only in Jesus Christ. He has given us fully of Himself. He wants us to enjoy the riches of our faith relationship with Him.

That's why we need to bolster our minds with the truths of God's Word about our spiritual resources. Sometimes God has to strip us bare, as it were, before we come to grips with the fact that Jesus is more than sufficient to meet all of our needs.

Introduction for Youths

Topic: *A Full Life in Christ*

Enjoying a full life in Christ is something like enjoying a full tank of gas. What a thrill it is to joyride around town, or spin around the countryside, knowing your tank is full. But the laws of physics soon catch up with us. No matter how sporty or powerful our car is, it won't run on empty.

When we confess our faith in Christ, He gives us all the fuel we need for time and eternity. The full tank is there all the time, whenever we need it. But sometimes we try to run on a foreign fuel. We think we've outgrown our need of Jesus. Or, we'd like to try some alternatives to Him.

Sooner or later, that false gas will let us down. For awhile we try to run on empty, because we refuse to turn on the fuel that is Jesus. He lives in us, but sometimes because of our sin and neglect we cannot tap into it. Our lives rust away like an abandoned car in a vacant lot.

Paul reminded us that we have to drive our roots of faith deeply into Jesus. We cannot afford to lose vital connection with Him. Therefore, every spiritual discipline we find in our church and among our Christian friends must be welcomed. This includes worship, Bible study, prayer, and Christian service. When we engage our minds and hearts in serving Jesus, our joyride with Him will go on forever.

Concepts for Children

Topic: *Jesus Wants Us to Be Faithful*

1. God calls us to drive deep roots of faith in Jesus.
2. Part of Christian growth is to pray for one another, as Paul prayed for Timothy.
3. We are also helped to be faithful to Jesus when our families serve Him together.
4. God gives us spiritual gifts to be used to help one another.
5. When we are tempted to doubt, we can remember that Jesus is faithful and we can maintain a firm grasp on Him.
6. The Bible is God's Word and it is important to study and memorize it.

The Lesson Commentary

I. LIVING IN CHRIST: COLOSSIANS 2:6-7

A. By a Personal Relationship: vs. 6

So then, just as you received Christ Jesus as Lord, continue to live in him.

In the first chapter of Colossians the apostle Paul declared that Jesus Christ is the living expression of God Himself. He also taught that Jesus is both creator and sustainer of everything in heaven and earth. Christ is supreme in existence, power, and position. He is also head of the church, the body of believers.

Paul's personal commission was to reveal the "mystery" of the Gospel, which is "Christ in you, the hope of glory" (1:27). However, false teachers had infiltrated the church at Colosse, trying to deceive the believers "by fine-sounding arguments" (2:4).

Paul responded to their challenge by emphasizing the overwhelming significance of Christ's incarnation. In Christ "are hidden all the treasures of wisdom and knowledge" (2:3). Therefore, he urged the Colossians not to waver in their faith. He took them back to their initial steps of faith by which they had come into a personal relationship with Jesus. They must not be swayed, but must go on living in union with Him.

To "receive" Christ Jesus indicates that Christian faith is a personal relationship of trust. We do not receive a religious theory, but a living person. This happened to Zacchaeus (Luke 19:1-6). When Jesus said He wanted to come to his house, the startled tax collector "welcomed him gladly." This is a picture of how we begin a personal relationship with Christ.

So we are to keep on living in Him. Jesus gave a beautiful metaphor of what this means: "I am the vine, and you the branches. He who dwells in me, as I dwell in him, bears much fruit; for apart from me you can do nothing" (John 15:5, NEB).

B. By Developing Spiritual Roots: vs. 7

Rooted and built up in him, strengthened in the faith as you were taught, and overflowing with thankfulness.

Continuing to live by faith in Christ requires deep, secure roots. We are rooted, built up, and established in Him. Our lives are the outflow of our faith decision to put down our roots in Christ. The result is spiritual growth, strength, consistency, fruitfulness, and overflowing praise.

Of course, deep roots are developed both intellectually and pragmatically. We grow in our knowledge of Jesus and in what it means to love and obey Him. Our Christian character grows as we grow in our understanding of His Word and how it applies to our lives.

In Paul's vocabulary, living in Christ means Jesus is both the life of the plant ("rooted" in Him) and the binding force of the building ("built up" in Him). Jesus gives us all we need to live a satisfying, purposeful Christian life.

II. FULLNESS OF LIFE IN CHRIST: COLOSSIANS 2:8-12

A. Wrong Philosophy: vs. 8

See to it that no one takes you captive through hollow and deceptive philosophy, which depends on human tradition and the basic principles of this world rather than on Christ.

After warning about humanistic false teaching, Paul gave a strong statement about Christ's supremacy. Christians need to be reassured that no other ideology comes close to the truth of the Gospel. The Colossians were endangered by teaching that was not according to Christ. Rather, it was based on human tradition, and it was deceptive. The false teachings had to be measured by the teachings of Christ.

The practical danger was made clear by Paul's warning against being taken captive. He pictured Christians as booty likely to be carried off if they were not careful. They had to be constantly vigilant against being taken in. Those who would capture them would do so with a philosophy of vain speculation, devoid of truth.

B. True Theology: vs. 9

For in Christ all the fullness of the Deity lives in bodily form.

Paul answered the false teachers with a powerful declaration of true theology: Why should the Colossians follow empty, worldly traditions and philosophies when the One in whom they had placed their faith possessed the fullness of God? The successful way to avoid being captured by false ideas is to grasp the overwhelming magnificence of the person of Christ.

Jesus is the source of all truth, and that truth is unchanging. Human philosophies constantly change. Each generation produces a better idea. Christian theology does not change because Jesus does not change. No human invention is able to surpass the truth of the Gospel. This truth about Christ is the bedrock of our faith and of our living. Anything less is a distortion, and will not serve us well.

C. The Gift of Fullness: vs. 10

And you have been given fullness in Christ, who is the head over every power and authority.

A complete life in Christ rests on the astonishing fact that God has given us "fullness in Christ." Paul used the same word "fullness" that he used to describe Christ's deity (vs. 9). Some translations use the word completeness for fullness. As the completeness of deity lives in Christ, so the completeness of Christ lives in us.

Our completeness rests on the fact that Jesus is supreme over all powers and authorities. Who He is and what He has done for us ranks above everything and everyone else. Therefore, we lack nothing for salvation, forgiveness, eternal life, and godly living. Sometimes we think God has short-changed us. "If only I had . . ." But when He gave us Christ, He gave us a complete resource! We have all we need, because we are linked to the One who has everything.

D. The Exercise of Fullness: vss. 11-12

In him you were also circumcised, in the putting off of the sinful nature, not with a circumcision done by the hands of men but with the circumcision done by Christ, having been buried with him in baptism and raised with him through your faith in the power of God, who raised him from the dead.

Having completeness in Christ means we are spiritually circumcised. Spiritual circumcision, in contrast to physical circumcision, gets rid of the fleshly roots of sin. Our completeness is demonstrated by the repudiation of our old sinful nature.

Spiritual circumcision is "in Christ" and not accomplished "by the hands of men." It is a spiritual act whereby the whole corrupt, carnal nature is put off like a garment. Just as we lay aside our dirty work clothes, so we put away our former lifestyle.

The rite of Christian baptism (vs. 12) signifies the passing from the old to the new. In baptism believers are united with Christ's death. We are buried with Him and raised to new life with Him. This is accomplished by our faith in God's power. When we confess our faith in Christ's resurrection, we acknowledge His lordship in our lives.

When we make a public profession of our faith in baptism, we are giving evidence that we have received completeness of life in Him. This becomes an outward "sign" of the inward reality of our relationship with Christ—just as circumcision was an outward sign for the Jews of being God's chosen people. In baptism, our faith union with Him means that our old sinful nature was put to death with Him and buried, so that our new nature may come forth.

III. VICTORY IN CHRIST: COLOSSIANS 2:13-15

A. Over Spiritual Death: vs. 13

When you were dead in your sins and in the uncircumcision of your sinful nature, God made you alive with Christ. He forgave us all our sins.

Paul continued to pile up more facts about our completeness in Christ. Because of our sins, we were spiritually dead and under God's just judgment of the death penalty. Paul called this "the uncircumcision of your sinful nature." But now, because of our oneness with Him, we are "made alive with Christ." We have conquered spiritual death.

Coming to Christ brings life. We pass from death to life, because in His death Jesus took the judgment due us because of our sins. In His resurrection He conquered the death penalty, enabling us to receive forgiveness for our sins.

B. Over the Law: vs. 14

Having canceled the written code, with its regulations, that was against us and that stood opposed to us; he took it away, nailing it to the cross.

Because we are sinners, the law declared us guilty and demanded our punishment. The law "stood opposed to us." However, once we are united to Christ, the law's power to condemn us is taken away. This demand is "canceled." God did this because Jesus fully met the law's demands. Paul said the law's demands were nailed to the cross. On the cross Jesus took our judgment on Himself.

C. Over Evil Powers: vs. 15

And having disarmed the powers and authorities, he made a public spectacle of them, triumphing over them by the cross.

The cross signifies Christ's victory over every spiritual power arrayed against God. Jesus "disarmed" them and humiliated them publicly. The word from the cross is that even the worst of human and satanic wickedness is no match for God's love and power in Christ.

God's triumph over evil came out of seeming defeat at the cross. But Satan's doom was sealed when God raised Jesus from the dead. Therefore, our completeness in Christ assures us of total victory. We can join Christ's victory procession.

IV. HOLDING FAST TO CHRIST: COLOSSIANS 2:16-19

A. Forget the Rules: vs. 16

Therefore do not let anyone judge you by what you eat or drink, or with regard to a religious festival, a New Moon celebration or a Sabbath day.

Paul briefly exposed one of the problems at Colosse. Certain unnamed persons were imposing rules that were a mixture of both Jewish and Greek ideas. The rules governed what you could eat and drink, what special days to observe, and the worship of angels (vs. 18). Those who kept them posed as being more spiritual than the apostles. They did not reject the Gospel, but added to it. Paul's solution was simple: Do not allow yourselves to be criticized for not keeping these rules.

B. Reality in Christ: vs. 17

These are a shadow of the things that were to come; the reality, however, is found in Christ.

The danger of these rules was that they overshadowed spiritual reality in Christ. To be complete in Him means we recognize that the old rules were a "shadow," not the real thing. Anything that detracts from Christ's supremacy must be rejected.

In effect, the rules keepers were denying the fullness of life in Christ alone. They still had one foot in the old pre-Christian traditions. "Reality" in this context is not outward but inward. Christ's strength and sufficiency are real, even though we can't see them. We accept them by faith.

C. False Worship: vs. 18

Do not let anyone who delights in false humility and the worship of angels disqualify you for the prize. Such a person goes into great detail about what he has seen, and his unspiritual mind puffs him up with idle notions.

Rules keepers were guilty of false humility and false worship. Some Colossian Christians were fearful of their salvation, because the false teachers had "disqualified" them from heaven. These false teachers also aroused fear because they claimed to have greater spiritual insights. However, Paul said their minds were "unspiritual" and puffed up with "idle notions."

D. Growth in Christ: vs. 19

He has lost connection with the Head, from whom the whole body, supported and held together by its ligaments and sinews, grows as God causes it to grow.

The capstone of Paul's warning is that the false teachers, angel worshipers, and legalists had cut themselves off from Christ. They had lost their spiritual grip. They thought they needed something more than Jesus, and so lost the only source of spiritual growth.

True spiritual growth comes from Jesus Himself. Believers who keep their faith in Jesus alone are "supported and held together" by Him. Christians who fully grasp all they have in Christ are not taken in by those who propound new rules about food and drink, religious observances, and visions that add to what God has already revealed in the Bible.

Discussion Questions

1. What does it mean for Christians to root their faith in Christ, and to be built up in Him?
2. In how many ways do we experience fullness of life in Christ?
3. How does our completeness in Christ help us to resist "hollow and deceptive philosophy"?
4. What difference does it make in our lives because we have put off the old nature and have been raised with Christ?
5. How can we help one another when we feel we lack something to be more devoted to Jesus?
6. How can we tell if new rules are of Christ, or of purely human origin?

Contemporary Application

God has made every provision for our spiritual vitality, yet many Christians often appear to be defeated. If not defeated, they do not seem to reflect much enthusiasm about their Christian commitment.

It's one thing to lose a battle if you lack adequate resources, but quite another if you have the resources but refuse to use them. Perhaps one reason for the church's lack of power is that too many Christians are not aware of all they possess in Christ. They lack the passion for discovering the wealth of their spiritual riches.

When we confess Jesus as Lord, we acknowledge that He alone can win our battles. Yet we seem to go on as if everything depended on our own cleverness and ingenuity. We find it hard to trust Jesus alone. We find it hard to discard human philosophies and traditions.

Jesus made a public spectacle of all of our enemies. The cross is our sign of triumph. Our sins are forgiven! Our old nature has been crucified! We are raised to new life in Christ! There is no excuse for settling for anything less than a victorious life in Christ.

The Way to Righteousness

DEVOTIONAL READING
Mark 12:28-34

DAILY BIBLE READINGS
Monday August 14
Colossians 3:1-6 Revealed with Christ in Glory

Tuesday August 15
Colossians 3:7-11 Put on the New Self

Wednesday August 16
Colossians 3:12-17 Live Faithfully, Joyfully, and Give Thanks

Thursday August 17
Colossians 3:18—4:1 Love and Honor All People

Friday August 18
Colossians 4:2-6 Live and Speak in Christian Love

Saturday August 19
Colossians 4:7-11 Paul's Faithful Support Community

Sunday August 20
Colossians 4:12-18 Paul's Final Greetings to the Colossians

Scripture

Background Scripture: *Colossians 3:1-17*
Scripture Lesson: *Colossians 3:1-3, 5-17*
Key Verse: *And whatever you do, whether in word or deed, do it all in the name of the Lord Jesus, giving thanks to God the Father through him.* Colossians 3:17.

Lesson Aim

To find joy in doing everything for Jesus.

Lesson Setting

Time: *A.D. 60-62*
Place: *Written to Colosse from Rome*

Lesson Outline

The Way to Righteousness

I. Raised with Christ: Colossians 3:1-3
   A. *Focus on Things Above: vss. 1-2*
   B. *Remember Your Destiny: vs. 3*

II. Put to Death . . . : Colossians 3:5-11
   A. *Sexual Immorality, Impurity, Lust, Evil Desires, and Greed: vss. 5-7*
   B. *Anger, Rage, Malice, Slander, and Filthy Language: vs. 8*
   C. *Lying: vss. 9-10*
   D. *Racial, Religious, Social, and Economic Distinctions: vs. 11*

III. Clothe Yourself with . . . : Colossians 3:12-17
   A. *Compassion, Kindness, Humility, Gentleness, Patience, Forbearance, and Forgiveness: vss. 12-13*
   B. *Love: vs. 14*
   C. *The Peace of Christ: vs. 15*
   D. *The Word of Christ: vs. 16*
   E. *The Work of Christ: vs. 17*

Introduction for Adults

Topic: *The Way of Life*

If you've been in a supermarket recently, you may have noticed the greatly expanded shelves of natural food supplements. These products have become big business. People pay high prices because they believe the nutritional values are worth the extra money. They put a high priority on their health.

On the other hand, you find the purveyors of so-called junk food are also doing very well. They cater to people who eat and drink anything, as long as it's filling and tastes good. They spend money, too, but not according to the rules of good nutrition. They go for whatever appeals to them, no matter if it is bad for them. Their priority is satisfying their taste buds.

In the supermarket of life, we have to make spiritual choices if we are going to follow the way of righteousness. Some people put a higher priority on godly living than others do. The apostle Paul made it very clear what our choices must be if we profess to be Christians. We can't go on consuming a diet of sin that will ruin us. The Bible tells us what those poisons are . . . and the overwhelming benefits of the healthy diet of positive Christian virtues.

Introduction for Youths

Topic: *Life on a Higher Level*

A missionary wrote to a friend about her son. "Isaac, at 6' 3" and 180 lbs., is looking forward to Duke basketball camp and hopes to get on his high school team this year. He just returned from a church mission trip to Jamaica. He'll be in the eleventh grade next year and hopes to maintain his straight-A record."

Isaac illustrates life on a higher level. What makes the difference? For one thing, his values and choices have been solidly anchored in Jesus Christ. Does this mean he has been spared problems and hardships? Not at all. He has been through some very rough patches.

The Bible spells out very clearly what we have to do to achieve life on a higher level. There are some really bad things we have to get rid of and some very choice things we have to learn and practice. If we are serious about following Jesus, we have to study these things and ask the Holy Spirit to lead us in paths of obedience.

Concepts for Children

Topic: *Jesus Tells Us How to Live*

1. The Bible helps us to recognize sinful practices in our lives.
2. When we choose to follow Jesus, He expects us to put away sin.
3. Some things like anger and bad language easily become bad habits.
4. We have to confess things that displease Jesus and ask Him for His power to live righteously.
5. By spending time with God in the Bible, we learn wise choices.
6. We are called to honor Jesus in everything we do and say.

The Lesson Commentary

I. RAISED WITH CHRIST: COLOSSIANS 3:1-3

A. Focus on Things Above: vss. 1-2

Since, then, you have been raised with Christ, set your hearts on things above, where Christ is seated at the right hand of God. Set your minds on things above, not on earthly things.

Following the way of righteousness is a journey that begins with total concentration on the Lord Jesus Christ. It's like following the signal of a lighthouse through the fog or an aircraft landing on instruments tuned to certain radio waves. Focus makes all the difference.

Paul's admonition to the Colossians started with their position in Christ. They had been raised to new life in Him (2:12; 3:1). The way of righteousness is hopeless if we do not have new life in Christ. There is not much point in telling people how to live if they have never committed themselves to Jesus.

Recognizing all that we have in Jesus—forgiveness, righteousness, eternal life—it is only logical that we should focus our hearts (vs. 1) and our minds (vs. 2) on Him. Jesus is in heaven at the Father's right hand, so that's where our thoughts and our love should be focused.

We have to choose between heavenly and earthly desires. The choices are tough, because earthly things look very attractive. They are here and now, while heaven seems a long way off. Therefore, we have to set aside time to think about Jesus, to pray, and to praise Him for all He has done for us. "Set your hearts . . . your minds" implies tough, consistent spiritual discipline.

B. Remember Your Destiny: vs. 3

For you died, and your life is now hidden with Christ in God.

Previously, Paul emphasized our completeness in Christ, which includes our identification with Him in His death. We were "baptized into his death" (Rom. 6:3), and "united with him . . . in his death" (Rom. 6:5).

When he wrote, "You died," he did not refer to physical death, but the death of self. Our real life, spiritually speaking, is with Christ. He sits in heaven. Because our life is really there, "things above" should be our primary concern.

Our comfort is that no matter what "earthly things" involve, real life is in heaven. Nothing can touch us there. "Hidden with Christ" means we are totally secure in His love, wisdom, and power.

II. PUT TO DEATH . . . : COLOSSIANS 3:5-11

A. Sexual Immorality, Impurity, Lust, Evil Desires, and Greed: vss. 5-7

Put to death, therefore, whatever belongs to your earthly nature: sexual immorality, impurity, lust, evil desires and greed, which is idolatry. Because of these, the wrath of God is coming. You used to walk in these ways, in the life you once lived.

Since Christians have died with Christ, and our focus is on heaven where He is, we can get rid of ("put to death") sinful earthly habits. We don't need to be in doubt about what practices are unfit for Christians. Paul gave us a valuable, practical checklist to review, and we shouldn't assume that we are immune. (1) *Sexual immorality.* Any illicit sexual intercourse. (2) *Impurity.* Any sexual or bodily perversion. (3) *Lust.* Any perverted or unnatural sexual desire. (4) *Evil desires.* Insatiable cravings; an appetite for wickedness. (5) *Greed.* The desire to have more and more. It is idolatry because it puts God in second place.

All of us are tempted by these things somewhere along the line. When the temptations hit us, we have to kill them right away and not even think about indulging or fantasizing about them.

Paul made clear that these practices bring God's wrath (vs. 6) and characterize the way unbelievers live (vs. 7). The way of righteousness is clearly different from the habits of unbelievers. We are also responsible to warn them about the consequences of their ungodly ways. God's wrath is certain and real. It will come. We can only be spared by trusting in Jesus.

B. Anger, Rage, Malice, Slander, and Filthy Language: vs. 8

But now you must rid yourselves of all such things as these: anger, rage, malice, slander, and filthy language from your lips.

These common sins are powerful roadblocks on the way to righteousness. Too often we think they are not as bad as the sins cited by Paul in vs. 5. Nevertheless, they contaminate us and cut off our fellowship with God and with each other. For example, slander includes insults and gossip. Filthy language includes dirty jokes. Christians living righteously do not tell them or want to listen to them.

In too many cases Christians find it easy to excuse these sins as simply bad habits. They claim these characteristics are just part of the way they were made. Evidently, to them Jesus is not strong enough to set them free from these things. Or, they simply like their sins and refuse to put them to death.

C. Lying: vss. 9-10

Do not lie to each other, since you have taken off your old self with its practices and have put on the new self, which is being renewed in knowledge in the image of its Creator.

Truthfulness and honesty are the cornerstones of righteous living. Lying is inconsistent with our new nature in Christ. Lying characterizes our old, pre-Christian lifestyle, which has been put to death. Paul said we have taken those things off. In their place we have been renewed in God's image. This is something like exchanging our dirty clothes for fresh, clean ones.

This exchange goes on every day. We are "being renewed" daily. Many times we put off the old and put on the new. Each temptation to sin requires us to recognize our new self. To understand what God's image means in us, we look to Jesus. We see His character in action. Our renewal in God's image results from incorporating the life and power of Jesus in our lives.

D. Racial, Religious, Social, and Economic Distinctions: vs. 11

Here there is no Greek or Jew, circumcised or uncircumcised, barbarian, Scythian, slave or free, but Christ is all, and is in all.

The way of righteousness stands squarely against our culture's prejudices. It is very easy to go along with racial stereotypes and to laugh at ethnic and religious jokes. But in Christ, we are called to a different standard. We do not allow ourselves to live in a world that erects all kinds of barriers between people.

In Paul's declaration, "Greek or Jew" refers to racial prejudice. "Circumcised or uncircumcised" refers to religious prejudice (Jews and Gentiles). "Barbarian, Scythian" refers to social prejudice. "Slave or free" refers to economic prejudice. The ungodly world separates people along these lines.

However, living in the way of righteousness means we cannot accept these sinful, man-made distinctions. Why? Because "Christ is all, and is in all." Jesus demands that we accept all people because of their value to God, and because He died for all.

III. Clothe Yourself with . . .: Colossians 3:12-17

A. Compassion, Kindness, Humility, Gentleness, Patience, Forbearance, and Forgiveness: vss. 12-13

Therefore, as God's chosen people, holy and dearly loved, clothe yourselves with compassion, kindness, humility, gentleness and patience. Bear with each other and forgive whatever grievances you may have against one another. Forgive as the Lord forgave you.

People who profess to be Christians should be able to be identified by certain righteous characteristics. We should put on or "wear" these qualities like our outward clothes which people see. Sinful habits must be replaced by these godly qualities.

We wear these habits because they are consistent with God's calling. Since we are holy and dearly loved, we are expected to reflect God's choice of us by the way we live. When we become Christians, we do more than give our assent to these things. We decide to adopt God's way of righteousness as our lifestyle.

When we examine these qualities, we see how revolutionary they are and what a significant difference they make in our lives. We won't insist on having our own way. We won't trample over the rights of others. We will yield to one another, show patience when we are tried, forgive one another, and not hold grudges. What a difference these qualities will make in our relationships!

B. Love: vs. 14

And over all these virtues put on love, which binds them all together in perfect unity.

Love is the capstone of the other qualities of a godly life. Love holds them all together, because in the church, we are bound to each other by our love. In fact, compassion, kindness, humility, etc., are all expressions of our love toward one another because of Christ. We cannot manufacture love, because it springs from hearts refreshed by the spirit of Christ.

This kind of love is not just a toothy smile of greeting. This kind of love springs into action for the sake of others. Love reaches out to others and goes beyond the routine. As Christians, the way of righteousness demands that we look for ways to help, to comfort one another, and to encourage and nurture as needed.

C. The Peace of Christ: vs. 15

Let the peace of Christ rule in your hearts, since as members of one body you were called to peace. And be thankful.

Paul listed three major principles to help determine our conduct in the way of righteousness. We can apply these principles when we have questions, because these principles cover everything we do.

The first principle is Christ's peace, which acts as our inner umpire in determining our activities. If we lack peace, the umpire says no. If we have peace, the umpire says yes. When His peace rules our conduct, we can be thankful.

When we are troubled about a proposed course of action, we must wait for Jesus to give us His peace. Unrest is our caution light. We must never violate the absence of His peace in our hearts.

This principle is both personal and corporate. In the church we are called to peace because we are members of Christ's body. The way of righteousness must be exemplified in the way we relate to each other in the church.

D. The Word of Christ: vs. 16

Let the word of Christ dwell in you richly as you teach and admonish one another with all wisdom, and as you sing psalms, hymns and spiritual songs with gratitude in your hearts to God.

The second principle is to be governed by the word of Christ. No decision or behavior can be justified that violates Scripture. The Bible is our yardstick for righteous living. Christ's words must dwell in us "richly," that is, in all their richness.

We can learn biblical truth by ourselves, but the church fosters teaching and admonishing one another. When we sit under the teaching of God's Word, we are learning more than facts. We learn to apply truths that change our lives. We need one another because each member has something to contribute to our spiritual growth.

We also learn as we worship together. Our music should teach us God's Word, and nourish us with the truths about Jesus. Then we can praise Him together.

E. The Work of Christ: vs. 17

And whatever you do, whether in word or deed, do it all in the name of the Lord Jesus, giving thanks to God the Father through him.

The third principle is to do everything in the name of Jesus. When we do that, our work becomes His work. Christians escape meaninglessness and achieve significance when we honor Christ in everything we say and do. Our words and deeds must speak of Jesus. Christians do their best at work because they are working for Jesus. They do not accept shoddy workmanship, or take shortcuts, because these things are not worthy of the name of Jesus.

Christians have long used this principle as a safety check against a proposed course of action. If what we propose to do cannot be done with honor to God, then we must back off and reconsider.

Thanksgiving undergirds each of these principles. "Be thankful" (vs. 15); "with gratitude in your hearts" (vs. 16); "giving thanks to God" (vs. 17). Praise transforms our lives. We thank God for His peace, for His Word, and for all He gives us to do.

Discussion Questions

1. What goals and ambitions are acceptable for Christians?
2. How can the church and the family develop spiritual goals that keep Jesus at the center?
3. What does it take to put to death the sins listed here? To clothe ourselves with the qualities of righteousness?
4. How can we keep our Christian families clean from sexual defilement in books, magazines, movies, and television?
5. What does it mean to have "the word of Christ dwell in you richly"?
6. How does giving thanks regulate the kinds of things we do?

Contemporary Application

Every day we seem to be confronted by a new crisis of some kind. What would the evening news be if there were no crises to report?

But perhaps the most significant crisis of all never makes the news. Our churches must realize that a crisis exists when Christians fail to follow the way of righteousness. It's a crisis when believers adopt a ho-hum attitude toward the principles and standards of godly living revealed in the Bible.

God has provided all we need to throw off the old life and put on the new one. There can be no doubts about His governing principles. But until we realize the danger of neglecting God's resources, we will not swing into action.

Action begins by evaluating how much time we spend feeding our hearts and minds on Jesus. Confession and repentance are demanded. We also have to use Paul's checklist regularly. Where we fall short, we must confess. We must seek the help of others to keep us on the road to godly living. As we rejoice and praise Him together, we allow the words of Jesus to penetrate our hearts and minds.

Welcoming Others in Christ

Scripture

Background Scripture: *Philemon*
Scripture Lesson: *Philemon 4-21*
Key Verse: *I pray that you may be active in sharing your faith, so that you will have a full understanding of every good thing we have in Christ.* Philemon 6.
Key Verse for Children: *If you consider me a partner, welcome him as you would welcome me.* Philemon 17.

Lesson Aim

To build strong relationships with others so we can take the risks of showing love to all people.

Lesson Setting

Time: A.D. *60-62*
Place: *Written from Rome to Philemon, who lived in Colosse.*

Lesson Outline

Welcoming Others in Christ

  I. Paul's Praise and Prayer: Philemon 4-7
    A. Praise for Faith and Love: vss. 4-5
    B. Prayer for an Active Faith: vs. 6
    C. Praise for Good Works: vs. 7
  II. Paul's Plea: Philemon 8-11
    A. On the Basis of Love: vss. 8-9a
    B. On the Basis of Spiritual Kinship: vss. 9b-11
  III. Paul's Plan: Philemon 12-16
    A. To Return Onesimus: vss. 12-13
    B. To Gain Philemon's Consent: vs. 14
    C. To Establish a New Relationship: vss. 15-16
  IV. Paul's Confidence: Philemon 17-21
    A. In His Partnership: vs. 17
    B. In His Ability to Repay: vss. 18-19
    C. In Spiritual Refreshment: vss. 20-21

Introduction for Adults

Topic: *The Grace of Life*

By God's grace we no longer have slavery in this country, though working conditions of migrant farm workers and so-called "sweat shops" take their human toll. But some employers make a special effort to treat even unskilled laborers in a "brotherly" way. One man recalls, "I'd never worked so hard when I was a youth as the summer I was hired out to a neighboring farmer. But he was a good man and treated me well. He was also a wise Christian and saw that I was not cut out for farm work. One day he relieved me of my summer's commitment and told me I would be happier doing something else, which was true. He was one of many people who graced my life. His wife was another. She taught Sunday school and paid my way to camp. They made a great investment in my spiritual well-being."

God gives us many opportunities to grace the lives of others. We have to see their potential as Christian sisters and brothers. The apostle Paul saw great potential in a runaway slave. He wanted the man's owner to see his slave in a new light—as a dear brother in Christ. When we see people that way, we can invest our lives in them.

Introduction for Youths

Topic: *A Plea for Acceptance*

All of us want to be accepted, regardless of our past mistakes. Tragically, the lives of many young people are scarred by sin before they come to Christ. Sometimes it's hard for older Christians to accept them. Imagine how hard it was for Philemon to take back the man who had robbed him and run away, and to treat him as a "dear brother."

As Christians, however, we are called to do the unthinkable and the impossible in human relationships. We don't keep bringing up past mistakes. We accept people because Jesus accepts them. Former enemies become fast friends in Christ. Such is the power of the Gospel.

When we cross boundaries to show Christian love, we gain new opportunities to point people to Jesus. Unbelievers find it hard to accept our Jesus if we do not first accept them.

Concepts for Children

Topic: *Jesus Wants Us to Be Friends in Christ*

1. Philemon's slave Onesimus stole his money and ran away, before he became a Christian.
2. At Rome, Onesimus became a believer in Jesus, and Paul sent him back to Philemon.
3. When we become Christians, we confess the wrong things we have done, and Jesus forgives us and accepts us.
4. We show Christ's love to others who have done wrong things to us.

5. In God's family, we welcome one another as partners.
6. We can pray for a change of attitude toward those we find it hard to accept.

The Lesson Commentary

I. PAUL'S PRAISE AND PRAYER: PHILEMON 4-7

A. Praise for Faith and Love: vss. 4-5

I always thank my God as I remember you in my prayers, because I hear about your faith in the Lord Jesus and your love for all the saints.

The apostle Paul's letter to Philemon gives an intimate insight into how personal relationships worked in the early church. It shows that the great missionary evangelist was a person of intense love. He paid attention to individuals and their needs.

This letter also shows how the Gospel transforms relationships. A runaway slave (Onesimus) became a Christian and therefore a brother in Christ. Paul sent him back to his owner (Philemon) and asked him to accept Onesimus "as a dear brother."

The story reveals that even in prison Paul continued to do evangelistic work. He continued to carry a heavy burden for the welfare of the churches he had founded. He kept on applying the truths of the Gospel to difficult situations. The Gospel shaped everything he did. Therefore, he chose to send his "son" back to Philemon's household in Colosse.

The church at Colosse met in Philemon's home (vs. 2). Paul sent his greetings to individuals—Philemon, Apphia, and Archippus—and to the church as a whole. Then he turned to prayers of thanksgiving and prayer for Philemon. Paul's prayers and praise were often very specific. What a great tonic it is for our souls when we take time to thank God for fellow believers by name. That's a sure cure for gossip and criticism.

Two things about Philemon stood out in Paul's mind—his faith in Jesus and his love for all "the saints," that is, all those who professed faith in Christ. Faith is the cornerstone on which we build our lives. Without our faith in Jesus we are nothing, but with our faith in Him we are everything. Therefore, it is good to thank God for the faith we see in fellow Christians. When we are tempted to criticize other Christians, we must first thank God for their faith.

Love for all the saints is praiseworthy because this is what distinguishes Christians from other people. Christians can learn to love one another, regardless of their differences, likes, and dislikes. Philemon set the example for the church at Colosse. Probably there were a few people who irritated him at times, but he loved them anyway. Christian love is demonstrated by deeds. It transcends feelings. No doubt Philemon had helped and cared for many people in the church.

B. Prayer for an Active Faith: vs. 6

I pray that you may be active in sharing your faith, so that you will have a full understanding of every good thing we have in Christ.

Paul prayed for Philemon to be a strong witness for Christ. He was to be bold in telling unbelievers about Jesus and the Gospel. While he was actively sharing his faith, Philemon would gain new insights into the riches of Christ.

This was the key to the growth of the church at Colosse. Everyone was responsible to spread the Gospel in the community. Paul was in prison. He could not do it. So he reminded Philemon of how important it was for him to set a strong example of bold witness.

C. Praise for Good Works: vs. 7

Your love has given me great joy and encouragement, because you, brother, have refreshed the hearts of the saints.

We see how Christian love works. Paul praised God for the joy and encouragement he had received from Philemon. This church leader not only loved his fellow believers, he "refreshed" their hearts.

Joy, encouragement, and refreshment are the staples of life together in the church. Paul was excited because he knew Philemon's good works personally. What did Philemon do to refresh others spiritually? In addition to caring for their needs, he prayed for them and urged them to continue strong in faith. As new Christians faced hostility, they needed to strengthen one another. No doubt Philemon told the story of Jesus over and over again. He rehearsed all he had learned from Paul.

II. PAUL'S PLEA: PHILEMON 8-11

A. On the Basis of Love: vss. 8-9a

Therefore, although in Christ I could be bold and order you to do what you ought to do, yet I appeal to you on the basis of love.

Paul recognized and confessed his spiritual authority over Philemon, but he refused to use it. As an apostle of Christ, he could have ordered Philemon to take back Onesimus. But Paul knew that such an order would be counterproductive, and contrary to the spirit of Christ.

He wanted Philemon to see that welcoming others in Christ is not about obeying orders, but acting in love. Having commended Philemon for his love for everyone in the church, Paul went a step further and laid the foundation for his appeal on the Christian virtue of love.

Paul did not command Philemon in this case; he appealed to him. Paul knew the power of love to change lives and attitudes. It seems risky to unbelievers to try to get something done on the basis of love, but that is the Christian way.

B. On the Basis of Spiritual Kinship: vss. 9b-11

I then, as Paul—an old man and now also a prisoner of Christ Jesus—I appeal to you for my son Onesimus, who became my son while I was in chains. Formerly he was useless to you, but now he has become useful both to you and to me.

Paul reminded Philemon of his advancing years and of his imprisonment. Certainly, these statements raised strong feelings of affection. Then Paul no doubt surprised Philemon by mentioning the man's runaway slave, Onesimus, who also apparently took some money (vs. 18).

However, it was more than the slave's name, but his relationship to Paul that must have astounded Philemon. The former slave had not only turned up in Paul's custody in Rome, he had become Paul's spiritual son. Twice Paul called him "my son."

So, Paul's unusual appeal was based on powerful bonds of spiritual kinship. Somehow, Onesimus had drifted under the sound of the Gospel from Paul's lips. Of course, many slaves had become Christians, but not in order to escape their masters. They sought freedom in Christ, and were taught to obey their masters as to "the Lord" (Col. 3:22-25).

Occasionally we hear criticism of the early church for not denouncing slavery. The church taught all people how to relate to others *in their present circumstances*, whether it was teaching honest service for slaves and workers, or fair and honest treatment for masters and employers. The story of Philemon and Onesimus shows what a difference the Gospel makes when love and spiritual kinship are the ruling factors even in a situation that could be much abused. As for the *institution* of slavery, however, Paul acknowledged, "if you can gain your freedom, do so" (1 Cor. 7:21).

The name Onesimus means "useful" and Paul played on that meaning. He reminded Philemon of how useful Onesimus had been to him. Now, with his new faith and relationship, Onesimus was useful to both Paul and Philemon.

III. PAUL'S PLAN: PHILEMON 12-16

A. To Return Onesimus: vss. 12-13

I am sending him—who is my very heart—back to you. I would have liked to keep him with me so that he could take your place in helping me while I am in chains for the gospel.

"I am sending him back" reveals the power of the Gospel and Christian love. Obviously, Onesimus didn't want to be a slave; he had run away! But now he was willing to go back. He had decided not to push his freedom and escape once again. Paul and Onesimus had become so closely knit together that Paul called him "my very heart."

Both Paul and Onesimus were paying a high price for Paul's plan to send him back to Philemon. Onesimus would go back to being a household servant; Paul would have to live in prison without his son's comfort. His first choice would have been to keep Onesimus. Apparently Paul and Onesimus had been so compatible that Paul found his companionship invaluable. It was as good as having Philemon himself on the scene.

Christian love enables us to meet the needs of others, regardless of their circumstances. We see clearly how welcoming others in Christ must be based on unconditional love.

B. To Gain Philemon's Consent: vs. 14

But I did not want to do anything without your consent, so that any favor you do will be spontaneous and not forced.

Paul could have acted independently, but he preferred to develop strong spiritual reasons for his plan. Just as God allows us to make a free choice whether to follow Him, so Paul wanted to give Philemon a free choice to do the right thing. Obviously, Paul's plan would take some time for Philemon to digest. What Paul proposed was absolutely revolutionary. We have to consider the risks he took—for himself, Onesimus, and Philemon. What assurances did he have that Philemon would treat his runaway slave with fairness, and not punish him?

To make sure this would not happen, Paul asked Philemon to act in accordance with the principles of Christian love. Philemon's voluntary consent was critical to the success of Paul's plan.

C. To Establish a New Relationship: vss. 15-16

Perhaps the reason he was separated from you for a little while was that you might have him back for good—no longer as a slave, but better than a slave, as a dear brother. He is very dear to me but even dearer to you, both as a man and as a brother in the Lord.

We might well ask what possessed Paul to return his "son" and "dear brother." Why didn't he keep him in Rome? Paul acted because of compelling moral reasons. He did not own Onesimus and had no right to keep him. Beyond that, however, he wanted Philemon and Onesimus to establish a new relationship.

Their new relationship was based on their common bond in Christ. Onesimus was still a slave, but Paul wanted to send him back "no longer as a slave, but . . . as a dear brother." Outwardly, nothing had changed, but inwardly everything had changed. Onesimus was still Onesimus the slave, but he was now a new person in Christ. He and his owner had a new relationship of love.

Paul recognized the economic and spiritual realities. Onesimus had been "very dear" to him, but even more so to Philemon on two counts: (1) "as a man," that is, the value of his work in the household; and (2) "as a brother in the Lord."

The Gospel changes everything. It overrides all human institutions. Even though we may function within those human institutions, our motivation and basis for relationship is different. Christian love and common faith build new relationships. The slave goes back "better than a slave" because he is a brother in Christ. Paul returned a man in better condition than when he received him.

We welcome others in Christ because we are all sisters and brothers in Christ. Old distinctions and barriers pass away. The love of Jesus is so strong that we look at human relationships in an entirely new and different light.

IV. PAUL'S CONFIDENCE: PHILEMON 17-21

A. In His Partnership: vs. 17

So if you consider me a partner, welcome him as you would welcome me.

Paul urged Philemon to welcome his slave as he would Paul himself. He did that because he considered Philemon his partner in the Gospel. This kind of strong partnership means that we work hard for the best interests and good of our fellow partners in the Gospel.

Their partnership was built on common goals as well as mutual love and respect. Philemon had supported, encouraged, and refreshed Paul. He had wanted to be with Paul in Rome. Their shared concern for the advancement of the Gospel and the building of the church drew them together. The challenge was: could Philemon welcome his slave with the same kind of respect and consideration?

B. In His Ability to Repay: vss. 18-19

If he has done you any wrong or owes you anything, charge it to me. I, Paul, am writing this with my own hand. I will pay it back—not to mention that you owe me your very self.

Paul offered to cover anything Onesimus had stolen. His letter was in effect an IOU, or promissory note. Apparently he signed his name to it. This was an open-ended promise, because Paul did not know how much Philemon thought Onesimus owed him.

It may seem strange that Paul took a business approach to an appeal based on love and partnership. But Paul didn't want a human debt to be a stumbling block to the relationship. However, he returned to their common bond in Christ by reminding Philemon how much he owed him—not in dollars, but in eternal life. "You owe me your very self." Philemon owed his salvation to Paul, who had brought him to the Lord. So Philemon probably took Paul's promise seriously, but with a hearty laugh as well. How could Paul ever owe him anything, when he owed everything to Paul? Here we have an interesting illustration of how Paul made a profound spiritual application out of his debt to Philemon for what Onesimus had done.

C. In Spiritual Refreshment: vss. 20-21

I do wish, brother, that I may have some benefit from you in the Lord; refresh my heart in Christ. Confident of your obedience, I write to you, knowing that you will do even more than I ask.

Paul exuded supreme confidence in his good friend and brother. He knew Philemon would go beyond his request, and do more. In the meantime, he longed for a personal visit from Philemon so that he could be refreshed in Christ.

Of course, by taking back Onesimus, Philemon would greatly encourage Paul. To take the slave back as a brother would be strong spiritual refreshment of the best kind. This no doubt would occur to Philemon as well.

Paul was so confident that he asked Philemon to get his guestroom ready (vs. 22). The brothers in Christ longed to be reunited. In the meantime, if Philemon took back Onesimus, Paul would rejoice in the power of the Gospel and Christian love.

Discussion Questions

1. How would you have felt, if you were Philemon, after receiving Paul's letter?
2. How do you think Onesimus felt about going back to Philemon?
3. What do Christians owe one another in Christ?
4. What differences keep us from developing strong bonds of love?
5. What obstacles did Philemon have to overcome to receive Onesimus back as a brother?
6. Why is welcoming others such a strong witness to the power of the Gospel?

Contemporary Application

What principles can we draw from this story to help us to welcome others in Christ? First, Paul asks all of us to lay aside prejudices and grudges. We have to allow the love of Christ to wipe the slate clean. As Christians we confess our sins to one another. We thank God that all of us can make fresh starts.

Another encouragement is that it is possible in Christ to develop very strong bonds of partnership, love, trust, and respect across barriers that normally keep people apart. We have to admire Paul's bravery in making such an audacious request of Philemon in that culture. But when we know our sisters and brothers in Christ, we can take such risks. We can trust our friendships to see us through tough times.

The world watches how we treat one another in the church. It's an amazing testimony to Christ's power when unbelievers see Christians overcome distrust and prejudice. When the unwelcome are made welcome, people see Jesus in us.